INTRAPSYCHIC
HUMANISM

INTRAPSYCHIC HUMANISM

An Introduction to a Comprehensive Psychology and Philosophy of Mind

MARTHA HEINEMAN PIEPER

WILLIAM JOSEPH PIEPER

The Falcon II Press

CHICAGO

Published by
The Falcon II Press, Inc.
9400 Sears Tower
Chicago, Illinois 60606

Book design: Cameron Poulter

Printed in the United States of America
1   2   3   4   5   6   7   8   9   10

Library of Congress Cataloging-in-Publication Data

Pieper, Martha Heineman, 1941–
   Intrapsychic humanism: an introduction to a comprehensive
psychology and philosophy of mind / by Martha Heineman Pieper
and William Joseph Pieper.
      p.   cm.
   Includes bibliographical references.
   ISBN 0-9624919-0-X
   1. Psychology.   2. Philosophy of mind.   3. Psychology,
Pathological.   4. Psychotherapy.   I. Pieper, William Joseph,
1929–.   II. Title.
BF121.P48   1990
150—dc20   89-29256
                                                       CIP

TO OUR CHILDREN

Contents

ACKNOWLEDGEMENTS

We could never have completed an undertaking of this breadth without the help of the friends and colleagues who were willing to read and comment on an evolving manuscript. We are especially grateful to our first reader, Fay Sawyier, who contributed invaluable suggestions to a very rough draft while maintaining an unfailing good humor. Other readers whose comments materially improved this book are Peter Feibleman, Thalia Field, Jessica Heineman-Pieper, Elizabeth Hersh, Lisa Maroski, Mark Steinberg, Katherine Tyson, and Donna Walker. They, of course, bear no responsibility for the final product.

During the many years we were writing this volume, we were sustained by the steady encouragement of Natalie and Ben Heineman.

ix

1
Introduction

This volume is an introduction to Intrapsychic Humanism, a general psychology that represents a unified theory of normal development, psychopathology, and treatment. In addition, Intrapsychic Humanism identifies a new ontology (reality) of subjective human experience and also a new epistemology (method) of knowing that experience. Intrapsychic Humanism evolved from our dissatisfaction with the guidelines for parenting, treatment, and self-understanding that are provided by other psychologies—most specifically psychoanalysis and other psychodynamic psychologies, cognitive psychologies, and behaviorism.[1] Intrapsychic Humanism provides an understanding of human development that gives parents the potential to raise children who can attain a conflict-free, pleasurable, self-regulated experience of self, even in a world of inescapable external loss. Intrapsychic Humanism also leads to a therapeutic approach whereby an individual with troubling psychic pain can achieve the same unconflicted, pleasurable inner well-being.[2]

Intrapsychic Humanism addresses many unresolved problems in psychology and philosophy. Examples from psychodynamic psychology include: (1) the inherent bias against women found in such global psychoanalytic constructs as penis envy and female masochism;[3] (2) the etiology and dynamics of psychopathology; (3) the presence of psychopathology in individuals whose parents were manifestly kind; (4) the unhappiness of many people in spite of their success in love and at work; (5) the exclusion of or unsatisfactory explanation for many crucial and universal aspects of child development, such as the smile response, stranger anxiety, separation anxiety, and the no response; (6) the disparity in psychodynamic metapsychology between objective and subjective viewpoints (e.g., ego and self); (7) the tenacity of psychopathology and the ineffectiveness of psychological therapies; (8) the un-

1

helpfulness of traditional nosological categories, which overlap and do not relate directly to therapeutic interventions; (9) the absence of a satisfactory, comprehensive understanding of the reason and timing for the psychotherapist's responses; and (10) the absence of a satisfactory explanation of the nature and cause of the therapeutic action of psychological treatment. In addition to the psychodynamic psychologies, other psychologies, such as the cognitive psychologies, are either restricted in scope, or, like behaviorism, have had limited applicability.

Examples of ongoing *philosophical* problems and issues addressed by Intrapsychic Humanism are: the mind-body problem, the problem of evil (of humankind's inhumanity to humankind), the need for an ontology and epistemology appropriate to psychic reality, the problem of the missing agent-self as agent-self reflection (that the agent-self has been knowable only as an object-self), the problem of ordering and regulating desire, the essence of human nature, and the nature of the good life.[4]

This chapter will introduce the key assumptions and concepts that underlie and inform Intrapsychic Humanism. We emphasize that, because Intrapsychic Humanism derives from our understanding of paradigmatic and psychopathological development, *the basis for and demonstration of the assertions and constructs offered in this chapter are the specifics of development and psychopathology presented in chapters 2–6.*

Some of the most significant and distinguishing tenets of Intrapsychic Humanism are:

1. The phenomena of the dynamic unconscious and psychic determinism, which Freud posited as intrinsic to human nature, are found only in psychopathological human nature.

2. The psychoanalytic construct of the oedipal conflict is neither the structural basis nor the primary cause of psychopathology.

3. In the absence of brain damage, psychopathology always results from caregiving that, despite the caregiver's best intentions, obstructs and distorts the child's psychic development.

4. The needs of intrapsychic consciousness (which is a type of consciousness we have identified) take precedence over all other needs.

5. From the perspective of the subjective experience of personal existence, the most important function of consciousness is to generate motives for personal meaning.

6. Paradigmatic development produces not what Freud saw as the normative subjective experience of "common unhappiness,"[5] but, rather, produces an inner well-being that is loss free, autonomous, divorced

from interpersonal success or failure, and immune to the vicissitudes of chance and the toll taken by entropy.

In the interest of streamlining the exposition of Intrapsychic Humanism, we have discussed, wherever possible, its philosophical and historical contexts in notes and appendices.[6] We stress that a background in psychology or philosophy is not necessary to understand the principles of Intrapsychic Humanism. Even so, because Intrapsychic Humanism offers an original theory of human nature, and, therefore, contains many new, unfamiliar, and interrelated assumptions, constructs, and terms, the reader initially may find reading this work somewhat arduous. In addition, because the exposition of Intrapsychic Humanism must proceed serially, the reader may at first need definitions or explanations that have yet to be presented. If the reader will bear with us, however, we believe all confusion will be resolved by the time the reader finishes the last chapter.

Parents and therapists need neither to have had a paradigmatic psychological development nor to have experienced the psychotherapy based on the principles of Intrapsychic Humanism (which we term Intrapsychic Treatment) to benefit from the insights Intrapsychic Humanism has to offer. Understanding the principles of Intrapsychic Humanism can aid even the parent or therapist who has psychic pain of her/his own to help the child or patient attain a life characterized by relatively stable inner well-being and a high level of social and cognitive functioning. In addition, even without Intrapsychic Treatment, an individual with psychic pain can use the principles and insights of Intrapsychic Humanism to increase the level and stability of her/his own inner well-being. A cognitive understanding of the principles of Intrapsychic Humanism can be exceedingly helpful because an individual experiences a world of difference between an inner well-being that rests largely on motives for pain in the service of pain relief and an inner well-being that rests largely on motives for pleasure in the service of pain relief (see chap. 6). This balance can be influenced positively by even a cognitive understanding of Intrapsychic Humanism.

The theories of psychological treatment and parenting advanced by Intrapsychic Humanism derive both from a new perspective on the essence of human nature and also from a new method for knowing that essence. Psychology is unusual in that the act of knowing uses the object of study (the subjective experience of personal existence) as the instrument of knowing.[7] For this reason, the philosophy of psychology (the study of the reality of subjective personal existence and the best way to

3

know this) has either been left unremarked or has been tailored to that aspect of mind that is logical and conscious.[8] In this chapter, we focus on the philosophy of psychology because a psychological theory can be no better than its definition of and method for knowing psychic reality.

The most relevant reality[9] for understanding the subjective experience of personal existence is the innate, consciousness-generated capacity for purposiveness.[10] Sentient biological existence can be understood as entailing that purposiveness that can be determined from an accomplished act. When used to understand subjective human experience, however, the construct of purpose acquires a unique meaning because the reference point is not the completed act but is, rather, the proposed, actively intended end. It is in this sense that we use *purpose* in reference to subjective experience. In these terms, purpose represents an intended, that is, efficient, cause which we term **agency.** The most significant category of agency is **regulatory agency.** As the name suggests, regulatory agency has hegemony over the individual's subjective experience of personal existence.

A **veridical,**[11] or nonillusory, act of knowing subjective personal existence must address the problem of solipsism and afford the observer a way to get sufficiently outside of her/his own personal motives to have an accurate awareness of them. An individual can only truly know and regulate *her/his own* motives if s/he originally had a veridical experience of being the agent cause of the primary caregiver's caregiving or, subsequently, had this experience with a therapist in Intrapsychic Treatment. In addition, s/he can only have a veridical perception of *another's* subjective personal experience if s/he has acquired the ability for veridical perceptions about her/his own motives and if, in addition, s/he has a parenting or a psychotherapeutic commitment to the person whose motives are to be known. The context of a caregiving commitment is necessary for the veridical perception of another's care-getting motives both because the other's motive for care-getting pleasure is a prerequisite for this knowing and also because only in a caregiving relationship does the caregiver have an operative nonpathological ideal to subjugate personal motives in the service of gratifying another's developmental psychic motives. Paradigmatically, the parent or therapist has a stable, hegemonic motive for the pleasure of helping the subject (child or patient) develop the capacity for effective agency with regard to the self-regulation of inner well-being. For this reason, the caregiver feels and conveys pleasure at putting aside personal motives in the service of motives for intrapsychic caregiving pleasure. The *subject's* resultant, veridical certainty of her/

4

his capacity to be the agent cause of the *caregiver's* caregiving equals an autonomous, self-regulatory capacity for an inner well-being that is mutualized and free of loss.

The principles of Intrapsychic Humanism lead to a revolutionary approach to childrearing. For example, the goal of psychological development is neither ego strength characterized by the capacity for aim inhibition and sublimation nor the ability to love and to work. Clearly, one can love and work effectively and yet feel significant inner disquiet. Paradigmatic development produces an individual with the capacity for a loss-free, autonomous, stable inner well-being divorced from chance, positive entropy, and interpersonal failures.[12]

CONSCIOUSNESS

In our view consciousness is, primarily, a type of reality to which the subject has a unique, privileged first-person accessibility.[13] Except when noted, we do not use *consciousness* in the sense of self-awareness or of conscious consciousness. Rather, consciousness is synonymous with the terms *mind* and *mental states*.[14] As will be seen, our construct of consciousness differs from other conceptualizations of consciousness.

In this century in the Western world, Freud's notion of consciousness has had the widest influence. He usually used the term consciousness to mean conscious consciousness, which he distinguished from a conflicted, instinctually driven, unconscious consciousness. While Freud thought conflicted unconscious consciousness accompanies all human experience, we believe it is found only in psychopathology. Following Nietzsche, who defined consciousness as a surface,[15] Freud defined consciousness as a sense organ, as an organ of perception. Freud conceived of consciousness as a window or an eye through which the ego witnessed, as an outsider, the worlds of external reality and, to a lesser extent, internal reality.[16] The internal reality perceived by the ego took the form of derivatives of the instinctual drives, which Freud posited as the *vis a tergo* (force from behind) which represents the substrate of human nature.

In contrast, with respect to understanding the subjective experience of personal existence (as opposed, for example, to understanding brain physiology), we postulate that consciousness functions above all as an organ of meaning and, accordingly, serves as a primary source of motive experience. Therefore, consciousness has causal efficacy and, further, causal-ontological status with regard to subjective personal existence. **Causal-ontological status** refers to the fact that one criterion for realness (ontological status) is the capacity to be an efficient cause—in this case, solely with regard to the regulation of subjective personal existence.[17] Moreover, subjective personal existence can best be understood as including a specific, qualitatively distinct, essential type of consciousness: ***intrapsychic*** consciousness.[18] Intrapsychic consciousness primarily generates those meanings that form the core of the subjective experience of personal existence.[19] Humans truly do not live by bread alone; essential human nature can most aptly be described as "the need to hunt and gather meaning." While bread is the necessary condition for physical survival, the capacity to sustain subjectively acceptable personal meaning provides the sufficient condition for physical survival.

Because one must rely on consciousness to know about consciousness, one cannot get outside of the experience of consciousness in any absolute sense.[20] Thus, in Intrapsychic Humanism, knowledge about one's own or another's agent-self experience refers to an inclusively subjective rather than objective type of knowledge. We term this unique type of subjectivity, which results from paradigmatic development rather than from the solipsistic, personal values of the knower, ***intrapsychic subjectivity***.[21]

Allowing for relative differences in phylogenetic form and structure, the concept of consciousness as an endogenous source of motive experience, as a generator of to-be-actualized ideals that must be matched with perceptual experience to produce structures of meaning, applies to all animals.[22] A ***perceptual identity process*** produces meaning when a ***percept,*** or registered experience, is signified as matching a ***precept,*** or ideal. ***Motives*** can be defined as the need for perceptual identity.[23] ***Meaning*** is the gratification produced by the completed process of perceptual identity. Experientially, then, motives generate meaning. The intrapsychic form of perceptual identity is the basis of an individual's experience of acceptable personal meaning (inner esteem). ***Regulatory agency meaning*** results from a special kind of perceptual identity process in which the precept being matched is an ideal of efficient causal capacity.

Intrapsychic consciousness is the most important regulating cause of and, therefore, essence of the subjective experience of personal existence.[24] The personal meaning generated by gratified intrapsychic motives constitutes the irreducible basis of human experience. Intrapsychic motive gratification always signifies mutuality; whether illusionally or veridically, the intrapsychic motive can only be gratified by intrapsychic care-getting. Thus, we can speak of the intrapsychic agent-self

6

as an *"I" of "we"ness*, or as the *"we"ness of the "I."*[25] The ideals and motives generated by intrapsychic consciousness can be transformed by experience with an intrapsychic caregiver. We chose Intrapsychic Humanism as the name of our psychology because intrapsychic consciousness potentially provides a loss-free, autonomous inner well-being that can be actualized only through a specific care-getting relationship with a parent or a therapist. In contrast to the psychoanalytic view that development commences with an autoerotic stage followed by the stage of primary narcissism, we believe that each infant enters the world with an innately determined, functioning perceptual identity process that affords her/him the phase-appropriate self-experience of being the regulatory, agent-self cause of being unconditionally cared for by the significant other.

Innately determined intrapsychic psychic structures can also be described as personal and caregiver meanings that impart an experience of ideal inner self-worth. *Psychic structure* is an experience of meaning with durable regulatory power. Intrapsychic motive gratification is experienced as a sense of stable, reliable self-worth. Each individual's private experience of personal existence rests on this innately determined sense of self-esteem and self-worth.[26] In paradigmatic development, these innately determined core meanings are confirmed by the caregiver,[27] who, by her/his caregiving, in effect conveys to the child, "You are experiencing an unassailable, loss-free sense of inner well-being because you can stably and purposively cause my unconditional motive for the pleasure of loving and caring for you."

Innate intrapsychic meaning structures determine and regulate subjective personal existence in the early stages of paradigmatic development and in all untreated psychopathology.[28] The term *innate intrapsychic meaning structure* refers to psychic reality, not to cognitive reality. Specifically, the term refers to intrapsychic regulatory agency reality, that is, to a unifying, acting self, rather than to the self as a thinking substance.[29] The postulation of innate intrapsychic meaning structures raises the fundamental issue of whether and how regulatory control over personal meaning structures is possible.

We assert that as the result of development that is paradigmatic in the terms of Intrapsychic Humanism,[30] an individual will possess a nurture-based, nonillusional *intrapsychic* agent-self and, thereby, gain a stable, loss-free capacity for self-regulatory control over her/his inner well-being. The loss-free quality of this inner well-being results neither from the abnegation of pleasure nor from the denial of the importance

7

of inevitable interpersonal loss. Rather, it stems from the child's empirical certainty that s/he is the agent cause of the caregiver's caregiving and, thereby, is that s/he is the agent cause of her/his own inner well-being.

The capacity for veridical regulatory agency that results from a paradigmatic developmental process leads to a subjective experience of personal existence devoid of delusion or subterfuge. The individual with a veridical regulatory agent-self neither knowingly nor unknowingly grapples with issues of appearance and substance with regard to motive choice; the individual's agent-self is not a proxy for motives prescribed by structurally unconscious sets of conflicted meanings. As a result, the individual will never select an interpersonal motive only to find that it satisfied a hidden agenda. An example of unintentionally selecting a motive that is in the service of an unacceptable ideal is the dieter who would not buy candy for himself, but felt comfortable about buying a bag of candy to bring home to his child; he then found himself eating the candy on the way home.

The recognition that intrapsychic consciousness both regulates subjective personal existence and also can be mutualized implies that human beings have the potential to regulate their own minds (to have minds of their own). We term the capacity for a veridical, regulatory-intrapsychic agent-self, *veridical intrapsychic self-caretaking.* It includes the ability to distinguish between veridical and illusional forms of agent-self regulation of subjective personal existence. Intrapsychic Humanism posits that every child goes through a phase in which her/his conviction of causing the caregiver's caregiving is illusional. This phase protects the child from two potentially destructive realities: (1) the fact that, even in paradigmatic development, the caregiver has personal motives and, therefore, may not always be available to the infant to provide veridical intrapsychic motive gratification and (2) the fact that the caregiver may have psychopathology that structurally prevents her or him, despite the best intentions, from having the conflict-free capacity to subordinate her/his personal motives to her/his motives for caregiving pleasure. The child's time-limited capacity for illusional intrapsychic agent-self experience permits the child's intrapsychic consciousness to continue to function while cognitive abilities, motor skills, and other interpersonal capacities become increasingly sophisticated. This period of illusional intrapsychic motive gratification, however, also establishes the structural basis for psychopathology.

In contrast to intrapsychic consciousness, the other form of consciousness, ***interpersonal*** consciousness, has two levels: regulatory and constitutive. What we term constitutive-interpersonal consciousness is the usual referent for consciousness. Like intrapsychic consciousness, the primary function of interpersonal consciousness is to generate meaning.[31] The following distinction receives detailed explication in chapter 4, but, in short, constitutive-interpersonal consciousness includes cognitive, physiological, and social-interpersonal motives, whereas regulatory-interpersonal consciousness generates the motive for the reflection of effective agency in relation to the choice and pursuit of constitutive-interpersonal motives.[32]

As will become clear, although they use memory, the meaning structures of *intrapsychic* consciousness are not organized by memory and, therefore, intrapsychic meaning does not signify time or finiteness. In contrast, interpersonal consciousness includes *memory* as it is traditionally defined. The nature of memory is that the self-reflective act of interpersonal introspection can make use only of short-term, not long-term, memory. Most significantly, only short-term memory has the quality of immediacy necessary to impart the meaning of interpersonal agency. But the nature of the brain is that in short-term memory only a limited series of sequentially regressive reflective steps can be managed at one time.[33] As a result, interpersonal consciousness cannot generate a simultaneous reflection of agent-self as agent-self; rather, interpersonal agent-self experience can be introspected only by making the agent-self the object of the introspective act.[34] When I think of myself thinking of myself, the thinking-of-myself self becomes an object. Thus, there are two types of introspected *interpersonal* meaning structures, agent-self and object-self, and there is always a missing personal meaning in terms of the last agent-self reflection in these sequentially regressive reflections. This causes the loss inherent in self-contained interpersonal self-recognition.[35]

Psychopathology is primarily a problem of deficit and malformation rather than of conflict. In other words, psychopathology is not primarily a conflict between opposing life-and-death instincts, between social demands and instinctual drives, or between learned ideals and social obligations. Psychopathology ultimately results from the phenomenon that survival depends on the acquisition of the meaning of effective intrapsychic agency; the motives of intrapsychic consciousness have hegemony over the motives of interpersonal consciousness. Examples include suicide, fatal forms of psychological marasmus,[36] and anorexia nervosa. Nonfatal psychopathology, on the other hand, can preserve physical survival by pathologically fixating the innately determined, illusional form of intrapsychic motive gratification, which preserves the child's conviction that her/his intrapsychic agent-self is the regulatory cause of the caregiver's intrapsychic caregiving in the face of the caregiver's inability to give intrapsychic care. Thus, the cause of nonorganic mental illness does not lie in the basic nature the infant brings into the world, but represents the interaction of traumatic nurture and adaptive, innately based psychic structure. Unlike paradigmatic development, in psychopathology nurture-based, veridical agency experience never replaces innately determined, illusional agency experience. One consequence of psychopathology, therefore, is that the individual does not achieve the species-specific potential for an autonomous, veridical, loss-free, pain-free, nurture-based, reflective regulatory control of her/his subjective personal existence.

In the absence of brain damage or the death of a parent, psychopathology has only one cause: the caregiver's inability, owing to her/his own intrapsychic incapacity, to provide the child with veridical caregiving.[37] The nonveridical caregiver cannot regulate her/his own subjective personal existence in a stable manner and, therefore, despite her/his best efforts, cannot provide the child with the veridical experience of having the stable capacity to cause the caregiver to choose caregiving pleasure over the pleasure of gratifying personal motives. The nonveridical caregiver's inability to provide (or even to know s/he cannot provide) veridical intrapsychic caregiving causes the child to develop a delusional form of intrapsychic agent-self. As we describe in the chapter on psychopathology (chap. 6), a pathological intrapsychic agent-self is sustained by an unconscious motive for a nonveridical type of intrapsychic well-being.[38]

There are two forms of psychopathology, intrapsychic and interpersonal. ***Intrapsychic psychopathology*** always underlies interpersonal psychopathology. The referent for intrapsychic psychopathology is the structurally illusional quality of an individual's intrapsychic agent-self experience. ***Interpersonal psychopathology*** has two referents: (1) behavior on the level of thought or action that transgresses average limits (e.g., obsessive compulsive behavior)[39] and (2) behavior on the level of thought or action that falls within average bounds but that is psychopathological by comparison with paradigmatic development as we define this (e.g., nightmares). Unless otherwise specified, we use the term interpersonal psychopathology to refer only to psychopathology as usually defined. As the length, complexity, and constant flux of standard psychiatric categorizations of abnormal behavior illustrates, interpersonal psychopathology is protean in form. *Interpersonal* psychopathology is the culmination of a host of factors. These include the degree of the caregivers' interpersonal psychopathology; the prevailing cultural values; and the child's biological endowment, socioeconomic opportunities, chance encounters, and other life experiences.

Intrapsychic psychopathology may or may not be accompanied by clinically manifest interpersonal psychopathology. The strength and also the potential downfall of the human species is that intrapsychic psychopathology can be accompanied by a superior level of interpersonal functioning that ultimately serves to gratify the intrapsychic motive. Precisely because intrapsychic psychopathology can coexist with and regulate excellent cognitive functioning, our planet may one day be blown up by atomic weapons or made uninhabitable by pollution.

Because we believe that the structure of intrapsychic psychopathology is unitary, we base our nosology on the determination of treatability rather than on the classification of interpersonal symptoms.[40] The determination of treatability occurs within diagnostic Intrapsychic Treatment sessions. Details of the process of determining treatability are provided in the chapters on psychopathology and Intrapsychic Treatment (chaps. 6 and 7).

EPISTEMOLOGY AND ONTOLOGY IN INTRAPSYCHIC HUMANISM

Empiricism and Mutuality

One major tenet of Intrapsychic Humanism is that in paradigmatic development and Intrapsychic Treatment the subject's intrapsychic regulatory agency reality is potentially both empirically knowable and mutualized. In contrast, introspection and empathy are nonempirical, solipsistic modes of understanding subjective human experience. Because they are inherently experience-distant ways of knowing,[41] introspection and empathy have proven to be incomplete, misleading and, therefore, destructive when used to understand the self and the other in psychological treatment and in childrearing.[42] In contrast, the intrapsychic knowing that a paradigmatic psychic development makes possible is a caregiving *activity* that imparts an experience-near, empirical knowledge of the subject's intrapsychic agency experience. Our assertion that, in an intrapsychic caregiving relationship, the subject's intrapsychic agency motives are empirically knowable does not contradict the observation that introspection in its usual sense is *solipsistic,* because the knowledge generated by intrapsychic caregiving relates solely to the subject's regulatory agency reality. Solipsism, literally the "alone self," traditionally refers to what is formally termed epistemological solipsism, which is the position that the human mind has no grounds for believing in anything but itself.[43] In common usage, solipsism connotes the inherent privacy of self-experience, which cannot be empirically known by another. From our perspective, the common usage of solipsism conflates pathological and paradigmatic self-experience. As a result of this conflation, the unalterable privacy of introspection that occurs within the constitutive level of interpersonal consciousness has been mistakenly understood to imply that all subjective experience of personal existence is permanently inaccessible.[44] In contrast, we distinguish between: (1) nonsolipsistic intrapsychic and regulatory-interpersonal levels of knowable agency reality and (2) the solipsism of constitutive-interpersonal introspection. Constitutive-interpersonal introspection remains entirely private in that no determination of veridicality is possible.[45]

As traditionally defined, the notions of solipsistic (nonempirical) and empirical (nonsolipsistic) have the over-arching referent of a loss-free means of achieving knowledge. Both solipsism and empiricism are usually characterized by what they are not: solipsism is often distinguished from empirical, which commonly is defined as the nonsolipsistic category of that which can be known. Experience is the etymological root of empirical, and common usage also specifies that empirical experience arises from publicly accessible data. The common referent for empirical is a to-be-known reality that originates in a locus that can be observed by another as well as by the knower and can be apprehended by an act of knowing that includes sensory experience. Empirical knowledge results from a perceptual experience that others can potentially replicate and validate. Put another way, in common usage all exteroception is nonsolipsistic and all introspection is solipsistic. In its common usage, introspection is existentially private both in the sense of being irreversibly shut off from directly shared personal experience and also in the sense of being a nonvolitional exclusion of external reality.[46]

The existentialists, among others, believe that solipsism is an etiological factor in the painful, alienated, divided, isolated condition of the inner self that, especially since the Enlightenment, is often attributed to the subjective experience of personal existence in Western society. We agree that it is not uncommon in Western culture for the individual to feel self-alienation, but we ascribe the cause entirely to the occurrence of psychopathological psychic pain in the context of the isolation intrinsic to introspective experience as traditionally defined.[47]

Intrapsychic Humanism characterizes solipsism and empiricism as follows. Knowledge is *empirical* when the substrate to be known is publicly accessible, that is, can be apprehended by more than one person. Knowledge is *nonempirical* when the substrate to be known is not publicly accessible in this manner. *Solipsistic* knowledge comprises that category of nonempirical knowledge in which the substrate to be known is an experience of consciousness accessible only to that consciousness. In its usual sense, introspection is an example of solipsistic knowledge. In contrast, knowledge is *mutual* when the substrate to be known is an experience of consciousness that can be known by a separate center of agency.[48] We propose that knowledge of another's intrapsychic motives is the only mutual form of empirical knowledge. One acquires it through the act of providing intrapsychic caregiving. In the veridical knowledge of another's intrapsychic motives that characterizes intrapsychic caregiving, empirical and mutual are equivalent and have the same referent.[49]

The to-be-known substrate of the intrapsychic form of psychic reality is the regulatory experience of agency, knowledge of which is limited to the mutuality of an intrapsychic caregiving relationship.[50] Veridical knowledge of another's intrapsychic agent-self differs entirely from notions that could be categorized as parapsychology or extrasensory perception. Most specifically, knowledge of intrapsychic consciousness is unrelated to mind reading. In contrast to the empirical-mutual knowledge of intrapsychic consciousness, mind reading implies the possibility of a nonvolitional communication of psychic reality. In other words, mind reading asserts that another's interpersonal consciousness potentially can be known by an empirical, mutual epistemic act.

One distinguishing characteristic of the empirical knowing of *nonagency* reality (e.g., the cause of earthquakes) is that the act of knowing itself cannot be empirically known. To know publicly accessible (empirical) nonagency reality is, accordingly, a solipsistic process. This is one reason why the methodology of the natural sciences does not produce certain knowledge.

Unlike extracranial nonagency reality (e.g., a tree), another's interpersonal agency experience is not empirically accessible. The phenomenon that one's interpersonal introspection remains private with regard to other minds can be illustrated by the potential disjunction between intention and language (the potential distinction between what is meant and what is said).[51] Excluding hallucinatory experiences, the nonempirical quality of interpersonal consciousness can be introspected by observing that no matter how many different conversational experiences occur within interpersonal consciousness, each one has the quality of originating intracranially. Even when a voice sounds just like someone else (e.g., a voice saying, "Enunciate clearly," may sound just like one's drama teacher), the "just like" has an as-if quality rather than an empirical quality. Unless one's cognition is fundamentally impaired, one does not believe that one is in direct contact with another's immediate interpersonal introspective experience. Even when there is a teacher in the room saying, "Enunciate clearly," the listener empirically experiences only the teacher's verbal behavior and not her/his interpersonal consciousness.[52]

Intrapsychic Caregiving Contrasted with Empathy

The notion of empathy has numerous referents.[53] For purposes of this discussion, we use empathy to denote the activity of knowing another as that activity is referred to in the psychoanalytic literature. There exists an active, ongoing debate in the psychoanalytic literature as to whether empathy is an instrument of or the very essence of the psychoanalytic process. Among American psychoanalysts, Kohut has been the most prominent proponent of the notion of the essential role of empathy in the psychoanalytic process. Kohut defined empathy as vicarious introspection.[54] He depicted two functions of empathy: information gathering and response.[55]

In our view, empathy is a product of the cognitive and social-interpersonal categories of constitutive-interpersonal motives. Given its solipsistic nature, empathy is inherently nonveridical. Empathy does not require an intrapsychic caregiving relationship, but only a unilateral motivation on the part of the observer to understand a specific, delimited dimension of the inner experience of the person being observed.[56] Because the other's interpersonal motives are solipsistic, empathy is necessarily experience distant and indirect; the subject's interpersonal motives can only be known to the other by deduction and can be related to only by interpretation. Consequently, empathy cannot yield reliable knowledge of another's mind.[57] When psychotherapists, including psychoanalysts, rely on empathy, their help is limited to interpretations that gratify the patient's cognitive and social-interpersonal motives, which are not veridical regulating causes of inner well-being. In parenting, when a caregiver relies on empathy exclusively, the caregiver misunderstands or overlooks the child's regulatory agency experience, which makes her/ his caregiving nonveridical and causes the child to develop intrapsychic psychopathology. On the other hand, veridical intrapsychic caregiving consists not of meaning structures that are indirect, deductive acts of interpretation, but rather of structuralizing, veridical acts of caregiving that advance the child's development of veridical regulatory agency. Veridical intrapsychic caregiving works in an analogous fashion between therapist and patient.

Veridical intrapsychic caregiving is the caregiver's or therapist's capacity to know accurately the child's or patient's intrapsychic motives and to make appropriate intrapsychic caregiving responses. In contrast to introspection and empathy, veridical intrapsychic caregiving does not entail an act of understanding. Rather, it is an *act of psychic structure building;* it is an active relationship that has the purpose of effecting the structural completion of the child's or patient's intrapsychic consciousness. This unique act of knowing is regulated by the caregiver's veridical intrapsychic caregiving ideals and motives, which make it pleasurable to subordinate personal motives to caregiving motives.[58] The compelling attractiveness of caregiving ideals can be illustrated by those non-human animals, such as chimpanzees, who spend years preferring caregiving motives over personal motives (e.g., to roam, to socialize).[59] In other words, while empathy gratifies constitutive-interpersonal motives for cognitive and social-interpersonal pleasure, veridical intrapsychic caregiving produces a superior pleasure, intrapsychic caregiving pleasure.

Because we posit that intrapsychic consciousness generates regulatory motives for mutualized, intrapsychic care-getting pleasure, we place the crux of psychic development within the mutuality of the intrapsychic caregiving relationship. The infant never lacks a subjectively experienced intimate relationship with the caregiver, which in paradigmatic development always has an orthogenic effect. This contrasts with psychoanalysis, which places the crux of psychic development in the ego's evolving responses to the psychosexual instinctual drive derivatives and to the impact of society's demands. Accordingly, the psycho-analytic constructs of an autoerotic stage and primary narcissism are misleading; they result from mistaking psychopathological for paradigmatic development.

If adhered to, Freud's principles of child development would cause psychopathology. For example, Freud emphasized the vital, developmental value of the ego's capacity for instinctual renunciation. He thought this renunciatory capacity helps the ego with its repressive function, thereby enabling the child to achieve developmentally successful, adaptive responses to the losses of instinctual gratification represented by toilet training and the frustration of oedipal motives. As will be explained in chapter 6, however, repression and renunciation are forms of psychopathological self-rage. In fact, all psychoanalytic descriptions of child development, including both those based on the drive model and those based on the object relations model, represent a conflation of psychopathology and normality.[60] Accordingly, such pain-dominated behaviors as oral rage, anal conflicts, temper tantrums, and adolescent rebellion, which psychoanalysis sees as the lot of every child, are actually an indication of psychopathology and, therefore, are not inevitable. This conflation of psychopathological and paradigmatic development also characterizes other developmental psychologies.[61]

Meaning Structures

A *meaning structure* is produced by an act of perceptual identity; it is a gratified motive. Overall, there are two categories of meaning structures: personal and nonpersonal. Personal meaning structures constitute the only meaning structures that are regulating causes of subjective personal existence. As regulatory causes of subjective experience, personal meaning structures have a reality equivalent to (just as real as) the reality of the nonpsychic type of physicality (e.g., a rock), which is the object of the natural sciences.[62] Because personal meaning refers to the subjective experience of regulatory agency, the study of personal meaning structures is equivalent to the psychology of regulatory agency reality. Intrapsychic Humanism focuses primarily on personal meaning structures and on how these originate, develop, and interrelate.[63]

In contrast to personal meaning structures, nonpersonal meaning structures, which are gratified constitutive-interpersonal motives, cannot regulate subjective personal existence.[64] Nonpersonal meaning structures may be composed of nonregulatory agency meanings (e.g., the "I" that is learning to play the piano) or nonagency meanings (the music being played). Nonpersonal meaning structures can causally affect the materialistic physical world (i.e., nonregulatory agency motives to understand or master the environment can result in the rearrangement of molecules in a chemical experiment).

In the psychoanalytic theory of instinctual drives, materialistic, non-agency reality is accorded the power to regulate the subjective experience of personal existence. Psychoanalytic theory grounds the psychic structure of the ego in the body. For example, the mouth is conceived of as a primal cavity that organizes early ego development by functioning as a template onto which early forms of ego structure can be copied. Piaget's essential conception of the origin of mind bears a striking resemblance to the psychoanalytic model.[65] Piaget posited that the mind develops through the child's integration of motor experience with cognitive-affective schemata. He concluded that mind, or intellect, arises by a process in which the earliest motor patterns are used to form cognitive-affective schemata that, in turn, function as templates for the development of isologous thought patterns. Piaget's developmental scheme resembles Freud's notion that thought represents experimental action, and both Freud and Piaget supposed that mind is epiphenomenal to matter. More specifically, though both Freud and Piaget assigned psychological significance to the products of mind, neither accorded the subjective experience of the mind the level of importance assigned to material reality.[66]

The conclusion that mind is epiphenomenal to matter in relation to the subjective experience of personal existence is equivalent to concluding that the tail wags the dog. It is a radically reductionistic understanding of subjective experience based on the value judgment that all valuable explanations are grounded in sensory experience associated with the materialistic, nonagency type of physical reality. Since such a view approaches the subjective experience of mind solely in terms of matter (the body), the understanding of personal experience it provides has an indirect, distant and incomplete quality.[67] Etymological dictionaries abound with instances of the common preference for grounding the intimacies of self-experience in impersonal experience. The psychological construct of *character,* for example, which denotes the typical, stable pattern of an individual's behavior, has its etymological root in the Greek word for the instrument that imprints a character on wax in order to identify a material object.[68]

Intrapsychic Subjectivity

Intrapsychic meaning represents an agent-self-caused caregiving relationship. Paradigmatic intrapsychic reality consists of a regulatory intrapsychic agent-self with the autonomous capacity for veridical agent causality with regard to acquiring the reflection of agent-self as agent-self. Intrapsychic regulatory agency reality is known by a unique subjectivity, **intrapsychic subjectivity.** Intrapsychic subjectivity differs from previous constructs of subjectivity in that it is the basis for a mutualized, empirical, nonillusional inner well-being.[69] Intrapsychic subjectivity encompasses: (1) the viewpoint we term intrapsychic caregiving, the caregiver's and intrapsychic therapist's empirical, mutual, veridical responses to the intrapsychic motives of child or patient in the context of an intrapsychic caregiving commitment; and (2) veridical intrapsychic self-caretaking, the stable inner well-being produced by the veridical regulation of one's own intrapsychic and regulatory-interpersonal motive gratification, a state that occurs conditionally during paradigmatic development and unconditionally after an individual has completed a paradigmatic developmental process.

The traditional referents for the knowing denoted by subjectivity have been empathy and introspection. As we said earlier, empathy is a nonempirical attempt to know another's constitutive-interpersonal motives. In its common usage, introspection represents the solipsistic attempt at self-knowledge by the constitutive-interpersonal "I." Empathy and introspection constitute the perspective of the creative arts, psychology, and that branch of philosophy concerned with the subjective experience of personal existence. While introspection and empathy can result in inferences about one's own or another's unconscious constitutive-interpersonal motives, this knowing is always problematic because it is solipsistic.

In the context of a focus on the subjective experience of personal existence, we ground the criteria we apply to reality testing in the veridicality of the intrapsychic caregiving relationship rather than in nonliving physical reality or within linguistic and mathematical logic.[70] In contrast to Intrapsychic Humanism, one mainstream tendency in Western thought is analogically and metaphorically to define living substance in terms of nonliving substance. We believe that the ideals of reality, validity, security, necessity, safety, truth, goodness, and certainty can be attained without grounding the meaning of personal existence in the supposed immutability of the nonliving, material stuff of the universe. In actuality, certain, real experience inheres only in a mutualized regulatory agency reality. In other words, the attribute *physical* should not only be defined in terms of *nonagency* physical reality, but also in terms of *agency* physical reality, which is an intrinsic component of the state of being alive.[71]

THE NEED TO EXPERIENCE A STABLE, EFFECTIVE AGENT-SELF

Teleology and the Perceptual Identity Process

The regulatory control of subjective personal existence is based on a unique teleological process specific only to regulatory agency reality.[72] We describe a teleological causality that occurs in the context of the intimate relationship between an individual's sense of personal agency and an intended ideal (motive). Intrapsychic teleological causality involves a motive (a consciousness-generated, to-be-actualized ideal of effective agent cause) that regulates the subjective experience of personal existence. We term this to-be-actualized ideal the intrapsychic motive.[73] The content of this potentially attainable, motivating ideal is that the agent-self will acquire a veridical reflection of agent-self as agent-self via the loss-free capacity to be the agent cause of the caregiver's intrapsychic caregiving love.[74]

The functional agent cause is stably located in the agent-self only after the completion of a paradigmatic developmental process. In psychopathology, actual regulatory control over the choice of the to-be-actualized ideal to be pursued resides in the power (appeal) of the ideal, which then acquires hegemony over choice. In this case, the vicissitudes of arbitrary desire regulate the agent-self. A dramatic clinical example is the condition of the impulse-ridden personality. On a less malignant level, an individual may explain, "I just couldn't resist buying that camera even though I want to save money." It should be noted that, even when the to-be-actualized ideal rather than the agent-self has agent-cause capacity, the agent-self has the illusion of having agent-cause capacity. (Even in the process of being unable to resist buying the camera, the individual has the experience that s/he is intentionally acquiring it.) In short, not all intentional acts (e.g., buying the camera) are intended acts (e.g., the individual intended not to exceed the budget). It follows that when acts of choice are regulated by a consciousness-generated ideal, the agent-self remains vulnerable to loss with regard to the consciousness-generated need for a stable, autonomous, agent-self, self-regulatory capacity.

At birth the consciousness-generated, intrapsychic motive (to-be-actualized ideal) is the regulating cause of intrapsychic motive gratification. In other words, from an intrapsychic caregiving perspective, agent cause lies outside the agent-self. Development represents a process whereby, from the viewpoint of the intrapsychic caregiver, intrapsychic agent cause shifts to the child's intrapsychic agent-self. This developmental achievement occurs in the second developmental stage, the regulatory-intrapsychic self stage (see chap. 3). A differentiated (regulatory) intrapsychic agent-self has a veridical, autonomous, loss-free capacity for intentionality, for regulating and owning its own mind experience; therefore, it is never vulnerable to losing the meaning of effective personal agency.[75]

Causality [76]

In early development and in untreated psychopathology, an individual directs her/his behavior toward a to-be-gratified ideal, which exerts a regulatory influence on that behavior. Purposive behavior is the sine qua non of human existence; without purpose the individual will not remain alive. Human experience is purposeful in that the individual pictures an accomplished end (a goal) in an as-yet-to-be-accomplished state. The not-yet-attained state of gratification represents an ideal state, which then becomes the purposive explanation for any given act. One consequence is that an effect can be designated erroneously as signifying the cause. The *whyness* form of causality contains the most intrinsic component of the subjective experience of personal existence and can reside either within or remain external to the agent-self. With regard to the intrapsychic motive, whyness and purposiveness refer to the need for the (illusional or veridical) capacity to be the cause of the caregiver's intrapsychic caregiving.

Purposiveness, or whyness, regulates the agent-self's view of itself and of the other's behavior in relation to the agent-self (as caused or not caused). The teleological viewpoint we introduce here explains the functioning of undifferentiated consciousness and the process by which consciousness can be differentiated (mutualized). In early development, the quality of the child's inner well-being is determined by the teleological principle that the child experiences any effect associated with the caregiver's behavior as signifying the caregiver's caregiving intentions. To the young child, then, effect can erroneously signify cause. The innately determined capacity illusionally to equate meaning and cause is the core problem of subjective personal existence.[77] The child equates all intrapsychic motive gratification, whether veridical or nonveridical, with the caregiver's intrapsychic intentions regarding the child's motive for effective intrapsychic agency. Because the operation of teleological principles causes children to accord unintended effects intentional significance, in psychopathology the child equates the psychic pain caused by the caregiver's unintentionally nonveridical caregiving with intentionally caused, veridical caregiving love. As a result, the child develops motives for nonveridical intrapsychic caregiving (for psychic pain), which the child perceives as caregiving love.

In other words, in early development and in all psychopathology, the locus of teleological causality that regulates subjective personal existence resides in the to-be-actualized ideal rather than in the agent-self.[78] From an intrapsychic caregiving perspective, in development (1) the to-be-actualized intrapsychic ideal *motivates* an agent-self to pursue intrapsychic motive gratification and (2) the percepts required to gratify the intrapsychic motive arise within the context of the caregiver's intrapsychic caregiving, which exists, of course, external to the child's agent-self. In psychopathology, the individual's experience of regulatory agency remains illusional. Thus, in early development and in psychopathology the individual does not have veridical regulatory control of her/his inner well-being, even though s/he introspectively experiences intrapsychic agent-self causal capacity (which equals the meaning imparted by intrapsychic motive gratification).[79]

Intrapsychic consciousness is undifferentiated in infancy and remains permanently undifferentiated in psychopathology. By *undifferentiated* intrapsychic consciousness, we mean that neither the to-be-actualized ideal (motive) for effective agency nor the percepts necessary to gratify this motive are within the regulatory capability of the agent-self. This missing reflection of veridical agency amounts to the missing reflection of agent-self as agent-self. A dramatic introspection of derivatives of this fundamental psychic pain occurred in the treatment session of a five-year-old child who had great difficulty in making decisions, and who invariably reversed decisions immediately after he made them. In this way, simple choices, such as what to eat, consumed most of his energy. He became increasingly aware of the conflicted nature of his daily experience, until one day he told his therapist, "I wish I could go in my mouth and up into my brain and make those guys in there stop fighting and leave me alone."

The term **intrapsychic agent-self** refers both to the meaning of personal agency produced by intrapsychic motive gratification and also to the agent-self's experience of agency in the pursuit of intrapsychic motive gratification. The quality of this agency experience is determined both by whether intrapsychic motive gratification is veridical or nonveridical and also by whether the agent cause of the gratification is veridically within the regulatory control of the agent-self or, from an intrapsychic caregiving perspective, exists external to the agent-self. The most important agent-self meaning with regard to any specific motive can be termed *regulatory agency capacity.* Intrapsychic motive gratification always (illusionally or veridically) imparts the personal meaning significance of an agent-self that possesses loss-free agent causality with regard to desire, choice, and purposive intentionality. The individual must have this self-experience of regulatory agency (the reflection of agent-self as agent-self rather than as object-self) in order to survive, but, during early development and in all psychopathology, this meaning is illusional. In paradigmatic development, the meaning of regulatory agency becomes internalized within the intrapsychic agent-self by means of a mutualizing process,[80] at which point the individual has the nonillusional, loss-free capacity for self-regulatory autonomy we term the *regulatory-intrapsychic agent-self.* The individual with a regulatory-intrapsychic agent-self veridically knows and owns her/his own mind. As will be explained in chapter 4, the regulatory-intrapsychic agent-self makes possible the onset of a veridical *regulatory-interpersonal agent-self.* Once this is securely established, the individual will never experience either loss due to her/his inability to follow chosen interpersonal motives or loss due to her/his pursuit of interpersonal motives s/he does not want to gratify. In other words, there will be no unintended, intentional acts. In addition, interpersonal motives that are chosen will be pursued effectively and without conflict. For example, if one has a job to do one will not put it off, forget it, do it incorrectly due to carelessness, or be overly obsessed with it. Veridical regulatory agent-self capacity also confers an invulnerability to nonveridical personal meaning experience (to illusional esteem).[81]

It can be seen that the essence of human nature, the hunting and gathering of meaning, differs in paradigmatic development and psychopathology. In paradigmatic development, intrapsychic hunting and gathering is under the hegemony of the loss resulting from the gap between the intrapsychic agent-self and the external location of the source of the reflection of effective agency, the caregiver's caregiving motives. As long as the source of the reflection of agent-self effectiveness lies external to the agent-self, the child will experience an ongoing sense of incompleteness. In contrast to psychopathology, in paradigmatic development this incompleteness will become reflectively recognized within the context of the child's empirically based conviction that a genuine, regulatory autonomy is being and will be acquired. This conviction is experientially grounded in the intrapsychic agent-self's sense that gratifying percepts, although external to the agent-self, are regulated by the caregiver's intrapsychic caregiving motives, which include the unconditional motive for the child's intrapsychic agent-self to regulate its own intrapsychic motive gratification. It should be emphasized that the conviction that the intrapsychic agent-self has effective agency capacity can be produced either by veridical or nonveridical intrapsychic motive gratification. Therefore, in development and psychopathology, the agent-self feels it has veridical agent-self capability even though, from an intrapsychic caregiving perspective, the intrapsychic agent-self remains structurally incomplete.

The intrapsychic to-be-actualized ideal initially exerts hegemony over the intrapsychic agent-self. Because of the mutualized nature of intrapsychic consciousness, the caregiver's intrapsychic caregiving ideals are an intrinsic component of the child's experience of hunting and gathering meaning. The content of the caregiver's intrapsychic caregiving ideals is that the child's agent-self attains veridical regulatory agency. The potential stumbling block in development is that the child can neither choose her/his parents nor regulate the parents' caregiving ideals without their consent. As a result, the child cannot protect her/himself against the psychic pain caused by caregivers who are unable to pursue the pleasure of intrapsychic caregiving mutuality.

In *psychopathology* the permanently undifferentiated, teleological nature of intrapsychic motive gratification results in two types of derivative interpersonal meaning: *paranoid* and *as-if*. The *paranoid* identity represents an externalization of psychic pain that occurs because the child's center of regulation with regard to purposive experience initially exists outside of the intrapsychic agent-self both intracranially in the to-be-actualized ideal and also extracranially in the caregiver's caregiving motives and ideals. On the other hand, the *as-if* type of personal meaning signifies a delusional sense of control that results from the fact that, given the meaning of intrapsychic motive gratification, the incompletely developed agent-self can experience an as-yet-to-be-attained ideal as if it had already been achieved.[82]

EPISTEMOLOGY AND ONTOLOGY IN PSYCHOANALYSIS

In part, the widespread influence exerted by psychoanalytic theory derives from Freud's claims that his conclusions were veridical because they were grounded in an ontology (essence) of psychic reality and an epistemology (knowing) of psychic reality that were scientifically acceptable by contemporary standards for the natural sciences.[83] Our conclusion that Freud's psychic reality and the method he advanced for knowing this reality cannot produce veridical knowledge about the subjective experience of personal existence was an important impetus stimulating us to develop a new psychology and philosophy of mind. In the service of describing the heuristic value of the ontology of psychic reality and the means of knowing that reality advanced by Intrapsychic Humanism, we present here a brief critique of Freud's claim that psychoanalysis is a veridical approach to knowing psychic reality.

Freud thought that by postulating that the instinctual drives were regulating causes of subjective experience he had made his model of psychic reality objective.[84] In consequence, he never systematically examined the process of the introspective act per se but instead adopted the bias that any psychology that uses the data of introspection as the main mode of knowing psychic reality is solipsistic and, hence, inherently defective. Freud did not realize that his version of introspection does not exhaust the possibilities of self-reflection—that there could be a form of introspection qualitatively different from the self-reflective act that stems from what psychoanalysis terms the primary autonomous apparatus.[85]

Freud organized and conceived his theories from a consistent philosophical viewpoint, the essence of which is that his entire psychological theory, including the metapsychology, is a science just like the natural sciences. Freud relied on the assumptions of nineteenth-century neural science as building blocks for his theory. However, that which Freud insisted is pure psychology (his metapsychology) is in fact a metaphysical statement that grounds psychic reality in positivistic neuropsychology.[86] Further, Freud's epistemology is unidirectionally determined by his ontology; his model of a somatic, positivistic, monistic psychic reality dictates his epistemology. After discarding his pre-1895 model of mind, Freud was determined not to rely on consciousness per se as the ultimate determinant of the subjective experience of personal existence. Ironically, Freud ultimately took the very position that he was certain he had avoided: his act of knowing uses the object to be known as the instrument of knowing.

Since Freud conceived the substrate to be known according to a paradigm organized by positivist principles, the act of knowing in psychoanalysis yields a remorselessly materialistic, reductionistic picture of human nature. Because Freud's epistemological options were severely restricted when he posited a psychic reality that conformed to the reality knowable by the natural sciences, Freud failed to realize that the single most important challenge in creating a psychological theory is to find a suitable epistemology for knowing psychic reality. As an inhabitant of the positivist, neo-Kantian period that arose as a response to the excesses of nineteenth-century idealism, Freud predictably assumed that empirical knowledge produced by the positivist principles of experimental science was the sole mode of reliable knowing. Consequently, Freud's method of apprehending the instinctual category of psychic reality is always experience distant.[87]

Freud's perspective is captured aptly in Sulloway's descriptive title, *Freud, Biologist of the Mind*. Freud saw the fabric of psychic reality as a product of instinctual drive derivatives, which he considered to be the end result of a biological process of primate evolution from the quadruped to the biped stage. He asserted that the societal product of this evolutionary process generates a species need to repress the animal, or quadruped, side of human nature. Freud conceptualized human nature as an uneasy truce between the individual's true, lower nature and the individual's learned, nonhegemonic, higher nature. He thought that each individual's psychic reality contains remnants of the whole evolution of lower animal life and that these remnants are recapitulated during childhood in the form of a permanently conflicted mental apparatus that poses a constant threat to the achievements of human evolution. Thus, Freud explained human nature by Lamarck's now discredited premise of the inheritance of acquired characteristics and by applying Haeckel's Law—that ontology recapitulates phylogeny—to the meaning structures of psychic reality. Accordingly, Freud asserted that cultural evolution is an extension of biological evolution. His version of cultural evolution was also shaped by his assumption of the universal reality of sexual conflict.

Lamarck's influence allowed Freud to postulate that phylogeny came to embody the father-son primal-horde behavior that supposedly occurred during the archaic history of the race.[88] The phylogenetic primal-horde stage includes two primordial types of drives—oedipal carnal desire and oedipal rage. Freud believed these attributes were ontogenetically recapitulated in every human. Accordingly, Freud concluded that transference phenomena result from an ontogenetic recapitulation of a species-specific phylogenetic stage that reflects a universal infantile neurosis and represents the basis of Freud's vision of a structurally flawed human nature. Freud thought repression was a natural, biologically based, inevitable condition produced as a by-product of a Darwinian selective process occurring in the context of sexual conflict between child and parent.

Freud's view of human nature exhibits an inverted Manicheanism;

he accords hegemony over psychic reality both to a lower animal side of human nature, which generates vegetative appetitive behavior, and also to the negative experiences of life (loss, conflict, pain, and rage). Freud initially used a topographical model of mind to account for his conclusion that all human existence was characterized by psychic pain. The topographical model included a repression barrier, which separates the instinctual unconscious containing the sexual drives from the rational, conscious ego, which includes the instinct of self-preservation and has the function of repression.[89] Freud's observations of the seemingly incorrigible human proclivity for self- and other-directed destructive behavior led him to conclude that humans possessed a death instinct.[90] He used the death instinct to account for the unconscious guilt that he thought was the chief cause of intense and intentional acts of self-hatred. When the topographic model proved inadequate to this new complexity, Freud developed the structural model of mind in which the ego (the organ of rationality) originates in the id (irrationality) and is regulated by the death instinct. In this model, the death instinct resides in the unconscious segment of the ego he termed the superego.[91]

Because he focused on the material level of human existence, which confronted him with the inevitability of corporeal death and decay (positive entropy), Freud eventually ceded ultimate power to Thanatos, the death instinct.[92] Freud relied on the death instinct to explain how humans can choose destructive behavior (meaning) over food or sex and over continued personal existence. In contrast to our view of the human as primarily a hunter and gatherer of meaning, Freud saw the human primarily as a driven hunter and gatherer of food, sex, or both. Freud overlooked the most relevant level of human existence—the giving and receiving of personal meaning in the intrapsychic caregiving relationship that makes the intrapsychic "I" an *"I" of "we"ness.*

Freud's materialistic definition of essential human nature led him to adopt a reductionistic epistemology, or way of knowing human nature. He used the sexual motives of constitutive-interpersonal consciousness as the key to knowing nontranscendental, psychic reality. The sexual drive is relatively plastic and displaceable and, while it is vital to species survival, it can go ungratified without posing a threat to the individual's survival. When Freud made the sexual drive the touchstone for the ontology of psychic reality, he necessarily downgraded relationship experience to an ancillary, even epiphenomenal level. In looking for truth about human nature, Freud concluded that an animal nature underlies human nature and that the instinctual drives are the bedrock of human mind experience. He explained the capacity for human relationship experience solely as a byproduct of biological drives rehearsed on the level of culture.

Freud's clinical and theoretical work occurred in the context of a series of influences that, although unrecognized by him, shaped and restricted his thinking. Some important aspects of the defining context of Freud's thought were: (1) his view that the subjective experience of personal existence includes inevitable psychic pain and "common unhappiness;"[93] (2) an epistemology that dictated a naive reductionism (of the psychological to the biological); (3) his conceptual bias, resulting from his professional identity as a biologist of the mind, that the development of psychic reality was the result of an enfolded phylogenetic process;[94] and (4) the fact that he worked in a post-Cartesian and post-Kantian era, which meant that his epistemology led him categorically to mistrust subjective experience as a way to understand the experience of mind.[95]

Freud saw transference as a normal, ineluctable, *permanent* component of human existence. He postulated that mind is the product of an innately determined, mechanistic, psychic apparatus and that the id (the dynamic unconscious) comprises the primary core of human nature. He asserted that transference experience is rooted in this conflicted unconscious. Thus, the human is a rational animal (secondary-process thinking) constantly beleaguered by the human as an irrational animal (primary-process thinking). Freud postulated that, because it originates in the conflicted, dynamic unconscious (which is forever kept from consciousness by a permanent repression barrier),[96] the primary process can be apprehended only indirectly in waking life through, for instance, manifestations of neurotic symptoms, transference processes, or the psychopathology of everyday life (e.g., slips of the tongue). Freud further asserted that primary-process thought could be best known through the waking recall of dream experience (the royal road to the unconscious) and, less effectively, in psychoanalytic treatment, via free associations and the transference neurosis. In dream analysis, in the psychopathology of everyday life, and in transference neurosis experience in treatment, Freud thought that he had found a sound epistemology for apprehending the hidden core of human nature.

Freud decided that the most reliable form of scientifically knowable psychic reality is the dream and its source, the dream work; from our perspective, however, this product of consciousness is actually the antithesis of a nonillusional, mutual subjective personal existence. Consequently, though psychoanalysis appears to take consciousness seriously, in actuality it has done more to retard a serious consideration of consciousness than, for example, the logical positivists, who in effect legislated consciousness out of existence. Because psychoanalysis does not believe that any consciousness-generated experience can veridically represent reality, it advances no ontology of nonillusional relationship experience. Genuine, loving, caregiving relationship experience, which we view as an intrinsic part of the reality of human existence, is denigrated by psychoanalysis as appearance, not reality—shadow, not substance. From the psychoanalytic perspective, consciousness represents an arena within which the vicissitudes of antagonistic instinctual drives clash with the conflicting demands of an external reality that is, at best, grudgingly recognized.

Freud sought an empirical explanation of the nature of psychic conflict. By the time he wrote *The Interpretation of Dreams*, however, he felt that he could also offer a broader explanation of human nature and the nature of mind. In our view, this took the form of reifying psychopathological psychic pain and according it the status of a normative, indigenous component of human nature. Freud thought that the goal of psychoanalytic treatment was to transform "hysterical misery into common unhappiness."[97] Freud said he told his patients that, "With a mental life that has been restored to health you will be better armed against that unhappiness."[98] He assumed that psychic reality is a biologically determined, physiological phenomenon rooted in materialistic physical reality and manifested within consciousness as derivative forms of visceral appetitive and aversive forces. In other words, psychoanalytic theory considers psychic reality to be composed of inherently conflicted meaning structures that are grounded in somatic structures, and consequently, are permanently outside the individual's agent-self, self-regulatory control. Freud had to take this position because he assumed that the consciousness manifested in sleeping dreams and incompletely captured by waking consciousness represents the purest example of the basal functioning of mind. He thought all introspected, waking consciousness was influenced by mental mechanisms that cloud, rather than elucidate, the fundamental workings of what he termed the psychic apparatus.[99] Accordingly, Freud said that secondary-process (rational) thought, which characterizes the conscious part of the ego, is an inherently defective mode of knowing one's own consciousness.[100]

While Freud concluded that rational, secondary-process thought was regulated by primary-process functioning, he also made rational thought the mediator of the process (e.g., dreams, free associations) by which primary-process thought becomes accessible. In this way, Freud thought that he had integrated his qualitatively distinct and opposed systems of meaning (primary process and secondary process) and had surmounted the related problems of solipsism and subjectivity. The unintended result, however, was that psychoanalytic theory embodies a materialistic reductionism of the psychological to the physiological and cannot provide a unified theory of human nature that can give an experience-near explanation of the sense of personal agency inherent in the subjective experience of personal existence.

Beginning in 1905, Freud's topographic model described human nature in terms of a psychic pain produced by the continuous, inescapable conflict between an irrational universe of instinctual drives (the id) and the rationality of an ego composed of self-preservative instincts and aims. The topographic model was superceded by Freud's 1923 structural model, which derived the structurally unconscious part of the ego from precipitates of the id's object cathexes that the ego has captured.[101] The structural model led Freud to add a new component, the superego, to his model of mind. The superego is a psychic structure created by a Lamarckian inheritance of a phylogenetically archaic unconscious. Freud placed the roots of the superego in the unconscious ego. As he defined it, the superego consists both of the phylogenetic precipitates of primary-process effects from inherited sources (the other minds in the archaic history of the species) and also of learned experience (from contemporary minds). Both sources are integrated and delivered to the child by means of cultural values. Freud's pessimistic view of human nature influenced him to make the punitive superego the mediating agency for the effects of historical consciousness on the ego.

Psychoanalysis conceptualizes the earliest developmental stages as objectless stages (autoerotic, pure pleasure ego) and sees motives for relationship and for meaning primarily as secondary, solipsistic phenomena, which represent reactions to the conflict between the instinctual drive derivatives' impact on consciousness and the demands of external reality. Accordingly, Freud modeled his thoughts about the relationship between love object as self (narcissism) and love object as other on the membranous behavior of the unicellular amoeba. He analogized the reciprocal, antagonistic movement of the amoeba's pseudopodal action with the reciprocal, antagonistic relationship between an individual's movement toward relationship experience and her/his withdrawal inward to a pure self-experience.[102] Given his postulation that love of self and love of other were implacably opposed, Freud concluded that caregiving pleasure between two human beings always represented epiphenomena of primary-process experience and could never be the basis for a nonillusional psychic reality.

Even after he described the superego, Freud continued to believe there could not be a primary, biological, nonmaterialistic, but physical source of regulatory motives. In fact, because his model of causal meaning (primary process) is rooted in the instinctual drives, Freud had to eschew the notion of motive. Even now, psychoanalytic theory cannot adequately account for the single most pertinent category of the subjective experience of personal existence, namely, the sense of personal agency.

In summary, Freud's decision not to accord epistemic and ontologic validity to any form of introspective experience of waking consciousness reflects his application of positivist scientific assumptions to mental phenomena. While dividing mind from body, psychoanalytic theory gives the body the status of the only true reality. This conceptual scheme manifests Freud's effort to explain the individual's and society's inability to exert regulatory control over the effects of the ubiquitous experience of loss and pain. He equates nonhuman animal behavior with a postulated lower human nature and attributes to this lower human nature hegemony over psychic reality. For Freud, human nature normatively and intrinsically includes an ongoing psychic experience of loss, pain, conflict, and rage.

This analysis of human nature excludes the potential capacity for reflective, ontological meaning experience and the capacity to mourn loss. As a result, Freud denied that the human's capacity and need for personal meaning could have ontological status in the sense of being an efficient cause of psychic reality. For example, Freud postulated that the infant turns from autoerotic pleasure to the external world only because s/he has to pay attention to external reality. Freud's hallucinatory breast model displays his conviction that reality testing occurs in response to instinctual loss.[103]

In contrast, we believe that a true mourning process allows the individual to experience inevitable constitutive-interpersonal loss without a corresponding loss of veridical (as opposed to illusional) inner well-being. We postulate a biological, physical, regulatory agency reality, which generates a motive for care-getting relationship pleasure and personal meaning experience. After the conclusion of a paradigmatic development, the gratification of this motive confers the capacity for a loss-free, agent-self, self-regulatory capacity. *To this day, mainstream psychoanalytic theory does not include a biologically based primary motive for social behavior and meaning experience, in spite of Spitz's recognition of the universality of the smile response.* [104]

The metaphysical presuppositions that underlie psychoanalytic theory ultimately are responsible for the harm caused by psychoanalytic treatment and by psychoanalytically guided childrearing practices. Psychoanalytic theory surmises that the core of subjective human existence contains biologically determined, uncontrollable sexual drive-derivative wishes, which constantly conflict both with the biologically determined death instinct in the structurally unconscious ego and superego and also with learned sets of cultural taboos and potentially controllable aims. In consequence, from the outset psychoanalysis forfeits the possibility that a person might aspire to, much less attain, a subjective experience of self characterized by an inner well-being based on a stable, loss-free, autonomous, pain-free personal agency. If one accepts psychoanalytic presuppositions about the essence of self-experience, one can never feel positively toward one's basic nature, but rather must live in fear and dislike of one's innermost essence. The highest goal of psychoanalytic treatment and child development is that personal subjective experience be composed of an inherently disappointing but not overwhelming struggle to manage inevitable psychic pain. Personal existence in effect represents a process of rehearsing roles prepared by a phylogeny molded by the current environment. Due to its hidden metaphysical assumptions, psychoanalysis promulgates as the highest attainable good the ability to love and work in the face of an ongoing and inescapable sense of inner misery. Since we believe inner disquiet is not an inevitable part of mature human existence, to accept fundamental psychic pain as paradigmatic in effect unnecessarily prescribes and endorses unhappiness.

The appeal of Freud's psychology is its nonmystical, nontranscendental, scientific approach to the problem that any psychological system must address, namely, humanity's inhumanity to itself. Explaining the problem of evil by man's evolution from lower animals provided a more humanistic approach to human suffering than did previous systematizations. However, in contrast to Freud's definition of psychic conflict as the result of opposing instinctual drive derivative wishes, we define psychopathological psychic conflict as the product of what is, ultimately, a learned, unitary motive. In our view, psychopathological psychic con-

31

flict has the meaning of psychic pain, which is a type of regulatory, personal meaning structure. While Freud viewed psychic conflict from an experience-distant vantage point, our approach places the observer inside the psychic conflict and in contact with the subject's sense of personal agency and motive for conflict and pain.

Nonpsychoanalytic Psychologies

We have focused on psychoanalysis because it is the first, most systematic, and most ambitious psychodynamic psychology. Subsequent developments and branchings in Freud's theories, which adopt his view of an inescapably conflicted, biologically determined, structural unconscious in combination with a psychic determinism forever beyond conscious control, are also subject to the above critique.

Nonpsychodynamic approaches attempt to explain the human mind and address the problem of regulatory control of subjective personal existence in at least one of four ways. Paradigmatic and nonparadigmatic forms of human experience are commonly seen as the result of: (1) learned behaviors resulting from social experience (e.g., some cognitive approaches, behaviorism); (2) some application of the principles of reductionistic biology (i.e., explanations based on genic, environmental, nutritional factors); (3) transcendental beliefs in a life force or a higher power; or (4) an existential form of will (intentionality), which provides the means to self-actualization.[105]

Some nonpsychodynamic approaches display a naive optimism about the perfectibility of human nature, while others manifest an unwarranted pessimism about the human condition. The unduly optimistic approaches do not appreciate the structurally unconscious nature of psychopathological motives. Overly pessimistic approaches accept the prevalence of psychic pain as a universal and ubiquitous condition of human existence and mistake interpersonal and intrapsychic psychopathology for normality. The consequence of the erroneous assumptions that underlie nonpsychodynamic psychologies, whether they operate in existential philosophies, general psychologies, theories of psychopathology, approaches to treatment, or childrearing guides, has been the promulgation of treatment and childrearing theories that are either of limited assistance or promote psychopathology.

THE SEARCH FOR CERTAINTY

The core of the quest for certainty and security is the need to avoid a sense of inner loss. The attempt to find certainty through constitutive-interpersonal motive gratification (the gratification of cognitive, physiological, and social-interpersonal motives), however, derives from intrapsychic psychopathology. In general, the cultural expression of conscious derivatives of this structurally unconscious, pathologically distorted need for agent-self, self-regulatory control of subjective personal existence depends on the prevalent and/or accessible technology and its associated *Weltanschauung* that a society has available at any given time and place.[106] In contemporary Western society, the need for this type of restitutional real usually takes the form of the technological manipulation of material, nonpsychic reality.

Derivatives of the unconscious, ongoing need to have an (illusional or veridical) agent-self, self-regulatory control of subjective personal existence are often expressed as the question of whether science, the problematic type of regulatory control of the external world conferred by reason, can insure the good life against unruly desire and unwarranted (capricious) loss.[107] Examples include the dispute between Plato and Aristotle over the possibility of basing the good life on rational self-sufficiency and the reaction of nineteenth-century idealism to the enshrinement of reason by the eighteenth-century enlightenment.[108]

With regard to the fundamental need to avoid inner loss, all previous societies, regardless of technological or other kinds of sophistication, can be divided into those with an outright mistrust of mind experience and those with a partial trust in the mind's efficacy to avoid inner loss. Those individuals who believe mind experience cannot protect the individual against inner loss can be divided into a form of the religious and the skeptical. An example of the religious category is Calvin's belief in predestination.[109] The skeptical category includes Freud and the positivists. Those who have a conditional trust in the sufficiency of mind experience to avoid inner loss can be divided into the optimistic and a second form of the religious. The optimists, the most prominent of whom is Plato, take a utopian position. Roman Catholic theology envisions salvation through a combination of good works (agency reality) and grace.

We assert unconditionally that mind alone can provide a stable, permanent experience of inner well-being. Further, we distinguish a species of mind experience that has no primary referent to pain. Our notion of paradigmatic intrapsychic motive gratification refers to an experience of inner well-being that has no reference to loss per se; unlike interpersonal pleasure, the experience of intrapsychic pleasure does not occur in a context defined by relief of, escape from, or absence of pain. We use the adjective "pain-free" to modify intrapsychic pleasure only in order to emphasize that postdevelopmental intrapsychic pleasure is both stable and also essentially unaffected by positive entropy and chance.[110] While interpersonal pleasure fluctuates according to circumstance, circumstance does not affect inner esteem because the stable well-being of the postdevelopmental intrapsychic agent-self is not contingent on interpersonal reality.

Because we understand mind and body as two types of a single physical reality, Intrapsychic Humanism is not a Manichean perspective. It stems from a radical view of human nature, based on the premise that the human is first and foremost a hunter and gatherer of meaning. From the viewpoint of inner personal meaning (regulatory agency physical reality), a mind-body distinction is artificial in that the distinction mistakenly assumes that the essence of psychic reality is either pure thought or material reality, which leads to a split and irreparably incomplete personal experience. We also avoid a reductionistic type of monism. We believe that mind-body dualism and reductionistic forms of monism are products of an act of knowing (epistemology) that is inappropriate to the to-be-known reality (ontology). Our distinction between agency reality and nonagency reality arises not from a dualistic world view but from our particular focus on subjective personal existence. For example, if the object of explanation were other than the subjective experience of personal existence (e.g., the causes and prediction of weather), the distinction between agency physical reality and nonagency physical reality obviously would not be heuristic.[111]

Pathological fixation at the level of nonveridical intrapsychic motive gratification can translate the remnant of the innate motive for veridical intrapsychic pleasure (for certainty and stability on the level of intrapsychic agency) into a search for validity in the form of cognitive certainty (about others, natural phenomena, transcendental phenomena, etc.). The ongoing, unconscious pain of intrapsychic loss (intrapsychic psychopathology) can make constitutive-interpersonal existence the arena for an unending compensatory search for the fulfillment of the need for certainty. Sought-for but elusive interpersonal certainty acquires the significance of the intrapsychic agent-self's delusional certainty of its ongoing, autonomous, loss-free capacity for a self-caused, other-given reflection of agent-self as agent-self. In other words, the driving ideal behind the futile quest for interpersonal certainty is the acquisition of an antidote to the pain inherent in the subjective experience of psychopathological intrapsychic agency.

The restitutional ideal of certainty is variously expressed as an ideal of validity, necessity, security, God, radical empiricism, radical idealism, or skepticism, among others. In both Eastern and Western thought, attempts to find a coherent, codified view of reality—specifically, the reality of subjective personal existence—can be distinguished by whether those attempts endorse the teleological process of an unending quest for the ideal, or take a position of radical skepticism. In the Eastern religion of Buddhism, the quest for the ideal typically endorses a nonrational, transcendental type of teleological experience that includes the capacity to negate or transcend material, corporeal reality and to inhabit that level of reality that can be termed the immaterial. In contrast, if one excludes the Manichean strain, postenlightenment Western thought generally credits material, nonagency physical reality with the potential to compensate for the loss represented by the effects of positive entropy on (constitutive-interpersonal) personal existence. By endowing nonagency physical reality with a substantiality not accorded agency physical reality, Western philosophy displays the effects of the unconscious conflicts that are indigenous to human nature in its pain-filled state on the quest for the ideal. As Heidegger observed, the Western quest for the ideal became reductionistically transformed into the quest for the tangible and the tactile. The fallibility inherent in constitutive-interpersonal introspection has repeatedly led Western thinkers to conduct their search for certainty on the level of the empirically provable.[112]

CHAPTER SUMMARY

Chapters 2–5 describe paradigmatic development. Chapter 2, "The Pre-Eidetic Stage," takes the infant from birth to about 12 months of age. In this period, the infant's smile response differentiates and the infant experiences the intrapsychic losses expressed as stranger anxiety and separation anxiety. The innately determined, nurture-facilitated grieving of stranger anxiety results in the phase-specific onset of an illusional process of intrapsychic motive gratification. The innately determined, nurture-facilitated grieving of separation anxiety makes it possible for the infant to have an internalized, though illusional, source of intrapsychic well-being in the form of memories of the caregiver that are available to recall.

Chapter 3, "The Regulatory-Intrapsychic Self Stage," takes the child from about 12 months to about 18 months. This stage includes transference and nontransference forms of care-getting anxiety, which represents the infant's third developmental intrapsychic loss. Care-getting

35

anxiety results when the caregiver temporarily pursues personal rather than caregiving motives and the child feels the loss of relative inner well-being pleasure. The caregiver's facilitative responses to the child's protests help the child have her/his first veridical, empirical, reflective awareness of the stability of the caregiver's intrapsychic caregiving motives. The child's empirical, veridical certainty of her/his intrapsychic agent-self's capacity to cause the caregiver to prefer the pleasure of intrapsychic caregiving over the pleasure of pursuing personal motives provides the child with a continuous and loss-free inner well-being. This veridical regulatory agency coexists throughout the next stage with the illusional form of intrapsychic motive gratification.

Chapter 4, "The Regulatory-Interpersonal Self Stage," follows the child from the age of about 18 months to six years. The first developmental event is the onset of interpersonal agency. This occurs as the result of the child's capacity to respond with a distinct and reflective "no" to the caregiver's necessary interference with the child's constitutive-interpersonal motives. At first, the child's regulatory interpersonal agency capacity is illusional in that it rests on constitutive-interpersonal motive gratification, which is inherently unstable because of its vulnerability to positive entropy and chance. Subsequently, the child develops a veridical regulatory-interpersonal agency capacity that derives its well-being from the intrapsychic agent-self's stable esteem. In the second half of this stage, the child is caught up in the dyadic and triadic forms of conjugal competitiveness. When the caregivers help the child become aware that the child's pursuit of conjugal motives is causing her/him to experience a loss of veridical well-being, the child develops a regulatory ideal of interpersonal relating we term the relationship ideal.

Chapter 5, "The Constitutive-Interpersonal Self Stage," concerns the phases of middle childhood and adolescence. There is an epigenetic unfolding of cognitive, social-interpersonal, and physiological motives, which at first are used for nonveridical regulatory agency gratification and, subsequently, become entirely free from illusional meaning. When this occurs, the individual has a stable inner well-being on both intrapsychic and interpersonal levels, and her/his pursuit of cognitive, social-interpersonal, and physiological motives is unconflicted and entirely unconnected to inner esteem.

Following the chapters on paradigmatic development, chapter 6 describes the etiology, nosology, structure, and dynamics of intrapsychic and interpersonal psychopathology, and chapter 7 is an introduction to Intrapsychic Treatment.

2
The
Pre-Eidetic
Stage

OVERVIEW OF THE PRE-EIDETIC STAGE OF LIFE

The pre-eidetic stage begins at birth and ends with a process we term *eidetic internalization,* which occurs roughly between the ages of 12 and 14 months.[1] The key intrapsychic events in this stage are behaviorally manifested as the smile response, stranger anxiety,[2] and separation anxiety. The pre-eidetic stage comprises two phases: the *veridical gratification phase* and the *illusional gratification phase.* The onset of the illusional gratification phase correlates with stranger anxiety.

The first intrapsychic milestone in the veridical gratification phase is the smile response,[3] which occurs in an undifferentiated form when the infant is about 10−12 weeks old.[4] When the smile response fully differentiates, the infant's smile becomes most intense in response to the caregiver's smiling face,[5] whereas, prior to differentiation, the smile response will occur even in response to a mask of mixed-up facial features.[6] The smile represents the ongoing interaction between nurture and nature. The caregiver's nurture matches the infant's innately determined, consciousness-generated, to-be-actualized ideal of being the agent cause of the caregiver's unconditional intrapsychic caregiving. The infant enters the world with a starter supply of intrapsychic self-esteem, which allows the merest of perceptual inputs (e.g., touch, taste, smell, sound, color) to have the meaning of intrapsychic motive gratification. However, as the infant's perceptual constitutive-interpersonal capacities mature, an increasingly specific caregiver percept is necessary to signify intrapsychic motive gratification.

Intrapsychic motive gratification is synonymous with the process of intrapsychic perceptual identity. The process of perceptual identity is powered by consciousness-generated components, namely: (1) precepts (ideals), (2) to-be-actualized ideals (motives), and (3) the interpretive process that signifies a percept (registered experience) as matching a precept (as actualizing the to-be-actualized ideal). In an act of perceptual identity, percepts are signified as identical with (as gratifying) consciousness-generated, to-be-actualized ideals (motives) when the percepts are compared with and match consciousness-generated ideals (precepts). An act of perceptual identity is experienced as an act of motive gratification, that is, it is an act of meaning attachment. The intrapsychic perceptual identity process produces the meaning of intrapsychic agency. A *percept* is any experience involved in the generation of meaning. A *caregiver percept* is any percept that matches the currently functioning intrapsychic precept and, therefore, signifies the infant's agent-self capacity to be the regulating cause of the caregiver's intrapsychic caregiving (causes the meaning of intrapsychic agency).

The infant's only intrapsychic structures in the pre-eidetic stage are the innately determined intrapsychic precept (ideal of effective intrapsychic agency) and the innately determined to-be-actualized ideal (intrapsychic motive to acquire this ideal agency capacity). The infant has no intracranial source of gratifying percepts during the pre-eidetic stage and, thus, no endogenous capacity to generate stable, reflective intrapsychic agent-self meaning. Since the infant must rely on extracranial gratifying percepts at this point, intrapsychic motive gratification is possible only so long as the caregiver provides minimally sufficient caregiving. If the infant is to avoid gross interpersonal psychopathology, the caregiver's attention must be sufficiently stable and responsive to the infant's care-getting needs to stimulate the differentiation of the infant's smile response. In conjunction with the caregiver's caregiving, as the infant's cognitive capacities mature, s/he becomes capable of more intricate discrimination, which allows her/him to smile most intensely and pleasurably in response to the caregiver's smiling face. In the pre-eidetic stage, the infant's visual experience of the face of the caregiver is the most important portal for the developmental process. Infants exhibit a marked preference for the human face, which they can distinguish and fix on in the busiest of backgrounds.[7] The most crucial meaning imparted to the infant by the caregiver's responsive smile is that the infant's appeal to the caregiver causes the caregiver to love being engaged by the infant's intrapsychic agent-self motive to receive intrapsychic caregiving love.

A paradigmatic psychic development in the pre-eidetic stage can best be described in terms of the vicissitudes of the process of the infant's intrapsychic motive gratification. In the first phase of the pre-eidetic stage, intrapsychic agent-self meanings are, in effect, transferred from caregiver to infant directly and experientially. From an intrapsychic caregiving vantage point, pre-eidetic experience has only intrapsychic meaning.[8] The infant has no capacity for reflective, interpersonal agent-self experience because the meaning structures of interpersonal consciousness that signify interpersonal agency do not function until the regulatory-interpersonal self stage (see chap. 4).

Although each infant is born with an innate set of intrapsychic self-identities and caregiver identities, these can only become autonomous when the caregiver helps the infant to discover the personalized form of her/himself (her/his agent-self causal capacity) represented within the caregiver's intrapsychic consciousness. The child's innately determined experience of the intrapsychic caregiving relationship and her/his own intrapsychic motive gratification process is phase-specifically nonreflective and structurally dissociated. Innate intrapsychic meanings are predetermined meanings that are attached to the child's perceptual experience of self and other.[9] The caregiver creates an atmosphere of caregiving mutuality that will allow the infant to discover a veridical, loss-free confirmation of her/his intrapsychic agent-self capacity.[10] This confirmation results from the *activity* of intrapsychic caregiving; each time the caregiver manifests the pleasure of intrapsychic caregiving mutuality (e.g., smiles at the infant, holds her/him lovingly), the infant experiences the pleasure of effective intrapsychic agency. This is the pleasure produced by the meaning that the infant is so appealing that s/he can cause the caregiver to prefer intrapsychic caregiving pleasure over all other pleasure. Two facts complicate this task: (1) ultimately, the infant will reflectively experience interpersonal agency as well as intrapsychic agency, and (2) the caregiver has personal (noncaregiving) motives in addition to caregiving motives. When we refer to the caregiver's *noncaregiving* motives, we mean that the caregiver has motives besides caregiving motives and not that the caregiver's caregiving is defective (nonveridical). Paradigmatically, the caregiver's motive for intrapsychic caregiving pleasure has stable hegemony over her/his motive for noncaregiving (personal) pleasure, which means that even when the caregiver pursues personal motives (e.g., watches the news on TV) the caregiver's intrapsychic caregiving motives can be engaged by the infant.

Analogous to the infant's need for an extracranial source of confirming percepts of her/his own intrapsychic agency is the fact that no human can directly see her/his own face.[11] This phenomenon is only one example of how the self-experience generated solely by the perceptual motives of constitutive-interpersonal consciousness intrinsically lends it-self to existential self-alienation. A dramatic illustration can be found in the myth of Narcissus, who was unable to recognize that the visage he adored and from which he could not part was actually his own re-flection in a pool. In contrast, innately based intrapsychic agent-self meanings can become transformed into noninnate, empirically based, mutualized personal meanings when the child discovers a personalized confirmation of the power (appeal) of her/his intrapsychic agent-self in her/his ability to cause the caregiver's intrapsychic caregiving.

Two Types of Caregiver Percepts

We term the first phase of the pre-eidetic stage the ***veridical gratifica-tion phase*** because the percepts used to gratify the infant's intrapsychic motive are phase-appropriately veridical. From an intrapsychic caregiv-ing viewpoint, caregiver percepts can be veridical or nonveridical. A *caregiver percept* supplies the infant with intrapsychic care-getting plea-sure by signifying that the caregiver is responding to the child's intra-psychic agent-self intentionality to be the regulating cause of the care-giver's unconditional intrapsychic caregiving love. Both veridical and nonveridical caregiver percepts occur in paradigmatic development.

A caregiver percept is veridical when it matches the phase-appropri-ately veridical ideal (precept) generated by the child's intrapsychic consciousness. An intrapsychic precept is veridical when it includes only information that phase-appropriately represents the caregiver's fo-cused intrapsychic caregiving. Because of the neonate's immaturity, the veridical intrapsychic precept is, initially, sufficiently diffuse that any pleasure (e.g., the caregiver's voice talking to someone else, the motion of a car) can signify the caregiver's intrapsychic caregiving attention. However, within the limits of the child's cognitive and perceptual ca-pacities, the veridical precept is an ideal of the caregiver's intrapsychic caregiving, as illustrated by the fact that the infant's most preferred veridical caregiver percept is a smiling face.[12] Soon after birth, the neonate's perceptual maturation causes the veridical intrapsychic pre-cept to become more specific about what constitutes intrapsychic care-giving and, thus, the range of acceptable veridical caregiver percepts narrows.

A ***nonveridical caregiver percept*** matches a phase-specific, nonverid-ical ideal (precept) generated by the child's intrapsychic consciousness. An intrapsychic precept is nonveridical when its informational content is unrelated to the caregiver's intrapsychic caregiving because of the information specified in the intrapsychic precept and not solely because of the infant's cognitive and perceptual immaturity. On a time-limited basis, the infant will accept the nonveridical caregiver percept as signifying the caregiver's focused veridical intrapsychic caregiving.

We stress that the referents for veridical and nonveridical caregiver percepts are meanings the child's perceptual identity process attaches to the child's experience and are not disparate caregiver behaviors. In paradigmatic development, the caregiver's intrapsychic caregiving remains stable in the sense that her/his motive for intrapsychic caregiving pleasure has stable hegemony over her/his personal motives. If the caregiver's motive for intrapsychic caregiving pleasure is conflicted (unstable), then the caregiving the child receives is nonveridical (psychopathogenic). *Nonveridical caregiving* and a *nonveridical caregiver percept* are, thus, entirely different. The former occurs only in psychopathology and is a function of the caregiver's psychopathology (see chap. 6), whereas the latter is a phase-specific component of paradigmatic as well as pathological development.

The intrapsychic precept, the intrapsychic motive, and caregiver percepts all have veridical and nonveridical forms. The child cannot reflectively differentiate between veridical and nonveridical caregiver percepts until the end of the second developmental stage (the regulatory-intrapsychic self stage) and, further, cannot distinguish between interpersonal and intrapsychic agent-self experience until the early part of the third stage (the regulatory-interpersonal self stage).

By definition, intrapsychic motive gratification provides the child with a sense of autonomous, self-regulatory intrapsychic agency even when her/his intrapsychic perceptual identity process is nonveridical. From the viewpoint of the child's subjective experience, the nonveridical caregiver percept appears isologous with (gratifies) the child's motive to experience an effective intrapsychic agent-self. For example, in the illusional gratification phase of this stage, when the infant's intrapsychic motive gratification process is nonveridical, even a percept of the caregiver reading the newspaper can signify the caregiver's focused intrapsychic caregiving attention. We stress that in paradigmatic development, even when the child's intrapsychic motive gratification process is phase-specifically nonveridical, the caregiver's intrapsychic caregiving motives are, in reality, available to be engaged by the child's needs and, therefore, the caregiver's behavior would be isomorphic with the veridical intrapsychic precept if this precept were functional. Even when the caregiver pursues noncaregiving motives, such as vacuuming the rug, her/his intrapsychic caregiving motives are stably available to be engaged by the child if the child were to need intrapsychic caregiving.

THE VERIDICAL GRATIFICATION PHASE

The veridical gratification phase begins at birth and ends five to eight months later, when the child grieves the intrapsychic loss expressed as stranger anxiety. During this phase, the veridical caregiver precept becomes progressively more specific with regard to the definition of ideal intrapsychic caregiving, that is, with regard to the information that has to be supplied by the caregiver percept in order for intrapsychic motive gratification to occur. The most representative and powerful veridical caregiver percept in this phase is the caregiver's smiling face. The infant's smile response displays the pleasure afforded the infant by the gratification of her/his intrapsychic motive by the veridical caregiver percept.

The smile response is differentiated when the infant responds with the most intense smile of pleasure to the caregiver's smiling face (rather than to a stranger's face, a picture, a doll, etc.). In the veridical gratification phase, while the range of caregiving that the infant's perceptual identity process will accept as veridical is very broad, the infant cannot develop in spite of traumatic intrapsychic caregiving. In contrast to *nonveridical* intrapsychic caregiving (which permits the smile response to differentiate but causes the infant to develop intrapsychic psychopathology), *traumatic* intrapsychic caregiving behavior prevents the differentiation of the smile response. In the veridical gratification phase, traumatic intrapsychic caregiving nearly always entails extreme neglect rather than abuse, because abuse that does not kill or cause brain damage to the infant will usually provide her/him with enough of a taste of relationship experience with the caregiver to allow her/his smile response to differentiate. Of course, the abused infant will usually exhibit sequelae of interpersonal psychopathology in the form of severe somatic symptoms, which can include functional pyloric stenosis, eating disorders, sleep disturbances, asthma, skin disorders, and delayed motor and speech development.

Traumatic intrapsychic caregiving in the veridical gratification phase causes the infant to ignore all current perceptual experience, including nourishment, in order to preserve some form of intrapsychic mutuality (intrapsychic motive gratification). In other words, faced with traumatic intrapsychic loss, the infant can maintain the meaning of effective intrapsychic agency only by regressing to an archaic form of dissociation. When the caregiver's caregiving does not elicit a differentiated smile response, the child can die of psychological marasmus even in the presence of adequate interpersonal care (nutrition, shelter, etc.).[13] Intrapsychic gratification (personal meaning) will always be chosen over the gratification of nonagency needs, even when the ultimate consequence of this choice is unintended death. Thus, what Freud called Thanatos or the death instinct is, in reality, a life instinct that has been rendered maladaptive by grossly defective nurture.

Spitz conceptualized the smile response as a precursor of the libidinal object,[14] which, in our terms, would make the smile response a product of constitutive-interpersonal motives. We understand the smile response as an expression of the infant's pleasure at the intrapsychic caregiving relationship (the meaning of effective intrapsychic agency). The universality of the smile response suggests that the smile response manifests innate, consciousness-generated intrapsychic meaning structures that are functional *before* exposure to the caregiver's smile. However, the caregiver's smile (the caregiver percept) is necessary if the child's innately determined capacity for intrapsychic motive gratification is to remain functional. In other words, while some caregiving interaction needs to occur for the infant to manifest a smile response, this caregiving can be exceedingly minimal and even of the sort that will ultimately prove psychotoxic. Even children who later develop severe forms of interpersonal psychopathology initially, at least, exhibit a rudimentary smile response. Psychopathogenic caregiver responses that are not so severe as to be intrapsychically traumatic permit the child's intrapsychic and interpersonal processes to unfold in an innately determined manner, but they are sufficiently ungratifying that the infant's psychic structure becomes pathologically altered so as to prevent the subsequent transformation from innate to nurture-based forms. An example is the caregiver who puts the infant on a rigid feeding schedule. While the infant's smile response may differentiate, the intrapsychic loss caused by the caregiver's unresponsiveness to the infant's cries of hunger is likely to result in intrapsychic psychopathology.[15]

Because of the child's immaturity, the ideal represented by the veridical caregiver precept is sufficiently unsophisticated that nearly any caregiver response will be signified as a gratifying, veridical caregiver percept. If the caregiver's intrapsychic caregiving is *nonveridical*, innately determined processes will modify the intrapsychic precept (ideal) with the following result: (1) the child's experience of being cared for in an ideal way will be delusional, and (2) the configuration of the perceptual experience of the caregiver (the percept), which paradigmatically is isomorphic to the innately based ideal (precept), is shaped by the caregiver's intrapsychic psychopathology rather than by veridical experiences with the caregiver's intrapsychic caregiving ideals. An analogy can be made with baby geese. The gosling's innately determined precept remains open to modification for a time-limited period. While goslings paradigmatically imprint on mother geese,[16] their to-be-actualized ideal (motive) to imprint is so compelling that, if the caregiving they receive immediately after birth is pathological (the mother goose is unavailable), they will imprint on any object that can establish what the gosling perceives as a caregiving relationship, even when the object belongs to a different species (e.g., humans).

A life-preserving evolutionary safeguard against experiencing unsupportable intrapsychic pain is that the child cannot distinguish between veridical and nonveridical intrapsychic caregiving until the differentiated regulatory-intrapsychic self stage. Regardless of the quality of the caregiver's intrapsychic caregiving, the evolution of intrapsychic meaning structures in infancy is primarily regulated by an innately determined process. Accordingly, in early infancy the effects of nonveridical intrapsychic caregiving are masked temporarily by the power of innate processes.[17] Because the infant has no endogenous source of intrapsychic caregiver percepts, the infant's inner well-being is vulnerable to the caregiver's motives from the very beginning of life.

Once the smile response differentiates, the infant experiences two levels of intrapsychic motive gratification: (1) that which occurs through the infant's actual experience of the caregiver's caregiving (which we represent by the percept of the caregiver's caregiving smile) and (2) that which occurs in the absence of the caregiver and in the context of the infant's lack of an endogenous capacity for structured mind experience. In the latter case, intrapsychic motive gratification occurs by means of the infant's nonfixated regression to the form of intrapsychic motive gratification that was functional before the differentiation of the smile response. During periods of regression, adequate caregiver percepts are provided by perceptual input of the minimal level of physiological functioning adequate for physical survival (e.g., being fed, seeing a pleasing color). Thus, when a two- or three-month-old infant who is alone in her/his crib smiles and laughs with pleasure at a colored mobile that turns about over her/his head, the mobile has acquired the meaning of a veridical caregiver percept.

The Intrapsychic Caregiving Relationship

The infant's smile response is a very early manifestation of the influence of the intrapsychic caregiving relationship on the innately determined form of the infant's intrapsychic agent-self. The signified meaning of the smile response is the sense of self-worth produced when the infant has the experience of the caregiver unconditionally gratifying the infant's agent-self motive to engage and regulate the caregiver's intrapsychic caregiving motives. The ecstasy of the infant's smile communicates the powerful pleasure of intrapsychic motive gratification. The term ***intrapsychic caregiving relationship*** emphasizes the reciprocal intrapsychic pleasure experienced by infant and caregiver and the mutual nature of the regulatory control of the relationship. The caregiver has hegemonic motives for intrapsychic caregiving pleasure, which can be gratified only by caregiving responses to the child's intrapsychic care-getting motives.

The intrapsychic caregiving relationship includes the broad spectrum of relationship experience between the infant and her/his primary caregiver that gives the child the reflection of having an effective intrapsychic agent-self that can cause the caregiver to prefer the pleasure of intrapsychic caregiving mutuality. From birth until the third stage, the regulatory-interpersonal self stage, while the caregiver's interpersonal caregiving (e.g., feeding the child, changing her/his diapers, keeping her/him warm, talking to her/him) must be minimally sufficient to allow the child to survive physically, the most important developmental significance of these caregiving behaviors is as a framework of interpersonal caregiving motives to which the child attaches the meaning of the caregiver's intrapsychic caregiving. From birth onward, a functional consciousness, and, therefore, physical survival, depends on the viability of the intrapsychic caregiving relationship.

The intrapsychic caregiving relationship differs from the interpersonal caregiving relationship in its mutual, empirical quality. Though the development of interpersonal consciousness depends on the maintenance of some type of intrapsychic motive gratification, cognitive (e.g., linguistic, logical) motives are relatively autonomous.[18] Further, interpersonal relationship experience plays a secondary, although clearly crucial, role in the development of cognition. In contrast, no cognitive structure exists within intrapsychic consciousness.[19] The knowing inherent in *matured* intrapsychic consciousness consists of a metacognitive, nonverbal sense of well-being that can roughly be translated as follows:

Because at one time I had the capacity to cause (engage) your response to my motive for you to care for me, I was able to develop the loss-free capacity to have the reflective, veridical experience of myself as agent-self and, therefore, I can own my own mind, al-

45

ways feel an ideal, mutualized inner well-being, which is no longer contingent on your caregiving motives or on my motives for interpersonal pleasure.

The construct of *mutualized consciousness* entails a radical assertion about human nature, namely, that the most hegemonic category of agent-self experience, intrapsychic agency, can become genuinely autonomous only when it is based on an empirical knowledge of the caregiver's intrapsychic caregiving motives. Because of the nature of intrapsychic motive gratification, the intrapsychic agent-self is always a self of "we"ness, which can also be described as the "we"ness of the "I." In paradigmatic development, the intrapsychic caregiving relationship matures along innately determined lines until it becomes nurture based. This shift from the innately determined to the reflectively experiential occurs in the differentiated phase of the regulatory-intrapsychic self stage.

Caregiving Opportunities in the Veridical Gratification Phase

The caregiver's caregiving advances the intrapsychic caregiving relationship by progressively modifying the infant's innately determined intrapsychic ideal (precept) to include only the caregiver's smiling face. Thus, by the end of the differentiated veridical gratification phase, only the percept of the caregiver's smiling face will match the infant's veridical intrapsychic ideal (precept) and provide the infant with optimal intrapsychic motive gratification. When the caregiver's smiling face is not in the infant's perceptual field, the infant achieves intrapsychic motive gratification by regressing to an earlier form of intrapsychic precept, which can be matched by a less specific percept, such as the infant's own experiences (e.g., sucking one of her/his fingers).

Since the child has no representational interpersonal agent-self experience until the regulatory-interpersonal self stage,[20] in the veridical gratification phase each gratified constitutive-interpersonal motive conveys the significance of an intrapsychic agent-self with the capacity to engage the caregiver's caregiving motives. Correspondingly, constitutive-interpersonal motive frustration signifies intrapsychic loss to which, if gratification is not forthcoming, the infant can only respond with intrapsychic regression. This phase, then, enables the caregiver to boost the infant's innately determined motive for veridical, relationship-oriented, intrapsychic motive gratification both by providing a nurturing awareness that helps the infant avoid constitutive-interpersonal loss and by providing bountiful relationship pleasure (talking to the infant, touching the infant).

Because the infant can only respond to ungratified constitutive-interpersonal motives with intrapsychic regression, keeping the infant happy and comfortable helps her/him become more functional and enhances her/his rate of development in all areas. Thus, for example, a caregiver should never let an infant cry with hunger until the "next" feeding time.[21] From an intrapsychic caregiving perspective, every cry of hunger expresses two separate losses: (1) the loss of the constitutive-interpersonal pleasure of satiety and (2) the intrapsychic loss of the meaning of having the agent-self capacity to engage the caregiver's intrapsychic caregiving motives (the loss of intrapsychic motive gratification). If the caregiver responds to the infant's cry, the infant experiences both the cessation of hunger pains and also a powerful perception of her/his intrapsychic agent-self's capacity to cause the caregiver to pursue the pleasure of intrapsychic caregiving. In contrast, if the caregiver has the misguided belief that deprivation builds character, independence, and so on, and leaves the infant to cry, the infant will have no choice but to regress to a less mature level of functioning.

Adultomorphizing in the Pre-Eidetic Stage

It may be helpful here to pause and contrast our view of the infant with the perspective of other developmental psychologies, which we term **adultomorphizing.** Adultomorphizing refers to the misunderstanding of child development that results from viewing the child as a small adult. This misunderstanding is due mainly to a primary reliance on clinical observation, constitutive-interpersonal introspection, and empathy to draw conclusions about children's motives. Empathy and constitutive-interpersonal introspection are solipsistic and nonempirical attempts to know agency reality (see chap. 1). Unless a person hallucinates, s/he recognizes that her/his constitutive-interpersonal introspection remains entirely private.[22] The inaccessibility of another's constitutive-interpersonal introspection contrasts with the empirical, mutual availability of another's *intrapsychic* agent-self experience in the caregiving relationships that constitute paradigmatic development and Intrapsychic Treatment. Constitutive-interpersonal introspection will never allow an individual to evaluate with certainty the veridicality of her/his own experience. As was made clear by Descartes, one can only be certain of one's own motive to evaluate that experience.[23]

While all intrapsychic motives are generated within and by intrapsychic consciousness and have the potential to be directly, consciously recognized within the caregiving relationship, this is not true of constitutive-interpersonal motives. With respect to the potential for conscious introspection, constitutive-interpersonal motives fall into two major categories: motives that are potentially knowable (the wish to see a basketball game) and those that are structurally, permanently beyond the possibility of direct introspective experience (e.g., tissue-based motives of the body that are part of an organ system whose sensory distribution precludes introspection).

Adultomorphizing is an interpretation of the child's behavior from an adult perspective which is determined by the cognitive and social-interpersonal categories of the observer's constitutive-interpersonal motives. These motives cannot provide veridical information about the quality of the child's intrapsychic agent-self experience or about the quality of the caregiver's intrapsychic caregiving. In adultomorphizing, the caregiver's intrapsychic caregiving motives are not distinguished from the caregiver's personal motives, and there is no touchstone by which to differentiate between the appearance and substance of veridical caregiving. In addition, interpersonal adultomorphizing focuses on the child's manifest behavior rather than on the child's agent-self experience.[24] For example, the child's motor efforts may be emphasized at the expense of her/his inner agency experience. The most heuristic view of human life from birth onward is that the infant constantly experiences a vital, ongoing intrapsychic caregiving mutuality with the caregiver.

The fact that the infant's earliest experience of caregiving mutuality is innately determined in no way implies an outlook that the caregiver can coast during the neonatal period. If the child is to have a paradigmatic intrapsychic development, the caregiver must have the veridical ability to discern within the universe of the infant's behavior the infant's purpose to acquire the extracranial reflection of agent-self as agent-self by engaging the caregiver's intrapsychic caregiving motives. Further, the caregiver must see this purposive behavior as consisting only of the search for positive care-getting pleasure. The child always phase-appropriately experiences the intrapsychic caregiving relationship as occurring between her/his own intrapsychic agent-self and the caregiver's intrapsychic agent-self. But the innately determined, veridical precept structure, which forms an ideal rendering of the caregiving relationship, is not, at this stage, very specific about the caregiver percept necessary to impart veridical caregiving pleasure. For example, any caregiver smile will be accepted as gratifying the infant's intrapsychic motive, regardless of the motive causing the caregiver to smile. Therefore, if the child is to avoid intrapsychic psychopathology, *the caregiver must respond to the child as if the child had the capacity to assess the veridicality of the intrapsychic caregiving relationship.* The caregiver must never experience the infant either as self-sufficient and hatching on her/his own or as organized by a primary narcissism that nurture can transform to a dyadic stage of secondary narcissism.[25] Rather, the caregiver must respond to the child as a reflectively intentional individual in search of agent-self control over intrapsychic care-getting pleasure. Thus, the caregiver will not relate to the child as if s/he were in a cocoon and did not have relationship purpose.

Due to an adaptive evolutionary process, the most minimal interpersonal caregiving will permit the child physical survival. The real challenge, however, is not that the child physically survive or even that s/he have a successful capacity for interpersonal performance (to love and to work). Rather, the goal is that the child develop the capacity for a nurture-based, veridical inner self-worth that is not intrinsically contingent on interpersonal satisfaction.

The mainstream psychoanalytic literature on child development contains an implicit assumption that no primary relationship motives (except motives which signify instinctual drive derivative behavior) operate within the infant at birth.[26] Psychoanalytic theory generally assumes that the infant's conflicted constitutive-interpersonal motives further development in and of themselves. Freud used, for example, the infant's hallucination of the gratifying breast to demonstrate that the frustration of instinctual (constitutive-interpersonal) motives is a necessary though not sufficient cause of the capacity for reality testing.[27] Freud used the hallucinated breast as a paradigm of the infant's developing capacity for an ego-based human relationship experience. Loss (lack of structure) generates structure through an intermediate, restitutional, intrasubjective, solipsistic product of the imagination. The failure of the imagined breast to be instinctually gratifying stimulates the child to perceive the presence or absence of an intersubjective reality.[28] In sum, Freud's hallucinated breast model posits that the infant's capacity for extracranial reality testing is an unintended effect of the hegemony of the pleasure principle over instinctual drive gratification, the referent of which is somatic nonagency reality.[29]

The hallucinatory phase is an adultomorphism that has the dream experience (itself the nonempirical, solipsistic product of constitutive-interpersonal consciousness) as its referent. Because he did not perceive the problems with his adultomorphic breast model, Freud used the hallucinated breast's failure to provide instinctual gratification as a necessary cause of the child's capacity for reality testing.[30] Freud's model precludes the most fundamental component of infant development, namely the self and caregiver meaning structures that occur in the context of the existence-at-birth of a preestablished, harmonious infant-caregiver relationship.

In contrast to psychoanalytic theory, we posit that the goal of psychic development is not self-regulatory stability with regard to tension regulation, but rather is the attainment and maintenance of an inner well-being and sense of self-worth that is tension free because it is affected neither by constitutive-interpersonal pleasure nor by constitutive-interpersonal loss. Because we believe that regulatory agency motives have hegemony over nonagency motives (e.g., physiological motives) with regard to the capacity for self-regulatory stability, our focus in the pre-eidetic stage is on innately determined internal meaning (the intrapsychic motive and the process of its gratification) and on the consequences of the vicissitudes of this gratification process for the infant's agent-self experience and manifest behavior.

Since World War II, there has been an increasing proliferation of experimental studies in the field of developmental psychology that share our viewpoint that the neonate begins life with an innate, preformed capacity for a caregiving relationship characterized by an inborn hunger for knowledge of the other. These studies conclude that the infant has an active agency capacity to regulate the caregiving relationship.[31] Investigators have propagated viewpoints concerning the ontogenesis of human nature that have several aspects in common: the premise that the neonate purposively tries to regulate the caregiving relationship, a focus on the intersubjective field of behavior, and the belief that infant motivational patterns are different from but akin to nonhuman (ethological) motivation.[32]

In our view, the various schools of developmental psychology all focus on manifestations of constitutive-interpersonal motives. In consequence, developmental psychologists often suggest or imply caregiving attitudes and behaviors that can potentially impair the child's psychic development. Terms like *hatching* or *infantile grandiose self* arise from the assumption that the child-caregiver relationship occurs on a constitutive-interpersonal level (on the level of cognition, language, and interpersonal social relationships).[33] Constitutive-interpersonal relating, however, can partake of intrapsychic meaning only indirectly. For example, in a nonveridical intrapsychic motive gratification process, constitutive-interpersonal experience acquires the *illusional* meaning of ideal intrapsychic caregiving, which, in turn, imparts the *illusional* reflection of agent-self as agent-self. One of the most serious defects in a caregiving approach derived from the view of child development as a hatching process is that conclusions about the child are based on the child's linguistic and cognitive motives and, therefore, are intrinsically tied to the child's social-interpersonal performance (constitutive-interpersonal motive gratification), which is mistakenly interpreted as signifying regulatory agency capacity rather than as the child's need to acquire the meaning of effective intrapsychic agency. When the caregiver approaches the caregiving relationship from the perspective of empathy, s/he mistakenly interprets the child's preverbal and paraverbal relationship behavior solely as a forerunner of verbal behavior rather than as a simultaneous manifestation of the motive for intrapsychic care-getting pleasure. This misconception is illustrated by the fact that the word *infancy* comes from the root meaning "incapable of speech."[34]

One consequence of an adultomorphic understanding of the infant has been the misapprehension that nonorganic forms of the pathological syndromes of primary and secondary autism, symbiotic psychosis, and other forms of childhood psychosis represent regression to or fixation at an isolated internal world. These syndromes actually represent regression to and fixation at an internal reality that provides the delusional experience of agent-self-caused, ideal caregiving mutuality. The infant's capacity to respond to extremely psychotoxic interpersonal caregiving with malignant mental illness is adaptive for the individual (although, arguably, not for the species) in that it permits the infant to survive. Survival occurs not by retreat to some caregiverless, mindless, objectless state (e.g., not to an "empty fortress"),[35] but rather by retreat to an innately determined, vivid, rich, actively functioning world of delusional intrapsychic mutuality with the caregiver. In other words, a psychologically ill child is isolated from the caregiver's actual, psychotoxic motives, not from a subjectively experienced intimate caregiving relationship. The most autistically withdrawn child maintains the representation of a vivid, pleasurable relationship with the caregiver and can use the most meager perceptual input to gratify her/his need for the (nonveridical) reflection of effective intrapsychic agency. However, this pathological, regressive gratification exacts the price of what, from an intrapsychic caregiving viewpoint, equals a psychotic subjective personal existence.[36]

In summary, the infant arrives into the world endowed with an ongoing sense of intrapsychic mutuality, that is, intimacy and involvement with the caregiver. Each subsequent perceptual experience conveys the meaning that the infant has already met the caregiver, is loved, and will continue to be the cause of the caregiver's intrapsychic love. The caregiver has the innately caused significance of being the extracranial center of intrapsychic caregiving from which the infant has been receiving the intrapsychic caregiving love s/he needs. Thus, the caregiver-child relationship gets under way with an extensive starter supply of goodwill and caregiving mutuality.

During the veridical gratification phase of the pre-eidetic stage, the most powerful caregiver percept is the caregiver's smiling face, which functions as the external stimulus for the differentiating smile response. In this phase, the percept of the caregiver's smiling face *matches* the infant's consciousness-generated, phase-appropriately veridical precept (ideal) of the caregiver and, therefore, gratifies the infant's consciousness-generated, veridical intrapsychic motive. In the beginning of life, the percept of the caregiver's smiling face fits into a prearranged set of meanings within the infant's psyche. The caregiver's smiling face becomes the primary percept that signifies the infant's intrapsychic agent-self causing the caregiver's caregiving pleasure. This match of percept and precept provides the basis for the increasingly intense intrapsychic pleasure expressed by the differentiating smile response.

The First Developmental Loss: Primary Stranger Anxiety

The maturation of the infant's cognitive and perceptual constitutive-interpersonal motives causes the infant to experience her/his first developmental loss. In the period just prior to stranger anxiety, when the infant's perceptual experience brought her/him a loss (the caregiver's smiling face was not in her/his perceptual field) and, in addition, the caregiver was not available to respond to the infant's expression of discomfort, the infant could regress to a form of intrapsychic motive gratification based on a less specific caregiver percept than the caregiver's smiling face (another smiling face, a bright color, food, etc.). However, as the infant's cognitive and perceptual constitutive-interpersonal motives continue to mature, they gain hegemony over the intrapsychic perceptual identity process. The evolving competence of the infant's visual system increasingly determines the segment of experience that is the focus of the infant's attention. While this maturation facilitates the differentiation of the smile response until the infant experiences the most intense pleasure in response to the percept of the caregiver's smiling face, there occurs a point at which the infant cannot escape from a loss-producing, nongratifying percept of a strange face. In other words, the same maturational process that allows the infant to differentiate the caregiver's smiling face from all others and, thereby, to have an increasingly intense and pleasurable experience of intrapsychic motive gratification, also makes the infant increasingly unable to ignore the non-gratifying percept of a strange face.

Obviously, in terms of overall survival value for both the individual and the species it is reasonable to conclude that, as the infant matures, the percepts produced by her/his constitutive-interpersonal motives to understand, master, and explore the external world could not be ignored through denial of current perceptual experience in the service of regression to archaic forms of intrapsychic motive gratification. The infant's constitutive-interpersonal capacities, such as speech, motor co-ordination, and visual discrimination, are all supported and facilitated by this new hegemony of gratifying constitutive-interpersonal percepts, which prevents regression to a diffuse source of intrapsychic motive gratification (regression to dissociative states that are antithetical to motives for the development of interpersonal capacities). However, the result of this new hegemony of gratifying perceptual constitutive-interpersonal experience over the intrapsychic perceptual identity process is that the infant experiences her/his first intrapsychic loss.

Primary stranger anxiety is the behavioral expression of the intrapsychic loss that the infant experiences when percepts that gratify constitutive-interpersonal motives for understanding, mastery, and exploration include information that does not fit or match the infant's veridical precept (ideal) of the caregiver's caregiving love.[37] From an intrapsychic caregiving perspective, the strange face means to the infant that s/he has failed to be the regulatory cause of the caregiver's intrapsychic caregiving. Part of the infant's innately determined, instantaneous grief work is her/his signs of distress, which Spitz called eight-month anxiety and which we call primary stranger anxiety.[38]

From an intrapsychic caregiving perspective, primary stranger anxiety signifies that the infant has begun an innately determined grieving process by bringing her/his phase-specific intrapsychic loss (the loss of the meaning of effective intrapsychic agency, which occurs when the infant perceives a stranger's face instead of the caregiver's smiling face) to the caregiving relationship for the express purpose of engaging the caregiver's intrapsychic caregiving. In paradigmatic development, the caregiver's intrapsychic caregiving relationship with the infant allows her/him to sense that the infant's dysphoria results from the infant's loss of the meaning of effective intrapsychic agency. The caregiver responds to the content of the infant's unease by removing the strange face from the infant's perceptual field and to the infant's loss of the reflection of effective intrapsychic agency by substituting the caregiver's own smiling, loving, gratifying face.

Loss and Mourning in Development

We emphasize loss and mourning in our exposition of a paradigmatic developmental process because they are most important from an explanatory viewpoint, not because they are quantitatively the most significant aspects of development. A *developmental intrapsychic loss* is a universal loss, the mourning of which advances the developmental goal of a differentiated, veridical, regulatory-intrapsychic agent-self.[39] We emphatically disagree with the notion that it is normal or healthy for a child to spend any significant amount of time crying or feeling unhappy. Pleasurable experiences between caregiver and child paradigmatically make up the vast part of development. The caregiver's stable preference for intrapsychic caregiving pleasure over the pleasure produced by the pursuit of personal motives provides the child with ongoing intrapsychic motive gratification. *Developmental mourning* is a special category of grief work that advances the developmental process by making the child invulnerable to further losses of the type being mourned. Mourning always occurs in the pleasurable context of the caregiving relationship.

Loss and mourning are critical explanatory concepts because the infant's innately determined subjective experience of intrapsychic motive gratification is developmentally dissociated and entails a nonveridical sense of effective agency. Intrapsychic loss and mourning provide the push that moves the infant from a dissociated type of innately based intrapsychic agent-self pleasure, based on the illusion of a self-regulatory intrapsychic agency capacity, to a reflective, developed type of agent-self pleasure, because intrapsychic loss and mourning intrude on the infant's illusional experience of regulatory agent-self capacity.

Phase-specific, developmental intrapsychic losses are an invariant characteristic of intrapsychic development. These losses are innately determined and, as such, are primarily due to the nature of human intrapsychic consciousness. Accordingly, developmental intrapsychic losses are in no sense a product of defective caregiving (of caregiver psychopathology) even though in paradigmatic as well as psychopathological development, the precipitating cause is often the fact that the caregiver has intrinsic personal motives as well as caregiving motives. Since, in paradigmatic development, the caregiver's intrapsychic caregiving motives are functionally available to the child at all times, developmental intrapsychic loss never entails intrapsychic alienation.

Intrapsychic loss can be primary or secondary. ***Primary intrapsychic loss*** entails a complete (though normative and short-lived) loss of intrapsychic motive gratification.[40] Primary intrapsychic loss includes only the two intrapsychic losses that occur in the pre-eidetic stage: stranger anxiety and separation anxiety. ***Secondary intrapsychic loss*** occurs in the undifferentiated phase of the regulatory-intrapsychic self stage and will be discussed in chapter 3.

All intrapsychic loss represents the loss of a crucial personal meaning structure. Intrapsychic personal meaning structures have the (veridical or nonveridical) significance of an agent-self with the capacity to regulate the subjective experience of personal existence via the experience of causing the caregiver's intrapsychic caregiving. Intrapsychic personal meaning structures arc as much a manifestation of a biological process as is the sensation of hunger. However, they are not primarily associated with any somatic level of physical experience. In other words, intrapsychic agent-self meaning and intrapsychic loss are not intrinsically connected to nonregulatory agency reality and nonagency reality and, therefore, are not proximally regulated by positive entropy.

Intrapsychic losses can be developmental or psychopathological. The psychic pain associated with developmental intrapsychic loss represents the loss of the phase-specific, intrapsychic mind experience that signifies having the agent-self capacity to be the regulating cause of the caregiver's stable preference for intrapsychic caregiving pleasure. Psychopathological intrapsychic losses will be discussed in chapter 6. In paradigmatic development, intrapsychic losses are never caused by a defect in the caregiver's intrapsychic caregiving. Therefore, the child can mourn each loss by engaging the caregiver's intrapsychic caregiving and experiencing an intrapsychic mutuality that reestablishes the reflection to the infant of effective intrapsychic agency. ***Intrapsychic mourning*** is an act of intrapsychic mutuality and, therefore, an expression of intrapsychic relationship pleasure. The child will not experience a paradigmatic intrapsychic development unless normative intrapsychic losses, such as the loss expressed as stranger anxiety, are mourned within the caregiving relationship. Otherwise, the infant has to handle the loss by regression, which becomes necessary and phase-specific at moments when the caregiver is temporarily unavailable. However, if regression results not only from the caregiver's temporary physical absence, but also from the caregiver's intrapsychic unavailability, then pathological regression becomes the child's only reaction to loss. At worst, pathological regression results in death by psychological marasmus and, at best, it produces an individual who is interpersonally successful, but who has intrapsychic psychopathology. Thus, those who advocate leaving the child alone when s/he is unhappy in order not to "spoil" the child, in order not to "reinforce" negative behaviors, or in order to "build character," are advocating caregiving behavior that is likely to cause intrapsychic psychopathology. While the child may seem to "shape up" by being isolated, this improved behavior actually represents compliance that stems from a pathological intrapsychic meaning structure of self-rage (see chap. 6). In the presence of nonveridical caregiving, the two phase-specific pre-eidetic losses expressed as stranger anxiety and separation anxiety can be grieved solely on the basis of innately determined responses. When the caregiver cannot help the infant mourn these two losses, while intrapsychic development will continue through the psychopathological equivalent of the undifferentiated phase of the regulatory-intrapsychic self stage, intrapsychic consciousness will become fixated and will never differentiate unless the individual receives Intrapsychic Treatment.

THE ILLUSIONAL GRATIFICATION PHASE

The illusional gratification phase of the pre-eidetic stage begins when the infant's innately determined response to the intrapsychic loss expressed as *primary stranger anxiety* causes the infant's veridical intrapsychic precept and associated, veridical intrapsychic motive to become phase-specifically nonfunctional. At the same time, the innately based, nonveridical intrapsychic precept and associated, nonveridical intrapsychic motive are activated. There are two mutually exclusive developmental lines of intrapsychic agency, veridical and nonveridical. These have a relationship of competitive inhibition. The *veridical* line becomes phase-specifically nonfunctional when percepts of the caregiver's mere presence (percepts regulated by constitutive-interpersonal motives associated with the system of visual perception) take precedence over percepts of the caregiver's intrapsychic caregiving (represented by the caregiver's smile) as a soothing experience for the baby. From the end of the veridical gratification phase of the pre-eidetic stage through the first half of the next stage (the regulatory-intrapsychic self stage), the veridical intrapsychic precept remains nonfunctional. The nonveridical intrapsychic precept is a nonspecific ideal that can be matched by percepts that gratify cognitive and perceptual constitutive-interpersonal motives as well as by percepts of the caregiver's focused intrapsychic caregiving. The basis for intrapsychic motive gratification (for the reflection of effective intrapsychic agency) is, therefore, nonveridical and, for a delimited period of time, the infant is structurally isolated from empirical contact with the caregiver's intrapsychic caregiving motives.

In the veridical gratification phase, the phenomenon that gratifying, caregiver percepts (e.g., a bright color) can be unrelated to the caregiver's actual caregiving is commensurate with the immaturity of the infant's perceptual capacities. As the infant's perceptual capacities mature, the caregiver percept becomes increasingly specific (stimulating isologous changes in the veridical intrapsychic precept) until the infant comes to prefer the caregiver percept of the caregiver's smiling face. In this sense, in the veridical gratification phase the infant's intrapsychic motive gratification is unsophisticated rather than illusional. In contrast, in the illusional gratification phase, because the functional caregiver percept is nonveridical, even though the infant's perceptual constitutive-interpersonal capacities continue to mature, percepts unrelated to the caregiver's intrapsychic caregiving (e.g., the caregiver talking on the phone) can signify the meaning of the caregiver's focused caregiving.

In the *illusional* gratification phase of the pre-eidetic stage, the infant is content merely to be in the presence of the caregiver. Because the caregiver's presence is the source of illusional intrapsychic motive gratification, we term the first developmental nonveridical caregiver percept the **presence caregiver percept.** A second type of developmental nonveridical percept, the **caregiving caregiver percept,** becomes functional in the next stage, the regulatory-intrapsychic self stage.[41]

In the illusional gratification phase of the pre-eidetic stage, since the caregiver's face is no longer the magnet it was in the veridical gratification phase, the infant can acquire from the presence of the caregiver a nonveridical version of the pleasure that was produced by the caregiver's face during the veridical gratification phase. Because the infant no longer needs to focus on the caregiver's face to obtain gratifying, caregiver percepts, s/he can now attend to her/his rapidly expanding interpersonal capacities, especially, those related to exploring, understanding, and mastering the surrounding world. Perceptual, motor, linguistic, and cognitive motives are all emphasized and occur in a context in which the infant has a phase-appropriate intrapsychic agency capacity that results from the ongoing pleasure of intrapsychic motive gratification.

Because percepts that gratify constitutive-interpersonal motives (e.g., for visual discrimination) acquire phase-specific hegemony over the intrapsychic perceptual identity process (are assigned the additional, non-veridical significance of percepts of the caregiver's intrapsychic caregiving), these nonveridical percepts are a time-limited source of the most profound pleasure the child can have, and, therefore, add a special pleasure to the child's development of social-interpersonal, motor, and cognitive capacities. Thus, in this phase of the pre-eidetic stage, teaching the child and introducing her/him to new activities in a pleasurable way has the double significance of constitutive-interpersonal motive gratification and intrapsychic motive gratification.

The nonveridical intrapsychic precept protects the infant from the loss expressed as primary stranger anxiety. Since the infant equates the caregiver's presence with the caregiver's focused intrapsychic caregiving, the infant no longer experiences primary intrapsychic loss in reaction to seeing a strange face. Despite the caregiver's optimal caregiving, the infant comes to rely for a time on an intrapsychic precept that, from an intrapsychic caregiving viewpoint, is exclusively nonveridical (although developmental and facilitative). *Facilitative* refers to any aspect of the caregiving relationship that furthers or stabilizes development. *Veridical* and *nonveridical* are always applied from an intrapsychic caregiving vantage point and refer to whether or not the intrapsychic precept is nonveridical, which, in turn, determines whether the infant is using nonveridical percepts to signify that her/his agent-self has the causal capacity to engage the caregiver's caregiving. The terms veridical and nonveridical refer to whether the reflection of effective agency (intrapsychic motive gratification) results from a phase-appropriately empirical contact with the caregiver's intrapsychic motives or from the illusional use of constitutive-interpersonal motive gratification to signify the reflection of intrapsychic agent-self as agent-self. To repeat, during early development, illusional experience is facilitative, innately determined, and time limited; it does not result from defective caregiving. The capacity for nonveridical intrapsychic motive gratification spares the infant the burden of external complexities for which s/he initially is poorly equipped. In paradigmatic development, the most important of these complexities is the existence of the caregiver's personal motives.[42]

Illusional Intrapsychic Mutuality

The structural shift to a nonveridical, nonspecific intrapsychic precept and caregiver percept, which is the infant's innately determined response to the loss expressed as stranger anxiety, makes possible the self-deception that is phase-specific in development and permanent in untreated psychopathology. The net effect of the mourning process initiated by primary stranger anxiety is that the infant will accept any experience of the caregiver, including the caregiver's mere presence (and, in psychopathology, even manifest rage), as signifying the caregiver's veridical intrapsychic caregiving. Percepts of the caregiver's presence, which gratify perceptual constitutive-interpersonal motives, acquire hegemony over percepts of the caregiver's intrapsychic caregiving as gratifying percepts for the intrapsychic motive.[43] We term the sum of the nonveridical personal meanings that result from this fusion the ***structure of illusional intrapsychic mutuality.*** It is a structure because it exerts regulatory control over the infant's intrapsychic perceptual identity process (inner well-being). The infant's experience of intrapsychic mutuality is illusional because the infant's intrapsychic agent-self is temporarily isolated from direct contact with the caregiver's intrapsychic caregiving (even though the infant continues to have the illusion that s/he has contact with and is the agent cause of the caregiver's intrapsychic caregiving motives). In other words, the term illusional intrapsychic mutuality implies neither that the infant does not enjoy a rich and facilitative intrapsychic care-getting pleasure nor that the caregiver's caregiving is nonveridical.

An illusional form of intrapsychic mutuality occurs in the context that the innately based motive for intrapsychic personal meaning has regulatory control of the subjective experience of personal existence. The infant will not survive unless some percepts can be accepted as matching the intrapsychic ideal (precept) of being the agent cause of the caregiver's intrapsychic caregiving. Until the onset of reflective interpersonal agent-self experience in the third developmental stage, only percepts that have the meaning of the caregiver's responsive intrapsychic caregiving can provide the necessary reflection of intrapsychic agency. The loss that precipitates primary stranger anxiety is resolved by an innately determined, structural shift in the intrapsychic precept, a shift that allows percepts that gratify perceptual constitutive-interpersonal motives to be illusionally interpreted as having the same intrapsychic significance as did percepts of the caregiver's intrapsychic caregiving (the most representative being the caregiver's smiling face) at the end of the veridical gratification phase. In other words, the infant responds to the intrapsychic loss that stimulates stranger anxiety with a nondiscriminating acceptance of constitutive-interpersonal information for the satisfaction of intrapsychic needs.

This shift from a veridical intrapsychic precept and its associated veridical intrapsychic motive to a nonveridical intrapsychic precept and its associated nonveridical intrapsychic motive results, in effect, in the *merger* of the infant's intrapsychic consciousness and constitutive-interpersonal consciousness. In the previous, veridical gratification phase, while the relationship between the infant's intrapsychic consciousness and constitutive-interpersonal consciousness is undifferentiated, it is not merged because the caregiver percept (the caregiver's smile) phase-appropriately conveys empirical information about the caregiver's intrapsychic caregiving motives. In the *illusional* gratification phase of the pre-eidetic stage, the relationship between intrapsychic consciousness and constitutive-interpersonal consciousness is both undifferentiated and merged.

When the merger of intrapsychic and constitutive-interpersonal consciousness occurs in the illusional gratification phase, the infant begins to experience intrapsychic loss in the caregiver's absence because the caregiver's presence is the phase-specific (nonveridical) source of the infant's intrapsychic motive gratification. Until eidetic internalization occurs at the end of the pre-eidetic stage, the infant has no intracranial source of caregiving percepts to provide (nonveridical) intrapsychic motive gratification in the caregiver's absence. Between the onset of illusional intrapsychic motive gratification and the onset of separation anxiety, at times when the caregiver temporarily removes her/himself from the infant's visual field, the infant regresses to a more primitive intrapsychic motive gratification based on undifferentiated caregiver percepts (e.g., shaking a rattle, cooing, and babbling). This is possible because, in the caregiver's absence, the infant has no overriding percepts of the caregiver to dilute the efficacy of undifferentiated caregiver percepts. The power of the *presence caregiver percept* form of the non-veridical caregiver percept to convey the significance of the caregiver's focused intrapsychic caregiving can be indirectly apprehended both by adult introspection and by the observation of all the common verbal expressions of the gratification provided by the mere presence of a loved one (e.g., the lyric, "just the sight of you").

Illusional intrapsychic mutuality can be viewed as an adaptive evolutionary resolution of the problems that can result from the inability to chose one's parents. In the face of nonveridical intrapsychic caregiving, illusional intrapsychic mutuality is a powerful force for physical survival because it enables the child to experience that harmony which is innately given within the intrapsychic precept and the intrapsychic motive. In psychopathology, the caregiver's nonveridical intrapsychic caregiving can be accepted by the child as veridical intrapsychic caregiving, because, no matter how sophisticated the child's perceptual capacities become, the nonveridical intrapsychic precept does not entail veridical information about the caregiver's intrapsychic caregiving. In effect, illusional intrapsychic mutuality endows every child with the ability to survive physically the caregiver's intrapsychic and, even, clinically manifest interpersonal psychopathology. Illusional intrapsychic mutuality provides a powerful source of protection for the child against having her/his wellsprings of personal meaning fatally poisoned by caregiver psychopathology.

The Two Forms of the Intrapsychic Motive

We identify two structurally distinct forms of the intrapsychic motive, which we term the **constitutive-intrapsychic motive** and the **regulatory-intrapsychic motive.** The former is most importantly determined by nature, the latter by nurture. The regulatory-intrapsychic motive does not differentiate until the second developmental stage, the regulatory-intrapsychic self stage (see chap. 3). The gratified regulatory-intrapsychic motive is the psychic structure we term the regulatory-intrapsychic agent-self. It entails the veridical capacity to own (regulate) one's own mind. The possession of a regulatory-intrapsychic agent-self changes the subjective experience of personal existence from one in which causality (regulation of gratification) is, from an intrapsychic caregiving perspective, external to the agent-self to a subjective experience of personal existence in which the locus of needed gratification is both structuralized within the agent-self and mutualized.

The constitutive-intrapsychic motive is the sole form of the intrapsychic motive until the regulatory-intrapsychic motive differentiates during the regulatory-intrapsychic self stage. The constitutive-intrapsychic motive provides the basis for the undifferentiated intrapsychic agent-self's ongoing conviction that it is engaging and regulating the caregiver's caregiving ideals and motives. The term **undifferentiated** refers to the phenomenon that the child's intrapsychic motive and associated intrapsychic precept are relatively indiscriminate with regard to the quality of the caregiver's gratification of the child's intrapsychic motive. The constitutive-intrapsychic motive is the only form of the intrapsychic motive that ever functions in untreated psychopathology.

There are two structurally distinct forms of the constitutive-intrapsychic motive, which are distinguished by whether the associated precept and gratifying percept are veridical or nonveridical. In the veridical gratification phase of the pre-eidetic stage, the precept, or template, is veridical in that its content (most representatively the caregiver's smiling face) phase-appropriately represents the caregiver's intrapsychic caregiving. However, because the infant's state of mind is phase-specifically dissociated, or nonreflective, the infant's smile response will differentiate even when the caregiver's intrapsychic caregiving is, from an intrapsychic caregiving perspective, as-if and nonveridical. In other words, *nonveridical caregiving* (i.e., a smile with anger behind it) can be accepted as a *veridical caregiving percept* because the veridical intrapsychic precept that is functional in the veridical gratification phase is developmentally unsophisticated. While the constitutive-intrapsychic agent-self motive must be gratified in order for an individual to survive, in the veridical gratification phase of the pre-eidetic stage, in order for an acceptable gratification of the constitutive-intrapsychic motive not to occur, the caregiver's interpersonal caregiving has to be so blatantly defective that it prevents the smile response from differentiating. The consequence is psychological marasmus. The most pathological kind of delusional gratification of the constitutive-intrapsychic motive consonant with physical survival produces the nonorganic form of primary infantile autism.

As we will describe in detail in chapter 3, in contrast to the diffuseness of the constitutive-intrapsychic agent-self motive, the *regulatory* form of the intrapsychic motive, which never differentiates in psychopathology and is activated in paradigmatic development only at the end of the regulatory-intrapsychic self stage, is informed by a precept (ideal) that entails a reflective, veridical agent-self experience based on veridical knowledge of the caregiver's actual intrapsychic caregiving motives. While constitutive-intrapsychic motive gratification is necessary for physical survival, regulatory-intrapsychic motive gratification is necessary for mental health. The regulatory-intrapsychic agent-self does not permit self-deception; it enables the individual to discriminate between actual and as-if types of intrapsychic care-getting pleasure. Conversely, the underlying defect in psychopathology is the fixation of the nonveridical form of the individual's constitutive-intrapsychic motive. As will be explained in chapter 7, in Intrapsychic Treatment the intrapsychic therapist's ability to arouse the agent-self potentially associated with the veridical constitutive-intrapsychic motive from its previous nonfunctioning state constitutes an integral part of the therapeutic action of an Intrapsychic Treatment process.

The Developmental Pretransference

The onset of illusional intrapsychic mutuality marks the beginning of the pretransference form of the developmental transference. In psychodynamic theory *transference* traditionally refers to an innately based misidentification which occurs by means of a transfer of meaning in which the significance of an experience is assigned (without the subject's awareness) an unapparent meaning of a forbidden gratification. In our use of the term, a nonveridical personal meaning significance of effective agency is unconsciously assigned to constitutive-interpersonal motive gratification. There are both intrapsychic and interpersonal categories of transference experience, and each of these has developmental and pathological forms. Transference does not exist after the completion of a paradigmatic development, which is why we term the stage of completed paradigmatic psychological development the posttransference stage.

In the illusional gratification phase of the pre-eidetic stage, the intrapsychic motive gratification process is *pretransference* because the infant does not yet possess an endogenous structure that can signify (nonveridical) intrapsychic motive gratification. The pretransference form of the intrapsychic perceptual identity process consists of the following components: (1) the nonveridical, consciousness-generated, to-be-actualized ideal of an effective intrapsychic agent-self (the nonveridical form of the constitutive-intrapsychic motive); (2) the nonveridical precept (ideal of caregiving mutuality), which forms the template for the perceptual identity process and which can be satisfied illusionally (by percepts unrelated to the caregiver's intrapsychic caregiving); and (3) the matching, gratifying, nonveridical caregiver percepts of the physical presence of the caregiver. At this point in development, even when the gratifying, caregiver percept includes the caregiver's actual intrapsychic caregiving responses, this information only signifies the caregiver's presence.

The Second Pre-Eidetic Loss: Primary Separation Anxiety

The illusional gratification phase of the pre-eidetic stage is the only period in life when the absence of the caregiver can cause the complete loss of intrapsychic agent-self meaning. Due to the infant's lack of an intracranial source of gratifying, presence caregiver percepts, in the illusional gratification phase, from an intrapsychic caregiving perspective, the disappearance of the caregiver from the infant's perceptual field has the meaning to the infant's intrapsychic agent-self of the loss of the capacity to cause the caregiver's intrapsychic caregiving. During these periods, the infant survives by relying on an innately determined grief work that entails an altered state of consciousness based on a nonfixated regression to an undifferentiated and, therefore, less specific intrapsychic precept. In other words, the successful mourning of the intrapsychic loss expressed as primary stranger anxiety enlarges the gratifying, caregiver percept from the phase-appropriately veridical percept of the caregiver's smiling face to a nonveridical percept that includes information related to the caregiver's mere presence. Although this change ends the infant's vulnerability to primary stranger anxiety, it leaves her/him vulnerable to a second developmental loss that occurs when the caregiver's personal motives cause her/him to remove her/himself temporarily from the infant's perceptual field. This second loss stimulates an expression of distress which we term *primary separation anxiety*. The loss expressed as separation anxiety is proximally caused by the personal motives of the caregiver, in contrast to the first intrapsychic loss, which was caused by the hegemony of the infant's maturing constitutive-interpersonal capacities over the infant's intrapsychic perceptual identity process.[44]

Primary separation anxiety occurs because the infant has no intracranial structure to provide phase-specific caregiver percepts (in this phase, nonveridical, presence caregiver percepts) during the caregiver's absence. Stated differently, the infant does not yet have any form of intrapsychic caregiver constancy. Each time the caregiver's personal motives remove her/him from the infant's perceptual field, the infant experiences intrapsychic loss, which always has the meaning of the loss of the capacity of the infant's intrapsychic agent-self to cause the caregiver's intrapsychic caregiving. This loss engenders an innately determined response, which is usually called infantile separation anxiety, but which we term primary separation anxiety in order to distinguish it both from other theories and from subsequent developmental or pathological forms of separation anxiety.

To summarize, the infant successfully mourns the first intrapsychic loss, manifested by primary stranger anxiety, by activating a new, innately determined, nonveridical intrapsychic precept and associated nonveridical intrapsychic motive. Because the nonveridical constitutive-intrapsychic motive is gratified by nonveridical caregiver percepts, the infant is, on a time-limited basis, structurally isolated from the possibility of direct contact with the caregiver's intrapsychic caregiving, which is the condition of illusional intrapsychic mutuality. The reliance on nonveridical, presence caregiver percepts for intrapsychic motive gratification in turn makes the infant vulnerable to the second intrapsychic loss, which is manifested by primary separation anxiety. Even though the infant introspectively experiences the nonveridical precept as an ideal of paradigmatic mutuality, this ideal lacks information about the caregiver's intrapsychic caregiving. This is only a seeming paradox, because intrapsychic motive gratification always entails the subjective experience of an intrapsychic agent-self with the capacity to engage the caregiver's intrapsychic caregiving and, therefore, to regulate its own intrapsychic motive gratification, whether or not, from an intrapsychic caregiving vantage point, this mutuality is veridical. In other words, at this stage the infant's agent-self reflection results not from the infant's veridical recognition that her/his agent-self is causing the caregiver's intrapsychic caregiving, but from the effects of intrapsychic motive gratification per se. Since the infant is not veridically in touch with the caregiver's intrapsychic motives (the caregiver's caregiving motives are signified by a presence caregiver percept of any aspect of the caregiver), the infant's development can progress beyond separation anxiety even in the presence of nonveridical intrapsychic and interpersonal caregiving that will cause the child to develop intrapsychic and, even, significant interpersonal psychopathology.

Primary separation anxiety is the infant's response to the loss of the phase-specific nonveridical caregiver percept (the presence caregiver percept), which causes the loss of the phase-specific reflection of agent-self as agent-self. The infant lacks any intracranial structure that can represent the caregiver's presence. When the caregiver leaves the infant's perceptual field, the infant does not have the capacity for an evocative memory of the caregiver that s/he can utilize to create the (illusional) experience that s/he continues to have the agent-self capacity to engage the caregiver's caregiving. In other words, the caregiver's personal motives, which render her/him absent, have the meaning to the infant of the infant's inability to cause the caregiver's intrapsychic caregiving and, therefore, have the meaning to the infant of the loss of effective intrapsychic agency.

Primary separation anxiety is precipitated by, but not substantially caused by, the caregiver's reasonable (i.e., consistent with a functional commitment to intrapsychic caregiving) but noncaregiving (personal) motive to be absent for limited periods of time. We emphasize that the term *noncaregiving motive* does not imply that the caregiver's caregiving is nonveridical. The paradigmatic caregiver has personal as well as caregiving motives (e.g., wants to spend time with other adults, likes to exercise, etc.). The paradigmatic caregiver differs from the nonveridical caregiver in her/his stable preference for intrapsychic caregiving pleasure.

Paradigmatically, the caregiver will respond to the infant's distress at separation in an understanding, accepting manner, perhaps by choosing a stand-in who can be comforting to the infant (even in the face of the infant's rejection) and by restricting her/his absences to relatively short periods of time.

Eidetic Internalization

As the child's constitutive-interpersonal cognitive capacities continue to mature, the infant responds to the intrapsychic loss expressed as primary separation anxiety by using her/his increasing capacity for evocative memory to recall images of the caregiver that are stored in long-term memory. The infant's constitutive-interpersonal representational capacities evolve from an enactive, to an iconic (pictorial), to a symbolic representation of the world.[45] Regardless of its representational form, if the recalled memory serves the purpose of signifying a caregiver percept, we term it an eidetic memory.[46] Intrapsychic motive gratification occurs when the infant's intrapsychic perceptual identity process assigns the significance of a gratifying, caregiver percept to the recalled memory. This intrapsychic use of constitutive-interpersonal evocative memory signifies the internalization of gratifying, nonveridical presence caregiver percepts. The term *internalization* denotes the process that produces nonveridical psychic structure.[47] Internalization occurs in both paradigmatic and psychopathological development. We use the term *eidetic memories* to refer to images of the caregiver that are generated during the pre-eidetic stage, are available for evocative recall, and can be assigned the meaning of caregiver percepts.[48]

The infant's capacity to recall memories of the caregiver has the illusional significance of the infant's intrapsychic agent-self causing the caregiver to reappear, which, at this point in development has the meaning of causing the caregiver's focused intrapsychic caregiving (causing intrapsychic motive gratification by presence caregiver percepts). In effect, the meaning of purposiveness associated with the intrapsychic motive is linked with the use of constitutive-interpersonal memory to gratify that motive, so that a given constitutive-interpersonal memory acquires the illusional significance of psychic structure (regulatory agency meaning). The nonveridical psychic structure that results from the eidetic internalization of the presence caregiver percept renders the infant less vulnerable to the personal (noncaregiving) motives of the caregiver.

Eidetic memories of the caregiver are stored in the infant's long-term memory and, when stimulated by the absence of the caregiver, become available to be recalled. When recalled, they signify the caregiver's reappearance in response to the infant's motive and, therefore, function as presence caregiver percepts and signify an extracranial reflection of intrapsychic agent-self as agent-self. In other words, the memory of the caregiver's presence provides the infant with an acceptable, though nonveridical, experience of regulatory control over the caregiver's intrapsychic caregiving motives. These afford the infant a limited capacity for an endogenously generated form of intrapsychic motive gratification even when the caregiver is absent on a time-limited basis.

We term the internalized structure produced by the act of eidetic internalization, the ***transitional intrapsychic caregiver.*** The appearance of the transitional intrapsychic caregiver marks the end of the infant's vulnerability to the intrapsychic loss expressed as primary separation anxiety. The caregiver's personal (noncaregiving) motives, which absent her/him from the infant's visual field for reasonable periods of time, no longer cause the infant primary intrapsychic loss. Because it is an internalized source of (nonveridical) intrapsychic motive gratification, the transitional intrapsychic caregiver represents the successful mourning of primary separation anxiety.

The transitional intrapsychic caregiver remains in place until the end of the regulatory-interpersonal self stage, during which time it affords the infant a continuous stream of illusional experience that signifies that s/he is continuously causing the caregiver to respond with intrapsychic caregiving even when the caregiver is temporarily absent. Although the transitional intrapsychic caregiver is the source of a nonveridical type of regulatory agency reality, it is a component of paradigmatic development.[49]

Summary of Innately Determined Mourning in the Pre-Eidetic Stage

Phase-specific, pre-eidetic intrapsychic losses result (1) from the developmental hegemony of cognitive and perceptual constitutive-interpersonal motives over the perceptual identity process of intrapsychic consciousness (the loss expressed as primary stranger anxiety) and, subsequently, (2) from the caregiver's absence, which (from an intrapsychic caregiving viewpoint) has the meaning to the infant of the loss of the nonveridical, presence caregiver percept necessary for intrapsychic motive gratification (the loss expressed as primary separation anxiety). The process of innately determined, pre-eidetic mourning makes possible a new, adaptive source of gratification of the infant's intrapsychic needs (a new source of caregiver percepts).

Pre-eidetic, innately determined intrapsychic developmental mourning occurs in five stages, which are described from the intrapsychic caregiving perspective and summarized as follows:

1. caregiver in sight—infant has no functional intrapsychic agent-self (stranger anxiety);

2. caregiver in sight—caregiver in infant's mind (mourning of [1]);

3. caregiver out of sight—caregiver out of infant's mind (developmental regression);

4. caregiver out of sight—infant has no functional intrapsychic agent-self (separation anxiety); and

5. caregiver out of sight—caregiver in infant's mind (eidetic internalization).

The first stage of developmental mourning (caregiver within sight, infant no functional intrapsychic agent-self) occurs because the immaturity of the infant's constitutive-interpersonal capacities for perceptual discrimination and cognitive awareness makes her/him vulnerable to a loss of inner well-being (loss of intrapsychic motive gratification, of self-conscious, agent-self experience) even in the caregiver's presence. This loss, which occurs when the infant cannot regress away from the ungratifying percept of a strange face, is manifested by primary stranger anxiety. The second stage (caregiver in sight, caregiver in mind) results when the infant mourns the loss of the first stage. In the second stage, any perceptual experience of the caregiver can be used for intrapsychic motive gratification. In the third stage (caregiver out of sight—caregiver out of mind), when the caregiver is not physically present, the infant simply regresses, so that any percept that gratifies a constitutive-interpersonal motive (e.g., a color, a smell) can signify the caregiver's intrapsychic caregiving. The fourth stage (caregiver out of sight—infant has no functional intrapsychic agent-self) consists of the loss expressed as primary separation anxiety, in which, when the caregiver is absent, the child experiences a loss of the presence form of nonveridical caregiver percept and a corresponding loss of intrapsychic well-being. The fifth stage (caregiver out of sight—caregiver in the infant's mind) resolves the loss that occurs in stage 4. The eidetic internalization of the transitional intrapsychic caregiver means that even when the actual caregiver is out of sight, the phase-specific, presence caregiver percept is still in mind. In other words, in the absence of the caregiver, the infant can still have intrapsychic well-being (although this well-being is nonveridical).

3
The
Regulatory-Intrapsychic
Self Stage

With the onset of eidetic internalization and the transitional intrapsychic caregiver, the child enters the regulatory-intrapsychic self stage. The regulatory-intrapsychic self stage generally begins when the infant is 12 to 14 months old and lasts four to six months. During this period, the intrapsychic caregiving relationship facilitates the emergence and structuralization of the child's capacity for intrapsychic reality testing of her/his own and the caregiver's intrapsychic motives. *Intrapsychic reality testing* is the capacity for veridical, reflective, self-regulatory intrapsychic agency.

Although the intrapsychic loss in this stage is universal, it has not been recognized as a developmental milestone. This loss is expressed as *care-getting anxiety,* which is the relative loss of pleasure the child feels when the caregiver pursues personal rather than intrapsychic caregiving motives. Unfortunately, care-getting anxiety is often misunderstood as a sign that a particular child is spoiled, mentally ill, narcissistic, willful, or in need of structure, control, or discipline. Care-getting anxiety occurs because the child develops the capacity both to distinguish the caregiver's choice of personal motives from the caregiver's choice of intrapsychic caregiving motives and also to realize that the pleasure derived from the caregiver's intrapsychic caregiving is infinitely more appealing than the pleasure that occurs merely by virtue of being in the caregiver's presence. The loss expressed as care-getting anxiety differs from the other two intrapsychic losses, expressed as stranger anxiety and separation anxiety. In care-getting anxiety, the child has a functional, though nonveridical, intrapsychic agent-self available to her/him both because of the presence of the internalized source of caregiver percepts, the transitional intrapsychic caregiver, and also because caregetting anxiety occurs when the child is with the caregiver and, therefore, the child has ongoing presence caregiver percepts available to her/him.

In many respects, the regulatory-intrapsychic self stage is the most fecund period of human development. If all has gone well in the pre-eidetic stage and the caregiver remains stable in her/his capacity for veridical intrapsychic caregiving, the child will now acquire the capacity for a nurture-based, reflective, veridical experience of her/his own intrapsychic agent-self and of the caregiver's intrapsychic caregiving motives. The regulatory-intrapsychic self stage is the only time when self-consciousness and intentionality are focused exclusively on intrapsychic agency (the intention to acquire the reflection of agent-self as agent-self via being the agent cause and regulator of the caregiver's intrapsychic caregiving).

During the regulatory-intrapsychic self stage three major intrapsychic events occur: (1) the activation of the *caregiving caregiver percept* within the transitional intrapsychic caregiver; (2) the reactivation of the *veridical intrapsychic precept* and the associated *veridical constitutive-intrapsychic motive;* and (3) the onset of the *regulatory-intrapsychic agent-self* (a differentiated, mutualized, intrapsychic agent-self).

THE UNDIFFERENTIATED PHASE

At the commencement of the regulatory-intrapsychic self stage, the child's intrapsychic perceptual identity process uses only the *presence* caregiver percept form of nonveridical caregiver percept to signify intrapsychic motive gratification. As we discussed in chapter 2, in paradigmatic development nonveridical caregiver percepts result not from inadequate caregiving but from the hegemony acquired by the child's perceptual constitutive-interpersonal motives over the intrapsychic perceptual identity process. From an intrapsychic caregiving perspective, the determination of the veridicality of a caregiver percept is made on the basis of the child's functional intrapsychic precept. Depending on the developmental stage, the same content (e.g., the caregiver's smiling face) can represent either a veridical caregiver percept or a nonveridical caregiver percept. Veridical and nonveridical caregiver percepts are distinguished by whether, from an intrapsychic caregiving perspective, the information included in the operative intrapsychic precept veridically, though phase-appropriately, signifies the caregiver's actual intrapsychic caregiving motives. The nonveridical caregiver percept generated within the child's intrapsychic consciousness is sufficiently diffuse in its representation of ideal caregiving behaviors that any percept of the caregiver (whether, from an intrapsychic caregiving viewpoint, the percept represents caregiving or noncaregiving, paradigmatic or non-veridical caregiver behavior) can illusionally signify the child's agent-self capacity to engage the caregiver's intrapsychic caregiving and, thus, can signify the reflection of intrapsychic agent-self as agent-self.

Nonveridical intrapsychic motive gratification facilitates paradig-matic development. When a percept that gratifies perceptual constitu-tive-interpersonal motives (e.g., a percept of the caregiver's mere physi-cal presence) acquires the significance of an intrapsychic percept (a percept of direct, causal contact with the caregiver's intrapsychic care-giving motives), extra pleasure accompanies the child's constitutive-interpersonal motive gratification. This boost enhances the child's de-velopment of important constitutive-interpersonal capacities, such as speech and motor skills. Because nonveridical intrapsychic motive grati-fication structurally isolates the child from direct contact with the care-giver's intrapsychic motives, the child can avoid coping with an impor-tant complexity before s/he is ready, namely the fact that the caregiver has personal as well as caregiving motives. Further, if the caregiver's caregiving is nonveridical, the child's reliance on a nonveridical form of intrapsychic motive gratification permanently shields the child from di-rectly experiencing the nonveridical quality of the caregiver's caregiv-ing, even though the price the child pays for this protection is a per-manent, psychopathological dissociation (mental illness; see chap. 6).

In the first, *undifferentiated* phase of the regulatory-intrapsychic self stage, the child has for the first time an internalized capacity for phase-appropriately continuous intrapsychic motive gratification, because of the transitional intrapsychic caregiver's potential to gratify the post-eidetic, nonveridical form of the intrapsychic motive in the caregiver's absence. In the pre-eidetic stage, the infant can only respond to the loss of extracranial caregiver percepts by a nonfixated regression. When nonveridical caregiver percepts are eidetically internalized and avail-able to motives of recall, they endow the infant with an internalized, incomplete, but functional intrapsychic self-regulatory control over her/his inner well-being. The eidetically internalized memories of the caregiver give the child a qualified experience of reliability with regard to the caregiver's physical presence. Because the caregiver's presence illusionally signifies the child's engagement of the caregiver's intrapsy-chic caregiving motives, the memories of the caregiver provide the child with an illusional sense of the stability of her/his capacity for effective agency. This dependability of nonveridical intrapsychic motive gratifi-

71

cation differs from the veridical reliability of intrapsychic effective agency that occurs at the end of this stage in that it does not confer a stable, autonomous, loss-free inner well-being. The percepts arising from the transitional intrapsychic caregiver do not have the experiential, extracranial power necessary for *stable* intrapsychic motive gratification because they are recollected percepts that have been eidetically internalized (stored in memory within constitutive-interpersonal consciousness). As a result, the capacity of the child's transitional intrapsychic caregiver to function as a source of gratifying, nonveridical caregiver percepts is limited in scope.

At the beginning of the undifferentiated phase of the regulatory-intrapsychic self stage, the caregiver's presence affords the child a transference type of intrapsychic motive gratification in a context in which the child no longer experiences primary stranger anxiety or primary separation anxiety.[1] The term **intrapsychic transference** refers to a transfer of meaning in which a constitutive-interpersonal experience acquires the meaning of an intrapsychic experience (e.g., a presence caregiver percept both satisfies constitutive-interpersonal motives and also signifies the caregiver's intrapsychic caregiving motive to gratify the infant's intrapsychic motive). The child's perceptual identity process attaches the significance of gratifying, caregiver percepts to the pre-eidetic memories of the caregiver internalized in the transitional intrapsychic caregiver.

Merger is a more generic term for the basis of nonveridical intrapsychic motive gratification than transference. Merger has two referents: (1) the child's inability to know the caregiver's actual intrapsychic motives in a context in which the child has the illusion that her/his agent-self is regulating the caregiver's intrapsychic caregiving motives and (2) the assignment of intrapsychic significance to percepts of the caregiver that satisfy perceptual constitutive-interpersonal motives. Merger experience occurs prior to transference experience. The developmental merger and the developmental transference ultimately lead to a nonmerged, nontransference form of the caregiving relationship. When this occurs, the child again has empirical contact with the caregiver's intrapsychic caregiving.

Transference experience can be developmental (mutualizing) or psychopathological (obstructive). The pathological transference form of the intrapsychic caregiving relationship permanently and structurally blocks the untreated individual from empirical contact with another's intrapsychic caregiving motives and, therefore, from veridical intrapsychic agent-self experience (see chap. 6). Developmental transference experience is functionally more akin to nontransference experience than it is to pathological transference experience. As we will see, the exposure of developmental transference experience to the caregiver's veridical intrapsychic caregiving facilitates the reactivation of the child's veridical intrapsychic precept. Because in *paradigmatic* development all caregiver percepts occur in a context in which the caregiver's motives for intrapsychic caregiving pleasure are, in reality, being engaged by the child's intrapsychic motives, the illusional meaning mandated by the nonveridical precept heuristically supports the evolution of the intra-psychic caregiving relationship. Since the caregiver's motives for intra-psychic caregiving pleasure are stable, they continue to have a devel-opmental impact on the child. The gratifying, nonveridical percept that the child's perceptual identity process signifies as having the meaning of the caregiver's intrapsychic caregiving love is never a percept of overt, interpersonal hostility, intrusiveness, or neglect, as may be the case in psychopathology. In a developmental transference, the cause of the nonveridical perceptual identity process resides within the child's intrapsychic meaning attachment process; the quality of the caregiver's actual intrapsychic caregiving remains unchanged. In a pathological transference process, however, a second component determines the nonveridicality of the perceptual identity process, namely the caregiv-er's intrapsychic and, sometimes, interpersonal psychopathology (see chap. 6).

The intrapsychic transference includes a consciousness-generated, nonveridical precept (ideal); a consciousness-generated, nonveridical to-be-actualized ideal (motive); and the eidetically internalized pre-eidetic caregiver imago, which becomes the internalized source of grati-fying, nonveridical caregiver percepts that we term the *transitional intra-psychic caregiver*. The intrapsychic transference endows the child with the phase-specific capacity for a *relatively continuous*, though illusional, intrapsychic agent-self experience, which is the most striking difference between the pre-eidetic stage (when the child could only respond to the loss of extracranial caregiver percepts by a nonfixated regression) and the undifferentiated phase of the regulatory-intrapsychic self stage.

The intrapsychic transference involves both primary and secondary sources of nonveridical caregiver percepts. The *primary* source of non-veridical caregiver percepts is the transitional intrapsychic caregiver. The *secondary* source of nonveridical caregiver percepts varies with the child's level of development. In the regulatory-intrapsychic self stage, secondary caregiver percepts are the product of actual perceptual experience with the caregiver. After the onset of interpersonal agency in the third developmental stage (the regulatory-interpersonal self stage), gratified interpersonal motives become the source of secondary caregiver percepts.

In the undifferentiated phase of the regulatory-intrapsychic self stage, the child's nonveridical intrapsychic motive ultimately needs secondary caregiver percepts (needs the caregiver's actual presence) for gratification. However, the child can have a functional, though illusional, agent-self experience in the temporary absence of the caregiver because the transitional intrapsychic caregiver affords a sufficient source of primary nonveridical caregiver percepts to allow intrapsychic motive gratification to occur without regression. The child can usually restitute the loss of the phase-specific secondary caregiver percept by utilizing the primary nonveridical caregiver percepts internalized in the transitional intrapsychic caregiver. For example, if the caregiver leaves the room, the child can generally combine primary caregiver percepts with some experience of pleasure, such as the pleasure derived from playing with a toy, to produce intrapsychic motive gratification. However, because the child's intrapsychic motive gratification is nonveridical and, therefore, unstable, the child is occasionally vulnerable to losses caused by the caregiver's personal (noncaregiving) motives to be absent.

The appeal of the presence caregiver percept provides an alternative explanation for Mahler's interpretation of the common observation that at this point in development the child moves away from the caregiver, returns, then moves away again. Mahler concludes that the child engages in these cycles of behavior to "refuel" in the service of growing out of a symbiotic merger with the caregiver.[2] In contrast, we believe that the child never tries to achieve independence in the sense of moving away from an inner closeness to the caregiver, but, rather, aims to maintain the pleasure imparted by the meaning of agent-self-caused ideal intrapsychic mutuality. When the child moves out of range of the caregiver, the ongoing, intense pleasure of effective intrapsychic agency, which has comprised the child's intrapsychic experience at least since birth and which, at this point, is generated by percepts of the caregiver's presence, becomes attenuated or interrupted because the child's exercise of motor agency has resulted in a noticeable lack of the phase-specific, presence caregiver percept. The resulting reduction in the inner well-being derived from the reflection of intrapsychic agent-self as agent-self motivates the child to return to the caregiver's presence in order to regain the lost pleasure. We believe the loss the child feels when s/he gets out of emotional range from the caregiver is not, as Mahler asserts, a loss of omnipotence, but, rather, the child feels a decrease in the pleasure of intrapsychic mutuality. There is clearly an adaptive quality to a form of intrapsychic motive gratification that both enhances the child's motives for exploration and mastery of the external world and also causes the very young but mobile child to remain close to the caregiver. The observation of the determination of other young animals, such as waterfowl, to remain in the presence of parents supports this conclusion.

In psychopathology, the presence caregiver percept form of intrapsychic motive gratification can be a powerful source of illusional well-being. The following vignette illustrates the pleasure provided by a presence caregiver percept form of intrapsychic motive gratification under the control of negative transference motives. A patient whose father had always been both overtly hostile to the patient and very self-involved called his father to tell him that he was going to graduate in June with his Ph.D. from what had been an arduous matriculation. The father gave this news short shrift and began a blow by blow account of a golf game he had played the day before. The patient observed that, while his feelings had been hurt when his father did not show enthusiasm in response to his good news, he had also felt happy just to hear his father's voice on the phone.

An example in which the presence caregiver percept form of nonveridical intrapsychic motive gratification is under the hegemony of positive transference motives is lovers who feel good just by virtue of being together, but who feel dysphoric (like "a part of myself is missing") and not in control of their inner well-being if one or the other has to travel. This transference relationship pleasure can be the basis for an extremely stable, functional, inner well-being. The drawback to this psychopathological esteem is, of course, that when the important person leaves, the pleasurable well-being that depended on her/his presence also disappears.

The transitional intrapsychic caregiver contains two types of nonveridical caregiver percepts, presence caregiver percepts and caregiving caregiver percepts. Caregiving caregiver percepts are not functional at the beginning of the undifferentiated phase, at which point the child's intrapsychic precept is too diffuse for the child to distinguish types of nonveridical caregiver percepts. In the course of the undifferentiated phase, the cumulative pleasure of the actual, ongoing intrapsychic caregiving relationship becomes so focused that the infant comes to recognize and prefer the bank of caregiving percepts of the caregiver's smiling face that were functional in the veridical gratification phase of the pre-eidetic stage and that are registered in memory. These percepts are termed *caregiving caregiver percepts* because the information used to signify intrapsychic motive gratification relates to the caregiver's intrapsychic caregiving (e.g., the caregiver's smile). Caregiving caregiver percepts are nonveridical caregiver percepts because they are now memories within the transitional intrapsychic caregiver, which is the internalized form of the structure of illusional intrapsychic mutuality. Though caregiving caregiver percepts are nonveridical, they are phase-appropriately reflective because they signify the caregiver's intrapsychic caregiving. In the undifferentiated phase of the regulatory-intrapsychic self stage, the child's experience of intrapsychic mutuality is nonveridical because all contact between the child's intrapsychic agent-self and the extracranial caregiver's intrapsychic caregiving motives is indirect, due to its mediation by the transitional intrapsychic caregiver. Thus, the pleasure of intrapsychic caregiving mutuality conveyed by all types of nonveridical caregiver percepts is as-if pleasure. Most importantly, caregiving caregiver percepts provide the child with the potential for a type of intrapsychic motive gratification, which, while nonveridical, produces more pleasure than the gratification provided by presence caregiver percepts. The caregiving caregiver percept is phase-appropriately reflective, since it conveys information about the caregiver's caregiving, while the presence caregiver percept conveys only information about the caregiver's physical presence or absence.

The child's capacity to use caregiving caregiver percepts as a form of transference intrapsychic motive gratification occurs in part because the phase-appropriately reflective mind experience provided by the transitional intrapsychic caregiver allows the child to discriminate on the basis of acquired experience among the caregiver's various behaviors. The paradigmatic caregiver's stable preference for caregiving intimacy also allows the child to recognize that nonveridical, caregiving caregiver percepts are infinitely more pleasurable than nonveridical, presence caregiver percepts. As a result of an innately determined process facilitated by the caregiver's ability to provide veridical intrapsychic caregiving pleasure, the caregiving caregiver percept becomes a distinct source of nonveridical intrapsychic motive gratification within the transitional intrapsychic caregiver.

In the absence of the caregiver, however, the child cannot yet use internalized caregiving caregiver percepts to provide intrapsychic motive gratification because the functional nonveridical *precept* (ideal) includes information that is too general to allow the child to distinguish between caregiving caregiver percept gratification and presence caregiver percept gratification without actual exposure to care-getting pleasure. The limited discriminatory capacity entailed by the precept structure is an important aspect of the intrapsychic isolation imposed by the structure of illusional intrapsychic mutuality. When the caregiver is present, though, the gratifying percepts that come directly from the transitional intrapsychic caregiver are stimulated and regulated by actual, focused care-getting pleasure and, therefore, the caregiving caregiver percept will convey a more powerful pleasure than the presence caregiver percept. In other words, the child becomes aware that focused care-getting pleasure (e.g., playing peek-a-boo) is more gratifying than the pleasure of merely being with the caregiver.[3] Once the child recognizes that the caregiving caregiver percept form of intrapsychic motive gratification produces more pleasure than the presence caregiver percept form of intrapsychic motive gratification, the child becomes vulnerable to a new intrapsychic loss, which is manifested by the behavior we term ***transference care-getting anxiety.***

Transference Care-Getting Anxiety

Transference care-getting anxiety is the behavioral expression of a phase-specific intrapsychic loss that differs from any previous intrapsychic loss because it occurs in the presence of the caregiver and in the presence of a functional caregiver percept (the presence caregiver percept form of nonveridical caregiver percept). Transference care-getting anxiety is a *secondary* intrapsychic loss rather than a *primary* intrapsychic loss. After eidetic internalization, intrapsychic losses are secondary because the transitional intrapsychic caregiver provides the infant with an ongoing source of caregiver percepts. In contrast, losses in the pre-eidetic stage are primary losses, because there is no internalized structure to afford the child a continuous experience of intrapsychic motive gratification in the absence of actual perceptual experience with the caregiver.

Transference care-getting anxiety directly results from the caregiver's temporary choice of personal over caregiving motives. For example, if the caregiver chooses to write a letter rather than to be actively engaged in caregiving behaviors, the child experiences a loss because the child has come to prefer the superior intrapsychic pleasure caused by caregiving caregiver percepts to intrapsychic pleasure caused by presence caregiver percepts.

In the undifferentiated phase of the regulatory-intrapsychic self stage, the loss caused when the caregiver pursues personal rather than caregiving motives is a transference loss because the sole functioning intrapsychic precept is a post-eidetic nonveridical precept and because the functioning intrapsychic motive is the post-eidetic nonveridical constitutive-intrapsychic motive. By definition, this motive can only be gratified by means of nonveridical caregiver percepts that are mediated by the transitional intrapsychic caregiver.

The child does not register every instance in which the caregiver's personal motives have temporarily superseded her/his caregiving motives because much of the time the presence of the caregiver and, therefore, the existence of presence caregiver percept gratification, can suffice to maintain intrapsychic motive gratification. The child can play by her/himself for relatively long periods of time in the caregiver's presence with little or no active caregiving input. For this reason, when the caregiver needs to attend to personal motives and, therefore, occasionally absents her/himself, episodes of *secondary separation anxiety* may occur. Secondary separation anxiety categorically differs from primary separation anxiety. It occurs only after eidetic internalization and is not a developmental intrapsychic loss because it does not further development. Secondary separation anxiety occurs in the absence of the caregiver, when the nonveridical, presence caregiver percepts provided by the transitional intrapsychic caregiver are, for some reason, not sufficient to provide the inner care and comfort needed by the child (e.g., the caregiver remains away too long, the child skins her/his knee, her/his toy breaks).

The child will be most likely to experience transference care-getting anxiety when her/his need for more focused caregiving is heightened, either because s/he has been actively engaged in the pleasure of caregiving mutuality with the caregiver, who then turns aside to pursue personal motives, or because the child has gone a relatively long time on presence caregiver percept gratification. In the latter case, the child may approach the caregiver wanting to "talk," to play a game, or even just to be held or nuzzled. If the caregiver does not put her/his personal motives aside and turn to her/his caregiving motives, the child experiences a loss of regulatory-intrapsychic agency (a loss of intrapsychic motive gratification) and responds with the manifest unhappiness we term transference care-getting anxiety. Unfortunately, this behavior is often entirely misconstrued. Instead of recognizing that the child who is experiencing transference care-getting anxiety needs refocused attention, caregivers and child development professionals alike often conclude that the child cannot tolerate frustration and needs to experience more of it in order to learn to live with it. Too often the conclusion is that the child needs less rather than more attention.

Transference care-getting anxiety categorically differs from Freud's description of what he considers the normative childhood experience that the child feels the loss of love when s/he recognizes that the parent can be angry with her/him. For Freud, this painful experience is a determinant of anxiety.[4] He thought the child's manifest anxiety in response to the caregiver's anger signifies dismay over the loss of the libidinal object of the child's instinctual drive derivatives. In contrast, transference care-getting anxiety is an expression of the loss the child experiences when s/he is temporarily unable to engage the caregiver's intrapsychic caregiving motives. It has a relationship meaning because it represents the child's attempt to reengage the caregiver's intrapsychic caregiving motives. Also, transference care-getting anxiety represents a relative loss of care-getting pleasure rather than pain caused by the caregiver's displeasure.

If the caregiver persists in pursuing her/his personal motives and does not immediately respond to the child's expression of transference care-getting anxiety by initiating or resuming her/his active caregiving—thereby, helping the child to complete the mourning of the loss—the child will experience the further loss of an aborted mourning process. This second intrapsychic loss will be grieved by a regressive use of presence caregiver percept gratification and of the illusional autonomy afforded by the transitional intrapsychic caregiver. Even in paradigmatic development, the caregiver will not always be able to drop her/his personal motives and resume active caregiving behavior. For that reason, the child's ability at this stage of development to grieve transference care-getting anxiety by resorting to her/his internalized transference gratification process is crucial for her/his survival. Paradigmatically, however, when the caregiver cannot respond immediately to the child's motives for active caregiving, the caregiver will understand that the child's transference care-getting anxiety expresses the frustration of a legitimate motive. The caregiver will not be angry at the child for rejecting the caregiver's noncaregiving behavior. The caregiver will give the child a positive recognition of the child's desire for a more intimate intrapsychic caregiving relationship, for the child's motive to communicate these needs to the caregiver, and therefore, for the child's increased capacity for effective intrapsychic agency.

A variant of this process occurs when the caregiver believes that s/he is being responsive to the child's transference care-getting anxiety but the child continues to exhibit this anxiety. The caregiver would not, at this point, feel irritated with the child for being dissatisfied, but would be stimulated to become more responsive to the child and more sensitive to the specific caregiving response required. For example, the caregiver is mowing the lawn and the child, who has been playing contentedly in the sandbox, wanders over and asks with some urgency that the caregiver stop mowing. The caregiver takes the child inside the house and gives her/him a cookie and a glass of milk and then returns to mowing the lawn. When the child continues to insist that the caregiver stop mowing the lawn, the caregiver realizes that the child needs focused caregiving and spends time with the child building a sand castle and playing with the hose. In other words, the caregiver will always take the child's expression of her/his agent-self motive to be the agent cause of the caregiver's intrapsychic caregiving seriously and at face value. Since the paradigmatic caregiver's motives for intrapsychic caregiving pleasure have regulatory control over her/his motives for personal pleasure, the caregiver will feel gratified both by the child's expression of care-getting anxiety and also by her/his own decision to choose caregiving pleasure over personal motives.

There are two common types of *nonveridical* caregiving responses to the child's expression of transference care-getting anxiety. In the first, more destructive response, the caregiver expresses manifest anger at the child. This anger is often rationalized by beliefs that the child is too spoiled, too demanding, too disrespectful, or does not have sufficient frustration tolerance. If the angry caregiver response is frequently abusive, the child will largely abandon the use of *caregiving* caregiver percepts and regress back to the predominate use of *presence* caregiver percepts for transference intrapsychic motive gratification. This child will be likely to have difficulty with interpersonal esteem and with future relationships. If the caregiver's responses are angry but not abusive, the child will be likely to be conflicted about positive relationship pleasure and about positive self feelings. In either case, the child's intrapsychic development will stop at this point and, in the absence of Intrapsychic Treatment, the individual will remain forever fixated at the level of transference intrapsychic motive gratification and, therefore, forever vulnerable to constitutive-interpersonal loss, which will always have the power to cause negative feelings about the self.

There is also a category of nonveridical response to transference care-getting anxiety in which the caregiver does not show displeasure at the child's demand for focused caregiving, but offers the child a soothing that is not developmentally facilitative. This nonveridical, as-if soothing will be accepted by the child's perceptual identity process as a veridical caregiver percept. The child can attach the significance of a veridical caregiver percept to interpersonally kind but nonveridical caregiver behavior because the caregiving caregiver percept is a form of nonveridical caregiver percept and, therefore, the child has no template to allow her/him to distinguish veridical from nonveridical caregiving behaviors. A caregiver's kind response to the child's expression of anger or unhappiness may be determined primarily by the unconscious wish to put an end to the child's dysphoria. For example, the caregiver may merely offer the child a substitute gratification, such as a new toy or some food, without offering the child the recognition that the caregiver endorses the child's intrapsychic motive for greater caregiving intimacy and without actually providing that intimacy. The child may accept this nonveridical caregiving response (the caregiver's personal motives, e.g., that the child not be uncomfortable or angry) as an adequate relief of the pain expressed in her/his transference care-getting anxiety. While the child with this type of caregiver may grow up to have seemingly pleasurable interpersonal relationships, all experiences of intimacy will be characterized by (conscious or unconscious) conflict. Because the caregiver who provides interpersonal kindness but nonveridical intrapsychic caregiving cannot recognize the true nature of the child's loss, the child will never have the reflective and veridical experience of being the agent cause of the caregiver's intrapsychic caregiving.

In paradigmatic development, the caregiver will not only respond positively to the child's expression of transference care-getting anxiety but also will feel an increase in caregiving pleasure at the child's progressive capacity for intrapsychic intimacy. This caregiving pleasure facilitates the caregiver's mourning of the fact that the child rejects the caregiver's choice of personal motives (e.g., to finish cleaning out a closet) and asks the caregiver to pursue intrapsychic caregiving motives and ideals. The caregiver either makes a positive choice of intrapsychic caregiving pleasure over the pleasure of the personal motive being pur-

81

sued at the moment or, if s/he is temporarily unable to put personal motives aside, recognizes that the child's disappointment is legitimate and, above all, developmental. Because the paradigmatic caregiver has a stable, differentiated, nontransference intrapsychic agent-self, s/he feels pleasure rather than pain when the child rejects the caregiver's temporary choice of personal motives and will make every effort to suspend the pursuit of personal motives and resume active caregiving. The paradigmatic caregiver easily mourns the child's rejection of her/his pursuit of personal motives because of the intensified relationship pleasure that arises from the child's increased motive for intrapsychic intimacy. In other words, it is important that the caregiver feel and express pleasure at being regulated by the child's intrapsychic agent-self. If some exigency prevents the caregiver from putting aside personal motives for caregiving motives, the caregiver will not be angry at the child for persisting in her/his expressions of transference care-getting anxiety, but rather will be aware of and understanding of the child's frustration and loss and will feel a loss her/himself for not being able to gratify the child's wish for increased caregiving mutuality pleasure.

The caregiver's choice of intrapsychic caregiving motives over personal motives results from the caregiver's recognition that this will provide the caregiver with a superior kind of pleasure. The paradigmatic caregiver is not a martyr who attends to the child out of a combined sense of deprivation and duty, but rather is a fulfilled, enthusiastic participant in the caregiving relationship. On the unusual occasions when a paradigmatic caregiver has negative feelings about giving up personal for caregiving motives, the caregiver would not conclude that the child caused this dysphoria, but rather would both understand that her/his own feelings were the result of her/his inner stability being temporarily out of joint and would also experience these negative feelings as a loss. Thus, feelings of irritation at the child's rejection of the caregiver's pursuit of personal motives would be extremely rare, would be responded to by the caregiver as a loss imposed on the child by the caregiver, and would be used by the caregiver as an opportunity for self-understanding.

The intrapsychic mourning process that begins with the child's expression of transference care-getting anxiety is completed by the caregiver's positive response. While a part of the child does experience intrapsychic loss, this does not cause a total loss of self-reflectiveness because the loss of the caregiving caregiver percept occurs in the presence of the caregiver, that is, in the context of the presence caregiver percept form of intrapsychic motive gratification. The child reflectively recognizes the loss represented by the caregiver's pursuit of personal motives when the child's (nonveridical) ideal of intrapsychic pleasure based on caregiving caregiver percepts is not attained because of the comparatively unsatisfying intrapsychic pleasure produced by presence caregiver percepts.

Transference care-getting anxiety is the first developmental mourning process in which the innately determined form of intrapsychic perceptual identity process is directly accessible to nurture in a positive way. Accordingly, this particular form of mourning represents a developmental watershed. The caregiver can help the child to progress toward the acquisition of a nurture-based, consciously reflective, veridical, agent-self, self-regulatory control of her/his intrapsychic reality. This process of enabling nurture occurs in the following manner. The most crucial aspect of transference care-getting anxiety occurs at the moment when the child protests and actively rejects the caregiver's substitution of personal for intrapsychic caregiving motives. In paradigmatic development, the child's expression of transference care-getting anxiety elicits a caregiver response that helps the child know not only that the intrapsychic care-getting pleasure conveyed by caregiving caregiver percepts surpasses the intrapsychic care-getting pleasure conveyed by presence caregiver percepts, but also that the mourning process that occurs with the caregiver is much more pleasurable than the mourning process that occurs by a regressive return to the presence caregiver percept form of intrapsychic motive gratification. The net result is that within the structure of the transitional intrapsychic caregiver the *caregiving caregiver percept* form of intrapsychic motive gratification becomes increasingly differentiated and preferred. The evolution of the transitional intrapsychic caregiver whereby caregiving caregiver percepts become distinguished from presence caregiver percepts marks the end of the undifferentiated phase of the regulatory-intrapsychic self stage.

We emphasize that though it is developmentally heuristic, the mourning process signified by transference care-getting anxiety is a type of grief work we call **intrapsychic pain relief,** which is a type of nonveridical intrapsychic motive gratification. Intrapsychic pain relief is the product of a motive for caregiver percepts which, from an intrapsychic caregiving perspective, are nonveridical but have the subjective meaning of veridical intrapsychic caregiving pleasure. In contrast to pain relief that results from the child's regression to the use of presence caregiver percepts internalized in the transitional intrapsychic caregiver, a superior type of soothing is produced by the pain relief that results when the child's ability to engage the caregiver's intrapsychic caregiving stimulates the child's internalized, caregiving caregiver percepts.

THE DIFFERENTIATED PHASE

The transitional intrapsychic caregiver has reached the end of its development. The differentiated phase of the regulatory-intrapsychic self stage affords the child her/his only developmental opportunity to recognize her/his own and the caregiver's intrapsychic caregiving motives and to know and own her/his own intrapsychic mind. Conversely, the differentiated phase of the regulatory-intrapsychic self stage marks the first time in development that (excluding the extreme caregiver psychopathology that produces marasmus or infantile autism) the child cannot move on to the next stage of intrapsychic development in spite of defects in intrapsychic nurture. If the caregiver does not her/himself possess a veridical regulatory-intrapsychic agent-self, the child can never have the empirical, veridical experience of causing the caregiver's positive, stable choice of caregiving over personal motives, which must happen for the child to develop a veridical regulatory-intrapsychic agent-self.

Empirical, mutual contact between the child's intrapsychic agent-self and the caregiver's intrapsychic caregiving motives occurs twice during paradigmatic development: (1) during the innately determined, veridical gratification phase of the pre-eidetic stage (when the child's intrapsychic agent-self experience is phase-appropriately dissociated) and (2) during the differentiated phase of the regulatory-intrapsychic self stage (when the child's intrapsychic agent-self experience is phase-appropriately reflective). During the veridical gratification phase of the pre-eidetic stage, the child's capacity for reality testing of the caregiver's intrapsychic motives is innately determined and, therefore, from an intrapsychic caregiving perspective, does not represent veridical intrapsychic agent-self intentionality. The veridical caregiver percept, while phase-appropriately reflecting the caregiver's caregiving motives (as represented by the caregiver's smile), is also exceedingly nonspecific (the caregiver's smile can be sufficiently effective to permit the child to survive, even if, from an intrapsychic caregiving viewpoint, it is merely pasted on). In the veridical gratification phase of the pre-eidetic stage, the infant has no capacity to discern interpersonal or intrapsychic psychopathology that might lie behind the caregiver's smile. In contrast, the differentiated phase of the regulatory-intrapsychic self stage affords a developmental, nurture-based opportunity for the child to gain reality testing of the caregiver's intrapsychic motives. As will be seen, one of the most adaptive aspects of the developmental process is that this reality testing can occur only if the caregiver's intrapsychic caregiving motives are veridical.

At the beginning of the *differentiated* phase of the regulatory-intrapsychic self stage, the child has no capacity for veridical intrapsychic self-awareness. The child's intrapsychic consciousness has been isolated from empirical, mutual contact with the caregiver's intrapsychic caregiving motives since the beginning of the illusional gratification phase of the pre-eidetic stage. At that point, the activation of nonveridical intrapsychic motive gratification shielded the infant from (1) the loss produced when percepts that are the products of perceptual constitutive-interpersonal motives acquired hegemony over the child's intrapsychic perceptual identity process, (2) the loss caused by the paradigmatic caregiver's temporary pursuit of personal motives, and (3) the potential loss caused by nonveridical caregiving. In the regulatory-intrapsychic self stage, however, because of the presence of an internalized source of gratifying, nonveridical caregiver percepts (the transitional intrapsychic caregiver), if the caregiver's caregiving is nonveridical, the child will not die, but rather will continue to use the caregiver's nonveridical caregiving (which the child accepts as ideal caregiving) for the gratification of her/his nonveridical intrapsychic motive. In other words, in this stage, nonveridical caregiving obstructs the emergence of the veridical, post-eidetic form of the constitutive-intrapsychic motive and causes the continuation of the child's nonveridical intrapsychic agent-self experience. The fact that the reactivation of the veridical constitutive-intrapsychic motive brings the child in empirical contact with the caregiver's intrapsychic caregiving motives poses no danger to the child's survival because this reactivation results from the child's capacity to distinguish the pleasure of veridical caregiving mutuality from the pleasure of nonveridical caregiving mutuality and, consequently, cannot occur unless the caregiver can provide veridical intrapsychic caregiving. We emphasize that a veridical, self-regulatory intrapsychic agent-self never occurs in psychopathology. When interpersonal psychopathology has its first manifestation in later life and it may appear that an individual has suddenly become mentally ill (e.g., anorexia nervosa during adolescence, clinical depression in response to the aging process), the affected individual has had intrapsychic psychopathology since childhood. As will be explicated in chapter 6, intrapsychic psychopathology can exist in the absence of behavior commonly defined as interpersonal psychopathology.

The nurture-based differentiation of intrapsychic consciousness commences because the child's increasing preference for the caregiving caregiver percept form of nonveridical percept stimulates the veridical intrapsychic precept (which became phase-specifically nonfunctional at the beginning of the illusional gratification phase of the pre-eidetic stage as part of the mourning of the loss expressed as primary stranger anxiety). This veridical intrapsychic precept is an ideal of empirical, mutual intrapsychic pleasure. When available, nontransference (non-dissociated) intrapsychic pleasure is superior to transference intrapsychic pleasure, which, by comparison, acquires the significance of loss. The child's intrapsychic agent-self begins to "wake up" (the phase-specifically dissociated state that is associated with transference experience is gradually dispelled) and to recognize the superior pleasure imparted by veridical caregiving percepts of the extracranial caregiver's actual intrapsychic caregiving. These had remained outside of the child's awareness because of the hegemony of the structure of illusional intrapsychic mutuality. The stimulation of the *veridical* precept initiates the beginning reactivation of the post-eidetic form of the veridical constitutive-intrapsychic motive.

We stress that the new, veridical intrapsychic agent-self does *not* evolve from the anlage of the transference intrapsychic agent-self. In fact, the veridical and the transference agent-selves are in a relationship of competitive inhibition and yield categorically different experiences of self and other. The developmental line of the veridical intrapsychic agent-self is discontinuous because it emerges from a latent form of veridical intrapsychic motive that can be reactivated only by veridical intrapsychic caregiving.

Initially, the post-eidetic veridical intrapsychic precept and veridical intrapsychic motive are functional only when the child directly experiences the pleasure of the caregiver's intrapsychic caregiving, that is, when the child receives the caregiver's focused intrapsychic attention. When the child loses these veridical caregiver percepts, which occurs when the caregiver temporarily pursues personal rather than intrapsychic caregiving motives, the child regresses to nonveridical intrapsychic motive gratification. Because of the superiority of the pleasure of intrapsychic caregiving mutuality, however, the child develops an increasingly stable recognition of and preference for nontransference (reflectively mutual and empirical) intrapsychic motive gratification. As a result, when the child regresses to a transference form of intrapsychic motive gratification in response to the loss of nontransference intrapsychic motive gratification, *s/he begins to experience increased loss of pleasure rather than a restitutional gain in pleasure.*

Nontransference Intrapsychic Care-Getting Anxiety

With the reactivation of the veridical form of the constitutive-intrapsychic motive, the child becomes vulnerable to **nontransference care-getting anxiety,** the fourth and last intrapsychic developmental loss. Nontransference care-getting anxiety expresses the loss of gratification produced by the post-eidetic veridical caregiver percept, which is an empirical percept of the caregiver's veridical intrapsychic caregiving.

Nontransference care-getting anxiety signifies a complex web of developmental achievements. Increasingly, the child becomes uninterested in pursuing the pleasure of pain relief (transference soothing). The nontransference form of care-getting anxiety in the differentiated phase of the regulatory-intrapsychic self stage categorically differs from the transference form of care-getting anxiety in the undifferentiated phase of the regulatory-intrapsychic self stage. Both forms of care-getting anxiety are triggered by the caregiver's temporary choice of personal over caregiving motives, but in nontransference care-getting anxiety, due to the functioning of the child's veridical intrapsychic precept, the child's veridical intrapsychic agent-self turns to the caregiver (to veridical, empirical caregiver percepts) rather than to nonveridical caregiver percepts internalized in the transitional caregiver. Nontransference care-getting anxiety represents a new type of mourning process that does not seek pain relief, but rather represents the child's active and confident attempt to acquire veridical intrapsychic pleasure by engaging the caregiver's intrapsychic caregiving motives.

When the caregiver responds to the child's motive for intrapsychic caregiving with personal rather than with intrapsychic caregiving motives, the child's veridical intrapsychic agent-self avoids the imminent loss by refusing to accept the caregiver's personal motives as intrapsychic caregiving and brings that rejection to the caregiver in the form of behavior which we term the **intrapsychic no.** The intrapsychic no expresses nontransference care-getting anxiety. It occurs when the child no longer responds to the loss of veridical caregiver percepts by the regressive use of nonveridical caregiver percepts. Intrapsychic no behavior represents the child's clear refusal to accept the caregiver's pursuit of personal motives as veridical intrapsychic caregiving and her/his clear demand that the caregiver turn to intrapsychic caregiving motives and behavior. For the first time, loss-generating caregiver behavior signals the child to continue to pursue veridical intrapsychic motive gratification. In other words, faced with the loss of veridical caregiving percepts due to the caregiver's pursuit of personal motives, the child's regulatory-intrapsychic agent-self refuses to fall back on transference forms of intrapsychic motive gratification.[5]

The intrapsychic no marks the end of the developmental line of intrapsychic mourning that began with primary stranger anxiety. The intrapsychic no represents the child's recognition of the unique intimacy that has always been associated with the caregiver's pleasure at putting aside personal for intrapsychic caregiving motives. The child's intrapsychic agent-self feels the caregiver's stable motive to pursue the pleasure of being engaged and regulated by the child's intrapsychic agent-self.

For the first time the child's intrapsychic agent-self can veridically recognize that the ideal of caregiving mutuality embodied in her/his veridical intrapsychic motive exerts hegemony over the caregiver's motives. The child now perceives that her/his intrapsychic agent-self-directed regulating purposiveness will be chosen preferentially by the caregiver as her/his regulating ideal. The caregiver chooses the regulating ideal within the child's intrapsychic agent-self in place of her/his own personal motives because of the superiority of intrapsychic caregiving pleasure. At this point in the child's development, when the caregiver happily puts aside personal motives and resumes focused intrapsychic caregiving, the caregiver's response has the significance of a ***structuralizing caregiver percept,*** because the child perceives that the efficient causality of her/his intrapsychic agent-self is a regulating cause of the caregiver's intrapsychic caregiving motives. For the first time, the child's agent-self reflectively experiences an extracranial, confirming reflection that empirically informs the child's intrapsychic agent-self of its functional capacity for effective regulatory agency.

The intrapsychic no is the child's way of turning to the intrapsychic caregiving relationship for intrapsychic nurture. The primary intention behind the child's intrapsychic no is not to reject the caregiver's personal motives per se, but rather to deny the appeal of the caregiver's personal motives as gratifying, caregiver percepts and to engage the caregiver's more gratifying, intrapsychic caregiving motives. The child's intrapsychic no indicates that a crucial developmental task has been accomplished; the child now possesses an actively functioning, structurally intact intrapsychic agent-self that autonomously and reflectively can distinguish veridical from nonveridical intrapsychic relationship pleasure.

The caregiver's facilitative response to the child's intrapsychic no provides a reality testing for the child that confirms the child's intrapsychic perception that her/his agent-self does indeed have a loss-free capacity for effective agency with regard to the autonomous capacity to experience the reflection of agent-self as agent-self. The child perceives that the caregiver has an unconflicted motive for intrapsychic caregiving intimacy that leads her/him to make a genuine, reflective choice between: (1) preserving the personal (noncaregiving) pleasure being pursued (e.g., reading a novel) and, thereby, rejecting the assertion of regulatory agency signified by the child's intrapsychic no and (2) placing the pursuit of her/his personal motives under the hegemony of the superior pleasure represented by her/his intrapsychic caregiving motives (under the hegemony of the child's intrapsychic agent-self) and, thereby, accepting the caregiving involvement that the intrapsychic no signifies.

This mutualizing process forms the basis both for the child's capacity for reality testing of the boundaries that separate her/his intrapsychic mind and the intrapsychic mind of the caregiver and also for her/his ability to be certain that this reality testing is veridical. From the onset of the structure of illusional intrapsychic mutuality in the pre-eidetic stage, percepts that are products of the child's perceptual constitutive-interpersonal motives have been used to signify percepts of the caregiver's intrapsychic caregiving. This meaning is nonveridical from an intrapsychic caregiving perspective but is convincingly veridical from the viewpoint of the child's subjective experience. Therefore, the child's sense of the boundaries between her/his intrapsychic motives and the caregiver's intrapsychic motives has been nonveridical because the signifier of the caregiver's intrapsychic motives was the child's own gratified constitutive-interpersonal motives. The child comes to know the boundaries of her/his own intrapsychic consciousness only through her/his ability to know the boundaries of the caregiver's intrapsychic caregiving motives. Intrapsychic mind boundaries are demarcated by the existence of cranially separate centers of initiative (regulatory agency reality). The child acquires the capacity for intrapsychic reality testing when (1) s/he reflectively rejects the caregiver's noncaregiving motives and, thereby, correctly distinguishes the ownership of intrapsychic caregiving motives (her/his agent-self) and the ownership of personal motives (the caregiver at that moment) and (2) s/he has this reality testing confirmed by the caregiver's acceptance and endorsement of the child's rejection of the caregiver's transitory choice of noncaregiving motives.

The developmental process whereby the child acquires the capacity to discriminate self and nonself differs for the intrapsychic and interpersonal forms of agent-self. As will be seen, in contrast to the constitutive-interpersonal agent-self, the process by which the intrapsychic agent-self comes to distinguish self and nonself does not intrinsically depend on language. In other words, it does not depend on personal pronoun usage associated with learning patterns based on reality testing of experience-near sensations that demarcate body boundaries. The acquisition of the capacity to discriminate intrapsychic agent-self from nonself entails the child's capacity to know her/his own mind by virtue of knowing that s/he cannot only own (regulate) her/his own intrapsychic motive for mutualized care-getting pleasure, but also, and equally important, that s/he does not have to accept the caregiver's personal (noncaregiving) motives at the expense of relinquishing the pursuit of her/his own self-caretaking motives.

We posit a specific, mutual, empirical dialectic of desire between child and caregiver, the loss-free focus of which is the regulatory center of the child's intrapsychic motive and its gratification.[6] The caregiver's affirmation that the child's ideal of intrapsychic care-getting pleasure surpasses the pleasure to be had by the pursuit of personal motives confirms the child's motive not to accept anything less than a veridical reflection for her/his capacity for intrapsychic reality testing (confirms the child's capacity to distinguish between veridical and nonveridical caregiver percepts). The child's intrapsychic no results from her/his veridical intrapsychic agent-self's recognition that the caregiver's pursuit of personal motives represents no loss to the child because the caregiver intrapsychic caregiving ideals remain stable and the caregiver continues to endorse the child's own act of veridical intrapsychic self-caretaking by responding to the child's intrapsychic agency. The child's awareness that the caregiver feels pleasure when the child rejects the caregiver's pursuit of personal motives liberates the child from the teleological regulation of her/his pursuit of intrapsychic motive gratification. The intrapsychic act of knowing, that is, the capacity for veridical intrapsychic self-caretaking, becomes the regulating cause and, therefore, the causal-ontological substrate of the child's personal existence.

The differentiated form of the veridical intrapsychic motive, which we term the ***regulatory-intrapsychic motive,*** marks the beginning of the child's capacity for a phase-appropriately conscious, reflective, and self-recognized participation in the intrapsychic caregiving relationship. The child's regulatory-intrapsychic motive for veridical intrapsychic mutuality focuses on the caregiver's and the child's intrapsychic caregiving motives and ideals and launches the child into a dialogue with the caregiver about how to increase the pleasure of the intrapsychic caregiving relationship. Because of the stable, mutual commitment of child and caregiver, this dialogue has no reference to paranoid or other concerns about the quantity (absence or presence) of intrapsychic caregiving pleasure. Rather, within a context of immutable, mutual commitment, the caregiving relationship is regulated solely by the participants' ideals of refining the pleasure of intrapsychic intimacy and availability.

Intrapsychic caregiving mutuality occurs in the context of the exigencies of the caregiver's interpersonal world and personal motives. As a result, the caregiver's intrapsychic caregiving *behavior* cannot always be actively engaged by the child, who now responds to the loss of veridical caregiver percepts by turning to the intrapsychic caregiving relationship. Whenever possible, the caregiver will gladly put her/his personal motives aside and resume intrapsychic caregiving. However, when the caregiver must continue to pursue personal motives (e.g., s/he must continue to cook dinner), because the child's regulatory-intrapsychic agent-self has no motive to fall back on nonveridical caregiver percepts, the caregiver's responsiveness and understanding can be used as a gratifying, veridical caregiver percept for the child's regulatory-intrapsychic agent-self motive. For example, the caregiver who must continue to cook will communicate to the child that s/he regrets that the child has to wait and that the caregiver is eager to play with the child and will be with her/him shortly. The child can now recognize that the caregiver's intrapsychic caregiving *motives* remain stable even when the caregiver cannot immediately refocus her/his behavior on the child. In other words, the child's veridical, regulatory-intrapsychic precept has the differentiated ability to specify the child's agent-self capacity to be the telic cause of the caregiver's stable intrapsychic caregiving *motives* rather than the caregiver's focused caregiving *behavior*. The caregiver, of course, has always endorsed the child's intrapsychic motive at times when the caregiver could not abandon personal motives, but, until this point in development, the child would respond to the caregiver's continued pursuit of personal motives by regression to nonveridical forms of caregiver percepts. Now, because regression to nonveridical intrapsychic motive gratification has assumed the meaning of loss, the child neither experiences the loss nor regresses. Because s/he is less dissociated, s/he can appreciate that s/he continues to be the agent cause of the caregiver's intrapsychic caregiving *motives* even when the caregiver's *behavior* continues to be regulated by the caregiver's personal motives. This moment is developmentally decisive because the child's veridical intrapsychic precept has become an empirically determined ideal of a mutuality that is functional and real even when the caregiver's focused intrapsychic caregiving behavior cannot immediately be engaged by the child. This modified precept includes the caregiver's stable motive to be regulated by the child's agent-self (the caregiver's stable preference for intrapsychic caregiving pleasure). In other words, the caregiver's intrapsychic caregiving precept and the child's intrapsychic precept share the same purpose, and the child's regulatory-intrapsychic agent-self's well-being no longer rests on the caregiver's focused intrapsychic caregiving behavior.

The caregiving response necessitated by the child's intrapsychic no is, clearly, more specific than caregiving responses to transference care-getting anxiety. Transference care-getting anxiety is an innately determined form of intrapsychic grief work. Because the nonveridical constitutive-intrapsychic motive is the form of intrapsychic motive that is functional in transference care-getting anxiety, the caregiver's *interpersonal* caregiving behavior represents a gratifying, nonveridical, caregiving caregiver percept. Nonveridical but kind caregiver responses to transference care-getting anxiety can include distraction, sympathy, substitute gratification, and nonspecific attention. If the caregiver resumes playing with the child out of personal motives that the child not be unhappy or angry, rather than out of the nontransference pleasure of being induced by the child's intrapsychic agent-self to subordinate personal to caregiving motives, the child will be unable to recognize the nonveridical quality of the caregiver's response. There are psychopathogenic caregivers whose motives for transference relationship pleasure are sufficiently unconflicted that they can respond effectively to the child's expressions of transference care-getting anxiety. Their children may develop a stable motive for transference intrapsychic motive gratification that occurs by means of nonveridical, caregiving caregiver percepts (via interpersonal relationship pleasure). Because the regulatory-intrapsychic agent-self motive cannot be gratified illusionally, however, if the child is to develop the capacity for veridical intrapsychic agency, the caregiver must respond to the child's intrapsychic no with genuine pleasure at the child's insistence on intrapsychic caregiving intimacy.

During the differentiated phase of the regulatory-intrapsychic self stage, the ***intrapsychic pleasure principle*** becomes functional. An innately determined, meta-regulatory precept structure, the intrapsychic pleasure principle, in effect, mandates a preference for the pleasure afforded by nontransference, empirical, mutual, nondissociated types of agent-self experience. Because veridical intrapsychic caregiving percepts are not filtered through the pre-eidetic caregiver imagos eidetically internalized within the transitional intrapsychic caregiver, veridical, regulatory-intrapsychic agent-self motive gratification is associated with a qualitatively different and infinitely more appealing pleasure than is transference intrapsychic motive gratification.

We stress that the superior pleasure the child experiences results from the child's decreasing dissociation and not from any change in the quality of the caregiver's caregiving. Once the child can recognize reflectively the superior nature of veridical intrapsychic caregiving pleasure, the intrapsychic pleasure principle causes the nonveridical intrapsychic motive for dissociated intrapsychic pleasure to operate at a disadvantage in its competition with the intrapsychic motive that pursues veridical intrapsychic pleasure. Thus, nature and nurture conspire to bring about the child's increasing capacity for phase-appropriate, reflective recognition and appreciation both of the caregiver's intrapsychic caregiving ideals and motives and of the child's own regulatory-intrapsychic agent-self capacity to engage these ideals and motives.

Veridical Intrapsychic Self-Caretaking

In traditional usage, self-knowledge is the knowledge we term *constitutive-interpersonal introspection*. Constitutive-interpersonal introspection aims for a veridical first-person knowledge of constitutive-interpersonal motives. In our terms, it is solipsistic and nonempirical. Further, unlike veridical intrapsychic knowledge of the self's and the caregiver's intrapsychic motives, the maturation of constitutive-interpersonal introspection does not depend on a paradigmatic caregiving relationship.[7] For example, many people with severe interpersonal psychopathology can be insightful about their motivation, even though they cannot regulate their motives in a stable, unconflicted manner. One patient who had a gambling addiction could be sensitively introspective about the process by which subtle pressures, such as the necessity to produce a long report at work, could precipitate a gambling spree. This capacity for constitutive-interpersonal introspection, however, did not enable him to stop gambling. Constitutive-interpersonal introspection is isolated from the outside world; it can never be directly perceived or experienced by any other than the agent-self doing the introspecting. In other words, constitutive-interpersonal introspection has only the introspector as a listener. This is the basis for both the truism that one can never really know another and for the universally recognized experience of being misunderstood.[8]

In contrast to constitutive-interpersonal introspection, *veridical intrapsychic self-caretaking,* which we also term *intrapsychic reflectiveness,* can occur only as a consequence of paradigmatic development. It results from the mutualizing of the child's intrapsychic consciousness and is a metacognitive, nonlinguistic form of certainty. Veridical intrapsychic self-caretaking results from veridical intrapsychic caregiving, in which the caregiver supplies the child with the veridical reflection of agent-self as agent-self by preferring the ideal of intrapsychic mutuality represented by the child's intrapsychic agent-self motive over the pleasure generated by the pursuit of personal motives.

There are two types of intrapsychic self-caretaking: innately determined (pretransference and transference) and nurture based (veridical). The innately determined type results from the epigenetic maturation of innate psychic structure that is exposed to minimally sufficient caregiving. Innately determined intrapsychic self-caretaking cannot be self-consciously conscious; it is a developmentally dissociated state of mind in which the inner sense of agency is tacitly felt and responded to, but the nonveridical quality of the agent-self experience is not reflectively known. In psychopathology, a pathologically dissociated type of innately determined intrapsychic self-caretaking forms the basis of the untreated individual's subjective experience throughout her/his lifetime.

Nurture-based, veridical intrapsychic self-caretaking enables the child to have a veridical self-regulatory autonomy based on the capacity to discriminate between veridical and nonveridical types of intrapsychic motive gratification. This capacity makes it possible for the child to discern the difference (1) between the caregiver's intrapsychic caregiving motives and the caregiver's personal motives; (2) between the caregiver's intrapsychic caregiving motives and the child's own intrapsychic self-caretaking motives; and (3) between the child's own transference and nontransference intrapsychic motives. The child's veridical intrapsychic self-caretaking precept now matches the caregiver's veridical intrapsychic caregiving precept.

At this point, pleasure rather than pain or the loss of nonveridical pleasure furthers the child's increasing self-reflectiveness. Subsequently, the caregiver's temporary pursuit of personal motives will not signify intrapsychic loss to the child's regulatory-intrapsychic agent-self, because the child's veridical intrapsychic precept now focuses on the caregiver's intrapsychic caregiving *motives,* which are immutable, rather than on the caregiver's intrapsychic caregiving *behavior,* which cannot always be available to the child. In other words, the child develops a regulatory-intrapsychic precept that informs her/him that to have any experience other than a loss-free, purposive experience of intrapsychic agency would be a self-induced, gratuitous loss.

The differentiation of the child's regulatory-intrapsychic precept ultimately results from the child's empirical experience of the stable, hegemonic functioning of the caregiver's intrapsychic caregiving ideals. It is proximally caused by the child's increasingly mature capacity for reflective communication with the caregiver, which allows the child to recognize the caregiver's stable preference for the pleasure of intrapsychic caregiving mutuality with the child. The transformation of the child's intrapsychic precept to reflect an increasing capacity for reality testing of the caregiver's intrapsychic caregiving *motives* is also made possible by the perceptual weight of the innumerable times that the caregiver has responded to the child's experience of intrapsychic loss with pleasure at putting aside her/his personal motives and providing the child with focused intrapsychic care-getting pleasure.

Veridical intrapsychic self-caretaking is, thus, a nurture-induced, autonomous capacity for veridical intrapsychic motive gratification. The child becomes free from the determinism of a nonveridical, teleological process because for the first time the child truly knows that effect does not necessarily signify intentionality. *The child realizes that the loss of focused care-getting pleasure, which results from the caregiver's pursuit of personal motives, does not signify any instability in the caregiver's ideals and motives and, therefore, does not signify any inadequacy in the regulatory capacity of the child's intrapsychic agent-self.* Whereas previously the caregiver's pursuit of personal motives had the significance of a loss, it now has the meaning of a signal that stimulates the child's pleasure that the caregiver's intrapsychic caregiving motives remain available to the child. Even when the caregiver cannot put aside personal motives for the moment, the child knows that the caregiver endorses and feels pleasure at the child's intrapsychic motive to engage the caregiver's caregiving. In other words, the child's regulatory-intrapsychic agent-self embodies a structuralized, internal, empirically based mutuality that removes the meaning of intrapsychic loss from the caregiver's temporary pursuit of personal motives. The regulatory-intrapsychic agent-self's loss-free capacity for reality testing of the stability of the caregiver's veridical intrapsychic caregiving motives is impervious to the vicissitudes of positive entropy and chance and is the source of the deepest, most pleasurable inner well-being possible. This subjective experience of personal existence can potentially be attained by every member of the human species.[9]

Much has been said about the importance of unconditional caregiving love to a successful developmental process.[10] In the child development literature, unconditional caregiving love refers to meaning structures that can, in a given instance, be free of loss but that are not intrinsically loss free. For example, the caregiver's unconditional love is usually paired with the inevitability of loss (e.g., of a toy, of not being able to have a specific desire gratified, etc.). In ordinary usage, the touchstone for unconditional love is the caregiver's response to the child's social-interpersonal behavior; unconditional love is also contrasted with earned love. In our usage, however, the referent for unconditional love is the *caregiver's* unconditional attraction to intrapsychic caregiving ideals. The unconditional love we describe refers specifically to the loss-free intrapsychic pleasure afforded by paradigmatic caregiving. Paradigmatic intrapsychic caregiving is unconditional because the caregiver's intrapsychic motive that the child develop the capacity for veridical intrapsychic agency is so powerful that the caregiver experiences pleasure when s/he puts aside personal motives for caregiving motives. This hegemony of caregiving pleasure over personal pleasure can be observed easily in those nonhuman animals who eschew other pleasures in order to remain with their young. Unconditional intrapsychic caregiving love has as its regulatory ideal the child's development of a regulatory-intrapsychic agent-self that can exert autonomous, veridical, self-regulatory control over the child's own subjective personal existence. For this reason, in paradigmatic development the child's regulatory-intrapsychic agent-self has a loss-free, veridical certainty that its agency will be vouchsafed a loss-free experience by the caregiver. This existential inner security represents the most important significance of the term regulatory agency and is *the one absolute certainty available to an individual.*

At the end of the differentiated phase of the regulatory-intrapsychic self stage, the child's regulatory-intrapsychic agent-self can respond in a trusting and unperturbed manner to the caregiver's temporary pursuit of personal motives. This confident, relaxed, and good natured response rests on the reality testing that the caregiver prefers the pleasure of intrapsychic caregiving mutuality and that the caregiver will never unduly deprive the child of focused intrapsychic caregiving attention. Henceforth, the child can autonomously generate her/his own inner well-being within her/his regulatory-intrapsychic agent-self, which has become a true "I" of "we"ness. The consequence is the child's capacity to own her/his own motives and the source of their gratification and, therefore, to own her/his own mind.

The child's ability to experience an ideal, veridical intrapsychic mutuality even at times when the caregiver pursues personal motives differs from the compliant behavior exhibited by children with nonveridical caregivers when these caregivers pursue personal motives. The compliant child's lack of objection stems from her/his belief that s/he can only win the caregiver's interest and good will by abandoning the effort to exert agent-self hegemony over the caregiver's choice of motives.

The Developmental Split

The developmental consequences of the onset of the child's veridical, regulatory-intrapsychic agent-self are as follows. First, the child begins to destructuralize: (1) the intrapsychic merger between her/his consciousness and the consciousness of the extracranial caregiver, (2) the intracranial intrapsychic merger between her/his own intrapsychic consciousness and her/his own constitutive-interpersonal consciousness, and (3) the intrapsychic developmental transference.

Second, there occurs the structure we term the ***developmental split,*** which is the intracranial coexistence of two categorically distinct forms of agent-self, one transference and the other nontransference. Although we have been describing the onset of the loss-free pleasure of the regulatory-intrapsychic agent-self, the nonveridical constitutive-intrapsychic agent-self remains functional and in a competitive relationship with the regulatory-intrapsychic agent-self until the end of the next stage. The developmental split occurs only in paradigmatic development; in untreated psychopathology there exists no veridical, regulatory-intrapsychic agent-self. The developmental split is more than a static boundary between two intracranial structures of agency. It denotes a dynamic, competitive relationship characterized by a unidirectional shift toward the hegemony of the veridical, regulatory-intrapsychic agent-self. As development progresses, the power that transference pleasure is able to exert over the quality of the individual's personal existence correspondingly decreases.

Because the transitional intrapsychic caregiver is a source of nonveridical caregiver percepts, transference agent-self experience has a kind of self-regulatory stability. However, this form of self-regulation is not autonomous and loss free. For example, since transference gratification generated solely by the nonveridical caregiver percepts internalized within the transitional intrapsychic caregiver does not evoke a sufficiently extracranial significance to be stably, autonomously effective, transference intrapsychic agent-self experience ultimately depends on the caregiver's ability to be physically available. In contrast, the child's regulatory-intrapsychic agent-self experience is phase-appropriately loss free and stably pleasurable. The child's regulatory-intrapsychic agent-self cannot attain optimal intrapsychic pleasure only because of the ongoing dissociation inherent in the transference gratification process on the transference side of the developmental split. This loss motivates the nontransference, regulatory-intrapsychic agent-self to persist in its efforts to gain increasing regulatory control over subjective personal existence. It should be noted that, unlike the developmental line of intrapsychic losses that ended with nontransference caregiving anxiety, this is a dynamic rather than a structural loss. It represents a relative loss of pleasure and is caused by the existence of an intracranial, transference-based agency that can temporarily preempt, but not establish hegemony over, subjective personal existence.

In summary, the regulatory-intrapsychic agent-self forms the basis for the child's reflective capacity for a mutualized, separate center of initiative and consciousness (an "I" of "we"ness). However, this capacity is incomplete because: (1) it coexists with a transference form of intrapsychic agent-self; (2) it includes only regulatory-intrapsychic agent-self experience and not regulatory-interpersonal agent-self experience; and (3) it involves a relationship focused on one caregiver at a time, without taking into account the caregivers' relationships with each other. At the close of the regulatory-intrapsychic self stage, there are two structurally distinct types of intrapsychic agent-self. The nonveridical constitutive-intrapsychic agent-self does not have autonomy with regard to the caregiver's personal motives, because it continues to operate by means of transference meaning structures rooted in the merger between the child's intrapsychic consciousness and constitutive-interpersonal consciousness and, therefore, it needs ongoing nonveridical caregiver percepts. The veridical, regulatory-intrapsychic agent-self has autonomy with regard to the personal (noncaregiving) motives of the caregiver. On the nontransference side of the developmental split, extracranial caregiver percepts are no longer used to gratify the child's regulatory-intrapsychic motive because these percepts acquired the significance of structuralizing reflections that stimulated the differentiation of the meaning structure of effective agency within the child's veridical, regulatory-intrapsychic precept. The child's veridical, regulatory-intrapsychic agent-self now has a phase-appropriate capacity for veridical intrapsychic agency regardless of the presence or absence of the caregiver's focused intrapsychic caregiving attention.

4
The
Regulatory-Interpersonal
Self Stage

This stage marks the onset of *interpersonal* agency. We emphasized earlier that before this point in development constitutive-interpersonal motives (including a nonreflective sense of constitutive-interpersonal agency, e.g., the intention to shake a rattle or to crawl) have served as gratifying, caregiver percepts for the intrapsychic motive.[1] Even before the occurrence of interpersonal agency in this stage, the child experiences constitutive-interpersonal motives in that s/he phase-appropriately knows, for example, that s/he feels hungry or wants to play. However, the child's pursuit of these motives has not been accompanied by a reflective experience of constitutive-interpersonal agency. In other words, while intrapsychic pleasure is always associated with a sense of intrapsychic agency, constitutive-interpersonal pleasure is initially associated with intrapsychic agency rather than constitutive-interpersonal agency. Thus, prior to the regulatory-interpersonal self stage, the infant is aware of pleasure that the caregiver knows represents constitutive-interpersonal motive gratification, but the infant is not aware of her/his interpersonal motives to be the agent cause that gratifies these constitutive-interpersonal motives.

Put another way, although from a viewpoint that excludes the child's agent-self experience, adult observations of infant behavior establish the existence of interpersonal motives as early as the prenatal stage; when one considers the child's *agent-self experience*, one finds that, prior to the occurrence of the **interpersonal no** in the regulatory-interpersonal self stage, the child's interpersonal motives do not manifest interpersonal agency but are subsumed under intrapsychic agency.[2] Until this point, the fundamental meaning of constitutive-interpersonal motive gratification is in terms of the intrapsychic caregiving relationship.[3] Although before the regulatory-interpersonal self stage the infant has interpersonal intentions—for example, to crawl, to walk, to reach, to babble, and to talk—we focus on the significance of this manifest intentionality for the regulatory control of subjective personal existence. The pleasure the infant experiences at being able to reach out intentionally, to grasp a ball, and to look at it confers the illusional reflection of *intrapsychic* agent-self as agent-self. Except on the nontransference side of the developmental split, the child's intrapsychic precept is sufficiently nonspecific that intentional acts and acquired pleasures of any kind can signify that the child's intrapsychic agent-self is exerting regulatory control over the caregiver's intrapsychic caregiving motives, which in turn signifies the capacity for the agent-self, self-regulatory control of subjective personal existence. In the previous example, the infant's undifferentiated intrapsychic agent-self experiences the "willingness" of the ball to be regulated by her/him as an affirmation of intrapsychic agency. Similarly, the appeal of the soothing blanket or other inanimate object, which Winnicott called a transitional object, is not that it represents the libidinal object per se, but that its presence confers the illusional meaning of effective intrapsychic agency.[4] The child's control over the blanket or teddy bear has the meaning to the child of the caregiver's pleasure at being regulated by the child's intrapsychic agent-self and, therefore, it signifies the causal efficacy of the child's intrapsychic agent-self to regulate her/his own subjective personal existence.

The child enters this stage with two functional intrapsychic agent-selves, one veridical and one nonveridical. The nontransference, regulatory-intrapsychic agent-self has a stable, veridical inner well-being based on its empirical knowledge that it is the agent cause of the caregiver's intrapsychic caregiving motives. The transference intrapsychic agent-self is the product of nonveridical caregiver percepts. As we will see, with the onset of interpersonal agency, the percepts that gratify the nonveridical intrapsychic agent-self motive change from percepts of the caregiver to percepts with the meaning of interpersonal agency.

Interpersonal consciousness has two levels—regulatory-interpersonal and constitutive-interpersonal. In this stage, the child begins to be aware of both constitutive-interpersonal and regulatory-interpersonal motives for agency meaning. Like the intrapsychic motive, the **regulatory-interpersonal motive** for the reflection of effective agency is a regulating cause of the subjective experience of personal existence. The content of the regulatory-interpersonal motive is homologous to the intrapsychic motive in that it is a motive for relationship pleasure (the motive for the reflective experience of agent-self as agent-self). However, because of the nonempirical nature of interpersonal consciousness, unlike veridical regulatory-intrapsychic motive gratification, veridical regulatory-interpersonal motive gratification is not produced by empirical relationship experience.[5] As we will explain shortly, veridical regulatory-interpersonal agency meaning is the mutualized product of the well-being structured in the regulatory-intrapsychic agent-self, and nonveridical regulatory-interpersonal agency meaning is the unstable product of nonveridical intrapsychic agency meaning and constitutive-interpersonal agency meaning.

In general, constitutive-interpersonal motives may be divided into social-interpersonal, cognitive, and physiological categories. The *cognitive* and *social-interpersonal* categories, while essentially distinguishable, are also interwoven. With respect to the subjective experience of personal existence, the cognitive and social-interpersonal motives together generate distinct types of meaning structures. Examples are (1) the self-reflective "I"ness that is the product of constitutive-interpersonal introspection, (2) language, (3) memory, (4) the capacity for abstract, logical thought and judgment (pure reason), and (5) the productive imagination (the source of creativity).

THE INTERPERSONAL NO PHASE

The first developmental event in the regulatory-interpersonal self stage is the onset of the child's capacity for interpersonal agency experience. This process begins when the child reacts to the caregiver's frustration of a given constitutive-interpersonal motive by shaking her/his head in negation of the caregiver's interference or uttering a distinct "no!" We term this negative response the *transference constitutive-interpersonal no.* An example is when the caregiver is with the child in the park and the child starts running toward a far-off scene of interest. The caregiver tells the child to return. The child proclaims an emphatic no and keeps running. Prior to transference interpersonal no behavior, the child, in her/his infantile zeal, may well have kept running despite the caregiver's calls. The child would have seemed either to ignore the caregiver or to make a game of not returning. The child no longer ignores or teases the caregiver while the child continues to run; rather s/he is compelled to respond with a no because, in addition to the threatened loss of gratification of the motive to run, the child is newly vulnerable to a second loss that occurs on the introspective level of constitutive-interpersonal agency. The caregiver's calls acquire the significance of loss to the child's emerging, nonveridical sense of effective interpersonal agency. The child's no response, therefore, represents the reaffirmation of the child's nonveridical sense of effective interpersonal agency by signifying the child's rejection of the caregiver's interfering motive. The child's constitutive-interpersonal no behavior represents grief work in response to two transference losses: of the gratification of the child's chosen constitutive-interpersonal motive, and of the caregiver's interference with the child's regulation of constitutive-interpersonal motive choice. These losses are illusional in the sense that nonveridical interpersonal agency meaning is produced by constitutive-interpersonal motive gratification rather than by the mutualized well-being of the regulatory-intrapsychic agent-self. Therefore, when the caregiver interferes with the child's constitutive-interpersonal motive choice and pursuit, the child's emerging nonveridical interpersonal agent-self experiences loss. Once it is functional, the child's veridical regulatory-interpersonal agent-self experiences no loss due to the caregiver's frustration of the child's constitutive-interpersonal motives, because the veridical regulatory-interpersonal agent-self does not use constitutive-interpersonal gratification to obtain its agent-self as agent-self reflection. In other words, the child only experiences loss on the transference side of the developmental split. On the nontransference side of the developmental split, the regulatory-intrapsychic agent-self continues to experience a loss-free, stable inner well-being, which is the gratifying, agent-self percept for the veridical regulatory-interpersonal agent-self motive. Therefore, all discussions of loss in this stage refer to interruptions that occur in the transference process that produces nonveridical forms of intrapsychic and interpersonal agent-self meaning. The nonveridical and veridical agent-selves remain in a relationship of competitive inhibition throughout this stage. Ultimately, the instability of nonveridical intrapsychic agent-self experience and nonveridical regulatory-interpersonal agent-self experience causes the child to develop the stable preference for veridical forms of agent-self meaning and, correspondingly, to experience nonveridical agent-self meanings as causing loss (pain) rather than pleasure.

The interpersonal motive with which the caregiver interferes may or may not involve her/him. Even when the child wants the caregiver to reach up and get her/him a toy, at this point in development, the child experiences the caregiver as instrumental to the child's constitutive-interpersonal motive gratification rather than as the fount of that gratification, as was the case in the earlier stages.

The proximal cause of the transference constitutive-interpersonal no is that the child's increasingly sophisticated motor and cognitive development stimulates motives whose consequences s/he is too immature to realize. Therefore, the caregiver must regulate certain of the child's constitutive-interpersonal motives that, unchecked, might lead the child to dangerous and, even, potentially fatal actions, such as running into the street, touching a hot stove, and climbing on unstable objects. The paradigmatic caregiver does not frustrate the child's constitutive-interpersonal motives gratuitously or with the belief that such frustration stimulates development; the caregiver does not believe that frustration can replace mutuality as the primary mode of regulation. Further, in frustrating the child's constitutive-interpersonal motives, the caregiver will avoid negative words and affect and will be as diplomatic as possible.[6] The caregiver knows or senses that the child's key task in this stage is to develop a stable, veridical, interpersonal agency to complement the child's regulatory-intrapsychic well-being, and, therefore, the caregiver has no wish to interfere with the child's developing self-confidence by gratuitously frustrating the child's choice of motives. In fact, the caregiver has an ideal of *facilitating* the child's constitutive-interpersonal motives when they are safe and do not conflict with the caregiver's most crucial personal aims. Consequently, the context for the interpersonal no is that the caregiver has interfered with the child's constitutive-interpersonal motive for one of two reasons: the motive entails danger for the child or the motive conflicts with a personal motive of the caregiver's that s/he cannot abandon at the moment.

The discussion of the emergence of interpersonal agency is necessarily from an intrapsychic caregiving perspective, because between the end of the regulatory-intrapsychic self stage and the interpersonal no, the child's developing sense of interpersonal agency functions outside of her/his reflective awareness. The child's ability to protest the caregiver's interference with her/his interpersonal motives results from the child's new capacity for interpersonal introspection, which allows the child to recognize reflectively her/his constitutive-interpersonal agency motives. The child can now retain the image of a given constitutive-interpersonal gratification as a to-be-attained ideal even in the face of the caregiver's denial of that gratification. Although from birth the child responds to the frustration of her/his constitutive-interpersonal motives with active unpleasure communicated by cries, negative communications, or irritability, from an intrapsychic caregiving viewpoint, these responses to interpersonal loss are qualitatively different from the interpersonal no response. The child's previous expressions of unpleasure or dissent were expressions of intrapsychic agency rather than of interpersonal agency. In addition to the meaning that the child is protesting the caregiver's interference with a specific constitutive-interpersonal motive, the child's transference interpersonal no comes to include the meaning of the child's negation of the caregiver's interference with the child's *choice* of interpersonal motive gratification. At this point in development, the child wants to preserve the belief that s/he can be the regulating agent cause of (have regulatory control over) constitutive-interpersonal motive gratification even more than s/he wants a specific gratification.

Personal Meaning Structures

Before we discuss the different levels on which the interpersonal no response occurs, we need to clarify the distinction between personal, self, and nonself meanings. Whether or not a given constitutive-interpersonal meaning has *self* meaning is determined by whether the individual experiences it as an inherent component of the self. Some self meanings are *intrinsic* in that the relevant constitutive-interpersonal self meaning structures convey an inherent sense of belonging to the self regardless of the perspective from which this meaning attachment is assessed. Examples of intrinsic self meaning structures are: (1) experiences with the representational significance of constitutive-interpersonal agency (e.g., the "I" of introspection) and (2) all subjective experiences of the body, regardless of whether the origin of the experience is externally imposed or internally induced. For example, an itch is an intrinsic self meaning structure regardless of whether it originates externally (e.g., an insect bite) or internally (e.g., jaundice).

A second type of subjectively experienced self meaning is illusional from an intrapsychic caregiving perspective. Examples of illusional constitutive-interpersonal self meaning structures include identifications with an aesthetically pleasing space, such as a home, a place of religious worship, or a particular outdoor setting. Illusional self meaning is attached to constitutive-interpersonal motive gratification when a given experience with significance *for* the constitutive-interpersonal agent-self acquires the added meaning *of* the constitutive-interpersonal self. An illustration is the adolescent patient who reacted to hearing anything even mildly negative about his high school by physically attacking the critic. One indication that an individual has attached illusional self meaning to constitutive-interpersonal nonself meaning is that s/he becomes irrationally defensive and upset if the value of the nonself entity is questioned.

Intrinsic and illusional self meaning structures are known in different ways. In principle, the individual has regulatory control over the *illusional* type of self meaning structure (e.g., over whether being a bowler has the core significance of self). In contrast, in the case of *intrinsic* self meaning (e.g., height) an individual cannot have regulatory control over the attachment of constitutive-interpersonal self meaning; s/he can control only the manner in which s/he reacts to this self meaning. As can be seen, knowledge of the intrinsic type of self meaning remains equally valid regardless of the perspective; one's eye color is accessible to consensual validation. However, with regard to understanding the subjective experience of personal existence, whether an individual has misidentified nonself meaning as intrinsic self meaning can be known with certainty only from an intrapsychic caregiving perspective.

A ***personal meaning structure*** is a specific type of self meaning structure in which the consciousness-generated ideals exclusively concern the meaning of regulatory agency. Personal meaning structures are not intrinsically linguistic. They are the essence of regulatory agency reality and, in postparadigmatic development, are the basis for knowing regulatory agency reality. There are four categories of personal meaning structure: nonveridical intrapsychic, veridical intrapsychic, nonveridical regulatory-interpersonal, and veridical regulatory-interpersonal.[7] Intrapsychic meaning is always personal meaning. ***Intrapsychic personal meaning*** refers to the meaning of loss-free, autonomous agency produced by the (illusional or veridical) experience of being the agent cause of the caregiver's intrapsychic caregiving. In contrast to intrapsychic consciousness, interpersonal consciousness generates both personal and nonpersonal meaning structures. Interpersonal *personal* meaning structures occur only on the *regulatory* level of interpersonal consciousness. The regulatory-interpersonal motive has the same general aim as the intrapsychic motive, namely, to acquire the autonomous, loss-free reflection of agent-self as agent-self. The meaning of regulatory-interpersonal agency entails the reflection of agent-self as agent-self with regard to being the agent cause of constitutive-interpersonal motive selection and pursuit. The regulatory-interpersonal agent-self has the (illusional or veridical) capacity to choose between competing constitutive-interpersonal motives and to determine the general manner in which the chosen motives are pursued.

Whether or not a nonself meaning structure, for example, a new bicycle, has the significance of illusional self meaning is a function of an individual's level of development and of the presence or absence of psychopathology. After the completion of a paradigmatic developmental process, no nonself meaning (e.g., the career success of one's spouse) will have illusional self meaning. Further, no self meaning arising from constitutive-interpersonal consciousness (e.g., the thought of being a good golfer) will signify (illusional) personal meaning. We stress that the distinction between self and nonself is only secondarily a cognitive act and is primarily a function of the veridicality of intrapsychic and regulatory-interpersonal motive gratification. In development and in psychopathology, illusional personal or self meaning is entirely consonant with a phase-appropriate capacity for cognitive reality testing. Though a child functioning on a transference level can unconsciously include any experience within the boundaries of her/his regulatory agency reality, if the child has reached the necessary level of cognitive development, s/he will easily distinguish the boundaries between another's body and the child's own body. For example, while the child consciously knows perfectly well that her/his doll is corporeally separate and inanimate, the possession of the doll can provide an illusory type of inner well-being.

Although all personal meaning structures are meaning structures of self, not all meaning structures of self are personal meaning structures. One's arm, for example, is a meaning structure of self that is not a veridical personal meaning structure. Constitutive-interpersonal self meaning structures may have illusional personal meaning. In paradigmatic development, the child's transference use of constitutive-interpersonal experience for intrapsychic and regulatory-interpersonal motive gratification progressively decreases. Once development is successfully completed, self meaning and personal meaning will no longer be illusional. For example, the individual will have the experience, "It feels good to run well," but will no longer have the experience, "I am good because I run well." In psychopathology, on the other hand, all constitutive-interpersonal motive gratification is ultimately in the service of regulatory-interpersonal and intrapsychic motive gratification.

To summarize, an individual can only derive intrapsychic or regulatory-interpersonal personal meaning from constitutive-interpersonal motive gratification (e.g., the presence of another, winning a game) in the context of the nonveridical form of intrapsychic motive gratification and the nonveridical form of regulatory-interpersonal motive gratification. Nonveridical intrapsychic motive gratification progressively decreases from the time of its onset in the pre-eidetic stage until the end of the regulatory-interpersonal self stage, at which point it has no further influence on inner well-being. Nonveridical regulatory-interpersonal motive gratification loses all appeal for the child by the end of the constitutive-interpersonal self stage. In psychopathology, however, nonveridical intrapsychic motive gratification and nonveridical regulatory-interpersonal motive gratification remain the sole forms of regulatory agency reality throughout the untreated individual's lifetime. In nonveridical intrapsychic motive gratification and nonveridical regulatory-interpersonal motive gratification, both nonagency reality and constitutive-interpersonal agency reality can be the source of percepts that convey the (illusional) reflection of agent-self as agent-self. For example, depending on the stage of development and the presence or absence of psychopathology, the gratification of constitutive-interpersonal motives for pleasurable oral experience may or may not represent illusional regulatory-interpersonal personal meaning significance and, in turn, illusional intrapsychic personal meaning significance.

Paradigmatic development confers a veridical capacity for reality testing that enables the individual to distinguish self from nonself meaning structures and personal from self and nonself meaning structures. The distinction between intrinsic and illusional self meaning structures uncovers a new dimension of the category of self meaning structure. Self meaning can be intrinsic (an absolute, structural category) or illusional (a functional, dynamic category). In a psychopathological subjective experience of personal existence, illusional self meaning structures play a very significant role in the individual's experience of agency.[8] The capacity conferred by paradigmatic development to recognize categories of nonselfness has a subtle but important significance with regard to the ability to distinguish between thoughts belonging to the self and thoughts belonging to another.

The constructs of personal meaning structure and of self meaning structure are distinct from cognates, such as personalized, personality, having a personal meaning, person, and self. For example, assuming a posttransference stage of development, amputation of one's arm is a tragic personal loss, but the mourning work attendant to this loss concerns intrinsic self meaning structures rather than personal meaning structures.[9]

The child's acquisition of the capacity to distinguish self and nonself is usually explained from a perspective that is essentially cognitive and, therefore, in our view, not heuristic.[10] On the level of constitutive-interpersonal existence, the capacity to distinguish self from nonself is proximally grounded in constitutive-interpersonal cognition. On the intrapsychic level of personal existence, however, the capacity to distinguish self and nonself is intrinsically metacognitive. The capacity to distinguish between intrapsychic agent-self cause and nonintrapsychic agent-self cause refers to the establishment of a structuralized self-regulatory autonomy of inner well-being, which becomes a veridical experience of regulatory-intrapsychic agency, or ownership of the intrapsychic motive and of the means of gratification of that motive. The capacity to distinguish intrapsychic agent-self cause from nonintrapsychic agent-self cause occurs only in paradigmatic development as the result of the child's recognition that the loss the child feels when the caregiver pursues personal rather than caregiving motives (the effect) does not signify an achieved ideal (the caregiver's intrapsychic caregiving intentions) and that the child, therefore, always remains the agent cause of the caregiver's intrapsychic caregiving motives.

In reference to the subjective experience of personal existence, after the completion of a paradigmatic development *regulatory agency reality constitutes the only fundamental, existential experience* (ontology). The regulatory-intrapsychic agent-self has a regulatory agency reality that is both empirical and mutual. The veridical regulatory-interpersonal agent-self has a regulatory agency reality that is mutualized by the well-being structuralized in the regulatory-intrapsychic agent-self but it is non-empirical in the sense that the caregiver's caregiving motives are not directly accessible to it. The constitutive-interpersonal agent-self is mutualized in the general sense that it is bathed in the well-being of the regulatory-interpersonal agent-self. The constitutive-interpersonal agent-self has only conditional regulatory agency reality with regard to constitutive-interpersonal motive gratification. For example, a fit 65-year-old man cannot outrun a fit 25-year-old man, no matter how effectively he pursues his motive to run competitively.

In paradigmatic development on the nontransference side of the developmental split, regulatory agency reality is phase-appropriately homologous to the regulatory agency reality in posttransference development. On the transference side of the developmental split, however, the child has an illusional form of regulatory agency. In the pre-eidetic stage and the regulatory-intrapsychic self stage, *caregiver percepts* are used to gratify the intrapsychic motive. Until the end of the regulatory-intrapsychic self stage, the caregiver provides the only source of (illusional or veridical) gratification of the child's intrapsychic motive. At the close of the regulatory-intrapsychic self stage, the child's regulatory-intrapsychic agent-self has become able to provide its own veridical intrapsychic motive gratification. With the onset of interpersonal forms of agency in the regulatory-interpersonal self stage, while the *primary* source of gratifying, *nonveridical* intrapsychic percepts continues to be the caregiver percepts that have been internalized in the transitional intrapsychic caregiver, the *secondary* source of gratifying, nonveridical percepts becomes the gratified nonveridical regulatory-interpersonal motive.

A second transference process, the **interpersonal transference,** now emerges. After the beginning of the regulatory-interpersonal self stage, the range of nonveridical percepts that can be used for illusional intrapsychic motive gratification and illusional regulatory-interpersonal motive gratification includes gratified motives that are generated on any level of consciousness. Therefore, with the onset of interpersonal agency, we broaden the term for gratifying, nonveridical percepts from nonveridical caregiver percepts to **nonveridical agent-self percepts.** In the regulatory-interpersonal self stage, constitutive-interpersonal motive gratification, which is a nonveridical agent-self percept for the nonveridical regulatory-interpersonal motive, also indirectly gratifies the nonveridical intrapsychic motive, because nonveridical regulatory-interpersonal motive gratification serves as a nonveridical agent-self percept for the nonveridical intrapsychic motive. Nonveridical agent-self percepts may arise in agency or nonagency reality. Those that arise in agency reality are the nonveridical intrapsychic agent-self, the nonveridical regulatory-interpersonal agent-self, and the nonveridical constitutive-interpersonal agent-self (which has proximal regulatory control with regard to cognitive, physiological, and social-interpersonal types of meaning structures). Nonveridical agent-self percepts that arise in nonagency reality, such as discursive and imaginative thoughts, may be consciousness generated; when they are not consciousness generated, they are either self meanings (e.g., toe sensations, genital motives) or nonself meanings (e.g., a character in a book or a beautiful seascape).

Levels of Interpersonal Consciousness

Interpersonal consciousness has constitutive-interpersonal and regulatory-interpersonal levels. One of the most important characteristics of constitutive-interpersonal meaning structures is that they are not regulating causes of subjective personal existence. In other words, constitutive-interpersonal meaning structures are not veridical personal meaning structures (although many are self meaning structures).

Physiological constitutive-interpersonal motives are either homeostatic (e.g., nutritional) or elective (e.g., genital). Though constitutive-interpersonal motives are not true regulatory causes with regard to the regulation of subjective personal existence, in development and in psychopathology they can exert powerful, transference-based effects on the quality of subjective personal experience.

Constitutive-interpersonal motives also have conditional causal power in relation both to nonregulatory agency reality and also to nonagency reality.[11] For example, the constitutive-interpersonal motives for cognitive and social-interpersonal pleasure that resulted in the creation of vaccines in turn exert a regulatory effect on individuals' nonagency reality by conferring immunity. Unfortunately, the power of constitutive-interpersonal motives to be regulatory causes in relation to nonagency reality can be exercised in the context of pathological transference motives for rage (see chap. 6). In this case, constitutive-interpersonal motives can lead to a destructive type of regulatory control (e.g., a bomb).

Interpersonal introspection originates in the innately determined capacity of interpersonal consciousness for reflective meaning experience. Constitutive-interpersonal introspection empowers the individual to experience consciously the variegated forms of the solipsistic, non-empirical "I"ness of constitutive-interpersonal consciousness. The "I" of constitutive-interpersonal consciousness is composed of interwoven social-interpersonal and cognitive motives. The introspected constitutive-interpersonal "I" has the meaning of executive function, of pursuing the gratification of constitutive-interpersonal motives, whereas regulatory-interpersonal agency conveys a meaning of self-worth that is associated with the meaning of self-regulatory stability (the sense that one can own one's own mind).[12] In paradigmatic development, both regulatory and constitutive categories of interpersonal agency have nonveridical and veridical forms. We term the nonveridical and veridical forms of *regulatory-interpersonal* "I"ness the **all-powerful agent-self** and the **veridical regulatory-interpersonal agent-self,** respectively. The nonveridical regulatory agency experience associated with the all-powerful agent-self is the illusion of effective agency founded both on nonveridical intrapsychic well-being and also on gratified constitutive-interpersonal motives. Because constitutive-interpersonal motives are proximally affected by positive entropy and chance, they cannot be a veridical, dependable source of the reflection of effective agency. The all-powerful agent-self has the illusion of having regulatory control over the choice and pursuit of constitutive-interpersonal motives. The transference-based, illusional quality of all-powerful agent-self, self-regulatory stability cannot be recognized by the all-powerful agent-self or by constitutive-interpersonal introspection.

Though transference-based interpersonal introspection may convey the felt distinction between the regulatory and constitutive levels of interpersonal consciousness (between executive and regulatory functions), it does not allow the individual to distinguish between personal and self meaning structures. In contrast, when interpersonal introspection is veridical the individual can distinguish between (1) transference-based and nontransference-based forms of "I"ness, (2) regulatory and constitutive levels of interpersonal consciousness, and (3) the personal meaning structures and self meaning structures signified by these respective categories of agency. The ability to make these introspective distinctions affords an individual the phenomenological basis for a loss-free interpersonal personal identity that is primarily based on the subjective experience of intentionality in contrast to the form of personal identity that primarily rests on memory.[13]

The *veridical* regulatory-interpersonal agent-self has veridical regulatory control over the choice and pursuit of constitutive-interpersonal motives and may be either conscious or preconscious. By **preconscious** we mean that a particular motive outside of ambient awareness can be veridically recognized by introspection, as when a person decides to go ice skating but, on reflection, concludes that paying the bills deserves first priority. The inner well-being structuralized within the regulatory-intrapsychic agent-self provides the source of gratification for the veridical regulatory-interpersonal agent-self motive. For this reason, inevitable interruptions in the gratification of constitutive-interpersonal motives, such as catching a cold and having to forego a chosen activity, do not affect veridical regulatory-interpersonal inner well-being. In other words, because the individual does not use constitutive-interpersonal motive gratification to gratify the veridical regulatory-interpersonal agent-self motive, constitutive-interpersonal loss does not affect her/his veridical regulatory-interpersonal well-being.

While gratified physiological and cognitive constitutive-interpersonal motives may acquire the illusional significance of gratifying, agent-self percepts for the nonveridical regulatory-interpersonal motive, in paradigmatic development their meanings have a relative stability. For example, in paradigmatic development, if a child feels hungry, s/he is hungry. The referents of constitutive-interpersonal meaning are nonregulatory agency reality (e.g. wanting to learn to read) and nonagency reality (e.g., hunger pains) in contrast to regulatory-interpersonal meaning the referent of which is regulatory agency reality. Because, paradigmatically, cognitive and physiological constitutive-interpersonal meaning structures are generally stable, they contribute significantly to the individual's capacity for reality testing of nonregulatory agency reality and nonagency reality.[14] In psychopathology, of course, these meanings are vulnerable to regulation by pathological psychic pain. For example, the addictive eater may feel hungry when in fact s/he has just eaten, and the anorexic may feel satiated when s/he is starving. In contrast to physiological and cognitive meaning structures, social-interpersonal meaning structures are not inherently stable and reliable. For example, the child's all-powerful agent-self illusionally believes that it controls the caregiver's personal motives.

When constitutive-interpersonal motives are used for transference well-being, they have illusional significance, that is, they are nonveridical agent-self percepts for the nonveridical regulatory-interpersonal motive. Constitutive-interpersonal motives may be conscious or unconscious. For example, hunger is usually conscious, whereas a child's motive to procrastinate in order to delay bedtime may be either conscious or unconscious. In paradigmatic development, this type of unconsciousness refers to an unavailability to awareness that is under the hegemony of the developmental transference and, therefore, this unconsciousness represents a pain-free, developmental dissociation that is not in the service of a psychopathological perceptual identity process. For example, in paradigmatic development the child's motive to delay bedtime will not be the product of an angry power struggle with the caregivers.

Constitutive-interpersonal introspection's structural inability to produce a direct, veridical reflection of agent-self as agent-self is a consequence of the fact that immediate, interpersonal self-consciousness occurs entirely within short-term memory, which can store only a small number of sequentially regressive operations.[15] By definition, interpersonal consciousness can never generate a completed veridical self-reflective act of effective agency. A completed self-reflective act always refers to effective agency, that is, to the capacity for self-regulatory stability conferred by the reflective experience of agent-self as agent-self. The combination of the nature of short-term memory and the inherent solipsism (isolation) of constitutive-interpersonal consciousness prevents the veridical reflection of constitutive-interpersonal agent-self as agent-self from coming from an extracranial source. On the other hand, without at least an illusional reflection of constitutive-interpersonal agent-self as agent-self, an individual cannot survive. In transference existence, constitutive-interpersonal agent-self well-being is the combined product of gratified constitutive-interpersonal motives and the well-being of the all-powerful agent-self.

In paradigmatic development during the regulatory-interpersonal self stage and the following stage, the constitutive-interpersonal self stage, the superiority of nontransference pleasure to transference pleasure causes an inexorable, unidirectional shift in which constitutive-interpersonal motives—initially under the hegemony of the transference regulatory-interpersonal agent-self—gradually come under the regulation of the veridical regulatory-interpersonal agent-self. This continues until, at the end of development, the interpersonal transference is completely destructuralized and interpersonal experience is composed only of the veridical regulatory-interpersonal agent-self and the constitutive-interpersonal agent-self, the latter of which is under the former's regulatory control.

Social-Interpersonal Motives

The social-interpersonal motive is that form of the motive for nonsexual relationship pleasure that is expressed on the constitutive level of interpersonal consciousness. The social-interpersonal motive is a constitutive-interpersonal form of the consciousness-generated need for relationship-based agent-self as agent-self reflections. The social-interpersonal motive represents the rendition within interpersonal consciousness of the innately based motive for appetitive but nonsexual relationship pleasure and also regulates both the physiological and the cognitive categories of constitutive-interpersonal motive experience. We posit an inherent relationship between the "I" of language and the social-interpersonal motive.

The social-interpersonal category of constitutive-interpersonal motives is the referent for the common term *intersubjective*, [16] which refers to the interaction between the subjective worlds of self and others. The social-interpersonal motive aims for interpersonal intimacy. Because it is generated by constitutive-interpersonal consciousness, from the perspective of agent-self experience, social-interpersonal intimacy (in the sense of attempting to know another's social-interpersonal motives) is nonempirical and solipsistic. This explains why it is possible for a person to make the painful discovery that others, whom s/he believed s/he knew well, had significant hidden motives.

In addition to being a primary source of social-interpersonal relationship experience, the social-interpersonal motive generates relationship experience whose purpose is to identify with the other.[17] The social-interpersonal motive is also the mode of expression for the other two categories of constitutive-interpersonal motives—the physiological and the cognitive. Examples of the expression of the social-interpersonal motive per se is the love relationship that in classical Greece was termed *philia* and the love relationship that in the early Christian era was termed *agape*. *Philia* refers to the type of love involved in friendship; *agape* refers to a sense of selfless love. An example of the social-interpersonal motive as a mode of expression for physiological motives is the love relationship the Greeks termed *eros*.

The social-interpersonal agent-self has the introspective experience of agency on the constitutive level of interpersonal consciousness. This self meaning structure is not a personal meaning structure because it does not regulate subjective personal existence. Though the social-interpersonal motive and the cognitive motive have different origins, there is an intrinsic relationship between the social-interpersonal motive and language, especially on the level of the "I." Though the "I" of language (which is part of interpersonal cognition) can be employed to signify the "I"ness of agency belonging to any category of consciousness, it primarily signifies the "I" of the social-interpersonal self.[18] Paradigmatically, the motive for social-interpersonal intimacy has hegemony over the sexual motive. In the posttransference stage of life, the aim of gratifying the sexual motive exerts a significant but nonhegemonic influence on social-interpersonal desire.

Physiological Motives

Of the three types of constitutive-interpersonal motives, the cognitive and social-interpersonal motives arise in agency reality, while the physiological motives arise in nonagency reality. Physiological motives can be categorized in many ways depending on the informing purpose. For example, physiological motives can be categorized by whether they are elective, semielective, or nonelective; by whether they are afferent or efferent; and by whether or not they are vital for the survival of the individual or the species. In terms of the subjective experience of personal existence, the most heuristic categorizations pertain to the elective quality of physiological motives and to their relevance for species and individual survival.

The *physiological motives* include the following characteristics: (1) physiological motives are generated by the effect of physiological functioning on constitutive-interpersonal consciousness; (2) unlike the cognitive and social-interpersonal motives, the physiological motives are noticeably fixed and limited by the innately determined "hard wiring" of the nervous system; (3) physiological motives are, by definition, signified by *sensation;* and (4) sensation can signify the meaning of the motive. Physiological motives are experientially more distant from the introspective eye of the constitutive-interpersonal agent-self than are the social-interpersonal and cognitive categories of constitutive-interpersonal motives. However, because strong sensations, such as hunger and those physiological experiences that qualify as affect, impart an experiential immediacy, they often obscure the experience-distant quality of physiological motives. Paradigmatically, the social-interpersonal motive imparts agent-self meaning to the entire spectrum of representational experience stimulated by physiological motives. An illustration is the statement, "I am hungry." Therefore, the physiological motives indirectly partake of agency reality. In spite of this, because the necessary (but not sufficient) cause of physiological motives is nonagency reality, physiological motives are, in part, always proximally regulated by positive entropy.[19] Physiological motives, as a result, have an inherent association with loss.

In paradigmatic development prior to the onset of concrete operational thinking,[20] the physiological category of constitutive-interpersonal motives plays its major role as an indirect, transference source of the reflection of effective intrapsychic agency via its role as a source of nonveridical regulatory-interpersonal motive gratification. Freud's perception of the importance of the physiological motives led him to construct an epigenetic, psychosexual model of polymorphously perverse infantile sexuality, which he used as an experience-near, behavioral construct to organize his experience-distant model of a psychic reality in which reason incompletely regulates the discharge of the instinctual drives. In contrast, in our view the nonagency reality of anatomic or physiological zones (e.g., oral, anal, and genital) does not significantly organize regulatory agency reality. Even in psychopathology, the specific physiological motives chosen as nonveridical agent-self percepts for the nonveridical regulatory-interpersonal motive are determined by the way in which the interplay of numerous factors (such as the stage of psychological and physiological development, genic inheritance, family structure, the caregivers' vocational and avocational choices, and cultural values) results in an idiosyncratic pattern of secondary identifications. In psychopathological development, physiological motives that an individual preferentially uses for transference gratification are typically those that are at least partially elective and in some way contingent on interaction with the caregivers' motives (e.g., food, smell, touch, elimination, and sexual desire).

Freud emphasized the relevance of the body's functioning in general and of infantile sexuality in particular to subjective experience. The genital motive, of course, is plastic in that it is elective and nonhomeostatic. It is also associated with a target organ that defines a gender-based identity and is affiliated with a universally appealing physical pleasure. Since the genital motive is vital to the survival of the species, the intensity of the pleasure associated with it has obvious adaptive significance. As will be discussed later in this chapter, in the conjugally competitive agent-self phase, a diffuse form of the genital motive plays a crucial role in paradigmatic development as the focus of a unique loss and mourning experience, which facilitates the child's acquisition of a transference-free subjective personal existence. In psychopathology, on the other hand, intrapsychic and regulatory-interpersonal motive gratification remain exclusively transference in nature and the special attraction of the pleasure associated with genital motive gratification is but one of a universe of motives available to be used as nonveridical agent-self percepts. In other words, contrary to Freud's central assertion, genital pleasure has no innately based hegemony over regulatory agency reality.

Physiological motives have a complex relationship with the constitutive-interpersonal agent-self. Paradigmatically, the constitutive-interpersonal agent-self proximally regulates all constitutive-interpersonal motives. In both developmental and pathological transference states, however, the physiological motives can exert hegemony over other constitutive-interpersonal motives. It is, therefore, not surprising that both psychoanalytic theory and Piaget's epigenetic epistemology postulate a body template as one of the regulatory causes of the development of mind. In fact, psychoanalytic theory places the origin of the ego in early physiological experience.[21] Although we recognize the importance of physiological motives to psychological development, we postulate that the regulatory cause of the development of mind in the first year of life is a unique, direct product of consciousness per se—the perceptual identity process of intrapsychic motive gratification.

The following is a list of characteristics that enhance the ability of physiological motives to serve as nonveridical agent-self percepts for the nonveridical regulatory-interpersonal motive:

1. The sensation of affect is associated with appetitive and aversive types of meanings that, in the presence of transference processes, can exert regulatory control over regulatory agency reality. Clinical examples are the person whose unprovoked anger regulates her/his treatment of others in ways s/he subsequently regrets and the person who becomes so elated when some things go well that s/he neglects to pursue other important interests.

2. Physiological motives characteristically convey an experience-distant introspective experience, which enhances their capacity to signify the (nonveridical) extracranial reflection of agent-self as agent-self.

3. Physiological motives are unique in that they are intrinsically regulated by two competing centers of regulatory control: agency reality (proximally in the form of the constitutive-interpersonal agent-self) and the forces affecting nonagency reality (e.g., the need for nourishment).

Any physiological motive can acquire the representational significance of extracranial agency that can supply the illusional reflection of effective agency for the nonveridical regulatory-interpersonal motive. An example from psychopathology is the hegemony exerted by the physiological pleasure of eating over the addict's regulatory agency reality. To the addictive eater, the pleasure of eating confers the meaning of agent-self, self-regulatory control, even though from any other perspective, including that of the individual's other self-caretaking ideals, the compulsive eating indicates that the individual is out of control.

The complex relationship between the two categorically distinct types of regulatory control, agency-based and nonagency-based, is amply demonstrated by the perennial discussion of the mind-body problem. The phenomenon of volitional starvation illustrates the potential for agency reality to exert regulatory control over nonagency reality. On the other hand, the fact that a person cannot voluntarily stop breathing to the point of asphyxiation illustrates that nonagency reality can acquire hegemony over agency reality. The aspect of the mind-body problem that concerns the relative strengths of agency reality and nonagency reality confuses different levels of causation with the essence of regulatory agency reality. Further, the thorniest aspects of the mind-body problem derive from the conflation of psychopathological and paradigmatic regulatory agency reality. For example, the conflict between the intentions of the mind (agency reality) and the desires of the body (nonagency reality) is not indigenous to human nature, but rather results from psychopathology, in which the individual never gains the capacity for veridical agent-self, self-regulatory control over her/his physiological constitutive-interpersonal motives.

Cognitive Motives

The regulatory-interpersonal self stage echoes the pre-eidetic stage in the prominent role played by the cognitive and social-interpersonal motives. We have emphasized that the necessary and sufficient cause of paradigmatic human development is the mutualizing and differentiation of intrapsychic consciousness. A *necessary cause* is a variable in the absence of which the event cannot occur but in the presence of which the event may or may not occur, and a *sufficient cause* is a variable in the presence of which the event will occur but in the absence of which the event may or may not occur. While the sufficient cause of intrapsychic mutuality is paradigmatic intrapsychic caregiving, intrapsychic mutuality has two *necessary* causes: (1) the paradigmatic development of cognition (which requires intact brain tissue) and (2) physical survival. The influence of cognition is most dramatic in the onset of primary stranger anxiety in the pre-eidetic stage and the onset of the interpersonal no in the regulatory-interpersonal self stage.[22] In the history of ideas, the capacity for agent-self regulation by means of the assertion of a no is often discussed in terms of negation.

Negation is associated most commonly with negative responses to a perceived loss. Negation is also used to explain the developmental achievement of the self acquiring the capacity for boundaries—the capacity to distinguish self from nonself, me from nonme.[23] Theories of human development that attach a developmental significance to negation all refer to what we would define as constitutive-interpersonal forms of negation and, accordingly, assert that the child's response to the pain of (constitutive-interpersonal) loss confers on the child the capacity to distinguish self from nonself by illustrating the distinction between her/his wishes for gratification and ungratifying reality. In contrast, we postulate that the child develops the freedom from illusional self meanings as a result of her/his awareness that veridical agent-self pleasure is superior to illusional agent-self pleasure.

Acts of negation can be classified as logical, psychological, or ontological. Any one of these types of negation can be used in the service of a pathological motive for rage. However, negation does not have the intrinsic significance of rage. *Logical negation* is a cognitive act and, therefore, is pertinent to cognitive development. It is vital for cognitive reality testing (learning presupposes the capacity to recognize contra-diction, incompatibility, incompleteness, etc. with regard to proposi-tions). Logical negation can have only illusional self or personal mean-ing; it cannot have veridical self meaning or veridical personal meaning.

Psychological negation represents an individual's reaction to the threat-ened or actual loss of the gratification of specific constitutive-interper-sonal motives (a reaction to ungratified desire). Like logical negation, psychological negation occurs on the constitutive-interpersonal level of consciousness and does not have veridical personal (regulatory agency) meaning. An example of psychological negation is the no expressed by the child in protest of the caregiver's interference with the gratification of the child's constitutive-interpersonal desire. Psychological negation need not be verbalized.

Freud defined negation as an ego defense whose purpose is to dis-avow or negate ungratifying external reality. He accorded negation a regulatory relationship to psychic reality. He thought that the differ-ence between healthy and pathological negation is quantitative, not qualitative; he posited that negation exists in both health and disease.[24] This assumption fits with the psychoanalytic viewpoint that normal and pathological varieties of psychic reality constitute one continuum. We would categorize Freud's version of negation as a pathological form of psychological negation.

Ontological negation refers to a negative act that in paradigmatic de-velopment establishes the ontological reality of the subjective experi-ence of personal existence. In our terms, it preserves or establishes the veridical reflection of agent-self as agent-self on the level of intrapsychic and regulatory-interpersonal meaning. It is intrinsically related to the child's developing capacity for veridical, agent-self, self-regulatory con-trol of subjective personal existence. In paradigmatic development, there are two ontological forms of negation: the intrapsychic no and the nontransference regulatory-interpersonal no.[25] The nontransfer-ence regulatory-interpersonal no, which will be discussed shortly, is not directed at the caregiver, but at the child's nonveridical regulatory-interpersonal motive to deny constitutive-interpersonal loss and to con-fuse constitutive-interpersonal loss with regulatory-interpersonal loss.

The intrapsychic no primarily represents an affirmation of the child's conviction of her/his regulatory-intrapsychic agent-self capacity to regulate the caregiver's intrapsychic caregiving motives.[26] The child's vital capacity to distinguish between her/his intrapsychic agent-self and the caregiver's intrapsychic agent-self results from the caregiver's confirming response to the child's intrapsychic no, which provides the structuralizing caregiver percepts discussed in chapter 3. The child's refusal to accept illusional reflections of effective intrapsychic agency represents intrapsychic rather than interpersonal negation. The intrapsychic no has the goal of mutualized pleasure in that: (1) the caregiver avoids the loss s/he would experience if s/he continued to pursue her/his personal motives at the expense of her/his motive for the superior pleasure of intrapsychic caregiving, and (2) the child receives the pleasurable, intrapsychically gratifying, empirical, mutual confirmation of the efficacy of her/his intrapsychic agent-self.

The child's intrapsychic no idealizes the child's agent-self capacity to regulate her/his inner well-being by affirming that the child will accept only veridical intrapsychic caregiving, and not the caregiver's personal (noncaregiving) motives, as gratifying the child's regulatory-intrapsychic motive. The caregiver wholeheartedly approves of and has her/his motives for intrapsychic caregiving pleasure gratified by the child's intrapsychic no because the intrapsychic no represents the child's acquisition of the capacity for regulatory-intrapsychic agent-self experience, which the caregiver has been working to help the child to develop.

In contrast, the *transference interpersonal no* is not an ontological form of negation. It is a product of the child's nonveridical interpersonal motives and has the goal of preserving the gratification of the child's constitutive-interpersonal motive choice in the face of the caregiver's opposing motive. The transference interpersonal no is not an attempt to engage the caregiver's caregiving motives. The caregiver may not agree with or accept the child's negation of the caregiver's interference with the child's constitutive-interpersonal motive (e.g., the caregiver will not change her/his mind and permit the child to cook on the real stove). Also, the transference interpersonal no does not have the consequence of strengthening the caregiving relationship. In fact, it results in a time-limited, partial alienation of the child from the mutuality of the caregiving relationship and in an increase in the as-if quality of the child's all-powerful agent-self.

The Emergence of Interpersonal Agency

Those authors who place the onset of interpersonal agency in the neonatal period prematurely impute to the infant's expressions of intentionality a reflective interpersonal agent-self meaning in a context in which only intrapsychic agent-self meaning exists. When the child is prematurely assumed to have the capacity for interpersonal agency, caregiving responses are often advocated that expect too much of the child and also fail to understand the child's need to have the caregiver respond to her/his expressions of intrapsychic intentionality. For example, if one believes that the infant has focused interpersonal agency from birth, one can easily experience the child's angry cry as an antisocial expression that needs to be regulated rather than as an expression of the loss of the crucial meaning of being the agent cause of intrapsychic caregiving love. From our perspective, the frustration of a specific constitutive-interpersonal motive (e.g., as manifested in the cry of hunger) carries with it the additional and, ultimately, more significant loss of the meaning of an agent-self with causal control over the caregiver's intrapsychic caregiving motives and, thereby, over the infant's own inner well-being. If one recognizes that the capacity for interpersonal agency does not appear until the regulatory-interpersonal self stage, and that in infancy constitutive-interpersonal motive gratification has illusional intrapsychic meaning, then one will focus not on *socializing* the infant but on helping her/him to establish the autonomous capacity for a veridical, mutualized, intrapsychic agent-self, which will be the basis for a subsequent capacity for genuine, nontransference interpersonal intentionality and pleasurable interpersonal relationships.

The child develops an introspectable constitutive-interpersonal agent-self before s/he has an introspectable regulatory-interpersonal agent-self. In other words, the child experiences a constitutive-interpersonal "I" that does not want to lose constitutive-interpersonal gratification before s/he experiences a regulatory-interpersonal "I" whose immediate aim of regulatory control over the choice and pursuit of specific constitutive-interpersonal motives is in the service of acquiring the autonomous capacity for effective agency. The purposiveness of the constitutive-interpersonal agent-self is strictly limited to the gratification of constitutive-interpersonal aims, although, on the transference side of the developmental split, the felt pleasure of this gratification functions as a nonveridical agent-self percept for the nonveridical regulatory-interpersonal motive, which, in turn, gratifies the nonveridical intrapsychic motive. The constitutive-interpersonal agent-self's no stimulates the child to introspect a transference regulatory-interpersonal agent-self.

Nonveridical Regulatory-Interpersonal Agency

The child's first sense of a *regulatory-interpersonal agent-self* is nonveridical. By definition, illusional regulatory-interpersonal agent-self experience is never fully and veridically subject to introspection, although its effects are nonreflectively felt. By *nonreflective,* we mean that, although this sense of agency can be felt, its illusional quality cannot be recognized. Therefore, though the nonveridical, all-powerful agent-self is structurally prevented from experiencing mutuality and veridical agency, the child does not notice this loss. The signified reflection of agent-self as agent-self is based on illusional sources of gratification (constitutive-interpersonal motive gratification and the nonveridical intrapsychic agent-self). As a result, the all-powerful agent-self is inherently unstable.[27]

Once the constitutive-interpersonal agent-self and the nonveridical regulatory-interpersonal agent-self (all-powerful agent-self) become functional, the gratifying percepts for the nonveridical *intrapsychic* agent-self motive change from caregiver percepts to gratified all-powerful agent-self motives. This alteration in gratifying percepts occurs because, once the constitutive-interpersonal agent-self becomes functional, the reflective interpersonal agency experience that accompanies the pursuit of constitutive-interpersonal motives prevents the direct attachment of nonveridical intrapsychic agency significance to the experience of constitutive-interpersonal intentionality. In the previous stages, constitutive-interpersonal gratification could have the illusional meaning of intrapsychic agency only because no competing agency experience accompanied the gratification. Now, however, the gratification of constitutive-interpersonal motives produces constitutive-interpersonal agent-self meaning, which, in turn, becomes a gratifying, nonveridical agent-self percept for the nonveridical regulatory-interpersonal motive. The gratified nonveridical regulatory-interpersonal agent-self motive, that is, the all-powerful agent-self, is, in turn, the sole gratifying percept for the nonveridical intrapsychic motive. Because the nonveridical intrapsychic motive no longer specifically needs caregiver percepts for gratification, but indirectly uses any type of constitutive-interpersonal motive gratification, the caregiver becomes only one of many possible sources of illusional pleasure. This shift has clear adaptational value, because it allows the child to widen her/his interests beyond the caregiver without experiencing a loss of (nonveridical) well-being. In this stage, however, the caregiver remains the most powerful source of transference gratification for the child. On the nontransference side of the developmental split, of course, the child's regulatory-intrapsychic agent-self rather than actual experience with the caregiver is the source of veridical intrapsychic well-being.

The transference interpersonal no marks the appearance of the interpersonal transference. In spite of the presence of the nontransference, regulatory-intrapsychic agent-self and the operation of the intrapsychic pleasure principle, developmental transference forms of gratification continue to have phase-specific attraction for the child. One reason is that the transference process of intrapsychic motive gratification is continuously fed by the progressive appearance of new sets of constitutive-interpersonal motives, each of which represents an innately determined and, therefore, nonreflective source of transference agent-self pleasure. In other words, the interpersonal pleasure of epigenetically unfolding constitutive-interpersonal motives is initially regulated by the structure of illusional intrapsychic mutuality rather than by veridical mutuality.

The gratification of intrapsychic and regulatory-interpersonal motives requires perceptual experience that can signify the reflection of agent-self as agent-self. On the transference side of the developmental split, all perceptual experience has the meaning of transference gratification or lack of gratification of the motive for effective agency. With the onset of nonveridical interpersonal agency, the transitional intrapsychic caregiver's only exposure to perceptual experience is mediated by the all-powerful agent-self, which in turn acquires (illusional) reflections of effective agency from the well-being of the constitutive-interpersonal agent-self. Because interpersonal agency represents a distinct (although intracranial) center of initiative and consciousness, it has a sufficiently external significance to meet the need of the nonveridical constitutive-intrapsychic motive for externally based reflections of effective intrapsychic agency. For this reason, interpersonal consciousness itself can be a source of gratifying, nonveridical percepts for the intrapsychic transference. At this point, thoughts (e.g., memories, fantasies, or hopes) can acquire the meaning of agent-self percepts that can be used for nonveridical regulatory-interpersonal motive gratification, which, in turn, gratifies the nonveridical intrapsychic motive. In psychopathology, this use of constitutive-interpersonal consciousness as a source of transference gratification persists. As a result, in benign psychopathology, a person can use pleasant or creative thoughts as nonveridical percepts for the pathological regulatory-interpersonal motive and, in more malignant forms of psychopathology, hallucinations and delusions can be sufficiently gratifying to maintain a life-sustaining level of intrapsychic and regulatory-interpersonal motive gratification (see chap. 6). In contrast, after the completion of a paradigmatic development, constitutive-interpersonal thoughts will provide only constitutive-interpersonal gratification (they will not have illusional regulatory agency significance).

Initially, interpersonal agency is nonveridical and is most acutely felt by the child at moments when the caregiver must frustrate her/his constitutive-interpersonal motives. As a result, the onset of the nonveridical interpersonal agent-self is a function not only of the child's new capacity for interpersonal introspection but also of the child's response to the caregiving relationship. The transference interpersonal no has a dual significance because the caregiver's attempted interference with the child's constitutive-interpersonal motives threatens the child with two types of transference loss. First, the child faces the frustration of the manifest constitutive-interpersonal motive to which the caregiver is reacting. More important, the child confronts the frustration of the non-veridical regulatory-interpersonal agent-self motive for regulatory control over the choice and pursuit of constitutive-interpersonal motives. Although the child may have to tolerate the ongoing frustration of the specific constitutive-interpersonal motive that s/he wants to pursue, the caregiver helps the child to realize that the loss of the reflection of regulatory-interpersonal agent-self as agent-self is not a necessary consequence of constitutive-interpersonal motive frustration. For example, the caregiver may have to stop the child from reaching for the sharp scissors which the caregiver is using. At the same time that the child experiences the constitutive-interpersonal motive frustration, the child can also have the experience that the caregiver is not angry at the child for her/his strong protests but rather appreciates these protests as representing a crucial, legitimate motive for regulatory-interpersonal motive gratification. As a result, the child begins to recognize that the caregiver's frustration of her/his constitutive-interpersonal motives does not entail a discouraging attitude toward the child's regulatory-interpersonal motives.

Cognitive and Social-Interpersonal Development

Between the onset of the regulatory-intrapsychic agent-self (at the end of the regulatory-intrapsychic self stage) and the transference constitutive-interpersonal no, the child's constitutive-interpersonal motives continue to mature, a process which results in the child's increasingly sophisticated capacity for language (e.g., naming self and others) and for motor activities. From an intrapsychic caregiving viewpoint, however, before the transference interpersonal no, the self-awareness that results from the maturation of cognitive and social-interpersonal capacities has the significance only of intrapsychic agent-self meaning, because as yet the child has no capacity for an introspective recognition of interpersonal personal meaning. Therefore, the vicissitudes (gratification or lack of gratification) of constitutive-interpersonal motive experience have illusional intrapsychic significance. Because the child's cognitive and social-interpersonal motives are not sufficiently developed to allow her/him to have a functional introspection of interpersonal motive frustration or gratification before the regulatory-interpersonal self stage, the child responds to constitutive-interpersonal loss by regressing to a dissociated state that allows the substitution of other forms of gratification, including gratifying percepts that come directly from the caregiver imago eidetically internalized within the transitional intrapsychic caregiver. Just before the onset of the interpersonal no, however, the child's maturation enables her/him to develop an incipient sense of constitutive-interpersonal agency.

The capacity for interpersonal introspection that makes possible the interpersonal no develops into the capacity to recognize potential loss on both regulatory and constitutive levels of interpersonal consciousness. The child's transference interpersonal no signifies a renewed pursuit of the frustrated constitutive-interpersonal motive by means of the rejection of the interfering motive asserted by the caregiver, which preserves a continued, unbroken transference experience of effective regulatory-interpersonal agency. In other words, the interpersonal agency experience entailed by the child's transference interpersonal no represents an attempt at self-caretaking.

The prominence of interpersonal introspection in the interpersonal no response motivates the child to become increasingly introspective, which results in the illusional reflection of regulatory agency we term *all-powerful agent-self experience.* The all-powerful agent-self preserves its well-being by maintaining the illusion of having unqualified control over the acquisition of one source of its gratifying agent-self percepts—constitutive-interpersonal motive gratification. The all-powerful agent-self's illusion of regulatory agency entails the belief that it can overcome any of the caregiver's motives that threaten its ability to choose and to gratify a constitutive-interpersonal motive. Accordingly, the all-powerful agent-self has the illusional belief that it will always prevail in a conflict with another and that another's independent motives generally signify a threatened loss. Psychopathological derivatives of this orientation abound. Examples range from the individual who inhibits her/his activities so as to avoid encounters that could potentially dispel the illusion of omnipotence, to the individual who cannot take no for an answer. In effect, then, all-powerful agent-self well-being rests on the illusion that the all-powerful agent-self can control the other's motives and that the other agrees to this regulation.

In contrast to *nontransference* mourning, *transference* grief work occurs in the context of a dissociated state of consciousness that allows the child to experience the caregiver's interference with her/his constitutive-interpersonal motive as regulated by the child's own agent-self. For example, in situations in which the caregiver insists on the interfering motive (e.g., the caregiver insists that the child leave the playground), since the child illusionally experiences the caregiver's motives as regulated by her/his all-powerful agent-self and, further, illusionally believes that s/he can, at some future point, reverse the loss, the child believes s/he has intentionally chosen the motive: s/he retains the experience of effective interpersonal agency on the level of the all-powerful agent-self.

This universal characteristic of interpersonal transference experience results both from the phase-specifically dissociated state of transference-regulated interpersonal consciousness and from the child's cognitive immaturity. The child's inability to appreciate the boundaries between cranially discrete centers of agency reality differs from the capacity to recognize the corporeal boundaries of others and results from the effects of transference. In keeping with this, transference-based interpersonal relationship experience entails the illusion that the other's behavior is always directed at the self.

The interpersonal no results from the epigenetic maturation of cognitive and social-interpersonal motives. This maturation enables the child phase-appropriately: (1) to recognize and appreciate the regulatory power of intentionality (choice regulated by purpose); (2) to have the judgmental capacity to compare one's chosen aim with an aim chosen by another; (3) to recognize the meaning of loss signified by the potential interruption of the continued pursuit of a chosen aim; and (4) to have a purposive intentionality that regulates and conserves the pursuit of the chosen aim even in the face of an oppositional and persistent aim asserted by another. The pleasure associated with constitutive-interpersonal intentionality is added to the pleasure produced by the gratification of specific constitutive-interpersonal aims. Subsequently, regulatory-interpersonal agent-self intentionality accompanies and regulates constitutive-interpersonal agent-self intentionality. At its onset, regulatory-interpersonal pleasure is transference pleasure.

The process level of the child's interpersonal developmental merger can be thought of in terms of the child's illusion of having mind control over the caregiver's personal motives, and the content level can be thought of in terms of the child's illusion that s/he can read the caregiver's mind and vice versa. The destructuralization of the mind-control form occurs at the end of the regulatory-interpersonal self stage and is synonymous with the destructuralization of the merger per se, because the mind-reading form of the developmental interpersonal merger is subsumed under the mind-control form. However, it is heuristic to separate these illusions because the destructuralization of the developmental merger includes developmental changes that are specific to each component of the merger.

As the child's cognitive abilities continue to mature, the child acquires the capacity to keep private a form of interpersonal no. The child becomes aware both that s/he has an unexpressed interpersonal no and that the caregiver does not know of this no. The child's awareness that s/he can decide whether or not to keep thoughts private enhances her/his social-interpersonal autonomy and contributes to the child's cognitive (in contrast to intrapsychic) capacity to recognize a physically separate center of agency reality.

The cognitive component of the transference interpersonal no significantly enhances the destructuralization of the developmental merger between the child's constitutive-interpersonal agent-self and the caregiver's constitutive-interpersonal agent-self. The child's ability to say no to the caregiver's interference with the child's intended regulation of her/his own constitutive-interpersonal motives enhances the child's capacity to differentiate between the imagined and the real, which in turn enables the child to recognize that s/he can know something that the caregiver does not.[28] When s/he discovers s/he has a thought of which the caregiver is unaware, the child feels a loss at learning that the caregiver is not omniscient. At the same time, on the non-transference side of the developmental split, this knowledge enhances the child's sense of regulatory control and increases her/his capacity for interpersonal intimacy. On the transference side of the developmental split, the child's recognition of the privacy of constitutive-interpersonal introspection, though devoid of paranoid aims, enhances the well-being of the all-powerful agent-self and the constitutive-interpersonal motives under its regulatory control. In paradigmatic development, of course, this nonveridical well-being ultimately will be destructuralized.

The developmental achievement of the capacity for an intentional privacy of interpersonal introspection is facilitated by playful behavior between child and caregiver focused on the exciting, suspenseful endeavor to guess what the other is thinking or knowing. As will become clear, the child's capacity to perceive the separation between self and caregiver, with regard to the privacy of interpersonal introspection, remains incomplete. It remains incomplete both because this reality testing is vulnerable to regression and also because, at this point, nothing in the child's experience conveys that s/he cannot read the caregiver's mind.

The child's awareness that s/he intentionally regulates the privacy of her/his interpersonal introspection is a type of interpersonal reality testing. The transference form of the child's new-found ability to appreciate the separation between her/his introspection and the caregiver's knowledge of that introspection also enhances the all-powerful agent-self's transference well-being. While the capacity to recognize constitutive-interpersonal privacy facilitates the destructuralization of the developmental merger, it has no regulatory agency significance, because it does not further the child's capacity to recognize that s/he cannot regulate the caregiver's personal motives.

Ongoing Effects of the Intrapsychic Transference

In the regulatory-interpersonal self stage, the transitional intrapsychic caregiver remains available to mediate between nonveridical agent-self percepts and the nonveridical intrapsychic precept. After the transference interpersonal no, the all-powerful agent-self becomes the gratifying, secondary nonveridical agent-self percept for the nonveridical intrapsychic motive. In turn, all-powerful agent-self motives are gratified by both gratified constitutive-interpersonal motives and also gratified nonveridical intrapsychic motives. This reciprocity between the developmental intrapsychic transference and the developmental interpersonal transference gives a boost both to the power of the all-powerful agent-self and also to the pleasure of the gratification of constitutive-interpersonal motives. Transference-dominated constitutive-interpersonal motives cause and, therefore, partake of the meaning of transference intrapsychic well-being and transference regulatory-interpersonal well-being. Thus, the intrapsychic transference process facilitates constitutive-interpersonal motive development and, therefore, effective constitutive-interpersonal agency. Each constitutive-interpersonal motive gratification (e.g., learning a word) conveys an added, transference pleasure, which aids the child in experimenting with and mastering the surrounding world and in determining her/his place in it. The change from a nonveridical intrapsychic perceptual identity process that uses nonveridical caregiver percepts, which are based on actual experience of the caregiver her/himself, to a nonveridical intrapsychic perceptual identity process that uses nonveridical regulatory-interpersonal agent-self percepts which are generated by constitutive-interpersonal success is clearly adaptive. A transference intrapsychic motive gratification that ultimately rests on constitutive-interpersonal pleasure enhances and encourages the child's motive to move away from an exclusive relationship with the caregiver into a world of objects, opportunities, peers, and school. The price paid for the transference rush of self-esteem associated with experiences of successful interpersonal performance is that constitutive-interpersonal losses, such as breaking a toy, cause the added pain of regulatory-interpersonal loss and intrapsychic loss. When a constitutive-interpersonal wish is not gratified, the child thus experiences three simultaneous losses: (1) the lack of gratification of a specific constitutive-interpersonal motive; (2) the loss of transference regulatory-interpersonal self-esteem (loss of the nonveridical reflection of effective regulatory-interpersonal agency); and (3) the intrapsychic loss of the (nonveridical) reflection of effective intrapsychic agency derived from the (nonveridical) meaning of effective regulatory-interpersonal agency.

Because the transitional intrapsychic caregiver contains eidetically internalized memories of the pre-eidetic gratified intrapsychic motive, it can serve as a nonveridical intrapsychic agent-self. Thus, when there is an interruption in constitutive-interpersonal motive gratification, the transitional intrapsychic caregiver can fulfill the need for agent-self percepts to gratify the nonveridical regulatory-interpersonal motive. In the regulatory-interpersonal self stage, then, the eidetically internalized transitional intrapsychic caregiver, which is the basis of the intrapsychic transference, functions both as a transference intrapsychic caregiver and also as a transference intrapsychic self. Therefore, we term this structure the ***transference intrapsychic self and caregiver structure.*** In other words, until it is destructuralized at the end of this stage, the transference intrapsychic self and caregiver structure both mediates transference intrapsychic motive gratification and also generates gratifying percepts for the interpersonal transference.

In paradigmatic development, the caregiver's caregiving response to the child's transference interpersonal no enhances the child's awareness of a (transference) form of well-being that has the significance of an agent-self, self-regulatory control over the choice and pursuit of constitutive-interpersonal motives. The constitutive-interpersonal agent-self represents the agency of introspective awareness of the wish to gratify a specific constitutive-interpersonal motive, whereas the all-powerful agent-self has the illusion of effective regulatory agency with regard to choosing among competing constitutive-interpersonal motives and selecting the general manner in which the chosen motive is pursued. Though the constitutive-interpersonal agent-self experiences loss, the child illusionally experiences the all-powerful agent-self as loss free. Because of its inherent dissociation, the all-powerful agent-self always has the experience of veridical regulatory control. Since the sources of gratifying, agent-self percepts for the all-powerful agent-self motive are both the transference intrapsychic self and caregiver structure and also constitutive-interpersonal motive gratification, the defectiveness of the all-powerful agent-self inheres, first, in its lack of reality testing (the all-powerful agent-self does not really have veridical regulatory control over the choice and pursuit of constitutive-interpersonal motives) and, second, in its vulnerability to the loss of gratifying, nonveridical agent-self percepts. In paradigmatic development, this vulnerability results from the fact that constitutive-interpersonal motive gratification is proximally subject to positive entropy, chance, and the vicissitudes of sociocultural reality that affect all nonregulatory agency reality. It is not caused by losses produced by nonveridical caregiving. The counterweight to the all-powerful agent-self's ongoing representation of veridical regulatory control is the developmental process by which the child comes to experience all-powerful agent-self well-being as the source of a loss that can be mourned through the child's choice of the superior well-being represented by veridical regulatory-interpersonal motive gratification.[29]

The all-powerful agent-self remains a transference source of continuous (but unreflective and unstable) well-being through adolescence and, in untreated psychopathology, for the individual's entire life. In psychopathology, the severity of the individual's *interpersonal* psychopathology will dictate the extent to which the all-powerful agent-self's response to inevitable constitutive-interpersonal loss will take on forms of crippling paranoia or self-rage. An example of paranoia in response to a small constitutive-interpersonal loss is the individual who, upon discovering that his plane will be delayed, verbally abuses the person behind the ticket counter as a way of reestablishing the experience of agent-self, self-regulatory control.

In psychopathology, because the all-powerful agent-self has a delusional experience of loss-free regulatory control, the individual's capacity for socially adaptive interpersonal functioning will depend on the degree to which s/he was forced by the nonveridical interpersonal caregiving s/he received to rely on dissociated states that sheltered her/his all-powerful agent-self's transference well-being and delusional sense of control from the discordant information generated by perceptual experience. The most extreme example of behavior regulated by this delusional well-being is suicide, which represents both an illusional regulatory control (the suicidal act) and also a defective reality testing that maintains the delusional conviction of effective agency (the conviction that the suicidal act will improve the quality of subjective experience).

Since, by definition, the all-powerful agent-self can only grieve by means of a restitutional process, the transference well-being that signifies a loss-free, all-powerful agent-self capacity plays a critical role when constitutive-interpersonal motives are frustrated. The dissociation that makes possible the ongoing well-being of the all-powerful agent-self is intensified by constitutive-interpersonal loss. Because a nonveridical regulatory-interpersonal perceptual identity process attaches the meaning of agent intentionality to the universe of experience that can be registered by the constitutive-interpersonal agent-self, the pain that results from constitutive-interpersonal motive frustration has the illusional significance to the all-powerful agent-self of the reflection of veridical regulatory capacity. Thus, the all-powerful agent-self experiences itself as having effective agency capacity in response to both constitutive-interpersonal motive gratification and constitutive-interpersonal motive frustration. This explains the delusion of invulnerability that can characterize psychopathological existence, examples of which may be found in chronic smokers' and reckless drivers' denial of the likely consequences of their behaviors. As will be discussed further in chapter 6, in psychopathology this delusion of invincibility is counterbalanced to a greater or lesser degree by cognitive and social-interpersonal reality testing, which acquires its power from the functional integrity of some remnant of the smile response and from constitutive-interpersonal identifications that are conducive to social-interpersonal adaptiveness. In paradigmatic development, the appeal of the all-powerful agent-self's illusion of loss-free regulatory control is outweighed by the onset and development of a veridical regulatory-interpersonal agent-self, which has the capacity for veridical social-interpersonal reality testing based on the capacity to mourn constitutive-interpersonal loss. Constitutive-interpersonal loss can only be mourned when the child has developed the capacity for veridical regulatory-interpersonal agency. As we will describe shortly, constitutive-interpersonal loss can be mourned when it exists in the context of the stable inner well-being provided by the regulatory-intrapsychic agent-self's ongoing, empirically based well-being, which, in turn, provides the veridical regulatory-interpersonal agent-self's ongoing reflection of agent-self as agent-self. Constitutive-interpersonal mourning is a process in which the individual has no motive to deny constitutive-interpersonal loss because her/his experience of effective agency is unrelated to constitutive-interpersonal motive gratification.

In contrast to the all-powerful agent-self, the constitutive-interpersonal agent-self does not invariantly deny constitutive-interpersonal loss. The child's constitutive-interpersonal agent-self realizes that it never got the cookie it wanted, even when the all-powerful agent-self maintains the conviction that it has the power to get what it wants. Also, unlike the all-powerful agent-self, the constitutive-interpersonal agent-self does not have a loss-free introspective experience. In psychopathology, however, the dissociated state associated with the all-powerful agent-self can nullify the introspective registration of loss by the constitutive-interpersonal agent-self. For example, in spite of all the perceptions to the contrary, the anorexic individual does not realize that s/he is dangerously undernourished.

The constitutive-interpersonal agent-self can experience two distinct types of loss. The first is the frustration of a chosen constitutive-interpersonal motive, which occurs both in paradigmatic and psychopathological development and results from inescapable moments of conflict with others' motives, from chance, or from the inescapable losses caused by the forces of positive entropy. The other loss experienced by the constitutive-interpersonal agent-self occurs only in psychopathology and occurs when the all-powerful agent-self's delusional reality testing exerts hegemony over the constitutive-interpersonal agent-self and causes an unstable form of constitutive-interpersonal agency. The loss stemming from an inherently unstable, pathological-transference-regulated form of constitutive-interpersonal agency is accented every time we follow a motive we did not "intend" or did not "want" to pursue, as well as when we are unable to follow a motive we have "chosen." The phenomenon of unstable constitutive-interpersonal agency can be illustrated by the fervent but ineffectual resolutions made every New Year's Day. This gap between the wish to control and the actual inability to control the pursuit of constitutive-interpersonal aims is usually seen by other psychologies and philosophies of mind as an ineluctable part of the human condition (often referred to as the problem of regulating desire) rather than as a product of inadequate nurture.

Previous Views of the Problem of Regulating Desire

Throughout Western history, the human inability to achieve regulatory control over desire has been so prevalent that most philosophers and psychologists have concluded that this condition inheres in human nature. Each culture develops its own accommodation to the problem of regulating desire. In general, these accommodations can be distinguished by whether or not the society separates the loss of regulatory control due to the inability to regulate everyday desire from the loss of regulatory control represented by death.

Systems of thought that include death in the problem of the regulatory control of desire often postulate some form of animistic spirituality or supernatural reality whereby the individual's relationship to a spiritual reality anchors a set of ethical ideals that have the aim of, but do not guarantee, the person's capacity to regulate everyday desire. In these systems of spirituality, the loss due to the defective regulatory control of everyday desire represented by death has the meaning not of loss per se, but rather of a rite of passage to some form of afterlife. In this view, then, the act of dying confers upon the individual a form of loss-free, self-regulatory stability.

Systems of thought that do distinguish between the problem of regulating everyday desire and the problem of the loss of regulatory control signified by death can be grouped into two main categories: (1) those that propose an attainable ideal of the capacity for the stable regulatory control of desire and (2) those that assert that the ideal of the stable, nonillusional regulatory control of desire is an impossibility. Systems of thought that envision the possibility of a stable capacity for the regulatory control of everyday desire can, in turn, be distinguished by whether they place the locus of regulatory control within the individual or within a social movement. Those systems of thought that assert that the individual can be the locus of regulatory control can also be distinguished by whether they are presented from a first– or third–person viewpoint and by whether or not the capacity for regulatory control rests on a precept of unqualified self-abnegation.[30]

We distinguish the loss resulting from the inability to regulate everyday desire from the loss signified by death. Although we posit the possibility of a loss-free regulatory control of desire, we are nonutopian both because we recognize that only regulatory agency reality is not proximally affected by positive entropy and chance, and also because we do not prescribe a specific, predetermined, to-be-achieved form of social and cultural reality. Constitutive-interpersonal loss is unavoidable (in the face of the most dedicated pursuit of constitutive-interpersonal motives, humans will always be vulnerable to losses, e.g., of a football game, a job, hunger, disease), but constitutive-interpersonal loss does not have to signify the loss of effective agent-self meaning, of inner well-being. The well-being of the regulatory-intrapsychic agent-self derives from its empirically based, mutualized certainty that it can cause the caregiver's intrapsychic caregiving love. This certainty is unaffected by the vicissitudes of positive entropy and chance and, therefore, remains stable and loss free even during times of constitutive-interpersonal loss. Intrapsychic well-being provides the reflection of agent-self as agent-self to the veridical regulatory-interpersonal agent-self, which, in turn, is a source of security for the constitutive-interpersonal agent-self, even during times of constitutive-interpersonal loss.

The Onset of the Veridical Regulatory-Interpersonal Self

In paradigmatic development, although the first introspectively experienced form of regulatory-interpersonal agent-self is nonveridical, this illusional form of regulatory-interpersonal agency comes to acquire the meaning of the loss of superior inner well-being because of the presence of the veridical, regulatory-intrapsychic agent-self. Concomitantly, the child develops a competing, nontransference experience of regulatory-interpersonal agency, which we term the *veridical regulatory-interpersonal agent-self.* The veridical regulatory-interpersonal agent-self derives its reflection of agent-self as agent-self from the veridical well-being structuralized within the regulatory-intrapsychic agent-self. The veridical regulatory-interpersonal agent-self has a stable inner well-being that does not depend on constitutive-interpersonal motive gratification. Therefore, the child's veridical regulatory-interpersonal agent-self experiences the transference interpersonal no as the loss of a superior, less dissociated type of well-being. As a result, the child responds with what we term the *nontransference form of the interpersonal no.* The nontransference interpersonal no is directed at the child's own transference-regulated motives to reject the caregiver's interfering motive, rather than at the caregiver. The child's veridical regulatory-interpersonal agent-self can recognize that the caregiver's frustration of the child's constitutive-interpersonal motives represents either an act of interpersonal caregiving or a personal exigency.

The nontransference interpersonal no represents the *veridical* regulatory-interpersonal agent-self's capacity to say no to the *transference* regulatory-interpersonal agent-self on the other side of the developmental split. The child's nontransference interpersonal no plays an important role in determining the child's capacity for *interpersonal* intimacy—for an interpersonal closeness that includes another's potentially nongratifying interpersonal motives. The nontransference interpersonal no sets the stage for interpersonal closeness based neither on domination nor on submission.

Unlike the all-powerful agent-self, the veridical regulatory-interpersonal agent-self is not the product of an illusional perceptual identity process. It is itself a source of veridical, reflective awareness. Paradigmatically, at the onset of the transference interpersonal no, the child already has a functional, nontransference, regulatory-intrapsychic agent-self under the hegemony of the intrapsychic pleasure principle. In other words, the child can phase-appropriately recognize not only that veridical pleasure is superior to transference pleasure but also that transference pleasure signifies a relative loss of pleasure and should be avoided. On the nontransference side of the developmental split in the differentiated regulatory-intrapsychic self stage, the child has had an ongoing, veridical, empirical knowledge of the stability of the caregiver's intrapsychic caregiving motives. This unmediated knowledge carries over into the regulatory-interpersonal self stage and facilitates the veridical regulatory-interpersonal agent-self's assumption that the caregiver's frustration of the child's constitutive-interpersonal motives does not signal any instability in the caregiver's caregiving intentions. The child's all-powerful agent-self and veridical regulatory-interpersonal agent-self respond entirely differently to constitutive-interpersonal loss. We stress that the resolution of the conflict inherent in the transference interpersonal no is an act of mourning (a choice of superior, veridical regulatory-interpersonal pleasure); therefore, the transference interpersonal no is not a paranoid type of conflictual experience. After the regulatory-intrapsychic self stage of paradigmatic development, there are two types of mourning. Constitutive-interpersonal mourning is a process in which the stable well-being provided by the regulatory-intrapsychic agent-self to the regulatory-interpersonal agent-self allows constitutive-interpersonal loss to be experienced reflectively with no effect on the individual's regulatory agency reality (inner well-being). The second type of mourning process is the child's recognition of the superiority of veridical agency meaning over illusional agency meaning. The transference system of illusional agency meanings is destructuralized when nonregulatory agency percepts and nonagency percepts cease to have any appeal as gratifying percepts for the intrapsychic motive or the regulatory-interpersonal motive.

All-powerful agent-self well-being derives its appeal from: (1) the innately determined power of the *transference* system of *intrapsychic* motive gratification, which is a gratifying, nonveridical agent-self percept for the all-powerful agent-self motive, (2) the pleasure of gratified constitutive-interpersonal motives, and (3) the fact that the all-powerful agent-self is an innately determined form of self-experience, which means that, from its onset, the all-powerful agent-self is a familiar self. The veridical regulatory-interpersonal agent-self, on the other hand, is nurture based and offers the superior pleasure of stable, veridical, non-dissociated, pain-free and loss-free regulatory agent-self pleasure. Because the *regulatory-intrapsychic* agent-self is mutualized by empirical contact with the caregiver's intrapsychic caregiving, it has a sufficiently extracranial quality to gratify the *regulatory-interpersonal* motive for the veridical reflection of regulatory-interpersonal agent-self as agent-self. Though the veridical regulatory-interpersonal agent-self is a structure of interpersonal consciousness and, therefore, is not empirically accessible to the caregiver's interpersonal caregiving motives, it functions in a mutualized context. This makes it possible for the veridical regulatory-interpersonal agent-self to maintain stable esteem (to have ongoing regulatory-interpersonal motive gratification) even in the face of constitutive-interpersonal loss. The stable well-being, in turn, imparts an atmosphere of mutuality to the constitutive-interpersonal agent-self.

The nature of the nontransference interpersonal no is that, although the child's constitutive-interpersonal loss may or may not be reversed, the child's veridical regulatory-interpersonal agent-self experiences no loss. The gratification the child's veridical regulatory-interpersonal agent-self continues to experience via the uninterrupted pleasure provided by the well-being structuralized in the regulatory-intrapsychic agent-self allows the veridical regulatory-interpersonal agent-self to retain the meaning of the capacity for effective agency in the face of the frustration of constitutive-interpersonal motives. The mutual though nonempirical relationship between the regulatory-intrapsychic agent-self and the veridical regulatory-interpersonal agent-self and, in turn, between the veridical regulatory-interpersonal agent-self and the constitutive-interpersonal agent-self under its regulatory control is the sole exception to and means of escape from the inherent solipsism of interpersonal consciousness. The nontransference interpersonal no is the foundation of an interpersonal intimacy based on a veridical regulatory-interpersonal agent-self, whose reflection of agent-self as agent-self is not derived from the gratification of constitutive-interpersonal motives. This makes it possible for the individual to remain intimately involved with another even when the other has conflicting motives. For example, disagreements between friends over where to eat or what movie to see will not cause ill feelings and alienation.

The contrast between the all-powerful agent-self's illusion of having the loss-free capacity for the regulatory control of constitutive-interpersonal motive gratification and the veridical regulatory-interpersonal agent-self's loss-free capacity for inner well-being can be illustrated by the consequences of constitutive-interpersonal motive frustration for each agent-self. On the nontransference side of the developmental split, the constitutive-interpersonal agent-self registers the loss of the pursued gratification within the context of the pleasure it derives from the veridical regulatory-interpersonal agent-self's stable well-being. This enables the constitutive-interpersonal agent-self to mourn, that is, to maintain a stable sense of self-confidence in its capacity for intentional agency, without denying the loss of the specific gratification. In this way, constitutive-interpersonal loss does not acquire illusional agent-self meaning. In contrast, on the transference side of the developmental split, because constitutive-interpersonal gratification is used as an agent-self percept for the regulatory-interpersonal transference and, in turn, for the intrapsychic transference, the loss of gratification experienced by the constitutive-interpersonal agent-self has the meaning of both regulatory-interpersonal pain and intrapsychic pain. The denial inherent in the all-powerful agent-self's response causes the constitutive-interpersonal agent-self to have unreflective feelings of self-doubt in combination with the renewed determination to achieve gratification at any cost.

Caregiver Responses to the Transference Interpersonal No

After the transference constitutive-interpersonal no, percepts of the caregiver are no longer secondary nonveridical percepts for the nonveridical intrapsychic motive, nor is the caregiver any longer an empirical source of intrapsychic motive gratification for the veridical regulatory-intrapsychic motive. The child's veridical, regulatory-intrapsychic agent-self, which embodies the structuralized, mutualized effects of the caregiver's nurture, assumes intrapsychic caregiving functions more effectively than the caregiver ever could. The caregiver has motives for personal pleasure (e.g., sometimes takes a walk, goes to work, needs a nap) but the child's regulatory-intrapsychic agent-self represents an empirical knowledge of and identification with the caregiver's veridical intrapsychic caregiving motives. Therefore, the regulatory-intrapsychic agent-self represents the steadiest, most stable source of intrapsychic care-getting gratification.

Further, due to the nonempirical nature of interpersonal consciousness, the caregiver cannot be a direct source of gratification for the regulatory-interpersonal agent-self's needs, although the caregiver can support an already functional regulatory-interpersonal agent-self. This does not mean, however, that the caregiver's role at this point in development is less important than before. On the contrary, if the child is to develop a stable, nontransference capacity to mourn constitutive-interpersonal loss, that is, to experience constitutive-interpersonal loss in the context of stable regulatory-interpersonal well-being, the caregiver must respond in an accepting manner to the child's negative responses to the caregiver's inevitable frustration of the child's constitutive-interpersonal motives. Regardless of whether the caregiver allows the child the constitutive-interpersonal motive in question or continues to frustrate it, the caregiver's facilitative response can confirm the efficacy of the child's regulatory-interpersonal agent-self.

The child with a psychopathological regulatory-interpersonal agent-self often responds to the transference loss entailed by constitutive-interpersonal motive frustration by pursuing her/his chosen motive even in the face of manifest caregiver disapproval. Many children with psychopathological agent-selves exhibit contrary behavior that is typically labeled "willful" or "headstrong." Such children are so sensitive to loss that even the possibility of interference with their motives often causes them to experience significant psychic pain. They frequently choose motives merely because they have been forbidden. An example drawn from an incident observed in a grocery store illustrates this phenomenon. A mother said to her two-year-old daughter, "Don't touch anything here." The two-year-old, who had been walking peacefully up and down the aisle, immediately touched the wrapper on a loaf of bread on the shelf. The mother rushed over and said angrily, "I told you not to touch that. Why don't you do what I tell you to?" The child, who did not shed a tear at being rebuked, said defiantly, "Because I don't want to."

Unfortunately, many child development theorists assume that this sort of conflict between toddler and caregiver is inevitable. McDevitt and Mahler, for example, conclude:

> The toddler cannot always have his mother's attention, the toys he desires, or the space he would like to occupy; he may become jealous of the interest mother pays to siblings or other children. Forced to limit the toddler's activities and demands, the mother cannot restore his former sense of omnipotence, nor is she able to relieve his sense of aloneness and helplessness. The junior toddler comes to feel hurt, frustrated, and angry with his mother. As a result he is negativistic and provocative, or he clings helplessly to his mother.[31]

If the caregiver cannot provide the child with a veridical mutuality that enables the child to mourn loss, one possible consequence is that the child may become more concerned about preserving her/his transference sense of self-esteem than about gratifying her/his phase-specific needs for various kinds of interpersonal success. Because they are afraid to fail, children with this psychopathological adaptation are afraid to try and, often, to learn. Manifest remnants of a pathological interpersonal no phase also can be seen in individuals who, because of an inability to mourn, cannot abandon the pursuit of a constitutive-interpersonal motive, even when the attainment of the motive is impossible or would be self-destructive (e.g., the person who continues to pursue an operatic career even after it becomes clear s/he does not have the necessary talent, or the person who cannot give up her/his plan to go skiing in spite of an avalanche warning).

Paradigmatically, in response to the child's transference interpersonal no, the caregiver either changes her/his mind and gratifies the motive in question (assuming this motive is not a dangerous or unwise one) or persists in frustrating the motive in question (either because the motive entails danger or because the caregiver feels unable to abandon the personal motive s/he is pursuing). In either case, the caregiver's response facilitates both the child's development of a nontransference form of interpersonal no and, ultimately, the child's capacity for interpersonal self-regulatory stability. The caregiver aims to help the child develop and retain the capacity for veridical regulatory-interpersonal agency and constitutive-interpersonal agency in the face of constitutive-interpersonal loss. The child comes to realize that her/his inability to gratify a specific constitutive-interpersonal motive (e.g., to stay in the park and play) has no significance for regulatory-interpersonal and constitutive-interpersonal well-being (has no agent-self meaning). To further this process, in those instances in which the caregiver must interfere with the child's constitutive-interpersonal motives, the caregiver will attempt to mitigate the ache of the loss in order to help the child to preserve a sense of interpersonal well-being. The most obvious way to achieve this is to offer the child another constitutive-interpersonal gratification to pursue. For example, in the context of explaining to the child why s/he cannot pursue her/his motive to cook on the real stove, the caregiver can offer the child a play stove or some real pots and pans to play with.

This way of handling the child's protests differs from the goal of substitute gratification that is commonly advocated. The caregiver's goal is to help the child to realize that constitutive-interpersonal gratification is not a veridical gratification of the child's motives for effective constitutive-interpersonal agency and effective regulatory-interpersonal agency. For this reason, if the caregiver can help the child actively choose another constitutive-interpersonal motive, the child will have the dual experience of partial constitutive motive frustration and interpersonal agent-self efficacy. In contrast, psychoanalytic theorists, such as Hartmann, advocate substitute gratification because they see the child as possessing a pool of libidinous or aggressive energy seeking a gratifying discharge (with the specific object being less important to the child than the general aim of discharge). From this perspective, the caregiver is advised to offer the child a substitute gratification in order to avoid especially harsh repression and subsequent symptom formation. In other words, the caregiver is advised to use substitute gratification to facilitate the child's denial of the loss. A child who is responded to in this manner will never come to know that constitutive-interpersonal loss is not equivalent to constitutive-interpersonal or regulatory-interpersonal agent-self meaning.

If the child will not accept another constitutive-interpersonal motive in place of the constitutive-interpersonal motive s/he is pursuing, the caregiver must respond with understanding to the child's strong protest of what s/he illusionally experiences as the loss of the reflection of agent-self as agent-self on both constitutive-interpersonal and regulatory-interpersonal levels. The child's negation of the caregiver's motives provides illusional gratification of the child's all-powerful agent-self motive. This grief work rests on denial; specifically, the content of the denial is that the child feels s/he is so powerful that s/he cannot, in any inherent way, be interfered with.[32]

The following illustrates a developmental (paradigmatic) *transference interpersonal no response*. The caregiver of an 18-month-old child sees that the child looks tired and says, "It's time for bed." The child says, "No." The caregiver says affectionately, "You don't want to go to bed?" The child repeats, "No." The caregiver gently picks the child up and starts carrying him to bed. The caregiver says, "Sometimes it's hard to go to bed when you don't want to." The child replies playfully, "No bed." The caregiver responds, "I can really recognize that you don't feel like bed right now. Shall we read a story?" The child points and says, "That one." The caregiver says, "OK," and reads it. When the story is finished, the caregiver says, "Well, its time for bed now. Let me tuck you in." The child replies, "No." The caregiver says, "You still don't feel like bed, huh?" The child says, "No." The caregiver replies, "Well, have a good night and I'll see you in the morning." The child remains in bed singing cheerfully to himself the words, "No, no, no, no, no, no."

This is an example of a *transference* interpersonal no because the child retains the belief that no one can interfere with his motives (the child retains the illusion that he has the power to choose the motive to stay up). Because of the way in which the caregiver responded, however, s/he helped the child to live with the constitutive-interpersonal loss (going to bed when he does not want to) without experiencing a corresponding loss of inner well-being.

Six months later, when the same child is told it is time for bed, he says, "I don't want to go." When the caregiver replies, "Well, you have a big day tomorrow and it's probably a good idea to get enough sleep," the child smiles and says, "Big day . . . okay, but one story first." The caregiver says, "Sure," and reads the story. Then the caregiver kisses the child and says, "Night, night," and the child replies, "Night, night." The caregiver leaves and the child sings and talks happily until he falls asleep.

This illustrates a *nontransference* interpersonal no response because the child's veridical regulatory-interpersonal agent-self can appreciate the caregiver's ability to make decisions that are in the child's interest. The child can make the self-caretaking decisions both to endorse the caregiver's perception that the child should go to bed and also to say no to the child's own motives for the transference gratification produced by the all-powerful agent-self's denial that its power of choice can be interfered with.

There is a clear contrast between the affection and trust between child and caregiver evidenced in this example and pathological transference interpersonal no experiences. The latter are characterized by a spectrum of responses. Struggles around bedtime provide a good illustration. At one extreme, the child stays up interminably, a caregiver sleeps in the child's room, or the caregivers take the child into their bed. At the other extreme, the caregiver becomes angry and punitive and the child responds with anger, copious tears, or rigid compliance.

The caregiver's task is to help the child to recognize rather than to deny constitutive-interpersonal loss by helping the child to understand that the pain of constitutive-interpersonal loss does not equal the loss of veridical interpersonal agent-self pleasure. The capacity to detach illusional agent-self meaning from constitutive-interpersonal loss forms the basis for an increasingly veridical regulatory-interpersonal agent-self, which, in turn, produces an increasing capacity for interpersonal reality testing. Unlike those who define interpersonal reality testing in terms of cognitive awareness of the external world, we define it as the stable capacity to choose constitutive-interpersonal motives which represent self-caretaking ideals rather than illusional agent-self meaning. This is equivalent to the capacity for stable, veridical, self-regulatory control over regulatory-interpersonal agency reality.

The caregiver performs a crucial function as a source of secondary, confirming percepts for the child's veridical regulatory-interpersonal agent-self. The superior pleasure the caregiver experiences at choosing interpersonal caregiving motives over personal motives provides the child's veridical regulatory-interpersonal agent-self with a facilitative, though nonempirical, reflection of effective agency capacity. The child's certainty that, within the context of the exigencies of the caregiver's personal needs, her/his regulatory agent-self can be the agent cause of the caregiver's interpersonal caregiving provides a source of interpersonal care-getting reflections that encourages and confirms the child's capacity for effective regulatory-interpersonal agency, which is independent of constitutive-interpersonal motive gratification.

In paradigmatic development, the vast majority of the interactions between child and caregiver are thoroughly pleasurable and unconflicted. At those times when the child's needs for interpersonal care-getting and the caregiver's personal motives conflict, and the caregiver responds to this conflict either by switching to caregiving motives or by responding with understanding to the child's protests, the child has the ongoing experience of interpersonal effective agency because s/he is the agent cause of the caregiver's interpersonal caregiving motives. For example, caregivers who enjoy socializing in the evening may find that the child needs help with her/his homework or wants the caregivers to be at home to read a story or to play a game. The caregivers will respond to the child's verbal request that they spend more time at home by restricting their social schedule to a level the child can comfortably tolerate. A caregiver may also perceive that the child's regulatory-interpersonal agent-self does not sufficiently control certain constitutive-interpersonal motives, for example, to do her/his homework, or generally to function autonomously in the caregiver's absence. In this instance, even though the child has not asked the caregiver for help and attention, s/he will make her/himself available in a relaxed way so that the child realizes that the caregiver is happy to postpone personal motives to help the child's regulatory-interpersonal agent-self gain increasing veridical regulatory control over constitutive-interpersonal motive choice and pursuit.

Paradigmatically, the caregiver does not relinquish personal motives in favor of interpersonal caregiving motives with a sense of anger, martyrdom, irritation, or the need to depreciate the child for needing help. Rather, while the caregiver may feel a loss at abandoning a given personal motive, s/he will feel that the choice of the interpersonal caregiving motive results from a desire for the pleasure of caregiving intimacy and the pleasure of actualizing her/his caregiving ideals to help the child to develop a veridical regulatory-interpersonal agent-self. The caregiver will feel that the ultimate cause of her/his choice of caregiving over personal motives inheres in her/his own caregiving ideals and motives rather than in the child.

The evolutionary specialization and elaboration of cognitive and social-interpersonal motives has created the potential for uniquely reflective, veridical, mutualized, highly pleasurable constitutive-interpersonal agent-self experience. At the same time, however, the specialization and elaboration of human cognitive and social-interpersonal motives are responsible for the degree of intrapsychic and interpersonal psychopathology found in the human species.[33] *Humans have available to them a variegated, seemingly infinite array of motives that are not directly related to survival or caregiving.* Motives for recreational pleasure, for example, can be satisfied in innumerable ways. As a result, human *caregiving* motives are in constant competition with a virtually unlimited spectrum of *personal* motives (to watch TV, to play golf, to travel). In contrast, many birds sit on their eggs for weeks at a time and, subsequently, remain close to their nests and dedicated to the care and feeding of their nestlings, with little or no competition from motives for cognitive or recreational pleasure; the chimpanzee mother rarely is more than a few yards from its infant until the infant is over nine months old.[34] The consistency of much nonhuman parenting may explain why, in contrast to human society, there seems to be relatively little aberrant behavior in the animal kingdom other than that related to environmental factors. Only the human caregiver has available to her/him highly pleasurable personal gratifications that directly compete with caregiving gratification.[35] In other words, the human capacity for symbolic representational thought is a major contributor to human psychopathology.

There exists a wide range of psychopathological caregiving responses to the child's need for the caregivers to relinquish some personal motives in order to provide the interpersonal caregiving necessary for the paradigmatic development of the child's regulatory-interpersonal agent-self and constitutive-interpersonal agent-self. The extremes of this spectrum are the caregiver who can neither separate from the child nor pursue any personal motives, and the caregiver who never relinquishes her/his personal motives in the service of caregiving ideals. The latter caregiver either neglects the child (this includes the caregiver who leads a whirlwind life and leaves the child to be raised by sitters as well as the caregiver who simply leaves the child physically alone) or expresses extreme hostility to the child, who is blamed for the loss of the caregiver's personal gratification. This caregiver may tell the child, "I gave up my movie and you're not really trying hard to solve that problem," or, "I have a lot of work to do, and I can't believe you couldn't do that puzzle yourself." At the other extreme is the caregiver who abandons her/his personal motives to an inappropriate extent, which gives the child's interpersonal agent-self the message that it is defective, incompetent, or not to be trusted. This caregiver may use the child as a rationalization to avoid personal motives about which s/he is conflicted (such as conjugal intimacy); s/he may use the child as a vehicle for transference gratification based on self-rage (as a reason not to gratify important personal motives of her/his own); or s/he may use the child to deny her/his own psychic pain (exemplified in "if it weren't for you" statements).

Only the caregiver with the capacity for veridical intrapsychic self-caretaking and veridical regulatory-interpersonal self-caretaking can distinguish accurately times when relinquishing or postponing personal motives supports the child's regulatory-interpersonal agent-self and times when this choice depreciates the child. When the caregiver responds veridically to the child's need for interpersonal care-getting, the child will experience the caregivers as allies of her/his motive to gain a veridical interpersonal agent-self stability. The child will experience the caregivers' attention and offers of help as facilitative, not as intrusive, rage filled, or depreciating.

The child's experience of the caregivers as fostering rather than as hindering the growth of her/his regulatory-interpersonal agent-self is exceedingly important to the development of the child's capacity to learn. The child whose caregivers made veridical perceptions about when and how to aid the child's development of effective interpersonal agency carries the expectation of this relationship pleasure into school situations and approaches the student role with confidence and optimism. In contrast, the child whose caregivers were hostile, neglectful, anxious, or intrusive may approach the learning situation with such maladaptive behaviors as a paralyzing fear of failure, an inability to ask for help, the refusal to learn, inhibitions that culminate in a lack of curiosity, or desperate and unregulated demands for attention.[36]

The child's capacity to engage the caregiver's interpersonal caregiving ideals is the only specific (though nonempirical) extracranially generated confirmation of veridical regulatory-interpersonal agent-self capacity. The nonempirical quality of this regulatory-interpersonal motive gratification results from the nonempirical nature of regulatory-interpersonal consciousness. As a consequence, the child can never have the empirical knowledge of the veridicality of the caregiver's interpersonal caregiving motives that s/he had of the caregiver's intrapsychic caregiving motives. The caregiver's interpersonal caregiving can function both as a gratifying, agent-self percept for the child's all-powerful agent-self motive and as a confirming reflection for the veridical regulatory-interpersonal agent-self. If the caregiver has intrapsychic psychopathology, s/he will use her/his interpersonal caregiving for transference intrapsychic and regulatory-interpersonal well-being, and the child will have no way to distinguish the caregiver's psychopathologically motivated interpersonal caregiving from paradigmatic interpersonal caregiving. The exceptions are those instances in which the caregiver's intrapsychic psychopathology is accompanied by interpersonal psychopathology that includes overt hostility, neglect, intrusiveness, or pathological placation. While the child may then become cognitively aware of the defective quality of the caregiver's interpersonal caregiving, this recognition does not give the child the capacity for veridical regulatory agency because it can not convey the superiority of veridical care-getting pleasure. Therefore, this knowledge does not lessen the appeal of the caregiver's nonveridical caregiving as a nonveridical agent-self percept.

The most damaging caregiver responses at this stage come from: (1) caregivers who are unable to interfere with any of the child's motives out of an inability to tolerate either the child's unhappiness or being deidealized by the child and (2) caregivers who use excessive force (psychological or physical or both) in response to the child's transference interpersonal no. The caregiver who cannot interfere with the child's motives exposes the child to potentially lethal consequences, such as falling out of a window, pulling a pot of boiling water onto her/himself, or getting hit by a car. S/he also gives the child such a powerful reinforcement for the all-powerful agent-self form of well-being that the child's capacity for cognitive interpersonal reality testing becomes severely compromised. If such a child does not accidentally die or become disabled, s/he will be grossly impaired psychologically and socially. For example, a four-year-old child, on a warm spring day, wanted to open the office window in her psychotherapist's fourteenth floor office and sit on the sill. When the therapist responded that the child would be in too much danger of falling, the child insisted that she could sit there because even if she fell, she would be able to land on her feet unhurt. This child had already broken a number of bones when she fell out of a tree, when she tipped over a chair, and when she slipped on ice. In milder instances of this form of caregiver psychopathology, the child becomes "unmanageable," which makes her/him the object of a great deal of hostility from peers and adults.

On the other hand, the caregiver who responds to the child's transference interpersonal no with overwhelming force and hostility also produces a child with severe interpersonal pathology. One example is the five-year-old patient who would circle his therapist's office until he saw an object that took his fancy. He would then walk up to it, slap the back of his left hand hard with his right hand, and say in a gruff voice to himself, "No! Don't touch anything!"

The child may respond to nonveridical interpersonal caregiving with compliance, which can appear to be healthy reality testing. The test of whether the child's capacity to give up a thwarted motive without undue distress represents pathological compliance is whether the child has manifestly mourned the experience by expressing the pain of the loss within the caregiving relationship.

Many possible nonveridical caregiver responses to the child's transference interpersonal no response are not as extreme as the ones just described. These responses generally fall into two major categories: too little regulation of the child's constitutive-interpersonal motives or anger at the child's "disobedience." The nonveridical caregiver responds to the child's transference interpersonal no with personal motives aimed at preserving the caregiver's own psychic comfort.

In psychopathology, the interpersonal no has only a pathological transference form; there is no nontransference interpersonal no. Consequently, the child can only grieve constitutive-interpersonal motive frustration with a pathological form of grief work. In psychopathology, the interpersonal no often acquires the meaning of anger with the caregiver. The nonveridical caregiver's psychic pain makes her/him likely to respond to the child's expressions of anger with personal motives aimed at restoring her/his own damaged self-esteem, rather than with caregiving motives. For example, the nonveridical caregiver's principle interest may be to stifle the child's resistance to having her/his constitutive-interpersonal motives regulated by the caregiver. This nonveridical caregiving response further alienates the child and increases her/his losses. Nonveridical caregiving reactions to the child who continues both to assert her/his own motives and to reject the caregiver's motive to interfere with the child's constitutive-interpersonal motives most often take the form of anger or of appeasement. In this stage, children commonly react to nonveridical caregiving with temper tantrums, accidents, learning disabilities, toilet choosing problems, nightmares and night terrors, phobias, psychotic denial, extreme compliance, and unbridled aggression toward animals, peers, or material objects.

Toilet Choosing

We term the developmental event that is conventionally known as toilet training, **toilet choosing,** because we do not believe it has to involve either loss for the child or conflict with the caregiver. Paradigmatically, toilet choosing does not fall under the heading of interpersonal negation because it does not involve the caregiver's interference with the child's constitutive-interpersonal motives. If the idea of using the toilet is presented to the child by a caregiver who has heretofore provided the child with paradigmatic caregiving, the child will experience pleasure and a heightened sense of (transference and nontransference) regulatory-interpersonal agency in response to what s/he will experience as actively choosing to use the toilet. This paradigmatic experience of toilet choosing can occur only when the child considers the caregiver to be a stable ally and proponent of the child's regulatory-interpersonal agent-self. In this case, the child will experience the caregiver's suggestion of the toilet as a new source of interpersonal motive gratification. In psychopathology, however, the child often experiences the caregiver as a depriver and a foe of the child's need to experience effective interpersonal agency; therefore, the mere suggestion that the child pursue a new constitutive-interpersonal behavior may cause the child to respond as though s/he were being threatened. This response may take the form of rebellion, rigid compliance, or "accidental" wetting and soiling.

The Developmental Split in This Stage

The developmental split begins in the regulatory-intrapsychic self stage and undergoes an evolution that corresponds to the child's increasing capacity to mourn developmental loss. Each stage brings a greater capacity for stable veridical intrapsychic and interpersonal motive gratification. The developmental split refers to the phenomenon that, in a paradigmatic developmental process, the child simultaneously experiences both transference and nontransference forms of agent-self, each of which forms the basis for a categorically distinct subjective experience of personal existence. By definition, the structure of illusional intrapsychic mutuality has hegemony over the inner well-being associated with transference agent-self experience. However, in a context of veridical caregiving, the transference intrapsychic and interpersonal agent-selves will not have any motive (need) for pain.

After the regulatory-intrapsychic self stage, development becomes a process of undoing (destructuralizing) the developmental split until the child develops a unitary, nondissociated, and nontransference subjective experience of personal existence. This is achieved through an epigenetic but categorically distinct series of mourning experiences, each of which produces an increasing structuralization of the capacity for stable inner well-being.

The regulatory-interpersonal self stage provides the context for the destructuralization of the developmental merger in the child's mind between the child's and the caregivers' interpersonal personal motives. Since the child's all-powerful agent-self has the illusion of having regulatory control over the caregivers' personal motives, on the transference side of the developmental split, the child cannot distinguish between her/his own and another's motives. Because the child has had the empirical experience of exerting hegemony over the caregivers' intrapsychic caregiving ideals, initially the child does not recognize that her/his agent-self capacity for regulatory control over personal motives refers only to her/his own motives. The destructuralization of the interpersonal form of the developmental merger involves both personal and cognitive meaning structures. The interpersonal no helps the child begin to test the locus of the veridical regulatory control of interpersonal

personal and self meaning structures. The child's introspective recognition of her/his capacity for private thoughts, that is, for thought experience that becomes publicly accessible only by virtue of her/his intentional act, contributes to the destructuralization of the developmental interpersonal merger.

If the background of the *interpersonal* developmental process is formed by the caregiver's facilitative interpersonal caregiving ideals and motives, then the foreground is the developmental grief work instigated by various phase-specific types of loss experience. This developmental grief work enables the child to experience the pain of a given constitutive-interpersonal loss without experiencing a corresponding reduction in the pleasure of intrapsychic and interpersonal agency meaning. Through this process, the child's consciousness becomes less dissociated, e.g., less innately regulated and more reflective. The nurture-directed mourning of constitutive-interpersonal loss teaches the child that the optimal subjective experience of personal existence is the loss-free intrapsychic and regulatory-interpersonal pleasure generated by caregiving mutuality, which increasingly becomes the child's most sought-after experience. As a result, constitutive-interpersonal psychic pain is never associated with regulatory agent-self meaning—with the loss of inner well-being. The superior pleasure of the nontransference mourning of constitutive-interpersonal loss is termed the ***regulatory-interpersonal pleasure principle.*** In effect, the regulatory-interpersonal agent-self experiencing this nontransference regulatory-interpersonal pleasure discovers that transference pleasure always has the meaning of the loss of veridical agent-self meaning and, therefore, always represents an inferior type of regulatory-interpersonal agent-self meaning. Veridical intrapsychic and regulatory-interpersonal mourning processes are equivalent to veridical intrapsychic and interpersonal self-caretaking processes. In a nontransference regulatory-interpersonal mourning process, the loss being mourned occurs within a pain-free, mutualized context. This, of course, does not imply that an individual with a veridical regulatory-interpersonal agent-self will never be frightened by events or that constitutive-interpersonal losses are not painful. Obviously, the pain of constitutive-interpersonal loss can range from basically inconsequential (the loss of a pencil) to great (the loss of a loved one, a crippling accident). Veridical interpersonal mourning will not involve the denial of the pain of constitutive-interpersonal loss. Unlike transference grief work, it will not be worsened by denial (dissociation) or a diminution of inner well-being.

Innately directed, phase-specific developmental intrapsychic losses, such as the loss expressed as transference care-getting anxiety, cease to occur after the regulatory-intrapsychic self stage; the veridical regulatory-intrapsychic agent-self experiences no intrapsychic loss. After the regulatory-intrapsychic self stage, the nontransference, regulatory-intrapsychic agent-self generates reflections that enable the child to mourn the loss represented by the continued use of transference (nonveridical) gratification. The transference intrapsychic agent-self, of course, remains vulnerable to intrapsychic loss resulting from the inherent instability of nonveridical intrapsychic motive gratification. It cannot, by definition, mourn this loss, but rather must deny it and restitute it. To the extent that constitutive-interpersonal gratification functions as an agent-self percept for the child's nonveridical regulatory-interpersonal motive and nonveridical intrapsychic motive, constitutive-interpersonal loss affects the child's inner well-being, and the child responds to this loss with a renewed desire for the original gratification, with regression, or with the pursuit of a substitute gratification. Thus, after the end of the regulatory-intrapsychic self stage, developmental losses and grief work always refer to a process initiated by: (1) constitutive-interpersonal loss, which, in turn, causes loss to the all-powerful agent-self and the transference intrapsychic agent-self, and (2) the continued existence of transference (nonveridical) intrapsychic or regulatory-interpersonal motive gratification, which has the meaning to the veridical intrapsychic agent-self and the regulatory-interpersonal agent-self of the loss of regulatory control over inner well-being.

Developmental transference grief work does not directly promote intrapsychic and regulatory-interpersonal development, but it does promote the development of constitutive-interpersonal capacities. Given the enormous number of mistakes (e.g., falls, incorrect answers) a child makes in the process of developing mature motor, social-interpersonal, and cognitive capacities, the motive to find a restitutional solution to these losses clearly has adaptive value. Developmental transference grief work differs from pathological transference grief work in that developmental grief work does not foster destructive or obstructive types of agent-self experience. Developmental transference grief work does not interfere with the process that ultimately destructuralizes all nonveridical agent-self experience. This destructuralization results from the facilitation of the intrapsychic and regulatory-interpersonal pleasure principles through the caregiver's caregiving availability.

THE CONJUGALLY COMPETITIVE AGENT-SELF PHASE

In the second phase of the regulatory-interpersonal self stage, the child's transference constitutive-interpersonal agent-self comes to view the heterosexual caregiver as a source of personal as well as of care-getting gratification. We term this phase the **conjugally competitive agent-self phase,** both in order to avoid the bias against women implicit in the psychoanalytic terms phallic and oedipal, and also because it bears only a superficial similarity to the phallic, double dyadic, and oedipal stages posited by psychoanalytic theory. In this phase, the child's transference constitutive-interpersonal agent-self is *competitive* because, first, it competes to win the heterosexual caregiver's conjugal favors and, subsequently, it competes for these favors against the isosexual caregiver. It is by now a truism that psychoanalysis, with its roots in Victorian culture, largely ignored the genital motives of girls and focused mainly on the genital motives of boys—hence Freud's choice of the masculine terms phallic and oedipal to refer to a phenomenon that is, in reality, equally pertinent to female development.

The conjugally competitive agent-self phase is divided into dyadic and triadic components. The dyadic subphase has dyadic and differentiated dyadic components. Although for heuristic purposes we will discuss the dyadic and differentiated dyadic components as if they were distinct, in reality considerable overlap exists.

The genital category of physiological motives is crucial to the successful completion of the regulatory-interpersonal self stage. In the context of her/his private world, the child may directly gratify her/his genital motives through masturbation. In the context of the family setting, however, the child's genital motives take a diffuse form we term *conjugal* motives. The child wishes to have the same relationship with the heterosexual caregiver as s/he perceives the isosexual caregiver to have. The child has a very nonspecific idea of this relationship, which incorporates elements of possessiveness, romance, nonspecific libidinal gratification, and, in the triadic phase, exclusivity. Adultomorphic interpretations of the child's behavior in this phase often lead to the misunderstanding of the child's behavior as being seductive in a fully genital, adult sense. Extreme forms of this misunderstanding result in the rationalization used by child abusers that the child actually wanted to have sexual intercourse with an adult.

We term the constitutive-interpersonal agent-self whose focus is conjugal gratification the ***conjugally competitive agent-self***. Between the ages of three and six years, the child's conjugal motives episodically exert hegemony over her/his cognitive and social-interpersonal constitutive-interpersonal motives. For example, the motive to be a successful competitor for the heterosexual caregiver can occasionally interfere with the child's pleasure and comfort as a student. The immaturity of the child's cognition reinforces the child's illusion of invincibility.

While the vicissitudes of the conjugal motives are a necessary cause of psychic structure building, these motives do not have inherent regulatory power. In contrast, psychoanalysis assumes that the axis of psychic development in early childhood consists of biologically determined, sequentially unfolding psychosexual stages organized by instinctual drive derivatives that constitute the basis of psychic reality. However, to the degree that motives associated with what psychoanalysis terms psychosexual motives, such as excretory motives, stimulate representational experiences (e.g., wishes, fantasies) which have ongoing hegemony over the child's inner well-being, development has gone awry. In fact, psychic conflicts around oral or excretory motives are products of nonveridical interpersonal and/or intrapsychic caregiving, that is, these conflicts are products of the caregivers' needs to use the child's behavior to soothe their own psychic pain (see chap. 6). As will be detailed in chapter 6, the conjugally competitive agent-self motive does not cause psychopathology. Its importance in paradigmatic development is limited to the part it plays in the destructuralization of the intrapsychic transference and the establishment of the psychic structure we term the ***relationship ideal***.

The Dyadic Conjugally Competitive Agent-Self Phase

The child's self-representation of conjugal attractiveness is inherently associated both with the wish to be recognized by the heterosexual caregiver as conjugally appealing and also with an increasing recognition of her/his own wishes that the heterosexual caregiver be a source of pleasure that gratifies the child's personal as well as care-getting motives. One byproduct of this phase is that during the times when the child's nonveridical constitutive-interpersonal agent-self focuses on regulating the caregiver's personal motives, the child's own self-caretaking functions are strengthened.

Since the child's choice of constitutive-interpersonal motives is vulnerable to the hegemony of the conjugal motive, the caregiver needs to be aware that during this phase the conjugal motive may affect any aspect of the child's experience, including experience that seems unrelated in content. For example, a child who shows an intense, seemingly irrational need to be admired for her/his ability to draw, may be displacing her/his wish to receive the kind of admiration s/he sees the isosexual caregiver receive from the heterosexual caregiver.[37]

For the first time, the child pursues the caregiver's interpersonal *personal* motives as well as her/his interpersonal *caregiving* motives. The child comes to recognize that important personal motives of the heterosexual caregiver are directed at the isosexual caregiver. The child's motive to regulate the heterosexual caregiver's conjugal motives initiates the commencement of the *dyadic* part of the conjugally competitive agent-self phase. In addition to having fantasies of being idealized for conjugal attractiveness by the heterosexual caregiver, the child begins to recognize that a mutual, special, conjugal admiration exists between the caregivers themselves. In the dyadic phase, the child's realization that s/he is not the center of the universe with regard to the heterosexual caregiver's admiration causes her/him a transference loss. The child comes to realize that the caregivers' feelings about each other are akin to the way the child illusionally experiences the heterosexual caregiver as feeling towards the child.

The dyadic phase becomes differentiated when the child realizes that the nurturing family unit consists of parallel dyadic relationships between the child and each caregiver and between the caregivers themselves. The differentiated dyadic part of the conjugally competitive agent-self phase represents an important developmental step in its own right and also leads to the triadic part of the conjugally competitive agent-self phase. The child is experiencing a psychic Copernican revolution, and the caregivers need to be exceedingly sensitive to the child's psychological vulnerability. In general, the child may exhibit a need for increased attention and, when the caregivers are involved with each other (even in seemingly mundane tasks such as housecleaning), the child may exhibit seemingly irrational bouts of crying, anger, whining, or general dysphoria. The caregivers need to realize that the child's irritability does not occur because the child is spoiled, willful, obstinate, or babyish; the child's lability results from neither abnormal development nor willfulness, but rather is a manifestation of a developmental, differentiated dyadic loss. The caregivers should communicate to the child both their understanding of the intensity of the child's feelings of loss and also their belief that the mutual involvement the caregivers have with each other can enhance rather than diminish the care-getting pleasure available to the child. The caregivers' responses facilitate the child's first reflective recognition that the intimacy of exclusivity is not inherently superior to the intimacy of shared involvement.

All developmental transference responses to loss are characterized by a restitutional form of grief work. Thus, the child's conjugally competitive agent-self mây respond to her/his losses by turning to one caregiver or the other in an attempt to form a special, even potentially collusive, relationship. The potential pitfall of the attractiveness of this alliance to the heterosexual caregiver is well-known, namely, that the child brings to this caregiver not only positive transference longings based on social-interpersonal choice, but also positive transference longings based on the child's conjugal motives toward the caregiver. The potential pitfall for the isosexual caregiver who receives the child's preferential attentions is often overlooked. If the isosexual caregiver encourages the child's attempt to avoid conjugal loss through an exclusive involvement with the isosexual caregiver, the child may have a difficult time establishing conflict-free heterosexual relationships in later life. There is, however, nothing inherently pathological about the child's intense, phase-specific focus on one or the other caregiver.

Nonveridical caregivers often have a very difficult time with the intensity of the child's feelings during this phase. Sometimes the caregiver being singled out for affection cannot tolerate the child's intense, worshipful attention and feels pressured by the child and irritated that the child will have nothing to do with the other caregiver. Such a caregiver may describe the child in this phase as "clingy," "needy," or "never leaving me alone for a second."

Paradigmatically, the caregiver being "rejected" remains available to the child because s/he knows that the child's behavior is a function of a temporary phase and has no implications for the child's true feelings for the caregiver. Caregivers who have a stable preference for veridical caregiving pleasure can accept with equanimity and understanding the child's temporary refusal to have anything to do with them; such caregivers will not react to the child's rejection with counter-rejection, such as, "I don't want to be with you either," or, "Well, then I'll take your brother/sister," nor will they force the child into interpersonal relating against her/his wishes.

Paradigmatically, in the differentiated dyadic phase, the caregivers will respond with sufficient availability, flexibility, and comfort to allow the child to continue to feel their interpersonal caregiving pleasure and involvement. In paradigmatic development, the child will have a dual response to the transference, differentiated dyadic loss that s/he is not the center of the heterosexual caregiver's universe: on the nontransference side of the developmental split, the child will turn to both caregivers for care-getting pleasure, and, on the transference side of the developmental split, the child will continue to pursue her/his conjugal aims. In a pathological form of transference grief work, the child may make a fixated, collusive alliance with one caregiver, or even with a sibling, another family member, or an outsider; s/he may significantly inhibit her/his conjugal motive in an attempt to resolve the loss through regression; or s/he may assign exaggerated importance to her/his conjugal motive in an attempt to deny the transference regulatory-interpersonal loss (which is nonconjugal) through fantasies of irresistible conjugal potency.

The Triadic Conjugally Competitive Agent-Self Phase

The triadic form of the conjugally competitive agent-self motive occurs because the all-powerful agent-self cannot mourn the loss that accompanies its inability to regulate and cause the gratification that the dyadic conjugally competitive agent-self passionately seeks. The transference-regulated, conjugally competitive agent-self, therefore, concludes that the reason for the loss is the isosexual caregiver's interference with the heterosexual caregiver's gratification of the conjugally competitive agent-self's conjugal wish. Thus, in its restitutional response to differentiated dyadic loss, the conjugally competitive agent-self superimposes the added need for exclusiveness, invidious comparisons, and competition on the dyadic relationship. In the triadic phase, the two aims most intensely pursued by the child's conjugally competitive agent-self are the gratification of the child's conjugal motive by the heterosexual caregiver and the heterosexual caregiver's rejection of the isosexual caregiver as a conjugal partner. The triadic conjugally competitive agent-self motive, therefore, inherently includes the wish for a conjugal pleasure that is accompanied by anger.

On the transference side of the developmental split at the beginning of the triadic phase, the all-powerful agent-self still smarts from the hurt of the differentiated dyadic loss and determines to resolve this loss by besting the isosexual caregiver. It pursues this aim because it still believes in its illusion of hegemonic regulatory control over the caregivers' personal motives and, therefore, over its ability to gratify the conjugally competitive agent-self motive.

At the beginning of the triadic phase, the conjugally competitive agent-self motive remains the source of the child's most appealing non-veridical agent-self percepts. This dominance results from the visceral attraction of the conjugal motive and is enhanced by the transference power that still inheres in the all-powerful agent-self. Paradigmatically, however, the context of the child's transference interpersonal self-experience is nontransference interpersonal self-experience composed of: (1) the veridical regulatory-interpersonal agent-self; (2) the constitutive-interpersonal agent-self under the regulatory control of the veridical regulatory-interpersonal agent-self, which is the product of the cumulative process of mourning nonconjugal, constitutive-interpersonal loss; and (3) the interpersonal care-getting pleasure the child continues to experience with the caregivers.

Its inability to mourn the differentiated dyadic loss leads the conjugally competitive agent-self to conclude that the cause of the loss is external and contingent—namely, the isosexual caregiver. This nonveridical grief work is the basis of triadic anger. In psychoanalytic theory, the oedipal experience, by definition, remains unresolved and it always ends as an "infantile neurosis,"[38] which Freud saw as innately determined, structuralized pain that inheres in human nature. We believe that the infantile neurosis described by Freud is actually a continuation of already existing psychopathology (see chap. 6). Although a paradigmatic triadic mourning process encompasses the frustration of the child's conjugally competitive agent-self motive and the absolute deflation of the child's all-powerful agent-self's belief that it can regulate the caregivers' personal motives, the result of this paradigmatic mourning process is to strengthen the child's veridical regulatory-interpersonal agent-self and to eliminate the pain that derives from the fruitless attempt to exert regulatory control over the caregivers' constitutive-interpersonal, conjugal motives.

In paradigmatic development, the conjugally competitive agent-self's competition with the isosexual caregiver and this self's resultant anger and fears of retaliation are primarily caused not by the process of competing for the heterosexual caregiver but rather by the all-powerful agent-self's ongoing determination to regulate constitutive-interpersonal motive gratification. Because the all-powerful agent-self experiences the caregivers' personal motives as under its regulatory control, on the transference side of the developmental split the child's relationship with the caregivers is conflicted in nature (in psychopathology, this conflict has a paranoid cast). The child's all-powerful agent-self enters the triadic phase reacting to the loss of a type of constitutive-interpersonal motive gratification that cannot occur unilaterally, but requires a gratifying response from the heterosexual caregiver. The all-powerful agent-self's illusion that it has the capacity for regulatory control over the caregivers' personal motives is, of course, enhanced by the fact that the child can cause the caregiver to put aside personal motives in the service of intrapsychic and interpersonal caregiving motives.

The triadic conjugally competitive agent-self phase results from both nature and nurture. The child's all-powerful agent-self responds to the differentiated dyadic loss experienced by the conjugally competitive agent-self with an *innately determined,* restitutional grief work that leads to the triadic form of conjugally competitive experience. The triadic phase proves developmentally heuristic, however, because the child's transference losses occur in the context of the caregivers' ongoing interpersonal caregiving and the child's veridical intrapsychic and veridical regulatory-interpersonal agent-self experience.

The triadic phase is entirely different from the oedipal stage described in psychoanalytic theory. For example, whereas psychoanalytic theory asserts that the child reacts to the oedipal experience with oedipal rage and castration anxiety, we believe that these reactions do not describe paradigmatic development because they connote a degree of alienation and fear that can only result from intrapsychic isolation based on an obstructive rather than a developmental transference process (see chap. 6). In other words, while conjugally competitive agent-self anger inevitably occurs in paradigmatic development, the type of hatred described in psychoanalytic theory is psychopathological. Whereas psychoanalytic theory places the origin of the oedipal motive in the instinctual drives (nonagency reality), we understand the triadic conjugally competitive agent-self as a nonveridical meaning structure that is caused by a nonveridical type of agency reality. Further, though triadic loss constitutes a critical component of paradigmatic development, it does not, as psychoanalytic theory posits, play a central role in psychopathogenesis, because intrapsychic psychopathology is set in place in the pre-eidetic stage. Since there is no developmental split (no nontransference agent-self experience) in untreated psychopathology, a triadic conjugally competitive agent-self experience occurs only on a fantasy level and does not have regulatory agency meaning.

Loss and Mourning in the Triadic Phase

There are numerous *transference* losses in the triadic part of the conjugally competitive agent-self phase. On the constitutive-interpersonal level, the conjugally competitive agent-self experiences both the loss of not getting the conjugal preference sought from the heterosexual caregiver and also the loss that it cannot bring about the heterosexual caregiver's rejection of the isosexual caregiver as a conjugal partner. While the conjugally competitive agent-self experiences dysphoria, only in psychopathology does the child experience the misery portrayed in psychoanalytic descriptions both of castration anxiety and of the child's generalized alienation from the caregivers.

Triadic transference losses are associated either with the heterosexual caregiver or the isosexual caregiver, and are manifested as ***triadic rejection anxiety*** and ***retaliation anxiety,*** respectively. Triadic rejection anxiety involves both the transference loss entailed by the heterosexual caregiver's denial of conjugal gratification and also the transference loss that the isosexual caregiver acquires the conjugal gratification denied to the child. We use the term *retaliation anxiety* rather than the psychoanalytic term *castration anxiety* both to emphasize that girls have the same fears about the isosexual caregiver as do boys and also because the child's fantasies about the nature of the isosexual caregiver's anger at the child for the child's conjugal motives toward the heterosexual caregiver tend to be more diffuse than the term castration anxiety implies.[39] Retaliation anxiety stems from the anger directed at the isosexual caregiver by the child's conjugally competitive agent-self, which needs to feel superior to the isosexual caregiver. Projected anger due to the frustration of this need traps the conjugally competitive agent-self in the conviction that the isosexual caregiver owns a retaliatory motive toward the child. On the transference side of the developmental split, the gratifying reflection of effective agency being pursued by the conjugally competitive agent-self entails meanings of invidious comparison, the need for exclusivity, and emotions of jealousy and envy, which lead to an inescapable drivenness for a winner-take-all type of competition and set the child up for inevitable loss.

The psychic pain produced by retaliation anxiety does not result, as psychoanalytic theory suggests, from a phylogenetically based, species-specific fear of punitive genital mutilation, but rather from a combination of the conjugally competitive agent-self's transference-based fantasies and the all-powerful agent-self's inability to mourn loss. Unlike triadic rejection anxiety, which is based on the child's awareness of the heterosexual caregiver's refusal to gratify the child's conjugal motives, the loss signified by retaliation anxiety occurs exclusively on a fantasy level. The *veridical* regulatory-interpersonal agent-self, however, is not directly affected by retaliation anxiety, because the constitutive-interpersonal motives under its control are not linked to transference motives for conjugal gratification within the family setting. The child's veridical constitutive-interpersonal agent-self never loses the pleasure of care-getting involvement with the caregivers, even when the caregivers frustrate transference-dominated, conjugally competitive agent-self motives. The ongoing, stable, unconflicted quality of the relationship between the child's veridical constitutive-interpersonal agent-self and the caregivers most significantly distinguishes a paradigmatic from a psychopathological triadic phase.

An example of retaliation anxiety in the paradigmatic context of a developmental split is as follows. A girl of three, who had just had an outing alone with her father in the country and who had never previously reported a nightmare, woke one morning and told her mother that she had had a "bad dream." She said she had dreamt that she was walking in a field when suddenly a big, scary, grimacing cat head, like the Cheshire Cat in *Alice in Wonderland*, floated up above the horizon and started heading toward her. She was very frightened, until, as the cat loomed overhead, it suddenly deflated and the child realized it had only been a balloon.

Within the dream, the transference-based isolation from and fear of the isosexual caregiver represented by the scary cat face was a loss to the child's veridical interpersonal agent-self, which responded by *deflating* the projected anger to allow the child once again to feel close to the mother. The mourning work that was begun in the dream was solidified when the child told her mother the dream and the mother helped the child to understand both that the pain in the dream was a reaction to the fun the child had had with the father the previous day and also that the mother was not only not threatened, but was actually happy about the child's pleasure with the father. The mother's caregiving response strengthened the child's nontransference perception that the mother was understanding of rather than angry at the child's transference, conjugally competitive agent-self wishes.

Psychopathological retaliation anxiety is illustrated by the actions of a five-year-old girl whose fears of the mother's retaliation were stimulated when she discovered that she had a loose tooth. In spite of the fact that this child had friends and older sisters and brothers who had recently lost teeth, she became quite determined that the tooth was not going to come out. She refused to chew on the side where the loose tooth was or to eat any hard food, and she maintained that, by taking these precautions, she could prevent the tooth from coming out. The child accused her mother of trying to feed her food that would dislodge the tooth. The child's anxious preoccupations with the tooth continued until it fell out a month later, at which time the child became upset for an entire day.

In paradigmatic development as the triadic phase progresses, the child comes to mourn the all-powerful agent-self pain that results from the irrevocable rupture of the illusion that was the basis of the all-powerful agent-self's sense of indomitable inner well-being, namely, the illusion of having regulatory control over the caregivers' personal motives as well as over their interpersonal caregiving motives. The mourning process takes place in spite of the context of alienation from the caregivers that exists on the transference side of the developmental split. As will be seen shortly, this process leads to the unique identification we term the *relationship ideal* and to the child's structuralized capacity to distinguish boundaries between cranially separate regulatory-interpersonal centers of regulatory agency reality.

The agent-selves associated with veridical inner well-being are the regulatory-intrapsychic agent-self, the veridical regulatory-interpersonal agent-self, and the constitutive-interpersonal agent-self under the hegemony of the veridical regulatory-interpersonal agent-self. The veridical regulatory-interpersonal agent-self has a categorically different triadic experience than does the all-powerful agent-self. As we said earlier, the veridical regulatory-interpersonal agent-self does not attempt to regulate the heterosexual caregiver's personal motives and, consequently, the constitutive-interpersonal agent-self under its regulatory control experiences no triadic loss and, therefore, neither triadic rejection anxiety, nor triadic anger, nor retaliation anxiety. The veridical regulatory-interpersonal agent-self's function in the triadic phase is to mourn the loss of regulatory control represented by the transference-based well-being of the all-powerful agent-self and the conjugally competitive agent-self. The veridical regulatory-interpersonal agent-self also furthers the child's sustaining and confirming relationship with both caregivers, whose interpersonal caregiving motives are stably available to the child. Thus, the veridical regulatory-interpersonal agent-self becomes increasingly able to distinguish between the loss produced by the all-powerful agent-self's attempt to regulate the caregivers' personal motives, and the pleasure of being the agent cause of the caregivers' interpersonal caregiving.

The veridical regulatory-interpersonal agent-self experiences no fundamental loss during the triadic phase. This loss-free experience occurs because the veridical regulatory-interpersonal agent-self receives ongoing reflections of effective agency both from the mutual intracranial pleasure it gets from the stable well-being possessed by the regulatory-intrapsychic agent-self, and also, indirectly, from its recognition that it has the stable capacity to engage the caregivers' interpersonal caregiving. The only loss to the veridical regulatory-interpersonal self is the existence of ongoing transference pleasure and pain that it cannot regulate.

The mourning process initiated by the veridical constitutive-interpersonal agent-self is facilitated first by the fact that this agent-self is neither angry at nor alienated from the heterosexual caregiver and, second, by the veridical constitutive-interpersonal agent-self's dual experience of the isosexual caregiver. This dual experience involves, on the one hand, the loss caused by the dissociated state represented by retaliation anxiety and, on the other hand, respect and admiration for the isosexual caregiver's capacity to be an attractive conjugal partner to the heterosexual caregiver. The veridical constitutive-interpersonal agent-self comes to value the privacy of the caregivers' conjugal intimacy and the durability of their commitment. Therefore, the crucial dimension of triadic loss is not the child's loss of the fantasied pleasure of conjugal gratification, but rather the loss caused by the all-powerful agent-self's inability to regulate the gratification of constitutive-interpersonal motives via the regulation of the heterosexual caregiver's conjugal motives. In order for the all-powerful agent-self to be unable to deny or to restitute on a fantasy level its loss of the reflection of effective regulatory-interpersonal agency capacity, it must experience the caregiver's no as based on the caregiver's regulation of her/his own personal motives, in contrast to a no based solely on a sense of loyalty and commitment to the other conjugal partner.

In paradigmatic development, the child will experience absolute loss both on the level of the conjugally competitive agent-self and, most important, on the level of the all-powerful agent-self. The child's conjugally competitive agent-self cannot acquire its version of conjugal gratification. The all-powerful agent-self experiences the loss that it does not have regulatory control over the caregivers' personal motives and, therefore, that it does not have agent-self, self-regulatory control over the child's own constitutive-interpersonal motive gratification.

The absolute loss experienced by the child's conjugally competitive

163

agent-self and, in turn, by the child's all-powerful agent-self is that the heterosexual caregiver will neither gratify the child's conjugally competitive agent-self motive nor reject the isosexual caregiver as a conjugal partner. We believe that the mourning of triadic loss results not from fear of the isosexual caregiver, but rather from an ongoing, mutual, care-getting, loving relationship with both caregivers, which produces structuralization and increased reflectiveness rather than repression. An important cause of triadic resolution is the unfailing warmth the child experiences from the isosexual caregiver, which allows the child to recognize retaliation anxiety as a projection. The child is amazed that the isosexual caregiver responds with loving nurture both to the child's anger at the isosexual caregiver and also to the child's desire for what the transference part of the child views as the isosexual caregiver's "property." In contrast, psychoanalytic theory posits that castration anxiety is the primary causal factor in the ego's renunciation of the instinctual, drive-derivative-based, oedipal wish.

Despite such positive experiences, the paradigmatic conjugally competitive agent-self can experience a negative, passionate intensity. This intensity mainly results from the fact that conjugally competitive agent-self anger is produced on the transference side of the developmental split, which means that it is produced in isolation from the caregivers' actual motives and represents a singleminded focus on winning. As a result, the child's phase-specific dissociation can allow her/him not only to feel intense anger at the isosexual caregiver but also to assume that the isosexual caregiver naturally returns this anger.

In summary, the child incurs several types of *transference* interpersonal losses as a result of the unavoidable, absolute loss of gratification of the triadic form of the conjugally competitive agent-self motive. Examples are: (1) the frustration of the conjugally competitive agent-self's wish for the inappropriate and exclusive gratification of the child's conjugally competitive agent-self motive by the heterosexual caregiver; (2) the loss resulting from the heterosexual caregiver's preference for the isosexual caregiver as a conjugal partner, which, on a transference basis, is experienced by the child's conjugally competitive agent-self as occurring at the expense of the choice of the child as conjugal partner; (3) the all-powerful agent-self's lack of regulatory control over the heterosexual caregiver's personal motives; and, finally, (4) the loss that arises from the frustration of the conjugally competitive agent-self's wish to be conjugally more attractive than the isosexual caregiver. This last loss entails a further loss based on the fantasy that the isosexual caregiver has retaliatory motives toward the child.

If the heterosexual caregiver does not help the child recognize that the primary cause of the child's triadic loss resides in the heterosexual caregiver's personal as well as caregiving motives, then, to the extent that the child does recognize triadic loss, her/his focus will likely be on differences in body size or sexual organ size and on paranoid feelings of exclusion and victimization. In this case, the biological component of the triadic loss will assume the burden of efficient causality. The child's pathological denial will be facilitated by the fact that inherent in the triadic wish is the conjugally competitive agent-self's delusional representation of an all-powerful body image, which more than counterbalances the undeniable differences in physical size and power between the child and the isosexual caregiver. Paradigmatically, the child reflectively faces the inescapable fact that her/his triadically organized, intensely experienced conjugal wish will never be gratified. The heterosexual caregiver's rejection of the child's triadic conjugally competitive agent-self motive triggers the pain of triadic rejection anxiety, which in turn precipitates triadic mourning. It should be emphasized, however, that the triadic loss concludes a cycle of intense caregiving.

When the losses inherent in triadic relationship experience are not mourned, in effect they become a rage-based and pain-based model for future relationship experiences. For example, the outlook that winning is everything, winner takes all, and might makes right creates a model of relationship experience that uses others for transference gratification. In this model of relationship experience, the individual cannot embrace an ideal of the other owning her/his own motives.

The child cannot mourn her/his triadic loss unless s/he can reflectively recognize and continue to feel good about her/his conjugal motive and potential capacity for satisfying conjugal relating. This ability is fostered by a developmental atmosphere that encourages the child to regulate her/his own mind and not to choose and pursue constitutive-interpersonal motives that are primarily in the service of isolation from the caregivers and of pain soothing. If the child's all-powerful agent-self chooses motives in the service of anger, the caregivers will respond with availability. The rejection of the child's triadic motive does not represent a rejection of the child's future potential to be a conjugal partner to a heterosexual peer but, rather, represents the rejection of the child's unrealistic belief in the possibility that her/his triadic conjugally competitive agent-self wish will now or ever be gratified by the heterosexual caregiver. The caregiver must convey the absoluteness of her/his personal choice not to gratify the child's triadic wish while, at the same time, s/he makes clear to the child that the wish to be a mature and functional partner in a conjugal relationship will one day be gratified.

Triadic mourning involves the child's perception of (1) the loss of actual conjugal gratification, (2) the child's transference-based alienation from the isosexual caregiver caused by triadic anger, and (3) the internal dissonance between the child's transference and nontransference selves. Triadic mourning occurs because the phase-appropriately functional regulatory-interpersonal pleasure principle allows the child to experience transference pleasure as a relative loss of the superior pleasure to be found in an atmosphere of anger-free mutuality. The child deliberately and reflectively chooses the social-interpersonal motive embedded in the intimacy of the caregiving relationship with the caregivers, which the veridical regulatory-interpersonal agent-self pursues, over the triadic conjugally competitive agent-self motive, which the all-powerful agent-self pursues. In other words, in paradigmatic development the child resolves the triadic conflict through the reflective choice of pleasure and an accompanying decrease in dissociation, rather than through an involuntary reaction to pain and an increase in dissociation (repression).

Additionally, the child becomes able to distinguish between the regulatory control of caregiving motives and the regulatory control of non-caregiving (personal) motives. In other words, s/he comes to recognize the parameters that distinguish conjugal versus caregiving relationship commitments. Therefore, the child comes to understand the true scope of her/his interpersonal regulatory control and also comes to appreciate that the heterosexual caregiver's commitment to the conjugal relationship is an important part of the caregiver's caregiving because good caregiving precludes the gratification of the wishes of the child's conjugally competitive agent-self. The child realizes that gaining regulatory control over the triadic conjugally competitive agent-self motive and relinquishing the gratification of the triadic wish cultivates a sense of security that is exemplified by the regulatory-interpersonal agent-self stability demonstrated by both caregivers. This capacity to appreciate the separateness and stability of the caregivers' regulatory-interpersonal agent-selves becomes the basis for the crucial identification we term the relationship ideal. Above all, the child's veridical constitutive-interpersonal agent-self feels an increased sense of well-being based on both the capacity to accept itself as it is at this point in development and also on the sense of a potential capacity for heterosexual relating to be striven for, pursued, and achieved.

Triadic mourning differs from differentiated dyadic grieving both because it intrinsically includes competition with the isosexual caregiver for the heterosexual caregiver and also because the transference losses are absolute in nature. From a developmental standpoint, it is crucial that the child conclude that the cause of her/his triadic loss is the heterosexual caregiver's personal motives to gratify her/his own conjugal motives as well as the heterosexual caregiver's caregiving motives. The child's ability to experience triadic loss as grounded in the personal, noncaregiving motives of the heterosexual caregiver rests on two types of perceptions. The child must recognize that the cause of the triadic loss is more than and, therefore, other than her/his own immaturity. The child must also be enabled to make a subtle but, nonetheless, definite perception that the triadic loss results from the caregiver's active personal motives rather than from a technical commitment the caregiver has made to her/his conjugal partner.

In paradigmatic development, conjugally competitive agent-self loss is not fundamentally the product of the child's physiological immaturity, but occurs when the child has to acknowledge the love relationship between the caregivers and their commitment to their own personal, noncaregiving motives as well as to their caregiving motives. The child will reflectively experience the loss to her/his all-powerful agent-self produced by each caregiver's regulatory-interpersonal agent-self capacity to regulate her/his own constitutive-interpersonal motives, both caregiving and noncaregiving. In psychopathology, however, the child may persevere indefinitely in intense forms of conjugally competitive behavior or may hide all overt competitive feelings.

Because of the child's veridical constitutive-interpersonal agent-self's stable, nurture-based confidence in its unshakable care-getting alliance with the heterosexual caregiver (which revolves around its capacity to be the agent cause of the caregiver's interpersonal caregiving), the child's veridical constitutive-interpersonal agent-self experiences the caregiver's no to the child's conjugally competitive agent-self motive as an act of loving caregiving aimed at sparing the child further transference-based pain. Thus, the caregiver's no is a form of nurture. It facilitates the child's recognition that the triadic aspect of her/his conjugally competitive experience rests on anger and represents a motive to interfere with the intimacy of the caregivers' conjugal relationship in the service of the motive to use conjugal intimacy for transference restitution of the differentiated dyadic loss.

The developmental process in the regulatory-interpersonal self stage causes the destructuralization of the intrapsychic transference. Conjugally competitive agent-self loss gives the child the opportunity for a reflectively conscious recognition of a constitutive-interpersonal loss that is perceived as unavoidable and absolute in that, even by the wildest stretch of the child's imagination, no restitutional or substitutional avoidance of the loss seems possible.

The triadic phase facilitates the developmental process that ends in the posttransference stage of development, when the individual experiences the caregivers as friends and can have interpersonal relationships that are appropriate and mutual rather than manipulative and/or conflicted. A nontransference experience of her/his conjugal motives helps the child realize that the conflict between the caregiver's personal motives and the child's personal motives does not entail a loss for the child, because the caregiver's personal motives do not fundamentally conflict with the caregiver's caregiving ideals. The child comes to recognize the difference between (1) having the veridical regulatory-interpersonal agency capacity to cause the caregiver's interpersonal caregiving and (2) lacking regulatory control over the caregiver's personal (e.g., conjugal) motives. Consequently, the child's nontransference experience of her/his conjugal motives provides a sufficient basis for the structuralization of the capacity to recognize distinct (self and other) centers of regulatory-interpersonal agency, which leads to the capacity for nontransference interpersonal intimacy.

As we described earlier, Intrapsychic Humanism's construct of transference does not refer to the oedipal transference form of relationship posited by psychoanalytic theory. The construct of transference in psychoanalytic theory is grounded in an innate relationship structure produced by a Lamarckian inheritance from a primal horde stage of human culture. In its clinical application, therefore, the psychoanalytic construct of transference is understood both as inevitable and also as stemming from an essentially inaccessible part of the mind. In our view, the transference structure of which the triadic relationship is a manifestation is ultimately a product of the nonveridical gratification process inherent in illusional intrapsychic mutuality and internalized in the transference intrapsychic self and caregiver structure. Paradigmatically, transference is an innately based phenomenon that becomes destructuralized through nurture.

Conjugally competitive agent-self loss is a sine qua non for paradigmatic development. It is the only psychic pain that can stimulate a mourning process that will destructuralize both the intrapsychic form of the developmental transference and also the developmental merger between the child's interpersonal consciousness and the caregivers' interpersonal consciousness. This mourning process enables the child to see as illusional and, therefore, as representing loss, the all-powerful agent-self's conviction of its capacity to regulate the caregivers' personal motives.

The loss to the all-powerful agent-self caused by the loss to the conjugally competitive agent-self is the only absolute all-powerful agent-self loss the child will ever reflectively know. The loss of this gratifying, nonveridical agent-self percept for the nonveridical regulatory-interpersonal motive (and, in turn, for the nonveridical constitutive-intrapsychic motive) causes the destructuralization of the transference intrapsychic self and caregiver structure.

The Relationship Ideal

The relationship ideal is the only constitutive-interpersonal *identification* that (1) is a personal meaning structure, (2) has hegemony over the veridical regulatory-interpersonal agent-self, (3) results from a triadic, rather than a dyadic form of relationship, and (4) occurs by means of structuralization rather than by internalization.[40]

Triadic conjugally competitive agent-self mourning makes the child's consciousness less dissociated and more flexibly available. The child's conjugal motives ultimately make the child aware of the breadth of relationship experiences within the nuclear family. As a result, certain of the caregivers' ideals, which have momentous significance for the child's future, become apparent and appealing to the child. These are ideals both of the pleasure of the dyadic intimacy of the caregivers' conjugal relationship and also of the pleasure of the caregiving intimacy of the caregivers' mutuality with the child. The identification process that produces the relationship ideal constitutes part of the mourning of the triadic form of conjugally competitive agent-self loss. The relationship ideal results from a process in which the caregivers' caregiving and personal ideals shape the child's nontransference constitutive-interpersonal motive for relationship pleasure. The mourning process occurs incrementally, through a progressive decrease in developmental dissociation.

The only *interpersonal* identifications that have veridical regulatory capability in relation to psychic reality are the veridical regulatory-interpersonal agent-self, which occurs on the level of regulatory-interpersonal consciousness per se, and the relationship ideal. These two identifications are categorically dissimilar in that the veridical regulatory-interpersonal agent-self receives its agent-self reflections from an intracranial structure (the regulatory-intrapsychic agent-self), whereas the relationship ideal results from identification with the extracranial caregivers.

The relationship ideal is composed both of a phase-appropriately actualized, posttriadic form of ideal personhood and also of to-be-actualized ideals (motives) for postdevelopmental, ideal self-experience. These ideals concern paradigmatic regulatory capacities for intimacy and commitment in romantic relationships, friendships, and caregiving types of interpersonal relationships. The relationship ideal emerges from the child's opportunity to experience the various types of intimacy involved in a conjugal relationship in which the child, though intrinsically involved, does not actually participate. In treatment, a patient may experience the same quality of *intrapsychic* caregiving as a child with a paradigmatic childhood experience, but the patient will have only an indirect understanding of the ideals and motives that regulate a paradigmatic parental conjugal relationship.

The relationship ideal fosters a self-caretaking capacity whose ideal is shaped by the caregiver's specific relationship ideals and capacities. The relationship ideal directly results from the child's nontransference, self-reflective acceptance of the caregiver's rejection of the child's attempt to gratify her/his conjugally competitive agent-self motives in the family setting. In the process of reflectively assenting to the caregiver's frustration of her/his constitutive-interpersonal motive, the child recognizes that the caregivers' caregiving and personal motives represent an ideal subjective experience of personal existence. The relationship ideal consists of nontransference triadic identifications made with caregivers who offer a rage-free, genuine, manifest, affectionate love and nurture in the face of being the object of the child's anger and ungratifiable demands. As a result of their caregiving ideals regarding the child and also of the ideals that inform their commitment to the conjugal relationship, the caregivers give the child an enduring self-idealization that transcends the pleasure of the child's transference-driven need for conjugal gratification. One important characteristic of the relationship ideal is that, because it originates in extracranial agency reality, it includes meaning structures that involve the intimacy of a veridical mutuality that occurs not only within paradigmatic caregiving relationships but also within personal, noncaregiving, social relationships.

The relationship ideal joins the regulatory-intrapsychic agent-self as a source of veridical, gratifying percepts for the veridical regulatory-interpersonal agent-self motive. The relationship ideal offers the regulatory-interpersonal agent-self constitutive and regulatory reflections. The constitutive reflections consist of specific ideals of relating, whereas the regulatory reflections promote the loss-free regulation of constitutive-interpersonal agent-self experience.[41] The constitutive reflections originating in the relationship ideal represent the third component (in addition to the regulatory-intrapsychic agent-self and the veridical regulatory-interpersonal agent-self) of an integrating, unifying set of personal meaning structures. These form the basis for a continuous experience of personhood that retains the characteristic of unchanging sameness even in the face of the entropic flux that affects both the individual's nonregulatory agency reality and also the individual's non-agency reality. The constitutive reflections from the relationship ideal are paradigmatic past, present, and future forms of agent-self experience (ways of being, personhood), that is, they are persisting identities to be pursued and cherished.

Veridical regulatory control over both intrapsychic and interpersonal personal meaning occurs only as a result of paradigmatic development or Intrapsychic Treatment. The domain of the regulatory control exerted by the relationship ideal is the constitutive level of interpersonal consciousness. Like all constitutive-interpersonal experience, the relationship ideal is itself ultimately regulated by the regulatory-intrapsychic agent-self. Because it provides a type of regulatory control over desire, the relationship ideal has a regulatory relationship with the veridical regulatory-interpersonal agent-self.

The problem of regulating desire presents the most important challenge to the individual and to the species. Previous solutions have consisted of forms of self-directed or other-directed rage that range along a continuum with extreme abnegation at one end,[42] and essentially unregulated, impulsive, self-indulgence at the other end.[43] We suggest that only the superior pleasure provided by veridical regulatory agency can stably and autonomously regulate other forms of desire.

In contemporary, nonreligious, nonbehavioristic approaches to the problem of regulating desire, Freud's notion of the superego provides a dramatic example of the view that espouses rage as the most effective source of regulatory control. Freud posited a phylogenetic, genic basis for the regulating use of rage, namely, the ego's capacity for instinctual renunciation and the superego's regulatory control of the ego. He also saw parental displeasure as the primary cause of the formation of ego and superego functions that pertain to the capacity for the regulatory control of desire. Specifically, Freud posited two explicit effects of parental anger with the child that were intrinsic to the child's acquisition of regulatory control functions: love-loss anxiety and castration anxiety.

In contrast, the relationship ideal makes possible a rage-free, pleasurable regulatory control of desire. The motives that compose the relationship ideal are themselves under the hegemony of the regulatory-interpersonal and intrapsychic pleasure principles. The regulatory reflections from the relationship ideal, drawn from paradigmatic interpersonal agent-self ideals, are identifications that originate in the caregivers' veridical caregiving and personal ideals and, therefore, crucially determine the ultimate balance between the individual's caregiving and personal motives.

The regulatory control exerted by the relationship ideal over the social-interpersonal agent-self is a primary cause of the individual's capacity to respond to the most unique, absolute, and unwanted loss in personal existence, namely, the loss caused by the hegemony of positive entropy over nonagency reality. Death is the most compelling manifestation of this loss. In the context of the relationship between the regulatory-interpersonal agent-self and the regulatory-intrapsychic agent-self, the relationship ideal allows the individual to recognize the loss of interpersonal personal identity signified by the inevitability of nonexistence while still maintaining an ongoing, stable intrapsychic and regulatory-interpersonal form of personal identity. This self-regulatory stability enables the individual to respond to death with a mourning process that is regulated by the individual's veridical agent-self experience, that is, without a loss of inner well-being.[44]

In psychoanalytic theory, regulatory control of desire is always incomplete and occurs by means of oedipal identifications, which result from failed desire (pain) and fantasied revenge (fear). In our view, oedipal identifications occur only in psychopathology. They are produced by a psychopathological transference process and represent a psychopathological type of grief work. We assert that Freud's definition of identification as the response to object loss refers only to psychopathological identifications and, further, that all of the identifications described by Freud are produced by restitutional, psychopathological grief work. Freud never envisioned the possibility of a pain-free and rage-free subjective experience of personal existence. Only a pain-free and rage-free introspective reflective experience, however, enables an individual to develop identifications that result from the veridical pleasure of caregiving mutuality rather than from loss.

The fact that the conjugally competitive agent-self occurs before the child acquires the capacity for symbolic thought associated with concrete operational thinking (which occurs between the ages of seven and eleven) adds to the unique and powerful meaning of the triadic experience.[45] The preoperational level of the child's thinking facilitates the child's capacity to experience triadic loss with a dimension of absoluteness necessary to effect an optimal triadic mourning process. Preoperational thinking helps the child to have the experience of pursuing her/his conjugally competitive agent-self motives with the sense that the competition is real and that the stakes are high.

Consequences of Triadic Mourning

A paradigmatic triadic loss experience causes the destructuralization of those ideals that involve a yearning for a competitive, triadic intimacy. That is to say, paradigmatic triadic identifications produce ideals and capacities for noncaregiving as well as for caregiving relationships based on a capacity for unconflicted availability, involvement, intimacy, and mutuality. A paradigmatic triadic experience plays a critical part in the developmental process, because it endows the child with a phase-appropriate capacity to mourn constitutive-interpersonal loss, that is, to divorce it from illusional agent-self meaning and to experience it within the context of the ongoing inner well-being ultimately provided by the regulatory-intrapsychic agent-self. One of the most critical types of constitutive-interpersonal loss that an individual must be able to mourn is the loss produced by the fact that significant others have constitutive-interpersonal motives that the individual cannot regulate. In psychopathology, this loss cannot be mourned, which accounts for the existence of relationships characterized by ongoing friction over habits that one person tries, without success, to regulate, such as ongoing strife with a spouse over whether the spouse will pick up after her/himself.

The net effects of a successful triadic mourning process include: (1) the child's capacity, on other than a strictly cognitive basis, to distinguish boundaries between her/his regulatory-interpersonal motives and another's regulatory-interpersonal motives; (2) the relationship ideal; (3) the phase-appropriate completion of the nontransference system of loss-free, autonomous intrapsychic and interpersonal well-being; and (4) the capacity to mourn constitutive-interpersonal loss.

In its completed form, paradigmatic regulatory agency reality consists of: (1) the structuralized, veridical, regulatory-intrapsychic agent-self; (2) the structuralized, veridical regulatory-interpersonal agent-self; and (3) the relationship ideal. The regulatory-intrapsychic and regulatory-interpersonal agent-selves are in a direct, mutual caregiving relationship with each other.

This completed structuralization of intrapsychic and interpersonal consciousness makes it possible for nontransference intrapsychic and interpersonal pleasure to gain hegemony over the remnants of the intrapsychic transference. With the onset of the relationship ideal, the all-powerful agent-self (which gained hegemony over transference functions within the intrapsychic transference self and caregiver structure at the beginning of the regulatory-interpersonal self stage) is now destructuralized with regard to its capacity to serve as a hegemonic source of gratification of the intrapsychic motive. The all-powerful agent-self loses its power as a gratifying, nonveridical intrapsychic percept once it becomes decisively clear to the child that the all-powerful agent-self cannot exert regulatory control over the caregiver's personal motives and that the all-powerful agent-self cannot regulate constitutive-interpersonal motive gratification, which is the source of its well-being. As a result, the child's developmental dissociation is increasingly dispelled and the inferiority of nonveridical intrapsychic motive gratification produced by all-powerful agent-self gratification becomes patent. Accordingly, the eidetically internalized memory traces of the transitional intrapsychic caregiver cease to have any personal meaning significance; they have no regulatory power to serve as gratifying, agent-self percepts. This marks the end of the intrapsychic transference process.

The end of the intrapsychic transference signifies the beginning of the end of the interpersonal transference, which does not become completely destructuralized until the end of the next stage, the constitutive-interpersonal self stage. During this next stage, the interpersonal transference becomes progressively less functional because the destructuralization of the intrapsychic transference leaves the all-powerful agent-self motive without any nonveridical agent-self percepts that originate in intrapsychic consciousness. Accordingly, constitutive-interpersonal motive gratification becomes the sole source of nonveridical regulatory-interpersonal agent-self meaning. Due to the proximal effects of the child's immaturity, others' personal motives, social and cultural restrictions, positive entropy, and chance, however, constitutive-interpersonal motive gratification remains very unstable. Therefore, without transference intrapsychic motive gratification to augment constitutive-interpersonal motive gratification as a source of illusional agent-self percepts for the interpersonal transference, nonveridical regulatory-interpersonal motive gratification becomes increasingly unreliable. In addition, the all-powerful agent-self has been structurally weakened due to the triadic loss it sustained and the fact that conjugal constitutive-interpersonal motives now function under the hegemony of the regulatory-interpersonal agent-self and the relationship ideal.

The capacity to mourn constitutive-interpersonal loss, that is, to experience it in the context of ongoing inner well-being, gives the child the capacity for stable veridical regulatory agency experience. An insight into the power of this nontransference process can be gained when one contrasts it to transference existence, in which constitutive-interpersonal loss always entails the loss of both intrapsychic and regulatory-interpersonal motive gratification. Thus, interpersonal performance and success are conditions of transference self-esteem. The ability to mourn constitutive-interpersonal loss gives the child the capacity to feel bad about a constitutive-interpersonal loss without experiencing the loss of effective agency pleasure.

5
The Constitutive-Interpersonal Self Stage

The constitutive-interpersonal self stage extends from the end of the regulatory-interpersonal self stage, at about age six,[1] to the close of adolescence, which, in the United States at least, occurs sometime in the third decade of life. Although this is the shortest chapter, we do not judge this stage to be less important than the others. On the contrary, it is important not only in its own right but also because of the prevalent misunderstandings of this stage, which result from the fact that psychopathology has been mistaken for normality. In this volume, we limit our discussion of the constitutive-interpersonal self stage to the topic of psychic structuralization; we intend to discuss other aspects of this stage in a subsequent work.

The name of this stage comes from the fact that the child's developmental task is to bring all constitutive-interpersonal motives under the hegemony of her/his veridical regulatory-interpersonal agent-self and, therefore, to free constitutive-interpersonal agent-self experience from transference use. Thus, the constitutive-interpersonal self stage is a vital component in the developmental process because it is the sufficient cause of the individual's capacity for a thoroughly nontransference, mutualized, loss-free, self-regulatory stability of inner esteem.

In this chapter, we focus predominantly on the destructuralization of the developmental split between the veridical regulatory-interpersonal agent-self and the all-powerful agent-self rather than on the emergence and maturation of specific constitutive-interpersonal motives. There are two reasons for this focus. First, to describe the vicissitudes of the process by which the veridical regulatory-interpersonal agent-self gains complete hegemony over the all-powerful agent-self is to encompass the regulation of specific constitutive-interpersonal motives. Second, constitutive-interpersonal motives are not regulating causes of psychic reality and our overriding purpose is to offer a palpable, demonstrable explanation for the capacity for self-regulatory stability with regard to the subjective experience of personal existence. In and of themselves, constitutive-interpersonal motives do not shed light on paradigmatic development. Authors who describe child development as a process of unfolding constitutive-interpersonal motives overlook regulatory agency reality. Further, in our view, the constitutive-interpersonal motives focused on in most child development texts are psychopathological. One example is the widespread notion that rebelliousness, moodiness, and a need to maintain distance from the parents are normal in adolescence. A second illustration is psychoanalytic theory's assertion that the period from prepuberty through adolescence invariably entails a regressive recapitulation of the preoedipal and oedipal psychosexual stages.

In the constitutive-interpersonal self stage, the child's regulatory-interpersonal well-being becomes completely uncoupled from constitutive-interpersonal motive gratification and, therefore, becomes invulnerable to constitutive-interpersonal loss. On the level of interpersonal consciousness, being loss free has two referents: the regulatory control of desire and the individual's response to unavoidable constitutive-interpersonal loss (loss that is not the result of a defective regulatory control of desire). We do not imply, of course, that life can ever be guaranteed to be free of losses caused by chance, positive entropy, and others' malevolence, including such disasters as the death of a close relative or friend, a chronic, debilitating disease, and being the victim of a violent crime. An individual who has completed a paradigmatic development, however, will have divorced all constitutive-interpersonal loss from nonveridical agent-self meaning and, therefore, constitutive-interpersonal loss will always occur in the context of ongoing constitutive-interpersonal, regulatory-interpersonal, and regulatory-intrapsychic agent-self well-being. Thus, the person suffering a constitutive-interpersonal loss may feel very sad about the loss, but will never feel that s/he is a bad person, will never become irrationally enraged, and will never lose the inner experience of feeling loved or of caring for her/himself.

The context for the constitutive-interpersonal self stage is that the intrapsychic transference has been destructuralized as a set of motives that can exert regulatory control over the subjective experience of personal existence. The destructuralization of the intrapsychic transference structure began in the regulatory-intrapsychic self stage with the onset of the regulatory-intrapsychic agent-self. By the end of the regulatory-interpersonal self stage, the child can perceive boundaries between her/his own regulatory-interpersonal motives and those motives that are located in extracranial agency reality. For example, the child recognizes her/his inability to regulate the caregiver's interpersonal *personal* motives even as s/he recognizes that s/he is the agent cause of the caregiver's interpersonal *caregiving* motives. Because the intrapsychic transference is necessary for an intact interpersonal transference system, the destructuralization of the intrapsychic transference at the end of the regulatory-interpersonal self stage begins the destructuralization of the *interpersonal* transference. The destructuralization of the intrapsychic transference eliminates the most stable source of gratification for the interpersonal transference, the transference intrapsychic self and caregiver structure. The all-powerful agent-self becomes entirely dependent on inherently loss-filled constitutive-interpersonal motive gratification for its reflection of agent-self as agent-self.

When the constitutive-interpersonal self stage commences, the veridical regulatory-interpersonal agent-self is structurally anchored by the regulatory-intrapsychic agent-self and the relationship ideal. On the other side of the developmental split, the transference, all-powerful agent-self is maintained by the nonveridical agent-self reflections provided by the gratification of epigenetically unfolding constitutive-interpersonal motives. Because of the regulatory control exerted by the intrapsychic and regulatory-interpersonal pleasure principles, the veridical regulatory-interpersonal agent-self increasingly gains hegemony over a weakening all-powerful agent-self.

We use the terms **middle childhood** and **adolescence** to denote the two main phases of the constitutive-interpersonal self stage. Middle childhood denotes the developmental period between the conjugally competitive agent-self phase and adolescence. In contrast to middle childhood, the psychoanalytic term for this phase, latency, emphasizes the psychosexual, instinctual drives. Middle childhood is characterized by the appearance of concrete operational thinking. Adolescence is physiologically defined by the necessary (but not sufficient) condition of gonadotropic activity. Since adolescence (as contrasted with puberty) is a psychological phenomenon, its completion can functionally be defined as the structuralization (freedom from transference use) of constitutive-interpersonal motives. Paradigmatically, adolescence ends with a specific type of nontransference, fully autonomous, self-regulatory capacity for effective agency. The acquisition of this capacity has no obvious or even predictive association with a narrow age frame.

Development in the constitutive-interpersonal self stage builds on the successful mourning of triadic conjugally competitive agent-self loss (which occurred at the end of the regulatory-interpersonal self stage and resulted in the structuralization of the relationship ideal) and, thus, of the structuralization of present and future regulatory ideals of phase-appropriate forms of interpersonal intimacy. Interpersonal intimacy is mediated by social-interpersonal motives, which regulate the gratification of social, caregiving, and physiological motives. Intrapsychic intimacy, on the other hand, involves the capacity for veridical intrapsychic self-caretaking and also for veridical intrapsychic caregiving (in the context of parenting or Intrapsychic Treatment). This new availability for nontransference relating to self and others emerges directly from the successful mourning of triadic conjugally competitive agent-self loss. Above all, on the nontransference side of the developmental split, interpersonal intimacy is not used as a source of agent-self meaning.

The constitutive-interpersonal self stage can be subdivided both in terms of the child's age and in terms of developmental goals, because age and developmental goals are correlated with the onset of many emergent constitutive-interpersonal motives. The most important of the emergent motives are the genital and the cognitive motives, both of which are mediated by social-interpersonal motives.

In keeping with the usual psychodynamic view of adolescence, we view adolescence as a relatively prolonged phase, the onset of which is biologically, culturally, and socially determined. Adolescence includes: (1) the psychological response to puberty (including the maturation of the secondary sex characteristics that precede genital maturation); (2) the appearance of the capacity for formal operational thinking; (3) the increased demands and expectations imposed by most societies; and (4) increased opportunities for the exercise of initiative and creativity. Brain tissue maturation is most commonly completed in the early post-pubertal stage. The potential for a qualitative change in the nature of cognitive thought processes coincides with the final stage of brain tissue maturation. This potential can only be realized by the child's exposure to a facilitative interpersonal nurture. Piaget termed the final stage of cognitive development, formal operational thinking. Formal operational thinking is the capacity for "decentering,"[2] which is the ability to take an objective view towards oneself (i.e., to think about thought). That is, the child employs her/his capacity for symbolic thought as an analytic mode of thinking about hypothesized as well as empirically experienced phenomena.

The literature on adolescence generally characterizes adolescent behavior as problematic, because it assumes that the adolescent's capacity for self-regulatory control undergoes an innately based regression, which, in turn, leads to turbulence and turmoil. In contrast, we assert that in paradigmatic development the adolescent experiences a phase-specific regressive regulatory control over constitutive-interpersonal motives that does not affect the adolescent's capacity to participate in the mutuality of an age-appropriate interpersonal intimacy. The developmental regression associated with a paradigmatic adolescence is manifested as a lability that leaves the adolescent vulnerable to excessive sensitivity and excessive determination. Developmental adolescent regression results both from the time-limited hegemony of the transference pleasure associated with the adolescent's somatic and cognitive maturation over veridical regulatory agency pleasure and also from society's complex response to adolescent behaviors that are phase-specific but that arouse anxiety in many adults. Adolescent regression, or the strengthening of the innately determined, transference (all-powerful agent-self) meaning attached to newly emerging constitutive-interpersonal motives, is a temporary phase in which a regressively established, rage-free but unstable hegemony of constitutive-interpersonal gratification serves as a source of transference regulatory-interpersonal self-esteem.

The veridical regulatory-interpersonal agent-self anchors interpersonal self-regulatory stability. It progressively gains regulatory control over the cognitive, social-interpersonal, and physiological categories of constitutive-interpersonal motives. The veridical regulatory-interpersonal agent-self can regulate constitutive-interpersonal motive choice and pursuit in a pain-free and loss-free manner because it does not make self-destructive or self-defeating motive choices and because constitutive-interpersonal loss does not affect the well-being derived from its mutualized, structuralized relationship with the regulatory-intrapsychic agent-self. The veridical regulatory-interpersonal agent-self's stable well-being provides an ongoing source of well-being for the veridical constitutive-interpersonal agent-self, especially at moments of constitutive-interpersonal loss.

The constitutive-interpersonal self stage can also be depicted structurally. In the regulatory-interpersonal self stage, the existence of the transference intrapsychic self and caregiver structure perpetuated the interpersonal transference. However, there is no intrapsychic transference in the constitutive-interpersonal self stage. The all-powerful agent-self is the sole remnant of a destabilized interpersonal transference structure that is increasingly destructuralized due to the fact that the veridical regulatory-interpersonal agent-self has become the locus of regulatory control of interpersonal consciousness. As a result, the individual increasingly chooses constitutive-interpersonal motives that are under the hegemony of the veridical regulatory-interpersonal agent-self, which causes the all-powerful agent-self to lose regulatory power (become destructuralized).

THE ROLE OF CAREGIVING MUTUALITY

The constitutive-interpersonal self stage occurs in the dual context of a caregiving mutuality that is both intracranial (i.e., occurs between the regulatory-intrapsychic agent-self and the veridical regulatory-interpersonal agent-self) and extracranial. The caregivers remain crucial to the child's successful development throughout the entire constitutive-interpersonal self stage, especially during prepuberty and adolescence.

Some examples of the caregivers' role in this stage are as follows. The caregivers remain available to help the child to mourn loss, especially the loss of gratification of any constitutive-interpersonal motives not under the hegemony of the veridical regulatory-interpersonal agent-self. An example is when the caregivers help the adolescent to separate constitutive-interpersonal loss from regulatory-interpersonal loss when the adolescent's first meaningful romantic involvement ends abruptly. The caregivers remain available to help the child's veridical regulatory-interpersonal agent-self acquire regulatory control over newly emerging constitutive-interpersonal motives, as when the child expresses an interest in art and the caregivers help the child to pursue this interest by arranging lessons and providing materials and encouragement. If the caregivers' own psychic structures are nonveridical, of course, the caregivers may encourage the child to pursue particular talents (constitutive-interpersonal motives) because the child's success (e.g., being the school football star) provides the caregivers with pathological agent-self percepts. One indication of the veridical or nonveridical nature of the caregivers' support for the child's pursuit of constitutive-interpersonal motives is the nature of the caregivers' response to the child's inevitable moments of failure or doubts about whether s/he wants to pursue these motives. When their support is nonveridical, the caregivers are likely to respond with anxiety, anger, or depression; when it is veridical, the caregivers' responses will be nurturing and understanding. Further, the caregivers' capacity to live a life of veridical regulatory control over their own constitutive-interpersonal motives provides the child with paradigmatic examples of the capacity to fulfill ideals.

The final structuralization of the caregiving relationship in the constitutive-interpersonal self stage occurs through an interrelated two-step process in which the complementary association between the relationship ideal and the veridical regulatory-interpersonal agent-self is structuralized through the gradual actualization of the ideals contained in the relationship ideal. This actualization occurs by means of paradigmatic regulatory identifications, all of which are guided by the mutuality between the regulatory-intrapsychic agent-self and the veridical regulatory-interpersonal agent-self. For example, the adolescent who falls in love for the first time and experiences transference-driven motives, including jealousy and the wish to control the loved-one's motives, can discover the nonveridical nature of these motives because of the relationship ideal, which provides a contrasting set of ideal ways of relating. These ideals include mutuality, consideration, and respect for others' motives. They are based on the veridical regulatory-interpersonal agent-self's capacity to distinguish boundaries between itself and the regulatory-interpersonal motives of another. When pursued, these ideals are experienced as infinitely more pleasurable than all-powerful agent-self pleasure, which is based on subjugation, control, possessiveness, and victory over others. Because the relationship ideal is a unitary psychic structure that originated within the agent-selves of the caregivers in the context of the conjugally competitive agent-self phase, it is an important source of the capacity for nontransference sexual and social-interpersonal intimacy.

The regulatory-intrapsychic agent-self's stable capacity to gratify the regulatory-interpersonal motive gives the adolescent the capacity to mourn any constitutive-interpersonal loss other than the unique situation represented by the death of a parent.[3] This capacity reflectively to experience constitutive-interpersonal loss without a corresponding loss in inner well-being is the basis for one of the key developmental goals of the constitutive-interpersonal self stage, namely, the acquisition of nontransference, self-regulatory control over all constitutive-interpersonal motives. This structuralization actualizes the capacity for the loss-free regulatory control of desire. Cognitive powers will be used for nontransference pleasure (e.g., thinking, learning, and creating in a conflict-free, curious, flexible way) rather than for transference pleasure (e.g., in a context of winner take all or reluctance to try, that is, as a means of furthering the all-powerful agent-self's illusion of agent-self, self-regulatory control).

The progressive structuralization of self-regulatory autonomy with regard to all categories of constitutive-interpersonal motive experience correlates with the progressive occurrence of sets of personal identifications that are organized by the aims of constitutive-interpersonal motives and are under the hegemony of the veridical regulatory-interpersonal agent-self.

PARAMETERS OF THE CONSTITUTIVE-INTERPERSONAL SELF STAGE

The significant parameters of the constitutive-interpersonal self stage may be summarized as follows. The child no longer experiences a developmental intrapsychic transference, and s/he has only a partial structure for the interpersonal form of the developmental transference. The truncated interpersonal transference is reduced to phase-specific all-powerful agent-self experiences, which occur in response to the epigenetic onset of new constitutive-interpersonal motives.

The constitutive-interpersonal self stage is also characterized by increased initiative and resourcefulness facilitated by a phase-appropriately nontransference pursuit of cognitive motives. The child is left free to use interpersonal consciousness (e.g., cognition, creativity) for nontransference pleasure. The specific choice of thought content, academic subjects, sports, modes of creativity, and so on, will be dictated by a host of factors, including the child's innately determined talents and life experiences. Because the child's thought processes are no longer used as gratifying, nonveridical agent-self percepts for the nonveridical intrapsychic motive, the child's failures will never entail the loss of inner esteem, and the child's successes will never cause nonveridical, intrapsychic transference pleasure. The child's interpersonal consciousness increasingly becomes a source of autonomous, transference-free, interpersonal pleasure.

The developmental goal of the constitutive-interpersonal self stage is posttransference existence (the posttransference stage). The term ***posttransference*** refers to a specific nontransference self-experience. Unlike the term nontransference, which always implies the possibility of a transference type of self-experience, the term posttransference refers to a subjective experience of personal existence characterized by an impossibility of transference experience even in the presence of extreme stress and trauma. The sweep of developmental process leading to this goal can be viewed from the perspective of the final destructuralization of the developmental split. The child increasingly realizes that motive choices that are regulated by the all-powerful agent-self's use of constitutive-interpersonal motive gratification for (nonveridical) well-being are the source of loss rather than pleasure. Specifically, they cause the child to lose the superior pleasure of nondissociated, veridical inner well-being. As a result, the remaining interpersonal transference motives are diminished and then extinguished.

THE DESTRUCTURALIZATION OF
THE DEVELOPMENTAL SPLIT

The progressive destructuralization of the developmental split entails the child's recognition that transference interpersonal pleasure, as well as transference interpersonal pain, represents a loss. The deidealization of transference pleasure as a source of inner well-being presents a greater challenge than the deidealization of transference pain. Both types of interpersonal transference meanings are destructuralized through the influence of the regulatory-interpersonal pleasure principle. Since, by definition, pain has more of a tendency to be associated with a motive for change than does pleasure, the child feels the influence of the regulatory-interpersonal pleasure principle more readily in association with the experience of transference pain than in association with the experience of transference pleasure. In other words, by its nature, the experience of transference pain is less likely to be subjectively invisible than the experience of transference pleasure. The attractiveness of transference pleasure—the all-powerful agent-self form of inner well-being—diminishes only as transference pleasure acquires the meaning of loss, namely, the loss of the pleasure of veridical regulatory-interpersonal agency.

During the constitutive-interpersonal self stage, transference, all-powerful agent-self well-being is renewed and stimulated by the epigenetic onset of new types of constitutive-interpersonal motives. These include motives for significant peer relationships, for increasingly sophisticated abstract thought, for accomplishment in specific skills, and for romantic relationships. Each of these emerging motives represents a de novo, gratifying, nonveridical agent-self percept, which, initially, provides transference regulatory-interpersonal motive gratification. The transference use of an epigenetically unfolding, constitutive-interpersonal motive is short-lived, however, due to the fact that the interpersonal transference structure lacks a structural grounding within the intrapsychic transference system. Because the all-powerful agent-self cannot rely on the intrapsychic transference for gratifying, nonveridical agent-self percepts, it is attenuated; gratified constitutive-interpersonal motives are its only source of well-being, and these are inherently vulnerable to positive entropy and chance. Thus, the child's veridical regulatory-interpersonal agent-self easily gains regulatory control over the emergent constitutive-interpersonal motives. The pleasure of veridical regulatory-interpersonal agent-self control over constitutive-interpersonal motives is superior to the pleasure of illusional all-powerful agent-self control because the veridical regulatory-interpersonal motive remains stably, autonomously gratified by the regulatory-intrapsychic agent-self, even in the face of inevitable constitutive-interpersonal loss.

The capacity for a nontransference friendship with the caregivers emerges as a consequence of the mourning of the triadic form of conjugally competitive agent-self loss. The nontransference side of the developmental split is the locus of the only veridical motives for relationship experience and, therefore, only the nontransference agent-self has the capacity veridically to register the value of the caregivers' inclusively nontransference motives. As we described, the interpersonal transference in the constitutive-interpersonal self stage entails cycles of developmental regression, which place some constitutive-interpersonal motives temporarily under the regulatory control of the all-powerful agent-self. Developmental regression is the antithesis of the structural regression that can occur in psychopathology, both because developmental regression is not regulated by pathological psychic pain and because the transference pleasure associated with any given regressed personal meaning structure ultimately acquires the significance of loss.

The constitutive-interpersonal self stage entails a process of personalizing each new set of phase-specific constitutive-interpersonal motives. Personalization is the acquisition of transference-free, autonomous, regulatory control over any and all experiences of constitutive-interpersonal consciousness.

THE POSTTRANSFERENCE STAGE

The individual reaches the posttransference stage of completed psychic development when the personalization process produces an autonomous, stable self-regulatory capacity for veridical effective agency with regard to all constitutive-interpersonal motive gratification. The individual no longer makes regulatory-interpersonal transference use of constitutive-interpersonal experience. The personal meaning structures of the posttransference stage undergo a final structuralization through the identification of the fully personalized, posttransference, regulatory-interpersonal agent-self with the relationship ideal. Throughout all the years of the constitutive-interpersonal self stage, the relationship ideal has served both as a source of ideal self-ideals (a regulative function) and also as a source of to-be-actualized ideal selves (a constitutive function). With the completion of the personalizing process, the relationship ideal becomes structurally identified with the posttransference, veridical interpersonal agent-self. The reflections supplied by the relationship ideal are now reflections about the forms of interpersonal agency that have actually evolved rather than reflections about a future selfhood. The posttransference interpersonal self has, in effect, grown into the projected agent-self of self-regulatory stability for which the relationship ideal acted as a kind of template. The structural identification between the veridical interpersonal agent-self and the relationship ideal is the culmination and the conclusion of a paradigmatic developmental process.

6
Psychopathology

Intrapsychic Humanism recognizes two types of psychopathology, *intrapsychic* and *interpersonal*.[1] Intrapsychic psychopathology is nearly universal and is compatible with a life of interpersonal pleasure and achievement. Intrapsychic psychopathology refers solely to the fixation of nonveridical intrapsychic agent-self meaning. Intrapsychic psychopathology always underlies interpersonal psychopathology. In the absence of clinically manifest interpersonal psychopathology, intrapsychic psychopathology can be detected by a formal diagnostic process or, often, by one's self-experience and/or others' comments about the self. For example, a person may have career success and loving family relationships, but be unable to regulate some aspect of her/his introspective experience. S/he may have occasional bouts of dysphoria (especially in relation to success or loss), be unable stably to pursue self-caretaking motives (e.g., staying trim), or be unable to abandon behavior patterns that are self-defeating or self-destructive (e.g., being overly self-critical, drinking too much). Sometimes those most intimately involved with the individual tell her/him that aspects of her/his personality of which s/he is unaware interfere with relationships or career success. For example, another person may observe that the individual is frequently insensitive, misses opportunities in business, works too hard, or cannot realize her/his potential. Because intrapsychic psychopathology structurally isolates the individual's intrapsychic regulatory agency reality, it is only amenable to change through an intrapsychic caregiving relationship in Intrapsychic Treatment (see chap. 7).

Interpersonal psychopathology has two referents: (1) behavior on the level of thought or action that exceeds average limits (e.g., manifest neurotic or psychotic behavior, addictions, and phobias) and (2) behavior on the level of thought or action that falls within average bounds but that is psychopathological by comparison with paradigmatic development as we define this (e.g., nightmares, temper tantrums, toilet choosing conflicts, negative feelings about the self, and adolescent rebelliousness). We term the former type of interpersonal psychopathology *clinically manifest interpersonal psychopathology.* Unless otherwise specified, in this chapter the term interpersonal psychopathology refers only to clinically manifest interpersonal psychopathology (to psychopathology in the usual sense). As the length and complexity of standard psychiatric categorizations of abnormal behavior exemplify, clinically manifest interpersonal psychopathology is protean in form. The fundamental cause of interpersonal psychopathology, however, is intrapsychic psychopathology.

Many factors determine the specific behavioral manifestations and the degree of severity of *interpersonal* psychopathology. Some of these include the extent of the caregiver's interpersonal mistreatment of the child; the child's biological makeup; social, economic, and cultural factors; and positive or negative chance experiences (e.g., a good teacher, a car accident). Interpersonal psychopathology is considerably more amenable to modification than is intrapsychic psychopathology. This accounts for the salubrious effects that friends, books, diverse psychological treatments, and. life experiences can have on interpersonal symptoms. The responsiveness of interpersonal psychopathology to external influences also accounts for the exacerbating effects on interpersonal psychopathology that can result from losses produced by positive entropy (e.g., the effects of aging), losses produced by chance (e.g., being in an earthquake), and losses of interpersonal gratification in general (e.g., losing a job, a girlfriend or boyfriend). Clinically manifest interpersonal psychopathology has been the sole focus of all psychologies, including those forms of psychoanalysis that aim at deep structural change. Because other psychologies focus on what we term pathological-transference-regulated constitutive-interpersonal motives, they do not account for the efficient cause of psychopathology, namely, the effect of nonveridical caregiving on intrapsychic and regulatory-interpersonal personal meaning structures.

Most people categorized as normal by the diagnostic criteria of other psychologies have intrapsychic psychopathology. The fact that intrapsychic psychopathology can coexist with exceedingly adaptive interpersonal functioning explains why an individual whose life is characterized by unfailing success may be prone to episodes of conflict-driven behavior and/or be vulnerable to unexpected occurrences of frank mental illness. Intrapsychic psychopathology can be coupled with a well-developed capacity for constitutive-interpersonal introspection, because constitutive-interpersonal introspection is primarily a function of cognitive motives, which are minimally dependent on the quality of the caregiver's nurture. From an evolutionary perspective, the fact that constitutive-interpersonal introspection can coexist with intrapsychic psychopathology illustrates the adaptive value of nonveridical intrapsychic motive gratification. In untreated psychopathology, for example, percepts that are the products of constitutive-interpersonal motives gain permanent hegemony over percepts of the caregiver's caregiving motives as a source of pathological intrapsychic motive gratification. In this way, constitutive-interpersonal motives can be gratified (giving the individual the tools for adaptive interpersonal experience with the world at large) at the expense of the veridical gratification of the intrapsychic motive. Given the spread of pollution and the proliferation of increasingly sophisticated and destructive weaponry, however, we speculate that postindustrial society is approaching the tipping point at which the adaptive advantage conferred by the pathological transference use of cognitive and social-interpersonal constitutive-interpersonal motives is being lost.[2]

Regardless of the level of her/his cognitive functioning, the individual with intrapsychic psychopathology is only conditionally a rational agent. Intrapsychic psychopathology is the ultimate cause of human cruelty and is a humanistic explanation for the problem of evil. Perhaps the most peculiar forms of human cruelty are parental cruelty and cruelty perpetrated in the name of religious ideals. The problem of evil reflects the recognition of the existence and irrationality of unprovoked and unwanted forms of aggression. The potentially global scale of the problem of evil is due to the uniquely human capacity for the gross manipulation of material, nonagency reality. An example is the danger of species extinction posed by chemical and biological warfare. The global destructiveness of which humans are capable results from the regulation of an evolved cognitive capacity by nurture-based pathological intrapsychic motives and pathological regulatory-interpersonal motives. The paradox that may eventually destroy both the human species and the environment is that, measured strictly on its own terms, human cognition can function effectively even when the content of this functioning is under the regulatory control of pathological intrapsychic and regulatory-interpersonal motives (e.g., the mad scientist).[3]

Intrapsychic Humanism's nosology is based on treatability rather than on categorizations or descriptions of psychopathological behavior. In a psychopathological as well as in a paradigmatic subjective experience of personal existence, our primary focus is the individual's regulatory agency reality, specifically, the process and meaning of her/his intrapsychic and regulatory-interpersonal motive gratification. We believe that the fundamental problem in psychopathology is a nurture-caused, structural defect in and malformation of the intrapsychic perceptual identity process.[4] The core internalized conflict in psychopathology is between: (1) motives derived from a nature-based, intrapsychic motive for veridical care-getting relationship pleasure and (2) psychopathological-nurture-induced motives for the pleasure afforded by delusional intrapsychic mutuality.[5]

The recognition that the nonveridical caregiving that is the structural cause of psychopathology is intrapsychic rather than interpersonal makes it possible to explain, without recourse to the catch-all that human nature is inherently flawed, why children whose caregivers are manifestly kind can develop psychic pain. Intrapsychic psychopathology is a function of the caregivers' incapacity for veridical regulatory-intrapsychic agency rather than of the caregivers' overtly noxious interpersonal behavior. From an intrapsychic caregiving viewpoint, the intrapsychically nonveridical caregiver's kind interpersonal caregiving is conditional on the child's modifying or relinquishing many of her/his own motives, particularly and most importantly the child's motive to reject the caregiver's choice of noncaregiving (personal) motives and the motive to be the agent cause of the caregiver's intrapsychic caregiving.[6] In other words, when interpersonal kindness accompanies nonveridical intrapsychic caregiving, the kindness is regulated by the caregiver's motives for personal comfort rather than by her/his motives for veridical intrapsychic caregiving pleasure. For example, the interpersonal kindness may be regulated by the caregiver's motive to be liked by the child or by her/his inability to tolerate the child's unhappiness rather than by the stable preference for the intrapsychic caregiving pleasure of helping the child to develop a regulatory-intrapsychic agent-self.

The distinction between (1) kind interpersonal caregiving and nonveridical intrapsychic caregiving and (2) kind interpersonal caregiving and veridical intrapsychic caregiving determines whether development is paradigmatic or psychopathological. Because pathological personal meaning structures are set in place before the child can introspect an interpersonal agent-self, the child cannot use her/his constitutive-interpersonal cognitive capacities to recognize that the caregiving s/he received was nonveridical and, hence, that her/his deep conviction of effective intrapsychic agency is illusional.

A structurally conflicted unconsciousness, which we term ***pathological dissociation,*** occurs only in psychopathology. Its imperviousness to change is due to the pathological-nurture-induced fixation of phylogenetically evolved intrapsychic meaning structures. The child is bonded to the conviction that s/he is authentically loved by a caregiver who, from an intrapsychic caregiving perspective, responds to the child with nonveridical intrapsychic caregiving and, possibly, with interpersonal hostility, intrusiveness, or neglect.

UNITARY CAUSE OF PSYCHOPATHOLOGY

All treatable patients initially want help with conscious psychic pain. This introspectable pain, however, is not the pain of the fundamental structural defect in the intrapsychic perceptual identity process. Intrapsychic Humanism's theories of psychopathology and treatment take into account both the meaning of intrapsychic pain caused by the individual's structural intrapsychic defect and also the strength of her/his innately based motive for the potentially attainable pleasure of veridical intrapsychic caregiving mutuality.

Ultimately, the cause of pathological psychic pain is that the child has no choice but to equate the nonveridical intrapsychic care-giving s/he received with caregiving love.[7] Accordingly, while psychopathology is not innately caused, the necessary (but not sufficient) cause of psychopathology is innately based in that nature leads the child to equate all caregiving behavior with intended, ideal nurture. Because the child cannot recognize the nonveridical nature of the caregiving s/he receives, from an intrapsychic caregiving perspective, nonveridical caregiving is experienced by the child as veridical caregiving. The child acquires motives for this delusional inner well-being, which occurs in the context of a structurally dissociated state that must be understood from the intrapsychic caregiving perspective. The irony is that one cannot experience the nonveridical quality of one's own intrapsychic agent-self unless one has received veridical caregiving.

The essence of nonveridical intrapsychic caregiving is that the caregiver's intrapsychic psychopathology prevents her/him from giving the child the veridical experience of intrapsychic agent-self, self-regulatory control with regard to engaging and regulating the caregiver's intrapsychic caregiving motives. Because the child has an innately based conviction that the caregiver has a self-regulated, intentional intrapsychic motive to care for her/him, the child attaches the meaning of veridical caregiving to any experience with the caregiver. Therefore, from an intrapsychic caregiving viewpoint, the child attaches the meaning of the caregiver's intentionality to the loss of veridical intrapsychic pleasure caused by the caregiver's nonveridical intrapsychic caregiving.

In other words, when caregivers have intrapsychic psychopathology, the child develops a delusional system of personal meaning structures. The child experiences the caregiver's inability to provide veridical intrapsychic caregiving as caused (regulated) by the child's intrapsychic agent-self. Thus, the child unknowingly attaches the meaning of the reflection of agent-self as agent-self to the caregiver's nonveridical intrapsychic caregiving. The child bases her/his source of inner well-being (and, consequently, her/his own continued existence) upon her/his learned capacity delusionally to experience nonveridical intrapsychic caregiving as loving, gratifying, veridical nurture. In consequence, the child's intrapsychic agent-self remains in the undifferentiated, pathological form it reached in the stage we term the ***pathological intrapsychic self stage*** (the stage that in psychopathology follows the pre-eidetic stage).

The Conjugally Competitive Self Phase and Psychopathology

The child's conjugally competitive agent-self motives are important in paradigmatic development, but they do not cause intrapsychic psychopathology. Intrapsychic psychopathology represents the fixation of intrapsychic motive gratification at a pathological transference level, and constitutive-interpersonal motive experience plays no causal role in this fixation. In fact, intrapsychic psychopathology occurs before the child has the capacity for introspectable interpersonal agent-self experience. However, conjugally competitive agent-self motives can contribute to *interpersonal* psychopathology in that, if the caregiver's psychic conflicts around the child's conjugally competitive agent-self motives are especially severe, the child may develop interpersonal symptoms that reflect conjugally competitive agent-self conflicts. Examples abound from the psychoanalytic literature, which has focused on phenomena such as frigidity and excessive or inhibited competitiveness.

As we described in chapter 4, in paradigmatic development triadic conjugally competitive agent-self loss results in the structuralization of the relationship ideal. Triadic loss does not paradigmatically result in the occurrence of what psychoanalysis terms an oedipal complex, or infantile neurosis.[8] If the caregiver does not provide veridical intrapsychic caregiving, the child never develops the capacity for nontransference agent-self experience. Pathological triadic experience, therefore, represents the continuation of previously established regulatory-interpersonal and intrapsychic psychopathology and does not constitute a distinct nosological category.[9]

STRUCTURAL CONSIDERATIONS

The primary referent for intrapsychic psychopathology is the nondifferentiation of intrapsychic consciousness due to the caregiver's nonveridical intrapsychic caregiving. Because the caregiver's intrapsychic caregiving motives do not have stable hegemony over her/his personal motives, the caregiver cannot respond adequately to the child's intrapsychic needs. Intrapsychic psychopathology is defined strictly in terms of the nature and quality of intrapsychic functioning and primarily refers neither to categories of abnormal behavior nor to the degree of adaptiveness of manifest behavior. When caregiving is intrapsychically nonveridical, the content and, therefore, the quality of the child's agent-self experience (viewed from an intrapsychic caregiving perspective) will include intrapsychic pain resulting from the child's early experience with the caregiver. The meaning of intrapsychic pain is never subjectively experienced, because the individual subjectively experiences intrapsychic pain as having the meaning of intrapsychic pleasure. Intrapsychic pain represents a loss of veridical pleasure, and, therefore, can only be recognized from an intrapsychic caregiving perspective. As will be described in chapter 7, Intrapsychic Treatment offers the patient a veridical intrapsychic caregiving relationship, which allows her/him to become aware of the nonveridical nature of her/his agent-self experience or, in other words, to become aware for the first time that s/he has intrapsychic pain.

The invisibility of psychic pain can be understood by analogizing it with the gosling that has imprinted on a human. The gosling has absolutely no idea that the human is not the ideal caregiver that it was innately programmed to expect upon hatching. It is a reasonable assumption that, from a perspective outside the gosling's experience, the human cannot provide the same quality of nurture as the mother goose and, therefore, that a gosling who has imprinted on a human has a less veridical well-being than the goose-imprinted gosling. Once the gosling's precept is pathologically modified, however, it regulates the gosling's behavior. If the mother goose is introduced to the gosling after it has firmly imprinted on the human, the gosling will continue to follow the human.[10]

Nonveridical intrapsychic caregiving modifies the child's intrapsychic precept to include motives for nonveridical intrapsychic caregiving and prevents the child's veridical intrapsychic precept and associated veridical constitutive-intrapsychic motive from being reactivated. Unless the individual receives Intrapsychic Treatment, these veridical structures remain forever nonfunctional. The regulation of motive experience is either consciously teleological (outside the agent-self), which leads to a paranoid orientation, or it is delusionally located within the agent-self, which leads to an as-if orientation. No developmental split can occur, because the child has no veridical intrapsychic agent-self. The child's intrapsychic agent-self is structurally isolated (protected) from the caregiver's intrapsychic motives (even though the child's experience of the caregiving relationship is always that it imparts an ideal mutuality). The child's regulatory-interpersonal agent-self and the child's constitutive-interpersonal agent-self ultimately serve the demands of the pathological intrapsychic transference. In untreated psychopathology, intrapsychic and interpersonal consciousness remain permanently merged, and all regulatory-interpersonal and constitutive-interpersonal experience has the added significance of intrapsychic motive gratification. Some authors have concluded mistakenly that constitutive-interpersonal derivatives of intrapsychic psychopathology result from normal development (represent the human condition). Examples are Freud's assumption that human self-experience is naturally unhappy and Melanie Klein's premise that the infant universally assumes a paranoid position.[11]

One illustration of the adaptiveness of the human species is the fact that the child's intrapsychic consciousness can develop to the point of transference intrapsychic care-getting anxiety even in the presence of nonlethal nonveridical caregiving. However, nonveridical caregiving prevents the occurrence of nontransference care-getting anxiety. The untreated individual's intrapsychic agent-self becomes irrevocably fixated at the point of transference intrapsychic care-getting anxiety, since the next step in intrapsychic development, the reactivation of the veridical intrapsychic precept and veridical constitutive-intrapsychic motive, is nurture based and requires veridical intrapsychic caregiving. Because the nonveridical caregiver's motives for intrapsychic caregiving pleasure are unstable and conflicted, the child cannot mourn the loss caused by the caregiver's nonveridical caregiving by engaging the caregiver's intrapsychic caregiving ideals and recapturing the veridical re-flection of agent-self as agent-self. Because the child never experiences the superior pleasure of veridical intrapsychic care-getting, the child remains unaware of the nonveridical quality of the caregiver's caregiv-ing. Even so, the child's innately determined belief is always that the caregiver's intrapsychic caregiving motives have hegemony over her/his personal motives and, consequently, that the caregiver intentionally provides ongoing, loss-free responses to the child's need to be the agent cause of the caregiver's intrapsychic caregiving. This is not to say, how-ever, that interpersonal psychopathology cannot be improved or made worse by an individual's subsequent life experiences. The plasticity of interpersonal psychopathology is important because, even in the pres-ence of *intrapsychic* psychopathology, the nature and degree of interper-sonal psychopathology is a major determinant of the quality of an in-dividual's subjective personal existence.

Overview of Psychopathological Structures

The following summary of psychopathological psychic structures as-sumes that the caregiver's interpersonal caregiving pathology, or the hegemony of the caregiver's personal motives over her/his intrapsychic caregiving motives, is not so malignant that the infant dies of marasmus because s/he cannot maintain the illusion of causing the caregiver's in-trapsychic caregiving. The first psychopathological psychic structure to develop is the structure of **delusional intrapsychic mutuality.** In paradig-matic development, illusional intrapsychic mutuality is a source of nonveridical intrapsychic meaning only because the child's constitutive-interpersonal motives have phase-specifically acquired hegemony as the percepts of choice in the child's intrapsychic perceptual identity pro-cess. If the caregiver's intrapsychic caregiving is veridical, the child soon has a competing, veridical source of caregiving percepts (the regula-tory-intrapsychic agent-self), whose superior pleasure ultimately causes the child to become uninterested in the pleasure provided by the struc-tural isolation entailed by illusional intrapsychic mutuality. In psycho-pathology, however, the structure of delusional intrapsychic mutuality retains its power and appeal because it has no veridical competition. Further, the nonveridicality of its internalized percepts is due to the caregiver's nonveridical caregiving as well as to the child's immaturity. Typically, however, the structure of delusional intrapsychic mutuality is sufficiently nourishing to preserve life and to allow the infant to pass through the stages of intrapsychic psychopathology without developing childhood forms of interpersonal psychopathology. The exception is the relatively infrequent case in which the caregiver's *interpersonal* caregiving is so psychotoxic that the child manifests aberrant behavioral forms of pre-eidetic development.

When the structure of delusional intrapsychic mutuality is eidetically internalized, it becomes the ***pathological intrapsychic caregiver*** during the pathological intrapsychic self stage and the ***pathological intrapsychic self and caregiver structure*** during the third and final stage in psychopathology, the ***pathological interpersonal self stage.*** The pathological intrapsychic caregiver forms the basis of a ***pathological intrapsychic transference structure.*** Pathological (obstructive) transference and pretransference processes structurally differ from developmental transference and pretransference processes. Paradigmatically, pretransference and transference intrapsychic agent-self experience is nonveridical but facilitative. In psychopathology, however, even before eidetic internalization pathologically fixates intrapsychic consciousness, the self-experiences of the paradigmatically and of the psychotoxically raised child are entirely different. Of course, the child who has received nonveridical intrapsychic caregiving has no idea that s/he has this loss because s/he has no comparison available to her/him.

When we describe nonveridical intrapsychic caregiving, we in no way imply that the caregiver lacks good intentions or fails to show the child manifest interpersonal kindness. In fact, every caregiver wants to do the right thing for her/his child(ren). Even the extremely abusive caregiver believes that s/he acts in the child's best interest. Exceptions, of course, include the caregiver whose pathological dissociation is so extreme that s/he does not even realize the child exists, the caregiver who projects other identities (e.g., Satan) onto the child, or the caregiver who loses control and then feels guilty. Most abusive parents believe the child *needs* discipline, education (to be *taught* a lesson) or that the child has caused the abuse by *provoking* the caregiver. When caregivers are interpersonally kind, the crucial distinction to be made is whether the caregiver's interpersonal kindness stems from veridical, self-regulated intrapsychic caring or from personal motives (e.g., to be needed and loved, to have a quiet or well-behaved child), which are in the service of pathological transference gratification. As we mentioned earlier, since the caregiver without a regulatory-intrapsychic agent-self has no veridical capacity for intrapsychic and regulatory-interpersonal self-caretaking, s/he might illusionally and understandably be convinced that her/his caregiving is exemplary.

The pathological intrapsychic transference persists as the sole mode of intrapsychic motive gratification past the point at which paradigmatically there would exist a competing, nontransference form of intrapsychic motive gratification. The child's inability to have a veridical agent-self experience creates a loss that cannot be mourned because it cannot be recognized consciously. Because the child experiences a delusional type of intrapsychic mutuality, s/he cannot recognize that this pleasure represents the loss of a superior, veridical type of inner well-being. In other words, from an intrapsychic caregiving perspective, the child acquires motives for delusional intrapsychic caregiving pleasure. However, from the viewpoint of the child's subjective experience, delusional intrapsychic mutuality signifies the caregiver's love and also self-love. In summary, the central consequence of intrapsychic psychopathology is structural isolation from the caregiver's nonveridical intrapsychic motives and, therefore, a structurally delusional agent-self experience.

Paradigmatically, in the regulatory-interpersonal self stage, the transitional intrapsychic caregiver takes on both transference intrapsychic self functions and transference intrapsychic caregiver functions. The transitional intrapsychic caregiver not only continues to mediate gratifying, nonveridical percepts for the intrapsychic motive but also, in its gratified form (which has the meaning of effective agency) serves as an internalized, gratifying, nonveridical agent-self percept for the nonveridical regulatory-interpersonal agent-self motive. In *psychopathology,* this dual function also occurs but, from an intrapsychic caregiving perspective, the innately determined intrapsychic motive for the developmental form of nonveridical intrapsychic caregiving relationship pleasure becomes altered to include a motive for pathological intrapsychic motive gratification, which, from an intrapsychic caregiving perspective, is equivalent to a motive for intrapsychic pain. Therefore, the pathological intrapsychic self and caregiver structure is a source of motives that generate a need to experience meaning structures of intrapsychic pain.

This defect affects the next regulatory psychopathological structure to develop, the **pathological regulatory-interpersonal structure,** which occurs as a result of the pathological interpersonal "no." The pathological interpersonal no occurs at the beginning of the pathological interpersonal self stage. It differs from the paradigmatic interpersonal no because the child has no veridical agency experience and, therefore, no stable inner well-being, and, often, because the child has acquired motives for interpersonal conflict with the caregiver. The conscious derivative of the pathological regulatory-interpersonal structure is the **patho-**

logical all-powerful agent-self. The pathological all-powerful agent-self resembles the paradigmatic all-powerful agent-self in that it uses both constitutive-interpersonal motive gratification and nonveridical intrapsychic motive gratification to acquire the (nonveridical) meaning of effective regulatory-interpersonal agency. The pathological all-powerful agent-self, however, does not coexist in a developmental split with a veridical regulatory-interpersonal agent-self. Its transference-based existence is rooted in the structure of delusional intrapsychic mutuality and, therefore, includes motives for delusional inner well-being (psychic pain). Nevertheless, there remains an innately determined, ongoing, though distorted, motive for veridical care-getting pleasure. In untreated psychopathology, this motive remains under the hegemony of the structure of delusional intrapsychic mutuality. As a result, the sought-for pleasure functions solely as a pathological agent-self percept.

After the onset of the pathological all-powerful agent-self, intrapsychic agent-self meaning is entirely contingent on regulatory-interpersonal motive gratification. This contrasts with paradigmatic development, in which, after the onset of the regulatory-intrapsychic agent-self, the veridical form of intrapsychic motive gratification is loss free and stable.[12]

In psychopathology, the pathological all-powerful agent-self is the last structure to occur on the level of regulatory agency reality. On the level of nonregulatory agency reality, the constitutive-interpersonal agent-self continues to be affected by the epigenetic unfolding and maturation of constitutive-interpersonal motives, pathological identifications, the child's innate endowments, social and cultural influences, and the effects of significant events. Pathological positive and negative constitutive-interpersonal identifications with significant others play a particularly important role in determining the constitutive-interpersonal agent-self.

In a psychopathological developmental process, constitutive-interpersonal motives, including motives for language, cognition, motor sophistication, and interpersonal intimacy, mature (with varying degrees of adaptiveness) in spite of the fact that they are ultimately dominated by the needs of the pathological intrapsychic transference and the pathological regulatory-interpersonal transference. The exception to this is childhood psychosis, in which the functioning of consciousness itself acquires the significance of the fundamental gratifying pathological agent-self percept and is entirely regulated by pathological transference needs.

The ***pathological constitutive-interpersonal structure*** is a nonregulatory structure of constitutive-interpersonal agency, which emerges just before the pathological regulatory-interpersonal structure. It comprises what we term the ***pathological pleasurable self structure*** and the ***dysphoric self structure.*** Both of these structures are pathological manifestations of social-interpersonal motives. The pathological pleasurable self structure is composed of constitutive-interpersonal motives for pleasure, which the child uses for pathological transference gratification. The dysphoric self structure is composed of constitutive-interpersonal motives for pain, which the child also uses for pathological transference gratification. The balance between the motives of the pathological pleasurable self structure and the dysphoric self structure, such as whether the person's most sought-after (transference) pleasure derives from the pleasure of being the best at everything or the pain of being the worst at everything, is a function of many factors. These factors include: (1) identifications with the caregivers' constitutive-interpersonal agent-selves, with cultural values, and with significant others; (2) the caregivers' conscious perceptions of the child; and (3) the child's genic endowments.

The conscious derivatives of the pathological pleasurable self structure and the dysphoric self structure are the ***pathological pleasurable self*** and the ***dysphoric self,*** respectively. Extreme examples of each of these pathological constitutive-interpersonal agent-selves are the excessively appetitive forms of personality organization, such as the so-called Don Juan who constantly seeks the constitutive-interpersonal pleasure of sexual conquests, and the so-called moral masochist, who constantly berates her/himself in a quest for constitutive-interpersonal pain that has a soothing effect (provides pain relief).

The main distinction between pathological and paradigmatic identifications is that paradigmatic identifications come under the hegemony of the veridical capacity to own one's own mind; they have a chosen rather than a driven quality. Conversely, the power of psychopathological identifications is teleological (external to the agent-self). An example is the man who always disapproved of his father's prejudice toward minorities but found himself recoiling when he was seated next to a minority person on a bus. In paradigmatic development prior to the posttransference stage, and in all psychopathology, constitutive-interpersonal identifications have conditional regulatory (personal) meaning because they function as nonveridical agent-self percepts. Developmental constitutive-interpersonal identifications and pathological constitutive-interpersonal identifications differ in that the former are time limited, pain-free, and ultimately regulated by the regulatory-intrapsychic agent-self and the veridical regulatory-interpersonal agent-self, while the latter are permanent, ultimately signify meanings of psychic pain, and are regulated by the pathological intrapsychic agent-self motive and the pathological all-powerful agent-self motive. In our view, negative constitutive-interpersonal identifications occur only in psychopathology and primarily represent identifications with the caregiver's dysphoric self and also with the caregiver's interpersonal mistreatment of the child. The other, pleasurable, type of psychopathological constitutive-interpersonal identifications (which would not be considered psychopathological by other psychologies) represents the child's identification both with the nonveridical caregiver's pathological pleasurable self and with the caregiver's kind interpersonal caregiving.

Whereas the occurrence of positive constitutive-interpersonal identifications intuitively seems logical (people want to emulate those whom they admire), the explanation for the occurrence of negative constitutive-interpersonal identifications is not at all obvious. Whereas Intrapsychic Humanism asserts that negative identifications, including the phenomenon of identification with the aggressor, occur only in psychopathology, psychoanalytic theory sees them as part of normative development. Freud based his explanation for negative identifications on the instinctual drives. In contrast, Intrapsychic Humanism grounds the construct of negative identification in an agency reality regulated by a biologically based, innately determined process (the to-be-actualized ideals and precepts generated by consciousness per se) that has been pathologically transformed by nonveridical nurture. The shared referent of psychoanalytic theory's construct of identification with the aggressor and Intrapsychic Humanism's construct of negative constitutive-interpersonal identifications is the phenomenon that a child with a pathological self structure, in an innately based, unconscious, driven manner, will, to varying degrees, seek to acquire an identity that conforms to the view of her/himself that is projected by the nonveridical caregiver.[13] Even though they occur exclusively on the constitutive-interpersonal level of consciousness, negative identifications function as conditional interpersonal personal meaning structures because they are gratifying, nonveridical agent-self percepts for the individual's pathological regulatory-interpersonal motive.

Pathological constitutive-interpersonal identifications contribute significantly to the specific content of the **character structure,** which is the composite of psychopathological meaning structures that occur on the level of constitutive-interpersonal consciousness and form the basis of the individual's identity. The character structure is a synthesis of: (1) the motives of the pathological pleasurable self structure and the dysphoric self structure and (2) negative and positive constitutive-interpersonal identifications with the caregivers and other significant people. The child with a character structure acquires her/his repertoire of constitutive-interpersonal motive experience in large part by: (1) copying the manifest behavior of her/his caregivers, (2) complying with the unconscious fantasies of her/his caregivers, (3) developing those innately given endowments of which the caregivers approve, (4) assimilating social and cultural values, and (5) responding to her/his own conflicting motives for transference pain and for transference pleasure.

Constitutive-interpersonal identifications based on the caregiver's socially adaptive or maladaptive characteristics constitute an important part of the character structure. For example, the child's identification with the caregivers' paranoid motives can serve an important regulatory function when it provides the basis for the child's acquisition of the capacity actively to dislike the caregivers in response to the interpersonal pain they inflict.

In psychopathology, all constitutive-interpersonal experience gratifies the pathological all-powerful agent-self motive, which, in turn, gratifies the pathological intrapsychic motive. Thus, in psychopathology constitutive-interpersonal, intrinsic and illusional self meaning structures retain conditional personal meaning as gratifying, nonveridical percepts for the pathological intrapsychic and regulatory-interpersonal motives. For example, the thought of pleasant weather can be an illusional self meaning that imparts the nonveridical reflection of effective agency for the pathological all-powerful agent-self, which in turn provides the reflection of agent-self as agent-self to the pathological intrapsychic agent-self.

The **character self** is composed of conscious derivatives of the character structure. It includes the pathological pleasurable self and the dysphoric self as well as conscious derivatives of positive and negative identifications. Examples are the "I" that consciously feels (delusional) self-esteem and the "I" that feels deficient or worthless.

In a *paradigmatic* self system, there is neither a character structure nor a character self. Rather, in the period from the end of the regulatory-intrapsychic self stage to the end of the constitutive-interpersonal self stage, there is a developmental split between mutually exclusive transference and nontransference agent-self experiences. Although only an individual with psychopathology develops a character structure and a character self, this individual's conscious self-experience need not be painful. The character structure can be the basis for a character self that is "sunny" and socially adaptive. Even in the best case, however, the individual with intrapsychic psychopathology and a sunny disposition will have a subjective experience of personal existence regulated by pathological pleasurable self longings and by the dysphoric self's reactive motives for the meaning of unpleasure. This reactive motive for dysphoria may not be recognized by the subject. For example, when a teenager with intrapsychic psychopathology who was very successful in school discovered that she had been accepted by the college of her choice, she left her purse on the seat of the bus she took home from school. She did not connect the loss of her purse with the good news until she entered Intrapsychic Treatment many years later.

This example also illustrates that psychopathology entails a structurally dissociated process of denial. Pathological denial refers to the disjunction between the regulatory agent-self meaning that is understood by the therapist from an intrapsychic caregiving perspective and the patient's subjective agent-self meaning. *Intrapsychic* denial makes the child structurally unaware of the caregiver's nonveridical intrapsychic caregiving, and, therefore, the individual with intrapsychic psychopathology cannot recognize the nonveridical quality of her/his intrapsychic agent-self experience.

ETIOLOGICAL CONSIDERATIONS

The cause and onset of pre-eidetic psychopathology can be discussed in terms either of the malformation and fixation of intrapsychic structure or of the behavioral manifestations of the intrapsychic defect. Intrapsychic malformation can be present without obvious behavioral manifestations; in fact, abnormal interpersonal behavior may not manifest itself until late in life (if at all).

The pre-eidetic stage is unique in that, due to the child's developmental immaturity, s/he has an exceedingly narrow behavioral repertoire in response to nonveridical caregiving. The generally accepted criteria for psychopathology are applicable and useful for recognizing and classifying clinically manifest infant psychopathology. Examples of manifest psychopathology in the pre-eidetic stage are: (1) deficits in a phase-appropriate capacity for intersubjective relating, including problems in any category of age-appropriate behavior, such as vocalization, the smile response, and "play" capacity; (2) deficits in age-appropriate cognitive development; (3) deficits in age-appropriate physical development, the most dramatic abnormality of which, aside from marasmus, is psychogenic dwarfism;[14] (4) functional syndromes (e.g., psychogenic colic); and (5) behavior disturbances (e.g., sleep problems, head banging).

In the veridical gratification phase of the pre-eidetic stage, while the child cannot survive traumatic intrapsychic caregiving, s/he cannot differentiate nonveridical intrapsychic caregiving from veridical intrapsychic caregiving. For example, the child cannot know when anger or indifference lies behind the caregiver's smile. Thus, the child can misidentify nonveridical caregiving as veridical caregiving which matches the veridical intrapsychic precept and signifies intrapsychic motive gratification. In this case, the child's smile response will fully (but not optimally) differentiate. Since the information required to match the veridical intrapsychic precept in the pre-eidetic stage is very general and unsophisticated (nearly any smile will do), the infant cannot discriminate between a caregiver percept that is nonveridical but permits the differentiation of the smile response and a caregiver percept that is veridical and fosters paradigmatic development. Pathological caregiver percepts are usually sufficiently gratifying to permit the infant's smile response to differentiate, but they alter the intrapsychic precept so that nonveridical caregiving becomes the infant's ideal of veridical caregiving and obstructs her/his capacity to assess the veridicality of the caregiver's caregiving.[15]

No one can consciously experience intrapsychic pain.[16] In psychopathology, restitution of intrapsychic loss by nonveridical means occurs as follows. Psychic pain goes unmourned because the child cannot engage the caregiver's intrapsychic caregiving motives in order to experience veridical intrapsychic pleasure. Because in development and psychopathology the child experiences all meanings (effects) as intentionally caused, unmourned intrapsychic pain has, from an intrapsychic caregiving viewpoint, the meaning that the caregiver caused it. Nonveridical intrapsychic caregiving is an all or nothing phenomenon; it occurs neither partially nor episodically. Therefore, when the caregiver has intrapsychic psychopathology, nonveridical intrapsychic caregiving becomes the one stable signifier that the caregiver is choosing to be regulated by the child's intrapsychic agent-self. In this way, nonveridical intrapsychic caregiving acquires the status of a gratifying, pathological caregiver percept.

While the structure of delusional intrapsychic mutuality is selectively adaptive in that it allows the child to survive toxic nurture, it also prevents the child who receives nonveridical intrapsychic caregiving from recognizing that her/his subjective experience of personal existence is being poisoned by the nurture that s/he is innately driven to identify as beneficial, desirable, and even ideal. The pathological intrapsychic caregiver becomes a fixated, permanent source of intrapsychic motive gratification, and the untreated individual's regulatory agency reality will always be the product of the merger between her/his intrapsychic consciousness and the caregiver's intrapsychic pain, rather than the product of the mutual recognition between child and caregiver of each other's intrapsychic needs and ideals. From an intrapsychic caregiving perspective, delusional intrapsychic pleasure is a psychopathological meaning structure that signifies veridical caregiving intimacy and furnishes the delusional reflection of effective agency.

Nonveridical intrapsychic caregiving has direct intrapsychic psychopathogenic effects only in the pre-eidetic stage (until eidetic internalization). After the eidetic internalization of the pathological intrapsychic caregiver, nonveridical intrapsychic caregiving directly affects only transference processes of the child's psyche, because the internalized, pathological intrapsychic caregiver mediates the perceptual identity process between empirical experiences with the caregiver and the child's pathological intrapsychic motive. After the onset of the pathological intrapsychic transference, perceptual experience no longer directly gratifies the intrapsychic motive. While this might seem an early point in development for psychopathology to be set in place, the sole referent is to *intrapsychic* psychopathology. The caregivers' interpersonal behavior will continue to have crucial positive or negative effects on the child's interpersonal ideals, goals, and identifications throughout the rest of development. Although intrapsychic psychopathology is structurally entrenched by the time of eidetic internalization,[17] if clinically manifest interpersonal psychopathology occurs, this may not happen until late in life. As we have emphasized, unlike intrapsychic psychopathology, interpersonal psychopathology is protean in form and can be modified by ongoing experience of all kinds (positive or negative). If all other factors are of average quality, the degree to which the caregivers' interpersonal caregiving is nonveridical most significantly determines the degree to which an individual's interpersonal psychopathology will severely disable her/him.

Another way to describe the essential meaning of intrapsychic psychopathology as it is found in *post-eidetic* development is that there is a fixation of interpersonal motive experience as a gratifying, nonveridical agent-self percept for the pathological intrapsychic motive. Thus, in psychopathology, thought processes are not autonomous; for the untreated individual's entire lifetime, every experience of constitutive-interpersonal consciousness, including her/his cognition, will serve as a gratifying, nonveridical agent-self percept for pathological intrapsychic motive gratification.

Since the nonveridical caregiver has no capacity for veridical intrapsychic self-caretaking and no regulatory hegemony of intrapsychic caregiving ideals (has no stable capacity to pursue the pleasure of intrapsychic caregiving), s/he has no capacity to know whether s/he is responding to the child with personal or caregiving motives. For example, when a young child expresses an emphatic and irritable "no" in response to the nonveridical caregiver's interference with her/his motive to stay in the park and play, if the caregiver lets the child remain, the caregiver cannot accurately determine the quality of the motives behind her/his decision. The caregiver cannot know if s/he lets the child remain because s/he has a veridical caregiving motive to give the child's regulatory-interpersonal agent-self a positive reflection for effective agency whenever possible, or because s/he has personal motives for the child not to feel unhappy or angry with the caregiver (i.e., needs to use the child for intrapsychic and interpersonal transference gratification). Similarly, if the caregiver insists that the child leave the park, s/he cannot veridically distinguish caregiving motives (i.e., the caregiver accurately perceives that the child needs a nap more than s/he needs to gratify the motive to stay and play) from motives based on the caregiver's need to use the child for transference gratification (i.e., the child's rebelliousness signifies a loss to the caregiver's pathological all-powerful agent-self and the caregiver attempts to restore the reflection of effective agency by overpowering the child's motives). In other words, even with every conscious motive to give veridical care, the caregiver without a differentiated intrapsychic self lacks veridical regulatory control over her/his personal motives. Without a regulatory-intrapsychic agent-self, the caregiver's intrapsychic pain is invisible both to her/him and to the child, for whom, from an intrapsychic caregiving perspective, the psychic pain induced by nonveridical caregiving acquires the meaning of intentionally caused, ideal intrapsychic caregiving love.

Psychopathological inner well-being always rests on the delusion that gratified constitutive-interpersonal motives convey the reflection of effective intrapsychic and regulatory-interpersonal agency. In other words, the invariant consequence of psychopathological development is the ongoing attachment of intrapsychic significance to interpersonal experience. From an intrapsychic caregiving perspective, the individual lacks any genuine, self-regulating identity and experiences the sense of self as composed of as-if identity states. In effect, the contents of the individual's consciousness become a function of the caregiver's intrapsychic (and, often, interpersonal) pain. The individual cannot regulate how s/he will feel about her/himself—of what the experience of her/his mind will consist. From an intrapsychic caregiving perspective, all constitutive-interpersonal loss causes regulatory-interpersonal and intrapsychic loss, to which restitution is the only possible response. An individual's restitutional responses to psychic pain can take the form of pain-seeking motives or of pleasure-seeking motives. In either case, these attempts at restitution ultimately rest on pathological motives for the meaning of delusional intrapsychic mutuality, which are equivalent to motives for intrapsychic isolation.

After the pathological interpersonal no ushers in interpersonal agency, the gratified pathological regulatory-interpersonal motive (the pathological all-powerful agent-self) becomes the gratifying, nonveridical agent-self percept for the pathological intrapsychic motive. Because the source of gratifying, pathological agent-self percepts for the pathological all-powerful agent-self motive is constitutive-interpersonal experience, any conceivable constitutive-interpersonal meaning, for example, even a fragment of a melody or a dissociated state of blankness, can serve as a pathological agent-self percept for the pathological all-powerful agent-self motive, which, in turn, is the source of gratification for the pathological intrapsychic motive. The phenomenon that in psychopathology any gratified constitutive-interpersonal motive can gratify the pathological regulatory-interpersonal motive provides a concise, unitary explanation for the range of interpersonal symptomatology.[18] Because constitutive-interpersonal motives can be gratified by a vast array of percepts, which, in psychopathology, include percepts with the meaning of pain, the content of fetishes, phobias, compulsions, obsessions, and other symptoms is only limited by the inventiveness of the human mind. Because symptoms are epiphenomenal, however, nosologies based on cataloging and classifying symptoms are, ultimately, unhelpful.

Intrapsychic trauma is an all-or-nothing phenomenon because the caregiver's inability to have a stable preference for intrapsychic caregiving pleasure prevents the child from developing a differentiated intrapsychic agent-self, regardless of whether the caregiver's intrapsychic defect is accompanied by interpersonal cruelty or by interpersonal kindness. As we have said, from the standpoint of the child's subjective comfort and social adaptability, the nature of the caregiver's interpersonal caregiving is crucial, because it shapes the interpersonal identifications that constitute the child's character structure and determines whether, for example, the child acquires a psychotic form of interpersonal psychopathology or has little or no clinically manifest interpersonal psychopathology.

Psychopathological Interpersonal Caregiving

There are as many *interpersonal* forms of pathological caregiving as there are varieties of character structure. These run a gamut from extreme interpersonal rage (e.g., infanticide) to extreme interpersonal kindness (the caregiver who never consciously feels or expresses anger toward the child). The intrapsychically nonveridical caregiver whose interpersonal behavior is manifestly caring gives the child opportunities for pleasurable interpersonal identifications that will tend to make the child interpersonally successful and relatively unconflicted in her/his motives for constitutive-interpersonal relationship pleasure. Paradoxically, however, the one drawback to having an intrapsychically nonveridical but interpersonally kind caregiver is that the child has difficulty understanding her/his conscious feelings of dysphoria. Because the nonveridical caregiver has no capacity for veridical intrapsychic self-caretaking, this caregiver cannot know that her/his intrapsychic caregiving ideals are not hegemonic (that s/he is not providing the child with a stable experience of having a veridical, effective intrapsychic agent-self). The interpersonally kind caregiver who feels only conscious love for the child and who spends much time with the child understandably is convinced that her/his caregiving is exemplary. Both caregiver and child attribute any dysphoria the child feels to essential human nature, the child's inborn temperament, or the child's willfulness.

Some nonveridical caregivers confine their expressions of interpersonal anger to times when the child is expressing transference caregetting anxiety and transference interpersonal no behavior, and to the subsequent elaborations of these negative responses to the caregiver in the conjugally competitive agent-self phase, middle childhood, and adolescence. Even though these caregivers feel and express conscious anger, they justify this anger by concluding that the child is at fault (e.g., the child is too spoiled, demanding, stubborn, needy, childish, unhappy, or willful). As the spectrum of pathological interpersonal caregiving behavior widens, caregivers can be descriptively classified according to the extent to which they are paranoid (blame the child for "evoking" their anger), guilty (feel bad about their outbursts but also cannot control them), or negligent (react to their negative feelings toward the child by failing to regulate the child's behavior or by withdrawing from the child).

Like the nonveridical caregiver, a therapist with intrapsychic psychopathology cannot offer the patient veridical intrapsychic caregiving; therefore, the patient will never have the stable, veridical experience of possessing an intrapsychic agent-self which can exert hegemony over the therapist's intrapsychic caregiving motives during the therapy hour. Therapists vary, however, in the degree to which their interpersonal behavior is pathological. Nonveridical therapists' interpersonal behavior toward their patients can range from unfailing kindness to extreme abusiveness. In current therapeutic approaches, it is particularly common for the therapist to blame the patient for the therapist's interpersonal expressions of anger by labeling the patient "resistant," "manipulative," or "provocative." An illustration is the therapist who fell asleep during a patient's session. When the patient woke him and said her feelings were hurt, the therapist responded that he had only fallen asleep because the patient's resistance had caused her to talk in a soporific monotone.

Caregiving Lapses

The structural loss caused by nonveridical intrapsychic caregiving differs from the loss caused in paradigmatic development by nontraumatic intrapsychic or interpersonal caregiving lapses. Nontraumatic caregiving lapses occur within a nurturing context in which the caregiver's intrapsychic caregiving ideals ultimately have hegemony over her/his personal motives. A nontraumatic caregiving lapse represents the temporary absence of an appropriate caregiving response. The loss (pain) that results from nontraumatic caregiving lapses does not pathologically modify the child's intrapsychic precept to include an ideal of nonveridical caregiving because the caregiver's intrapsychic caregiving motives remain available to be reengaged by the child. The paradigmatic caregiver always remains functionally available to put aside her/his personal motives (including the motive to be distracted or otherwise unavailable to the child) and to respond to the child.

Caregiving lapses occur when a caregiver with a stable motive for intrapsychic caregiving pleasure pursues personal motives at a time when the child needs intrapsychic or interpersonal caregiving responses. The loss to the child caused by caregiving lapses differs from *developmental* losses, which are inevitable, innately determined, and unrelated to the quality of the caregiver's caregiving. Nontraumatic caregiving lapses occur whenever a caregiver who has the capacity to offer the child veridical intrapsychic and interpersonal caregiving temporarily responds to the child with personal motives rather than caregiving motives. Examples are infrequent moments when the caregiver continues to clean out a closet when the child really needs focused attention, or thinks about something else when the child is talking. Nonstructural caregiving lapses are inevitable; the child's intrapsychic and interpersonal care-getting motives will at times not be gratified. Because the caregiver's caregiving ideals have hegemony over her/his personal motives, however, the child will have the veridical experience that s/he can engage the caregiver's caregiving motives by alerting the caregiver to the loss caused by the caregiving lapse. The caregiver's responsiveness is the result not of a technical commitment to care for the child but of the superiority of caregiving pleasure to the pleasure of gratified personal motives. In psychopathology, the superiority of caregiving pleasure is hidden from the caregiver, who feels conflict (pain) in relation to the stable pursuit of caregiving intimacy.

DYNAMIC CONSIDERATIONS

Psychopathology refers to an ongoing process as well as to the outcome of psychopathological development. No human life can continue in the absence of an ongoing experience of (illusional or veridical) caregiving mutuality sufficient to satisfy the ongoing intrapsychic and regulatory-interpersonal motive for the reflection of agent-self as agent-self. This holds true even in psychopathology, where the core meaning structure, the structure of delusional intrapsychic mutuality, entails intrapsychic isolation. Pathological intrapsychic isolation refers not to the absence of subjectively experienced relationship experience but rather to the absence of the empirical, mutual, veridical experience of being the agent cause of the caregiver's intrapsychic caregiving. The ongoing, primary loss in a psychopathological childhood is that intrapsychic development ceases even though interpersonal development continues (and, in fact, may result in great social and career success). The conjunction of interpersonal accomplishment and inner dysphoria is usually rationalized as the human condition, or, conversely, as the consequence of learned bad habits.

Rage

Rage is a meaning structure that occurs only in psychopathology. There are two categories of rage: rage that is a personal meaning structure (occurs on the intrapsychic or regulatory-interpersonal level of consciousness and is a regulating cause of the subjective experience of personal existence) and rage that is a nonpersonal meaning structure (occurs on the constitutive-interpersonal level of consciousness). Personal meaning structures of rage always represent self-rage. Constitutive-interpersonal meaning structures of rage can take the form of either self- or other-directed rage (paranoia). Personal meaning structures of self-rage are a product of the distortion of the child's innate intrapsychic perceptual identity process by the caregiver's nonveridical caregiving. Constitutive-interpersonal rage is proximally a function of negative constitutive-interpersonal identifications.

The notion of rage is easily misunderstood because it has many connotations and can be discussed from many perspectives. Examples are: personal meaning in contrast to self-meaning, intrapsychic and regulatory-interpersonal consciousness in contrast to constitutive-interpersonal consciousness, conscious consciousness in contrast to unconscious consciousness, introspectable in contrast to nonintrospectable, the relation to affect, the relation to anxiety and tension, the relation to intentionality, the target of the rage, and, finally, the perspective from which the construct of rage is discussed. In Intrapsychic Humanism, rage is discussed from the perspective of intrapsychic subjectivity (the perspective of intrapsychic caregiving and intrapsychic self-caretaking).[19]

We make an important distinction between rage and anger. Anger refers to intentional, aggressive behavior and/or feelings commensurate with unprovoked, painful events that are caused by another's rage (e.g., having an angry reaction to being mugged). We also distinguish rage from those affective experiences that are commonly referred to as anxiety or tension states. The distinction depends on the significance of the experience to the individual feeling the affect. Anxiety and tension may or may not have the meaning of rage; they represent rage if they signify a loss of the individual's inner well-being.

Intrapsychic self-rage and regulatory-interpersonal self-rage are pathologically dissociated personal meaning structures.[20] Consequently, they have no *inherent* association with affect, which is experienced solely on the constitutive-interpersonal level of consciousness. Intrapsychic and regulatory-interpersonal self-rage are structurally dissociated states and, therefore, can be known only from an intrapsychic caregiving perspective. Constitutive-interpersonal rage can be either conscious or unconscious and, therefore, can sometimes be conditionally known by introspection and empathy. Depending on an individual's capacity for concealment, her/his conscious constitutive-interpersonal rage may or may not be perceptible by another. In most instances, regardless of whether the self or another is the primary target, the initiator has no awareness whatsoever of her/his own rage. This lack of awareness is illustrated by the situation in which the individual feels the fury of her/his emotion, but ascribes this to an external cause (e.g., her/his boss) and, therefore, fails to perceive that the rage is self-generated.

The personal meaning structure of self-rage is invariantly a manifestation of psychopathology and a consequence of an obstructive transference process. As they grow older, all but the most disturbed children develop the ability to recognize crude forms of nonveridical *interpersonal* caregiving. Unfortunately, however, the child's capacity to recognize the nonveridical quality of some aspects of the caregiver's interpersonal caregiving has no restorative, beneficial effect on the motives for delusional intrapsychic mutuality (intrapsychic self-rage) s/he acquired before the end of the pre-eidetic stage, when the intrapsychic precept was pathologically distorted to include an ideal of nonveridical caregiving. The child acquires a motive for a continuous supply of this nonveridical caregiving, which becomes the fabric of the child's regulatory agency reality. The intrapsychic precept of psychopathological inner well-being is an intracranial agent cause that is located external to the agent-self.

From an intrapsychic caregiving perspective, in psychopathology the individual's intrapsychic agent-self and regulatory-interpersonal agent-self maintain a delusional, although dissociated, conviction of self-regulatory stability. This is the case even when the constitutive-interpersonal agent-self feels helpless and despairing. As will be seen, conscious constitutive-interpersonal experiences of psychic pain actually contribute to the delusional well-being of the pathological intrapsychic and regulatory-interpersonal agent-selves.

As personal meaning structures, intrapsychic and regulatory-interpersonal self-rage are regulating causes of the subjective experience of personal existence. We emphasize that when personal meaning structures of self-rage are viewed from the perspective of the individual's subjective experience, they represent personal meaning structures of ideal inner well-being. The innately determined intrapsychic motive and regulatory-interpersonal motive are to-be-actualized ideals of acquiring the ongoing relationship pleasure of the reflection of agent-self as agent-self; however, nonveridical intrapsychic caregiving distorts this need so that it can be gratified by nonveridical caregiving. In this sense, the regulatory agency reality of the individual with psychopathology is composed of personal meaning structures of self-rage, which, of course, the individual experiences as the source of her/his most pleasurable inner well-being.

Since personal meaning structures of intrapsychic and regulatory-interpersonal self-rage are defined strictly in telic terms (they are intracranial but external to the agent-self), there is no inherent contradiction in attributing to the construct of personal meaning structures of self-rage the characteristics of both intentionality and dissociation. We avoid the contradiction inherent in the construct of unconscious affect, which in part motivated Freud to replace the topographic model with the structural model of the psychic apparatus. Though he often alluded to unconscious affect, Freud took a position against this notion. He said that "Feelings cannot properly be described as 'unconscious.'"[21] In Intrapsychic Humanism, constitutive-interpersonal forms of rage not associated with affect refer not to unconscious affect but rather to the existence of the meaning structure of rage, which can be known by the effect that one person's interpersonal behavior has on another. For example, the other can feel assaulted by an interpersonal expression of rage of which the subject is entirely unaware. An illustration is the person who forgets to pick up a friend at the appointed time and leaves her/him stranded on a street corner.

Constitutive-interpersonal rage and constitutive-interpersonal self-rage can be known only conditionally because they can be known only through empathy or constitutive-interpersonal introspection. Knowledge of constitutive-interpersonal rage and constitutive-interpersonal psychic pain can be deduced only conditionally from reported introspection or manifest behavior. For example, a man who smiles and says he is glad to be leaving his job, but who toys with a letter opener while being fired, can reasonably be assumed to have hostile motives toward the person delivering the unpleasant news. The positing of hidden motives by the interpretation of manifest nonverbal and verbal behavior (e.g., malapropisms) is, of course, an established tradition in Western thought.[22] This hermeneutic understanding of hidden motives is categorically distinct from the understanding of hidden meanings made possible by the empirical mutuality of an intrapsychic caregiving relationship. Because of the nonempirical, indirect nature of empathic knowing, deductions about another's unconscious constitutive-interpersonal motives may be incorrect. In the above example, the motives of the person toying with the letter opener might run more in the direction of suicide than homicide.

An individual can use her/his cognition to make inferences about her/his own constitutive-interpersonal rage and self-rage. This is the type of introspection used by psychologists, philosophers, poets, and creative artists with an introspective orientation. Constitutive-interpersonal introspection is also the referent for the psychoanalytic construct of the self-analytic function, which is the stated goal of psychoanalysis. Like the use of empathy to make inferences about the constitutive-interpersonal motives of others, the use of constitutive-interpersonal introspection to understand solipsistic, constitutive-interpersonal self meaning structures may or may not be accurate. An example is the man who concludes that his true feelings for his lover are superficial because he forgot the woman's birthday. Constitutive-interpersonal introspection alone, however, will not enable him to verify this conclusion in the context of all the other possible hypotheses (for example, that the man really adores the woman and his psychopathological motives for isolation caused him to react aversively to the extent of his involvement).

The plethora of antithetical constitutive-interpersonal motives that can be posited as causes for a given behavior both fuels the cliché that psychodynamic theorists always see true motives as the opposite of apparent motives and also contributes to endless, unresolvable arguments over which competing interpretation of a given behavior is correct. Because of the solipsism and distance inherent in constitutive-interpersonal knowing, constitutive-interpersonal introspection and empathy cannot provide certain knowledge of agency reality even when they carry the conviction of unshakable accuracy. Thus, the conclusions of psychoanalytic theory, psychohistory, and applied psychoanalysis in general can never be verified. Only a caregiver who is engaged in a paradigmatic parenting relationship with a child, or a therapist engaged in a paradigmatic therapeutic process with a patient, can have certain knowledge of another's intrapsychic regulatory agency reality. As we will describe in chapter 7, however, since introspection can be made irrevocably private and pathological interpersonal meaning structures can exert hegemony over constitutive-interpersonal consciousness, prior to the differentiated developmental split that occurs late in treatment, the therapist can know only the patient's motives to be involved in or isolated from the intrapsychic caregiving relationship.

In psychopathology, every constitutive-interpersonal loss produces psychic pain on constitutive-interpersonal, regulatory-interpersonal, and intrapsychic levels of consciousness. At the same time, however, regardless of the form—conscious or unconscious, associated or not associated with affect—constitutive-interpersonal psychic pain serves as a gratifying, nonveridical agent-self percept for the pathological regulatory-interpersonal motive, which, in turn, serves as a gratifying, nonveridical agent-self percept for the pathological intrapsychic motive.

In a pathological transference process, the individual's intrapsychic motive is gratified by nonveridical intrapsychic caregiving. This phenomenon seemingly contradicts the assertion that continued physical existence rests upon the experience of feeling loved. However, as we have described, the individual's subjective experience of the meaning structures generated by the structure of illusional intrapsychic mutuality is an illusional intrapsychic well-being. The nonveridical intrapsychic perceptual identity process that becomes functional in response to stranger anxiety allows the child to survive nonveridical intrapsychic caregiving. The child will subjectively experience nonveridical intrapsychic caregiving as ideal caregiving love and will eidetically internalize it in the form of pathological caregiver percepts. From an intrapsychic caregiving perspective, however, the caregiver's nonveridical caregiving acquires the meaning of a caregiving frown. This meaning of caregiver displeasure, which contrasts to the meaning of caregiver love imparted by the nonveridical caregiver percept in paradigmatic development, will form the core of the eidetically internalized, pathological intrapsychic caregiver and, without intrapsychic therapy, will be the basis for the individual's intrapsychic agent-self experience.

Competition between Pathological Constitutive-Interpersonal Agent-Selves

A psychopathological subjective experience of personal existence is organized by two antipodal categories of social-interpersonal constitutive-interpersonal motives, which ultimately both serve and are regulated by the needs of the pathological intrapsychic motive. These antagonistic motives are the motive for constitutive-interpersonal pleasure and the motive for constitutive-interpersonal pain, both of which are used as gratifying, pathological agent-self percepts for the pathological regulatory-interpersonal motive. These competing constitutive-interpersonal centers of motive, the pathological pleasurable self and the dysphoric self, respectively, signify two separate and competitive intracranial centers of agency. While the introspectively inclined individual can experience the distinct difference between the dysphoric self and the pathological pleasurable self, from an intrapsychic caregiving perspective, these transference selves serve the same goal, namely, to gratify the pathological regulatory-interpersonal motive. The gratified regulatory-interpersonal motive, in turn, is the pathological agent-self percept for the pathological intrapsychic motive.

The pathological pleasurable self's motives for constitutive-interpersonal pleasure ultimately derive from the pathologically deformed intrapsychic motive for the pleasure of veridical intrapsychic mutuality. The extent to which an individual with intrapsychic psychopathology can have functional use of the motive for constitutive-interpersonal pleasure is largely a measure of the degree to which the caregivers' interpersonal caregiving was kind. A person with functional use of the motives of the pathological pleasurable self has intrapsychic psychopathology, but little or no clinically manifest interpersonal psychopathology. Such a person would be considered normal by the diagnostic criteria of other psychologies.

From an intrapsychic caregiving perspective, the pathological motive for psychic pleasure and the pathological motive for psychic pain represent ideals of two different types of caregiving intimacy and provide radically dissimilar types of care-getting pleasure. After the early part of the pathological intrapsychic self stage, if the caregiver's interpersonal caregiving behavior is relatively benign and positive, the nonveridical caregiver percepts used for intrapsychic motive gratification will be mainly the caregiving type rather than the presence type. The child will have predominantly pleasurable constitutive-interpersonal identifications and will have the capacity for pleasurable interpersonal self-experience and pleasurable interpersonal relationships. We emphasize, however, that transference pleasure is inherently unstable. Though the gratification of pathological pleasurable self motives has the introspective meaning of pleasure, from an intrapsychic caregiving vantage point, because this pleasure is used as a gratifying, pathological agent-self percept in the pathological transference process, from an intrapsychic caregiving perspective, it is in the service of psychic pain (self-rage). Regardless of how interpersonally benign the nonveridical caregiver was, the subjective personal existence of every individual who receives nonveridical intrapsychic caregiving will be regulated by motives for nonveridical personal meaning structures, which, from an intrapsychic caregiving perspective, are equivalent to motives for personal meaning structures of self-rage. Whether an individual's pathological pleasurable self motives or dysphoric self motives predominate, however, will significantly determine the relative pleasurableness or painfulness of the individual's conscious self-experience.

The individual who received traumatic interpersonal caregiving is likely to rely mainly on presence caregiver percepts for nonveridical intrapsychic motive gratification. This individual's constitutive-interpersonal identifications will be primarily dysphoric in nature, and s/he will be extremely conflicted about her/himself and about her/his motives for relationship pleasure (although the conflict will not necessarily involve career motives). The degree to which the motive for constitutive-interpersonal psychic pain controls a person's interpersonal functioning largely depends on the degree to which the caregivers' negative interpersonal caregiving behaviors forced her/him into negative constitutive-interpersonal identifications.

While psychopathology prevents an individual from developing the capacity for nontransference agent-self experience, it does not prevent the individual from developing an outstanding ability for *cognitive* reality testing. However, in psychopathology all social-interpersonal relationship experience is ultimately regulated by the solipsism that characterizes interpersonal consciousness when an individual lacks a regulatory-intrapsychic agent-self.

The Aversive Reaction to Pleasure

The subjective experience of psychopathological constitutive-interpersonal agency reality is regulated by an ongoing conflict we term the **aversive reaction to pleasure**.[23] The aversive reaction to pleasure reflects one side of the constantly shifting equilibrium between the motives of the pathological pleasurable self and those of the dysphoric self. The pathological pleasurable self and the dysphoric self continuously compete for hegemony over the individual's interpersonal behavior, including the individual's introspected thought processes. Subjectively, the individual's pathological pleasurable self has no motive for psychic pain. However, because in psychopathology the individual lacks a stable inner well-being that is unaffected by constitutive-interpersonal loss, the pathological pleasurable self can only respond to interpersonal losses in general or to losses incurred as a result of its competitive struggle with the dysphoric self with a renewed (restitutional) pursuit of interpersonal pleasure. Except through the mourning process made possible by Intrapsychic Treatment, the dysphoric self structure cannot be destructuralized, and the tug of war between the two centers of agency continues in a context in which, eventually, positive entropy favors the dysphoric self.

The pleasure seeking of the pathological pleasurable self includes an adaptive aversion to constitutive-interpersonal pain that can be observed in all life forms. An individual will avoid constitutive-interpersonal pain to the extent that early childhood nurture and extrafamilial influences encouraged her/him to pursue an adaptive, pleasurable interpersonal existence. The dysphoric self usually functions within an unobserved dissociated state; even when it is conscious, it is phenomenologically experienced as an alienated, or even alien, self-experience. Accordingly, while the individual is subjectively convinced that the psychic pain s/he feels is not the product of agency (is not purposeful), from an intrapsychic caregiving perspective, the dysphoric self pursues gratification that has the manifest meaning of self-rage. These sought-after experiences of loss may or may not be associated with affect, but, when present, the affect is always unpleasant. Constitutive-interpersonal pleasure always signifies a loss to the dysphoric self. The dysphoric self responds to this loss with a renewed striving for pain, which has the unconscious meaning of transference pleasure in that, from an intrapsychic caregiving perspective, the dysphoric self distorts the regulatory ideal of avoiding loss into an ideal which, ultimately, has the meaning of the delusional pleasure (pain) of nonveridical intrapsychic caregiving. The dysphoric self seeks a personal existence based on a cruelly ironic and paradoxical reality. The regulatory ideal of the human species that has hegemony over all other ideals is the ideal of avoiding intrapsychic loss and seeking the pleasure of the reflection of effective agency through intrapsychic caregiving mutuality. This ideal blindly and vigorously sustains, supports, and directs the dysphoric self to seek what, from an intrapsychic caregiving viewpoint, is self-directed rage. An example of the sort of distortion that can be caused by this capacity to use derivative, constitutive-interpersonal self-rage as a gratifying, pathological agent-self percept is taken from a radio interview with a woman whose father was blind. The woman said, "I always thought not that my father was blind, but that I was invisible."

An aversive reaction to pleasure is the dysphoric self's reaction to each instance in which the pathological pleasurable self successfully gratifies its motives for constitutive-interpersonal pleasure. The aversive reaction to pleasure, therefore, is a manifestation of endogenous motives generated by nonveridical nurture, which, from an intrapsychic caregiving viewpoint, tinge the individual's existence with the omnipresent threat or actuality of loss in the face of the most satisfying pleasure. Each time the individual has a deeply pleasurable and satisfying experience, whether it be a thought, a career achievement, or a moment of satisfying relationship pleasure, the individual will feel driven to experience a compensating dysphoria. In a person without clinically manifest interpersonal psychopathology, this dysphoria can be as subtle and unrecognized as a thought about an unpleasant weather forecast, or it may be apparent only to another person.

The inner well-being generated by the dysphoric self resembles that generated by the pathological pleasurable self in that it serves as a pathological agent-self percept for the pathological all-powerful agent-self motive. Thus, the categorical difference between the pathological pleasurable self and the dysphoric self appears not in their ultimate goal (which is the avoidance of pain and the pursuit of the reflection of agent-self as agent-self) but in the means to that end. The aversive reaction to pleasure is the product of a motive for constitutive-interpersonal unpleasure. This unpleasure subjectively signifies the pleasure of a caregiving intimacy which, from an intrapsychic caregiving viewpoint, is based on intrapsychic and regulatory-interpersonal psychic pain. In other words, the dysphoric self restitutes the loss represented by pathological positive transference pleasure by actualizing motives for the meaning of unpleasure. This meaning of unpleasure (which signifies pleasure to the dysphoric self) restores the historically established atmosphere of nonveridical caregiving mutuality with the caregiver, because, from an intrapsychic caregiving perspective, the meaning of unpleasure characterized the intrapsychic relationship with the original caregiver and is, therefore, the means by which the dysphoric self can get the (illusional) reflection of effective agency.

Suicide

Every instance of constitutive-interpersonal pleasure or pain is a nonveridical agent-self percept for the pathological all-powerful agent-self motive and, in turn, for the pathological intrapsychic agent-self motive. Regardless of whether the individual consciously experiences constitutive-interpersonal loss as signifying victory or defeat, from an intrapsychic caregiving perspective, this loss can serve as a gratifying, nonveridical agent-self percept for the pathological regulatory-interpersonal motive and, thereby, become a source of intrapsychic motive gratification. For example, when an individual with psychopathology does not receive an expected promotion, the keen sense of loss that ensues provides a source of well-being for the individual's dysphoric self and, ultimately, for her/his intrapsychic agent-self. This pain-regulated gratification process partially explains why more people do not commit suicide. In part, the human species has been protected from self-extinction because only the rarest and most malignant forms of psychopathology necessitate a suicidal level of self-rage in order to preserve the illusion of regulatory, effective agency. It is unusual, in other words, for an individual to preserve the integrity of her/his agency reality only at the expense of her/his nonagency reality.

Another reason that suicide does not occur more frequently is the existence of the regulating ideals of the pathological pleasurable self structure. As stated before, the dynamics of the pathological split are such that constitutive-interpersonal loss stimulates the pathological pleasurable self to find a restitutional solution, which entails obtaining conscious constitutive-interpersonal pleasure. The regulating ideals of the pathological pleasurable self structure impel the pathological pleasurable self to avoid constitutive-interpersonal loss. To return to our example, not only can the person who is not selected for a promotion use the pain caused by this loss as a gratifying, pathological agent-self percept for the dysphoric self motive and, in turn, for pathological regulatory-interpersonal and intrapsychic transference gratification, but the pain can also stimulate the pathological pleasurable self to attempt to restitute the loss. This restitution might take the form of a renewed striving for the next promotion. Cases in which the person who has been fired or not promoted returns with a gun and shoots her/his supervisor are extreme instances of the attempt by the pathological pleasurable self to restitute the loss by acquiring a positive reflection for its effective agency capacity.

We hypothesize that another reason that constitutive-interpersonal self-rage in the form of suicide does not occur more frequently is that constitutive-interpersonal self-rage can be blunted by the effects of psychosis. Psychosis is a severely disabling form of constitutive-interpersonal self-rage in which the individual sacrifices her/his cognition to gratify dysphoric self motives. Psychosis preserves the (illusional) meaning of effective agency and, thereby, preserves life, by functionally ablating interpersonal reality testing and facilitating a rich experience of delusional meanings. Because psychosis does not inherently affect either gonadal functioning or physical survival, it has probably been adaptive in terms of the preservation of the human species.

Summary: Three Types of Losses in Psychopathology

Psychopathology involves three types of losses. The first, which can be known only from an intrapsychic caregiving perspective, is the ongoing, structural loss that the signified reflection of intrapsychic and regulatory-interpersonal agent-self as agent-self is delusional. While the individual does not reflectively experience the lack of veridical regulatory agency, subjectively experienced derivatives of it are, as we have seen, paranoid, filled with self-rage, or as-if. An individual's self-experience can be characterized by uncertainty, a lack of autonomy, inner dissatisfaction, or a lack of control over her/his own destiny. Or, on the other hand, an individual's inner experience can be composed mainly of constitutive-interpersonal pleasure. Nonveridical intrapsychic and regulatory-interpersonal agency is entirely compatible with interpersonal success because constitutive-interpersonal consciousness can function relatively smoothly, though not autonomously, even in the face of a psychopathological fixation of intrapsychic consciousness.

The second type of loss in psychopathology results from the inherent instability of psychopathological motive gratification. Because constitutive-interpersonal motive gratification is proximally subject to positive entropy and chance, it cannot be stably gratifying. As a result, the pathological pleasurable self structure is periodically deprived of transference pleasure, which causes the pathological all-powerful agent-self and, in turn, the pathological intrapsychic agent-self to lose the reflection of agent-self as agent-self. Intrapsychic loss must be restituted immediately; most often this occurs by the use of the psychic pain as a gratifying, pathological agent-self percept for the motives of the dysphoric self structure. This gratification, in turn, represents a nonveridical agent-self percept for the pathological all-powerful agent-self motive and, in turn, for the pathological intrapsychic motive. Even though a person with intrapsychic psychopathology can have a minimal amount of interpersonal psychopathology and, therefore, can possess a relatively stable motive for interpersonal pleasure, this pleasure will be interrupted constantly because of the losses inherent in constitutive-interpersonal motive gratification. For example, the most successful businessman will encounter reverses, the most successful politician will fail to get a bill passed, and the most successful athlete will lose a game. When this happens, in addition to the frustration of a specific constitutive-interper-

sonal motive, the individual with intrapsychic psychopathology will experience an interruption of inner well-being.

The third categorical type of loss that results from a pathological
psychic structure is caused by the conflict between the aims of the
pathological pleasurable self for (transference) pleasure and the aims
of the dysphoric self for (transference) pain. Transference pleasure signifies a loss to the dysphoric self and transference pain signifies a loss
to the pathological pleasurable self. This conflict makes stable inner
contentment and well-being impossible. A dramatic illustration of this
conflict is found in Stevenson's novella *The Strange Case of Dr. Jekyll
and Mr. Hyde*. Jekyll explains that he was driven to create Hyde because
of the

> primitive duality of man; I saw that, of the two natures that con-
> tended in the field of my consciousness, even if I could rightly be
> said to be either, it was only because I was radically both; and from
> an early date . . . I had learned to dwell with pleasure, as a beloved
> daydream, on the thought of the separation of these elements. If
> each, I told myself, could but be housed in separate identities, life
> would be relieved of all that was unbearable; the unjust might go
> his way, delivered from the aspirations and remorse of his more
> upright twin; and the just could walk steadfastly and securely on
> his upward path, doing the good things in which he found his
> pleasure, and no longer exposed to disgrace and penitence by the
> hands of this extraneous evil. It was the curse of mankind that
> these incongruous faggots were thus bound together—that in the
> agonized womb of consciousness, these polar twins should be con-
> tinuously struggling.[24]

One of the more corrosive aspects of a psychopathological existence
is that ongoing intrapsychic loss is produced not only by reactions to
inevitable constitutive-interpersonal loss but also by an individual's
own aversive reactions to constitutive-interpersonal pleasure. Examples
abound of instances in which constitutive-interpersonal pleasure stimulates severe reactions, such as reversing an individual's success, inadver-
tently causing loss in some other area, depression, a reactive psychosis,
accidental death, and even suicide. In a milder form, the aversive reaction to pleasure can occur as a feeling of slight dysphoria or a sense that
the sought-for and acquired satisfaction was not as rewarding as originally thought, which is illustrated by the saying, "The grass is always
greener on the other side of the fence."

Constitutive-interpersonal consciousness encompasses specific cognitive, social-interpersonal, and physiological motives. In psychopathology, the expression of these motives is determined by the ongoing conflict between the dysphoric self and the pathological pleasurable self. Constitutive-interpersonal motives can range from the need for constant interpersonal pain and misery to a functional desire for pleasure. Because it gratifies the dysphoric self, the meaning of self-rage (pain) caused by an aversive reaction to pleasure can even produce a consciously experienced sense of well-being. Examples are individuals who react to a pleasurable achievement with a penitent act or a state of mind that produces the pleasure of atonement. A mild example of this phenomenon is the patient who, after achieving an important success, would feel satisfaction in reminding herself to be sure not to get a swelled head.

Because the individual with psychopathology uses constitutive-interpersonal motive gratification for regulatory-interpersonal motive gratification and, in turn, for intrapsychic motive gratification, s/he is constantly vulnerable to the loss of inner esteem. The dynamics of the aversive reaction to pleasure impel the individual to experience some form of dysphoria (if only in mild forms, such as sleep disturbances) in response to the acquisition of consciously wished-for pleasure. At the same time, constitutive-interpersonal loss represents the loss of regulatory control (the loss of the reflection of agent-self as agent-self) to the pathological pleasurable self. Thus, in psychopathology the individual's conscious experience always has an out-of-control aspect to it; even a successful person with little or no clinically manifest interpersonal psychopathology cannot consistently, autonomously, and veridically regulate her/his inner well-being.

In summary, depending on the degree of an individual's interpersonal psychopathology, which is determined in large part by the amalgam of pleasurable and negative constitutive-interpersonal identifications (which are to a large extent a function of the degree to which the caregiver's interpersonal caregiving was abusive, overbearing, or negligent), an individual's conscious interpersonal experience can be composed of a vast array of permutations and commutations of feelings about the self and of motives for pleasure and for pain. Regardless of the quality of life experienced by the individual with a psychopathological self system, the intrapsychic caregiving perspective reveals that the person will be unable to mourn (1) the loss that accrues from the presence of a delusional intrapsychic agent-self and a delusional regulatory-interpersonal agent-self; (2) the loss that results because the primary agent-self percept that determines the individual's inner well-being, namely, constitutive-interpersonal motive gratification, is proximally subject to positive entropy and chance, which makes transference gratification inherently unstable; and (3) the loss that occurs when interpersonal pleasure stimulates the reactive pain (however subtle) of an aversive reaction to pleasure. From the same perspective, it can be seen that two categories of constitutive-interpersonal psychic pain characterize a psychopathological personal existence: pain caused by constitutive-interpersonal loss that is not self caused and pain caused by self-induced constitutive-interpersonal loss.

Pathological constitutive-interpersonal introspection often includes feelings of shame, inferiority, or guilt. Guilt refers to a socially organized form of constitutive-interpersonal self-rage. Shame represents a complex phenomenon in that, while it is a form of constitutive-interpersonal self-rage regulated by ideals that refer to social-interpersonal experience, it is often partly the consequence of a reaction against (and therefore represents regulation by) the form of constitutive-interpersonal self-rage that is organized by paranoid ideals. In this variant of shame, the source of the mortifying feelings is externalized. An example is the person who feels shame when an indiscretion is discovered, but not when s/he commits it. Suicide is the most extreme form of constitutive-interpersonal self-rage. Suicide, psychotic depression, and nonpsychotic depression represent varying degrees to which the motives of the dysphoric self structure, in harmony with negative constitutive-interpersonal identifications, have hegemony over the motives of the pathological pleasurable self structure. In these clinical states, a gratifying, pathological agent-self percept of conscious constitutive-interpersonal self-rage is the primary mode by which the individual obtains the needed reflection of agent-self as agent-self. In this case, the pain of constitutive-interpersonal self-rage has the meaning of being both deserved and intentionally caused.

Paranoid Character Structure

In this section, we will focus on *clinically manifest* interpersonal psychopathology, the consequences of which can potentially be introspected by the subject or known by empathy. We stress that clinically manifest interpersonal psychopathology represents only one aspect of psychopathology, and that a person whose behavior falls within all social norms can nevertheless have a psychopathological form of intrapsychic agency and can exhibit behavior that would fall within Intrapsychic Humanism's definition of interpersonal psychopathology.

The two forms of rage that primarily organize psychic conflict on the constitutive-interpersonal level of interpersonal consciousness are self-rage and paranoid rage. Constitutive-interpersonal self-rage is a product of the motives of the dysphoric self in combination with negative constitutive-interpersonal identifications, which include identifications with the caregivers' dysphoric self motives for self-rage and paranoid rage. Because it represents the use of the meaning of pain for constitutive-interpersonal pain relief, constitutive-interpersonal self-rage gratifies the dysphoric self motive. Gratification of the dysphoric self motive, in turn, represents a loss to the pathological pleasurable self, which seeks transference pleasure in the service of pain relief.

Because it is composed in part of negative constitutive-interpersonal identifications, some of which can include the caregiver's paranoid orientation (the motive to explain inner pain as externally determined), an individual's character structure can represent the organization of constitutive-interpersonal self-rage into a paranoid, or other-directed, form of rage. Paranoid rage only occurs on the constitutive-interpersonal level of consciousness; in contrast to self-rage, there is no intrapsychic or regulatory-interpersonal form of paranoid rage. Paranoid rage pathologically soothes constitutive-interpersonal self-rage. Because its sole function is to offer relief for the pain of constitutive-interpersonal self-rage that results from the gratification of the motives of the dysphoric self, paranoid rage, ironically, always serves the motives of the pathological pleasurable self. Motives for paranoid rage combine the power of the pathological pleasurable self with negative constitutive-interpersonal identifications so as to (incompletely) regulate the dysphoric self's motives for constitutive-interpersonal self-rage. In other words, paranoid rage is a form of pathological grieving by the pathological pleasurable self in response to the losses represented by the pain of constitutive-interpersonal self-rage.

An individual with a *paranoid character structure* associates every personal experience with such an unrelieved interpersonal unpleasure that it is hard to see the effects of motives for pleasure. The interpersonal caregiving received by a person with a paranoid character structure was sufficiently traumatic that self-raging personal meaning structures form the basis of the individual's character self. In this context, the motives of the child's pathological pleasurable self for relationship pleasure find a singular gratification from the fact that the caregiver's motive to form a positive alliance with the child stems from the caregiver's paranoid motives. When a caregiver has a paranoid character structure, s/he often makes an ally of the child with regard to her/his paranoid vision of the world. For example, s/he may enlist the child in a project to spy on the neighbors.[25] If this mode of relating is not sufficiently counterbalanced by other relationships that offer a nonparanoid gratification of the individual's pathological pleasurable self motive, the child's negative identifications will be organized so that, behaviorally, the child will develop a paranoid character structure. Among nonpsychotic types of psychopathology, the individual with a paranoid character structure has the least ability to form a successful therapeutic relationship.

In contrast to the phenomenon of the paranoid character structure, a dynamic form of paranoia exists in all untreated psychopathology. The individual soothes the pain of ongoing intrapsychic and regulatory-interpersonal loss with delusional mutuality (isolation) rather than with the reflective pleasure of the human contact found in a mutual, veridical caregiving relationship. Dynamic paranoia is a consequence of the primary lesion in all pathology, namely, motives for the pleasure of delusional intrapsychic mutuality. Everyone with a pathological self system is phobic (paranoid) about her/his own or another's potentially rage-free caregiving motives because they threaten the perceptual identity process that provides the individual's inner well-being. Because pathological intrapsychic motive gratification produces the meaning of delusional mutuality, the individual is necessarily phobic about derivatives of the innately determined intrapsychic motive, which convey the wish for veridical intrapsychic motive gratification (which has come to signify the loss of inner well-being). Also, from an intrapsychic caregiving perspective, the dysphoric self must necessarily be phobic about any behavior of another that could serve as a model of veridical self-caretaking. To the dysphoric self, veridical inner well-being signifies the loss of the delusional well-being that provides the dysphoric self with its agent-self meaning. A dramatic illustration of this phenomenon is the dream of a mother who had brought her daughter for Intrapsychic Treatment because of the daughter's symptoms of agoraphobia and low self-esteem. During the two years the teenager had been in treatment, her symptoms had dramatically improved: she was no longer uncomfortable about leaving her house, she had friends she enjoyed, and she felt positively about herself. One day the girl told her therapist that her mother had had an "interesting" dream, which she then related. In the dream the mother, the father, and the brother had all died, but the patient remained alive. The mother, father, and brother were in heaven looking *down* on the patient and feeling sorry for her because she was alive and not with them. Within a week, the mother called the therapist to say that she was terminating her daughter's treatment because the daughter was doing "well enough."

Invisibility and Acceptability of Pathological Psychic Pain

Psychopathology is adaptive in that it permits the dependent young to survive nonveridical caregiving. However, one consequence of the effectiveness with which psychopathology shelters the child from nonveridical caregiving is that psychopathology is invisible and, therefore, tenacious. Psychopathology is invisible because the individual cannot know that her/his intrapsychic agent-self experience is nonveridical. Psychopathology can also be invisible in the sense that the individual may consider conscious derivatives of psychic pain to be acceptable or inevitable.

Masochism is not instinctual but results from internalized pathological personal meaning structures caused by traumatic intrapsychic caregiving. The most dramatic consequence of masochism is the universal phenomenon that, from an intrapsychic caregiving viewpoint, the child's primary reaction to the loss of veridical pleasure caused by the caregiver's nonveridical intrapsychic caregiving consists of love for that caregiver. Common sense would suggest that the child would recognize the caregiver as the cause of her/his pain and that reidealization of the self would occur by the deidealization of the caregiver. This would be possible, however, only if the child's agent-self could supply its own gratification needs. The child experiences nonveridical intrapsychic caregiving as ideal caregiving that s/he is causing and regulating. Because the child experiences every effect as intentionally caused by a paradigmatic caregiver, meanings which, from an intrapsychic caregiving perspective, represent psychic pain caused by nonveridical caregiving acquire the meaning of caregiving love. In this way, the child transforms the caregiver's nonveridical intrapsychic caregiving into delusional pleasure. This motive for nonveridical pleasure is the basis of masochism.

Motives for the pleasure of delusional reflections of agent-self as agent-self are the primary defect in psychopathology. They furnish the primary defense against the reflective recognition of the nonveridical nature of the caregiver's intrapsychic caregiving and, in turn, of the nonveridical nature of the individual's regulatory agency experience.[26] From an intrapsychic caregiving perspective, the referent for all psychopathological psychic pain is, ultimately, nurture-caused intrapsychic motives for delusional intrapsychic mutuality. The greatest difficulty in effecting structural, permanent therapeutic change results from the invisibility to the individual's unaided constitutive-interpersonal introspection of the delusional well-being that shapes pathological intrapsychic and regulatory-interpersonal personal meaning structures. Because the individual never received veridical intrapsychic caregiving, s/he has no standard of comparison that would allow her/him to recognize that even her/his most pleasurable (transference) inner well-being represents the ongoing loss of a superior type of pleasure.

The invisibility and acceptability of psychic pain, therefore, are caused by intrapsychic denial. In psychopathology, the inability to have a nondelusional intrapsychic self-experience illuminates the difference between veridical intrapsychic self-caretaking and constitutive-interpersonal introspection. Except in psychotic states, solipsistic, nonempirical, constitutive-interpersonal introspection is potentially unaffected by either the presence or the absence of psychopathological psychic pain. In contrast, veridical intrapsychic self-caretaking cannot occur in the presence of psychopathological psychic pain because it is predicated on an empirical, veridical experience of intrapsychic care-getting pleasure. Intrapsychic caregiving is an activity in which the caregiver (the listener) actively responds to the child's intrapsychic motive and also represents a separate center of regulatory agency reality. In constitutive-interpersonal introspection, both the reporter and listener reside within one and the same center of agency. Intrapsychic denial is, thus, the consequence of the fact that the individual never has had a stable, veridical, empirical experience of causing the caregiver to choose the pleasure of intrapsychic caregiving over the pleasure of pursuing personal motives. As a result, the individual can neither discriminate between veridical and nonveridical caregiver percepts nor know that s/he experiences the caregiver's unintended nonveridical intrapsychic caregiving as intentional caregiver love. The difference between intrapsychic and interpersonal denial is that the former is, most importantly, the result of a structure that has remained undifferentiated, whereas the latter is the result of an active (though unconscious) motive.

Since children will always accept nonveridical intrapsychic caregiving as veridical caregiving, and since they must have at least this delusional experience of being the agent-cause of the caregiver's intrapsychic caregiving love in order to survive, when the child receives nonveridical caregiving, psychopathology is the price s/he pays for physical survival. Whereas Freud concluded that masochism is a consequence of the death instinct, to which he granted ultimate hegemony over psychic reality,[27] masochism is actually a function of a life or survival instinct. This survival instinct causes the child to misidentify nonveridical caregiving as veridical caregiving and, therefore, to pursue nonveridical meaning structures that subjectively convey ideal inner well-being but, from an intrapsychic caregiving perspective, signify psychic pain.

The child's psychic reality is fixated because the nonveridical caregiver needs to use the child's mind as a (transference) means to her/his own inner well-being. The nonveridical caregiver, furthermore, experiences loss in response to the child's motive for intrapsychic caregiving intimacy (the motive to be the agent-cause of the caregiver's veridical intrapsychic caregiving). One unfortunate consequence of intrapsychic psychopathology is that it makes an individual relatively impervious to psychological treatment by preventing her/him from having an empirical knowledge of the therapist's intrapsychic caregiving motives.

The most consciously unpleasurable self-experiences, such as those manifested in clinical syndromes in which individuals constantly berate themselves, can remain invisible in the sense that they feel acceptable and/or inevitable. For example, many people do not realize that they are depressed (their constitutive-interpersonal self-rage is invisible to them), while others feel angry at themselves but believe they deserve this self-rage. In each case, the individual fails to perceive that extreme dysphoria gratifies an active motive for the meaning of pain. An individual may introspectively recognize the presence of constitutive-interpersonal psychic pain, but, since s/he has no idea that the intrapsychic caregiving s/he received was nonveridical, s/he has no idea that her/his intrapsychic motive for this nonveridical intrapsychic caregiving leads to a motive for constitutive-interpersonal pain.

Whereas Freud treated masochism as a distinct nosological entity, we consider the masochism he described to be nothing more than a constitutive-interpersonal expression of self-rage. Eventually, Freud placed masochism under the hegemony of the death instinct.[28] From an intrapsychic caregiving perspective, constitutive-interpersonal masochism reflects a character structure with powerful motives for the conscious experience of unpleasure. A diverse spectrum of interpersonal motives can be used to organize and constitute this need for self-rage.

There are two general categories of constitutive-interpersonal masochism: mediated and nonmediated.[29] Constitutive-interpersonal masochism is mediated when an individual induces other people to act as instrumental causes of her/his constitutive-interpersonal pain (e.g., the individual solicits others to abuse her/him sexually). Constitutive-interpersonal masochism is nonmediated when an individual directly causes her/his own constitutive-interpersonal pain (e.g., the individual constantly berates her/himself).

The distinction between mediated and nonmediated masochism sheds light on the degree of acceptability that motives for self-rage have within a person's overall character structure. More often than not, mediated masochism occurs within a character structure that functions with such apparent autonomy that the afflicted person rarely enters treatment and even more rarely makes a thoroughgoing therapeutic agreement. The mediated masochist usually comes for help because of an external crisis rather than as the result of an introspective awareness of internal conflict. The nonmediated masochist tends to have an introspectively oriented character self. S/he usually presents her/himself for help because s/he has an introspective awareness that her/his unhappiness results from an internal disturbance of her/his sense of regulatory control over her/his subjective experience of personal existence. The nonmediated masochist is difficult to treat because, though s/he can often engage in a serious treatment process, the power of her/his dysphoric self motives makes the motive to hold on to pain particularly tenacious, which threatens to make the treatment process interminable. Patients with nonmediated masochism often desire pain relief but not at the cost of relinquishing consciously experienced self-rage, which has become their gyroscope. One example is a patient who said, "I know I am extremely critical of myself and that I make myself miserable, but I also know that if I didn't drive myself this way I would never accomplish anything." A second example is the patient who concluded, "I am nearly always in a storm of internal rage, which I don't like, but I can't escape it, and so I just put up with it without much hope of escape."

These vignettes illustrate the phenomenon of **acceptable psychic pain**. Acceptable psychic pain is a form of **invisible psychic pain.** An individual experiences acceptable psychic pain as noxious and unwanted but can neither regulate it nor become uninterested in it. In contrast to acceptable psychic pain, which is specific to masochism, invisible psychic pain characterizes all psychopathology. As we just described, invisible psychic pain refers to an individual's inability to recognize that a conscious experience has acquired the meaning of a pathological agent-self percept. In contrast to invisible and acceptable psychic pain, ***pathologically dissociated psychic pain*** refers to structurally unconscious motives for delusional inner well-being, which, from an intrapsychic caregiving viewpoint, has the meaning of psychic pain.

Contrast between Intrapsychic and Interpersonal Irrationality

In addition to the irrationality identified by Freud,[30] Intrapsychic Humanism recognizes an irrationality that concerns a disorder of the personal meaning structures of intrapsychic consciousness (a disorder in the capacity of the intrapsychic agent-self for intrapsychic reality testing). ***Intrapsychic irrationality*** represents the individual's defective reality testing of the veridicality of the gratification of her/his motive for intrapsychic relationship pleasure. This type of irrationality cannot be identified conclusively by a hermeneutic process, but only by the knowledge that is produced by intrapsychic caregiving in Intrapsychic Treatment, which makes it possible for the therapist to perceive the motives for delusional intrapsychic mutuality that are the ongoing source of the individual's pathological intrapsychic transference gratification. As we have noted, the hegemony exerted by intrapsychic irrationality may never affect cognitive reality testing. Intrapsychic irrationality is, therefore, consistent with thought that does not manifest the Freudian type of irrationality (does not exhibit the psychopathology of everyday life).[31]

Intrapsychic Humanism's broadening of the definition of mental illness to include intrapsychic psychopathology makes possible a new focus on the motives driving cognition and other forms of knowledge. *Mental illness* usually refers to what we would term meaning structures of constitutive-interpersonal consciousness and implies a distorted interpretation of reality. The corresponding assumption is that people without clinically evident mental illness will fundamentally agree about reality. Because of the pervasiveness of intrapsychic psychopathology, however, for most people *all* interpersonal motives, including motives to understand external reality, are ultimately regulated by (are pathological agent-self percepts for) pathological intrapsychic and regulatory-interpersonal motives. The presence of intrapsychic psychopathology is compatible with an individual's capacity to make brilliant discoveries about the natural world (about nonagency reality) or about aspects of human nature other than agency reality (e.g., the nature of language). The existence of intrapsychic psychopathology, therefore, is not a valid criterion for evaluating the veridicality of such discoveries. For example, the nature of Einstein's intrapsychic perceptual identity process is irrelevant to an evaluation of the theory of relativity. However, the motives that exert regulatory control over the discoverer's quest for knowledge are sometimes relevant to the accuracy of the discovery. Although discussions of the extent to which an author's philosophical and psychological theories are products of a psychopathological self system have been fundamentally ad hominem in nature because they have been restricted to a focus on the author's constitutive-interpersonal motives, the intrapsychic and regulatory-interpersonal paradigm of irrational thought makes possible a nonpersonalized basis for evaluating a theorist's motives. For example, it is reasonable to assert that Descartes's search for a certainty that could inhere exclusively in a privileged first-person case (that could be reached by what we term constitutive-interpersonal introspection) was, by definition, a reflection of Descartes's intrapsychic psychopathology, which drove him to look to constitutive-interpersonal consciousness for an absolutely certain knowledge of (and, therefore, regulation of) his personal existence. If Descartes had had a veridical regulatory-intrapsychic agent-self, he would not have looked to constitutive-interpersonal consciousness for certainty.

These observations about Descartes differ from the reductionistic attempts by applied psychoanalysis to explain, for example, the content of da Vinci's art through an analysis of his psyche.[32] Due to the inherent fallibility of empathy, it is impossible to account for the specific relationship between constitutive-interpersonal psychopathology and creativity or other mental acts. It is impossible, therefore, to provide a one-to-one correlation between early life experiences and specific creative productions. However, it is possible to know that a given assertion about human nature is based on a psychopathological rather then a paradigmatic view of human nature.

We wish to emphasize that we do not take the position that anyone who disagrees with us is mentally ill. Since we have a more restrictive definition of mental health and a more inclusive definition of psychopathology than has been advanced by other authors, however, we would conclude that many philosophical and psychological assertions about essential human nature that have been examined only in a context divorced from psychopathology are the products of psychopathological motives and do not speak to paradigmatic human nature. Nevertheless, we do not presume to make judgments about the aesthetic value of a theory, the moral motivation of the theorist, or the veridicality of the theorist's capacity for cognitive reality testing. Creative ideas and art forms that we would term intrapsychically psychopathological in origin have made deeply moving, original contributions to an understanding of the common human condition. Yet philosophical and psychological discussions that are under the hegemony of the author's intrapsychic psychopathology, even though they can be regulated on a conscious level by the highest ideals, cannot directly facilitate an understanding of paradigmatic human nature (although they can shed light on specific forms of interpersonal psychopathology). One consequence is that the effects of intrapsychic psychopathology on the findings of studies of "normal" human subjects have not been recognized.

NOSOLOGY

In psychopathology, both conscious and unconscious forms of psychic pain ultimately result from the use of nonveridical intrapsychic caregiving for intrapsychic motive gratification. Psychopathological psychic pain represents the delusional use of the caregiver's nonveridical intrapsychic caregiving (which, from an intrapsychic caregiving viewpoint, causes the child to experience the loss of the pleasure of veridical intrapsychic agency) for gratification of the distorted intrapsychic motive for intrapsychic caregiving love. Motives for delusional inner well-being represent the attachment of delusional personal meaning significance to unrecognized and unmourned intrapsychic pain.

Nosologies based on behavioral description or psychodynamic principles enumerate the many epiphenomenal manifestations of constitutive-interpersonal forms of self-rage and other-directed rage.[33] These manifestations, or symptoms, are mainly caused by negative constitutive-interpersonal identifications with the caregivers' constitutive-interpersonal rage and/or self-rage. Also significantly contributing to an individual's constitutive-interpersonal expressions of psychopathology are (1) the individual's genic endowment, especially in relation to cognitive functioning, and (2) the quality and timing of the extrafamilial influences to which the individual is exposed.

As we have said, many expressions of interpersonal psychopathology are commonly mistaken for normal development or seen as a slight and not particularly significant deviation from the normal. Examples include the "terrible twos," nightmares, toilet training conflicts, fears and phobias, bed wetting, thumb sucking past the age of one, delayed speech, adolescent rebellion or expressions of low self-esteem. These manifestations of interpersonal psychopathology have been taken for normality because of their prevalence. Also, since intrapsychic consciousness has never previously been identified, interpersonal success at love and work has, understandably, been accepted as indicating mental health, and accompanying perturbations in inner well-being have been misunderstood as normal responses to constitutive-interpersonal loss or as essential human nature. The extent to which intrapsychic psychopathology and interpersonal success and adaptiveness can coexist has not been recognized.

Descriptive nosologies underestimate psychopathology both because they do not recognize intrapsychic psychopathology in a person whose interpersonal functioning is typical or adequate and also because they focus solely on constitutive-interpersonal agency reality, which is proximally affected by positive entropy and chance. Average or typical human misery ("common unhappiness") is considered unavoidable and normative.[34] One unfortunate consequence of such nosologies has been that psychopathological childhood unhappiness has been overlooked and many children who could profit from psychological treatment do not receive it.

Other psychologies use descriptive nosologies based on empathy and behavioral description. In contrast, the fundamental form of psychopathology in our nosology is the unitary meaning structure of intrapsychic pain that is due to a structural defect, namely, the fact that the child never develops a veridical intrapsychic agent-self because her/his intrapsychic agent-self cannot veridically regulate the caregiver's intrapsychic caregiving. Accordingly, nosological categories in Intrapsychic Humanism are determined by the patient's treatability rather than by, for example, the quality of the patient's interpersonal functioning. For example, our nosological categories are not determined by the presence or absence of psychotic thought processes or by the quality of cognitive thought processes. Treatability can only be determined from an intrapsychic caregiving perspective within a diagnostic process. Therefore, Intrapsychic Humanism's nosology cannot be applied to persons who do not voluntarily bring themselves for help. The use of biographical data to assess a person's psychic make-up, as in applied psychoanalysis, can have a descriptive utility, but it is ultimately unreliable as a diagnostic tool because biographical data is the product of a hermeneutic, cognitive activity and cannot conclusively establish the presence of a motive to develop a veridical type of regulatory agency reality through involvement in a therapeutic relationship.

Interpersonal psychopathology varies widely in its severity. For example, an individual with interpersonal psychopathology can experience great interpersonal success and have generally positive relationships, or an individual with interpersonal psychopathology can die from anorexia nervosa. In the presence of intrapsychic psychopathology, however, even a highly functional individual will occasionally have the sense of not being in control of her/his inner well-being and will not always be able to regulate her/his interpersonal motive choice. Further, in response to inevitable interpersonal loss, this person will be unable to experience genuine mourning and, therefore, will be unable to separate her/his inner esteem from the vicissitudes of her/his constitutive-interpersonal experience. The predominant psychic pain introspectively experienced by this individual will be a sense of incomplete regulatory control. For example, the individual can feel unaccountably depressed for short periods or find her/himself overreacting to certain losses, such as being delayed in traffic. Some individuals with intrapsychic psychopathology can even have a consistently unruffled constitutive-interpersonal introspective experience. However, this introspected sense of stable well-being is the product of dissociated states that can be recognized by external observers. An example is the individual who constantly gave advice and felt completely in control of himself. The advice, however, was a reaction to the anxiety aroused by others' potential or actual failures.

At the other extreme, the infant who dies of psychological marasmus cannot even use oral constitutive-interpersonal gratification for illusional intrapsychic pleasure because of the overwhelming toxicity of the caregivers' interpersonal behavior. This infant will reject all nourishment in order to remain connected to the only source of intrapsychic motive gratification available, the innate personal meaning structures with which s/he was born.

Treatability, which is the sole nosological discrimination made in Intrapsychic Treatment, refers to the patient's actual or potential ability to make developmental use of the therapist's veridical intrapsychic caregiving (to make use of the experience within the therapy session of the reflection of intrapsychic agent-self efficacy that results from being the veridical agent cause of the therapist's intrapsychic caregiving). This nosology follows from the goal of Intrapsychic Treatment, namely, to correct the patient's intrapsychic structural defect by reactivating her/his veridical intrapsychic precept and veridical intrapsychic motive and, subsequently, by making possible the differentiation of her/his regulatory-intrapsychic agent-self and veridical regulatory-interpersonal agent-self. Accordingly, as will be discussed more fully in chapter 7, the basis for the therapeutic action in Intrapsychic Treatment is the intrapsychic caregiving mutuality made possible by the therapist's regulatory-intrapsychic agent-self. The therapeutic action consists of a dual process of structure building and mourning. The therapist responds to the patient's need for help by offering the patient veridical intrapsychic motive gratification in the context that the therapist does not gratify the patient's motive for nondevelopmental interpersonal relationship pleasure.

The therapist uses the diagnostic interviews to assess the nature of the patient's motive for help and, thereby, to assess the patient's treatability. Patients can have two distinct motives for help: (1) pain relief, which may or may not be accompanied by (2) the functional or potentially functional motive for a pain-free (veridical, nontransference) agent-self experience. Without the potentially functional motive for veridical agent-self experience, a patient can only benefit from supportive Intrapsychic Treatment. While supportive Intrapsychic Treatment can effect a major reduction in this individual's symptoms (in the individual's constitutive-interpersonal dysphoria), once the individual's symptoms improve, s/he will be unaware of the remaining, ongoing loss caused by the existence of delusional regulatory agent-self experience.

In psychopathology, cognitive functioning can remain virtually unimpaired (although it ultimately serves pathological intrapsychic and regulatory-interpersonal motives) or it can be significantly compromised. Between these extremes, psychopathology often affects an individual's ability to exercise her/his cognitive capacities to the fullest. An example is the person who cannot think clearly in a testing situation. While all psychopathology results from the same intrapsychic and regulatory-interpersonal defects, it manifests itself in a wide variety of constitutive-interpersonal defects. Every instance of *constitutive-interpersonal* psychopathology presents a unique clinical picture of character self strengths and weaknesses, which in turn reflects the condition of the individual's cognitive functioning and the specific ideals and aims incorporated within the individual's constitutive-interpersonal identifications. A patient's motive for help accordingly reflects the degree to which the patterns of her/his character structure permit the therapist to have access to the latent, undifferentiated portion of the patient's intrapsychic motive. In other words, the patient's motive for help is a function of the degree to which the patient can tolerate and value the intimacy of the intrapsychic caregiving mutuality offered by the therapist. In clinical terms, the patient's motive for help is initially measured by the present outcome of the dynamic balance between the patient's motive for positive, pleasurable involvement that stems from the motives of the pathological pleasurable self and the aversive reactions to pleasure imposed by the dysphoric self.

The therapist assesses the patient's treatability by using the diagnostic interview(s) to ascertain the following:

1. Can the patient consciously recognize (feel gratified by) the therapist's veridical intrapsychic caregiving?

2. If not, does the patient have the *potential* capacity to feel gratified by the therapist's intrapsychic caregiving? and

3. Does the patient's motive for help include a goal of psychic pleasure other than pain relief?

The basic assessment of treatability must also include the following considerations: (1) a distinction between outpatient and inpatient treatment based on the extent to which the patient relies on forms of pain relief (restitutions) that are either destructive to her/himself or to others or cause a devastating loss of rational thought, and (2) the patient's ability to make a therapeutic commitment with respect to the use of the times the therapist has available, the ability to reach the therapist's office, and so on.

The nosology of Intrapsychic Humanism significantly increases the number of patients diagnosed as treatable. The great majority of individuals, including those with severe interpersonal psychopathology, can participate in an intrapsychic therapeutic relationship without becoming self-destructive or destructive to others and without losing the capacity for rationality. Further, most individuals who cannot meet the criteria for outpatient treatment could successfully have inpatient treatment.[35] Finally, nearly every one who wishes psychological assistance can benefit from supportive Intrapsychic Treatment. The only criterion for treatability in supportive Intrapsychic Treatment is that the patient have a reasonably stable motive to feel less dysphoria and more pleasure.

Contrast with Other Nosologies

Psychoanalytic theory posits that psychic pain is an intrinsic component of the fabric of psychic reality (of human nature) and, therefore, concludes that trauma is not a primary psychopathogenic agent. Psychoanalytic theory sees psychic pain as primarily biological in origin and as proximally caused by the unavoidable, innately determined conflict between the instinctual drives and the demands of external (social) reality. The ego functions as the seat of psychic conflict and pain, and an individual is thought to reach out for help when sufficient regression (libidinal or structural) occurs to interfere with the ego's normal mechanisms of defense. Psychoanalysis views the patient's suffering as primarily caused by the opposition of instinctual wishes that are forbidden both by the demands of society and also by the instinctually based rage of the structurally unconscious part of the ego and superego.

The superego and the repression barrier that psychoanalytic theory considers normative do not in fact exist in paradigmatic development. The superego described in psychoanalytic theory represents, we believe, a form of constitutive-interpersonal self-rage that functions as a gratifying, pathological agent-self percept for the pathological regulatory-interpersonal motive. The individual who has received paradigmatic caregiving can experience constitutive-interpersonal loss without any diminution in inner well-being. As a result, s/he has no need for pathological denial or other types of self-regulation based on self-rage, and s/he has no conflicted unconscious or superego. What Freud stipulated as the irreducible elements of his psychoanalytic theory, namely psychic determinism (the incorrigible control of constitutive-interpersonal behavior by structurally dissociated motives) and a dynamically conflicted unconscious, in fact occur only in psychopathology.

While psychoanalytic theory does point to nurture (trauma) as well as to nature as a cause of psychic pain, it subordinates nurture to nature and postulates that phylogenetically determined, inexorable psychic conflict forms the basis for the subjective experience of personal existence. The ramifications of the psychoanalytic model can be quite startling. An example is the assertion that the seemingly unnatural, antihumanistic experience of being abused by one's parents can exacerbate, but not be a primary etiologic agent of mental illness. Psychoanalytic theory posits two types of psychic pain: that which is innately determined (species specific) and that which the individual internalizes in the form of negative introjects of the caregiver. Consequently, even when the child is the object of extreme abuse, psychoanalytic theory asserts that the child's internalization of this abuse is regulated by an innately determined rage directed at the caregiver, which is ascribed either to the child's response to the intrusion of the external world into the autoerotic monadic self or to an innate force labeled the *death instinct*.

According to psychoanalytic theory, humans will always have psychic pain. Psychoanalytic theory views psychic pain as innately determined and also as the result of the world's reasonable response to the child's unreasonable, innately determined, instincts. Freud concluded that psychic pain is the price paid for civilization and the consequence of the positive entropy that rules physical existence (e.g., the death instinct).[36] In contrast, we believe that, in spite of the fact that positive entropy gives nonagency reality ultimate power over regulatory agency reality, intrapsychic and regulatory-interpersonal pain cannot occur once an individual completes a paradigmatic developmental process.

The difference between Intrapsychic Humanism's and psychoanalysis's nosologies can be illustrated by examining what psychoanalytic theory calls the obsessive-compulsive neurosis.[37] Psychoanalytic theory asserts that this nosological category represents a preoedipal defense to an oedipal conflict, specifically, that it is organized by conflicted psychosexual wishes that occur in the context of a fixated anal stage. The psychoanalytic construct of anal fixation illustrates the etiological significance ascribed by psychoanalysis to the conflict between the child's innately determined, pregenital sexual desires and the aims of the child's narcissistic libido. This explanation focuses on constitutive-interpersonal (psychosexual) motives rather than on the hegemonic motives and meaning structures of pathological forms of intrapsychic and regulatory-interpersonal motives. From our perspective, the pertinent dynamic cause of obsessive-compulsive behavior is a pathological transference process organized by the competing motives of the pathological pleasurable self and the dysphoric self. The doing and undoing of compulsive behavior is a repetitive cycle in which motives for constitutive-interpersonal pleasure that stem from the pathological pleasurable self trigger an aversive reaction to pleasure on the part of the dysphoric self, which takes the form of an undoing, self-raging set of motives for constitutive-interpersonal pain. In contrast to psychoanalytic theory, we assert that physiological motives have an etiological significance only to the degree that they are indications of the child's idiosyncratic interpersonal relationship with the primary caregivers and of the child's exposure to extrafamilial influences. In other words, the issue that psychoanalytic theory labels choice of neurosis or symptom specificity[38] is irrelevant to the fundamental etiology of psychopathology and can be discussed on the level of innate endowment and familial and cultural contexts.

In summary, we believe that psychopathology reflects the phenomenon that humans develop motives for the pleasure of delusional inner well-being in response to nonveridical (unstable) intrapsychic caregiving. As a result, in psychopathology the individual cannot experience stable inner well-being. For example, the individual cannot know for sure how s/he will feel upon awakening and can have trouble consistently making self-caretaking decisions (e.g., how much to eat, drink, or work). The individual manifests this lack of regulatory control of positive feelings about the self through a variety of dissociated states. Perhaps the most subtle, because most ubiquitous, example of the consequence of intrapsychic and regulatory-interpersonal psychopathology involves the distinction between foreseeing and intending. Often, people are aware that they will do something, but cannot decide not to do it. For example, someone on a diet might know s/he is about to eat but be unable to resist. Less common and, therefore, more obvious, are those subjective experiences that are sufficiently out of the ordinary that they are obviously pathological (symptomatic). Examples include a spectrum of manifest, constitutive-interpersonal self-rage that ranges from mild inhibitions to extreme self-hatred and suicide.

The following short clinical vignettes illustrate conscious derivatives of the loss that occurs in psychopathology due to the fact that regulatory control of the individual's intrapsychic and regulatory-interpersonal well-being is outside the agent-self. A five-year-old patient came in for her therapy appointment and announced that she had had a "bad day" and had gotten into all kinds of trouble at school. She said, "I feel like there's a little person inside me pulling strings." A 12-year-old patient was very worried that he would forget his lines in the play in which he was to perform that evening. At the same time, he felt that no matter how hard he rehearsed, he could not feel a sense of control over whether or not he would remember his lines when the time came to say them. He told the therapist he found himself commenting to himself, "I hope you don't forget your lines."

THE VALUE OF A COGNITIVE UNDERSTANDING OF INTRAPSYCHIC HUMANISM

The caregiver who lacks a regulatory-intrapsychic agent-self but has a cognitive understanding of the principles of Intrapsychic Humanism can help her/his child to develop the capacity to have a relatively pleasurable and successful, in contrast to a painful and unsuccessful, personal existence. Though this caregiver cannot, by definition, regulate her/his regulatory agency reality well enough to give the child veridical intrapsychic caregiving, the caregiver's good intentions, coupled with an understanding of Intrapsychic Humanism's principles of child development and psychopathology, can go a long way toward keeping the child's interpersonal psychopathology to a minimum.

For example, the caregiver's responses to the child's interpersonal expressions of intrapsychic pain makes a critical difference. If the child has temper tantrums, which, by definition, indicate the presence of intrapsychic psychopathology, the caregiver knows that the child is experiencing at least the following losses: (1) the loss of constitutive-interpersonal motive gratification, (2) the resultant pathological all-powerful agent-self loss of the signified meaning of agent-self as agent-self (the loss of not having regulatory control over the pursuit and gratification of constitutive-interpersonal motives), and (3) the resultant intrapsychic loss of effective agency, which is due to the loss of the nonveridical agent-self percept (pathological all-powerful agent-self gratification) that gratifies the pathological intrapsychic motive.

Authors on child development commonly recommend that caregivers respond to the child's temper tantrums with manifest expressions of disapproval or by ignoring or otherwise isolating the child. The consequence of disapproval or isolation, however, is that the child must either give the experience of unpleasure created by the caregiver's response the meaning of a gratifying, pathological agent-self percept for the motives of the dysphoric self (to use pain for pain relief) or the child must renew her/his efforts to gain the constitutive-interpersonal motive gratification that has not been forthcoming (e.g., to continue or escalate the tantrum) in order to get pleasure to use for pain relief. In either case, the child learns to respond maladaptively and painfully to constitutive-interpersonal motive frustration. The caregiver will respond quite differently, however, if s/he understands that the tantrum primarily represents the child's attempt to regain inner well-being by acquiring the reflection of effective agency and that the tantrum is neither an act of hostility and disobedience nor a character trait that must be eradicated. The caregiver will try to help the child to regain the reflection of effective intrapsychic and regulatory-interpersonal agency in a way that does not entail constitutive-interpersonal self-rage or desperate, senseless perseverance. For example, the caregiver will offer the child an ideal of mourning through interpersonal mutuality, which gives the child's pathological pleasurable self a boost (helps the child to respond to the loss with increased awareness rather than with denial). The caregiver might say, "It's very hard having to go to bed when you don't feel like it," and then show the child that the caregiver will do everything possible to help the child to respond to the loss with motives that stem from her/his pathological pleasurable self structure rather than with motives that stem from her/his dysphoric self structure. The caregiver might ask, "Would you like to come and choose a stuffed animal to take to bed with you and choose a story for me to read?"

It is always important to distinguish between behavior and motive. The act of offering the child a stuffed animal or a story can be justified in terms of the instinctual model of psychoanalytic theory as helping the child's ego in its attempt at instinctual renunciation. The caregiving based on this rationale, however, is not intrapsychically facilitative. Because the instinctual model does not include a recognition of the child's agent-self experience, the substitute gratification is in the service of helping the child renounce an ungratified motive rather than in the service of helping the child feel an ongoing sense of effective agency in the context of constitutive-interpersonal loss.

Even when the child with intrapsychic psychopathology seems happy, occupied, and self-sufficient, the caregiver can be very facilitative. For example, if the child is busily putting a puzzle together, the caregiver gives the child plenty of encouragement and appreciation of her/his accomplishments, not with a Skinnerian belief in reinforcing the behavior itself but with the goal of nourishing the pleasure-seeking motives of the pathological pleasurable self.

The phenomenon of aversive reactions to pleasure will allow a caregiver who cannot give veridical intrapsychic caregiving to give the child relatively veridical *interpersonal* caregiving. For example, the caregiver may take great pains to give the child exactly what s/he wanted for her/his birthday. The child may respond by focusing on something that is "wrong" with the gift, such as the color of the doll's hair or the model of the truck. The caregiver who is informed by the principles of Intrapsychic Humanism does not conclude that the child is spoiled, ungrateful, willful, or hostile, but understands that the child's behavior is an aversive reaction to pleasure. The caregiver can suggest to the child that the child is caught between two separate motives by saying, for example, "Perhaps one part of you feels pleased that we got you what you asked for, which might make another part of you believe that you feel bad about having gotten what you wanted." This response, if made with affection and understanding, can help the child to recognize this pattern of behavior and, thereby, help the child to gain the increased control that a cognitive understanding and positive constitutive-interpersonal identifications can impart.

While nothing will change intrapsychic psychopathology except Intrapsychic Treatment,[39] the caregiver can have a beneficial impact on the quality of the child's subjective experience of personal existence because s/he can affect whether the child's motives for constitutive-interpersonal pleasure or motives for constitutive-interpersonal pain will have proximal hegemony over the child's subjective experience of personal existence.

This discussion also applies to therapists who may not themselves have regulatory-intrapsychic and regulatory-interpersonal agent-self stability but who, if they know the principles of Intrapsychic Humanism, will be able to help their patients to rely more on the pleasure-seeking motives of the pathological pleasurable self than on the pain-seeking motives of the dysphoric self. While the process described above may resemble the well-recognized syndrome of transference cure, it differs categorically because it is based on an understanding of loss and on practice principles that lead to effective responses to loss. It also does not encourage dissociated states induced by pathological positive transference feelings. Most importantly, the therapist must understand both the phenomenon of aversive reactions to pleasure, specifically, aversive reactions to intrapsychic care-getting pleasure, and the fact that all psychopathology ultimately rests on a distorted motive for intrapsychic and regulatory-interpersonal caregiving pleasure. An understanding of aversive reactions to pleasure can aid those therapists who tend to grow discouraged or angry when patients enter periods of isolation, depression, or paranoia. By recognizing that aversive reactions to pleasure are as integral to the therapeutic process as pathological positive transference phenomena, a therapist will be better equipped to ride out these aversive reactions with a maximum of grace and a minimum of blame directed at her/himself or the patient.

Lastly, Intrapsychic Humanism can give an individual without a veridical agent-self a lever with which to help her/his pathological pleasurable self motive for constitutive-interpersonal pleasure gain hegemony over her/his dysphoric self motive for constitutive-interpersonal pain. For example, understanding aversive reactions to pleasure will help an individual who feels somewhat depressed after a big success or who continuously finds fault with her/his lover to make sense of these seemingly incomprehensible behaviors and to be generally aware that any pleasure will trigger a motive for psychic pain. Further, by understanding that constitutive-interpersonal motive frustration has the added meaning of both regulatory-interpersonal loss and intrapsychic loss, an individual can understand why s/he has an exaggerated response to constitutive-interpersonal loss. The individual will be helped to distinguish the *real* loss from the signified transference meaning of the loss (which can include feeling the end of the world is imminent or feeling extreme self-hatred).

In general, whether psychic pain is present in one's child, one's patient, or oneself, once aversive reactions to pleasure are understood and accounted for, success can breed success. The more an individual can be helped or help her/himself to gratify pathological pleasurable self motives rather than dysphoric self motives, the more s/he will be able stably to choose constitutive-interpersonal pleasure and avoid constitutive-interpersonal pain. Pathological intrapsychic motive gratification based on constitutive-interpersonal pleasure is fundamentally more pleasurable than pathological intrapsychic motive gratification based on constitutive-interpersonal pain (which has the subjective meaning of pleasure). In this sense, the pathological pleasurable self has the advantage over the dysphoric self, which explains why small inputs can have a huge effect on the balance between the pathological pleasurable self and the dysphoric self and, consequently, on the quality of the person's subjective experience of personal existence. For example, many people will say that a particular teacher, coach, or incident changed their entire lives. The meaning of this change, of course, lies in the shift in the dynamic balance between psychopathological motives for pain as pain relief and for pleasure as pain relief.

7
Intrapsychic Treatment

THE GOAL OF TREATMENT

Intrapsychic Treatment provides the individual who received non-veridical intrapsychic caregiving the opportunity to acquire the intra-psychic nurture necessary to develop the capacity for a stable, loss-free, pleasurable inner well-being.[1] Since all psychopathology is a manifes-tation of conflict caused by a nurture-induced structural deficit and malformation, the goal of Intrapsychic Treatment, psychic structure building, is analogous to the goal of child development, namely, the differentiation of a regulatory-intrapsychic agent-self and a veridical regulatory-interpersonal agent-self. We recommend supportive (in con-trast to structure building) Intrapsychic Treatment when, for some rea-son, the patient does not develop an operative motive for veridical in-trapsychic care-getting pleasure but has a stable motive to feel better through the medium of a reflective relationship experience. Supportive treatment may also be appropriate when an individual enters treatment with the sole goal of alleviating a specific symptom, such as agorapho-bia, or wants help with a time-limited crisis. Supportive treatment exclu-sively aims to help the patient's pathological pleasurable self achieve a relatively stable dominance over her/his dysphoric self. In this way, sup-portive Intrapsychic Treatment can produce beneficial and significant effects.

Except where otherwise stated, this chapter exclusively focuses on structure–building Intrapsychic Treatment, which both positively af-fects the balance between the patient's dysphoric self and pathological pleasurable self and, further, allows the patient to acquire stable, ve-ridical self-regulatory control over her/his subjective experience.

THE STRUCTURAL BASIS FOR INTRAPSYCHIC TREATMENT

Paradoxically, the innately determined intrapsychic perceptual iden-tity process that makes humans vulnerable to mental illness also contributes to the mentally ill individual's potential to complete her/his intrapsychic development through Intrapsychic Treatment. With rare exceptions, each individual with psychopathology can achieve the intrapsychic developmental goal that was denied her/him in childhood.

In contrast to paradigmatic development, in psychopathology the onset of the interpersonal self does not preclude the possibility of empirical, mutual contact between the individual's intrapsychic agent-self and another's intrapsychic caregiving motives. This is the structural reason for the efficacy of Intrapsychic Treatment. As long as an individual's intrapsychic consciousness remains structurally incomplete, s/he has no autonomous, empirically based reflection of intrapsychic agent-self as agent-self. As a result, an individual's nonfunctional veridical intrapsychic motive retains the potential for differentiation. Although the innately determined intrapsychic perceptual identity process makes the infant vulnerable to mental illness, in the context of Intrapsychic Treatment, pathologically distorted intrapsychic meaning structures also signify incomplete individuation actively seeking veridical completion (differentiation). Differentiation can occur only if the patient received sufficiently benign interpersonal caregiving that the pleasure-seeking motives of her/his pathological pleasurable self are powerful enough to leave the patient's intrapsychic consciousness functionally receptive to the empirical, mutual pleasure of the therapist's intrapsychic caregiving.

The therapist uses diagnostic interviews to assess the patient's treatability by determining the nature of the patient's motive for help. As described in chapter 6, there are two basic motives for help: (1) relief of the pain caused by the gratification of the motives of the dysphoric self and (2) the functional or potentially functional motive for a pain-free (veridical) agent-self experience. The latter is necessary for the patient to achieve the equivalent of a completed paradigmatic developmental process.

We hasten to add that no patient comes to therapy consciously, actively seeking intrapsychic structure building (seeking veridical intrapsychic pleasure rather than transference pleasure). Rather, every patient comes feeling dysphoria and wanting relief from this pain (wanting transference pleasure). The therapist both respects the patient's need for psychic pain relief and also understands that, from an intrapsychic caregiving viewpoint, pain relief that occurs by means of social-interpersonal relationship pleasure ultimately has the same meaning as does pain relief that occurs by means of social-interpersonal relationship pain, namely, the meaning of pain represented by delusional inner well-being.

The treatable patient has the potential or actual capacity to trust in and feel gratified by the therapist's veridical intrapsychic caregiving. An example of a patient in the process of actualizing this capacity to trust the therapist's veridical intrapsychic caregiving is a six-year-old boy who had great difficulty feeling he had any control over his own subjective experience. The boy came into a therapy session that took place after he had been in Intrapsychic Treatment for about a year looking very dejected. He had missed the previous session because of an illness. The therapist asked him how he was feeling and he replied, "There's nothing in my mind." The therapist said, "Oh?" and the boy went on: "Yes. You know the bad guy in my mind that is so mean to me?" The therapist nodded. The boy continued, "Well, he broke open the lock in my mind and let everything out. I need you to help me fill it up again."

The goal of intrapsychic treatment is neither to resolve what psychoanalytic theory terms intersystemic conflict nor to strengthen compensatory sectors of the self.[2] The intrapsychic therapist focuses on the patient's current reactions to the intrapsychic caregiving relationship.[3] The intrapsychic therapist offers the patient the veridical intrapsychic nurture necessary both to reawaken the patient's veridical constitutive-intrapsychic motive and also to help the patient mourn the loss represented by psychic pain, which has acquired the subjective meaning of pleasure. Intrapsychic Treatment makes it possible for the patient to acquire veridical agent-self, self-regulatory control over her/his inner well-being by virtue of the patient's veridical, empirical experience of being the agent cause of the therapist's intrapsychic caregiving. Whereas the primary tools of psychoanalysis (interpretation and the development of a transference neurosis) aim to help the patient relive her/his past in the present, Intrapsychic Treatment focuses on the future (the capacity for veridical intrapsychic self-caretaking) embodied in the present therapeutic relationship (the therapist's actual veridical intrapsychic caregiving). The stability of the therapist's intrapsychic caregiving motives allows the patient to know the pleasure of veridical intrapsychic caregiving intimacy and arouses the patient's dormant veridical constitutive-intrapsychic agent-self motive.

While a person in a psychological treatment other than Intrapsychic Treatment can report improvement in the self-regulation of interpersonal self-esteem, this improvement results from the strengthening of the patient's pathological pleasurable self motives vis à vis the patient's dysphoric self motives. This positive effect can also occur outside of treatment. It is not unusual, for example, to hear someone say that a particular relationship permanently changed the course of her/his life.

The kind of lasting improvement that can result when a significant person supports an individual's pathological pleasurable self is illustrated by the life of Jean Valjean in *Les Miserables.* Jean Valjean turns from a life of crime to a life of good works as a result of the caring he experiences from the bishop. When the police catch Jean Valjean with the bishop's silver basket, the bishop protects Jean Valjean by telling the police that he had given the basket to Jean Valjean as a gift.[4] When an individual's increased well-being results only from a shift in the dynamic balance between her/his pathological pleasurable self and her/his dysphoric self, however, s/he will never have the loss-free pleasure of stable, veridical, agent-self, self-regulatory control over her/his subjective experience of personal existence and will, therefore, remain vulnerable to inner disquiet due to aversive reactions to pleasure and also to inevitable interruptions in constitutive-interpersonal motive gratification.

Intrapsychic Treatment enables the patient to develop a veridical, regulatory-intrapsychic agent-self. Interpretation of unconscious motives plays a secondary role in an Intrapsychic Treatment process. Interpretation is one way to help the patient become aware of the nonveridical quality of pathological pleasurable self well-being and dysphoric self well-being. For example, the therapist makes interpretations involving the patient's childhood memories only when these memories function as nonveridical agent-self percepts to nurture the motives of the pathological pleasurable self and the dysphoric self. The patient's childhood memories have no dynamic significance other than as gratifying, nonveridical agent-self percepts for the here-and-now pathological regulatory-interpersonal motive and, in turn, for the pathological intrapsychic motive.

An example of the therapeutic use of childhood memories in Intrapsychic Treatment comes from the treatment of a patient whose life had been filled with interpersonal failures before she entered treatment. With increasing consistency she began to achieve interpersonal success both in her career and in personal relationships. Usually, when she told the therapist of a moment of interpersonal pleasure, she would (in a context of sharing her feelings within the framework of a positive alliance with the therapist) immediately associate to traumatic childhood experiences involving her parents. She felt that these memories, which she had never before recalled, were important contributions to the therapeutic work. In one representative instance, she associated to the verbal abuse she had received from her father on a day when her devotion to her studies caused her to be slow to finish her chores. Rather than explore the content of the memory and the role this traumatic interpersonal experience played in the etiology of the patient's psychopathology, the therapist helped the patient to realize that the association to the traumatic childhood experience was a form of aversive reaction to pleasure. The painful memories gratified the motives of the patient's dysphoric self, which was experiencing a loss due to the pleasure generated both by the patient's success and also by the act of sharing her newfound pleasure with the therapist.

All psychic conflict involves a clash between motives that derive from the innately determined desire for the pleasure of veridical caregiving mutuality and acquired motives for the pleasure of delusional caregiving mutuality (which, from an intrapsychic caregiving perspective, has the meaning of psychic pain). Motives for the pleasure generated by veridical caregiving have an innate power, of which the acquired motives for delusional intrapsychic mutuality partake when they become fixated at the point of the eidetic internalization of the pathological intrapsychic caregiver. Stated differently, because the child equates the caregiver's nonveridical intrapsychic caregiving with paradigmatic caregiving that s/he causes and regulates, the child harnesses the power of her/his innately based intrapsychic motive in the pursuit of gratification that, from an intrapsychic caregiving perspective, is delusional. The net result is that the individual develops a primary motive to acquire the pleasure of delusional intrapsychic mutuality. From an intrapsychic caregiving perspective, of course, delusional intrapsychic pleasure is equivalent to intrapsychic pain and, therefore, motives for delusional intrapsychic pleasure are equivalent to motives for intrapsychic self-rage.

The person who seeks psychological help is potentially treatable only because some of her/his motives are shaped by positive constitutive-interpersonal identifications and are ultimately regulated by transference intrapsychic motive gratification produced by the caregiving form of nonveridical caregiver percept. This context permits a developmental form of intrapsychic transference to emerge. From an intrapsychic caregiving perspective, patients initially enter psychotherapy in order to get relief from the unpleasure generated by the dysphoric self. Patients prove to be treatable because their innately determined ideals for a personal existence characterized by veridical autonomy and mutuality can be summoned and activated by the stability and veridicality of the therapist's intrapsychic caregiving ideals and motives. The intrapsychic therapist faces the challenge of providing the patient with intrapsychic caregiving in the context that the patient has a matured constitutive-interpersonal self with an acquired motive to experience unpleasure.

Pathological Dissociation

During a paradigmatic developmental process, some of the child's motives are structurally unconscious. This unconsciousness, which we term ***developmental dissociation***,[5] is phase-specific and results from immaturity. In psychopathology, however, psychic conflict occurs within a context of ***pathological dissociation***. We believe a permanently inaccessible unconscious (referred to in psychoanalysis as the "dynamically unconscious repressed") occurs only in untreated psychopathology.[6] In other words, whereas Freud considered a structural unconscious to be a universal, innately determined attribute of the human species, we equate a structural dissociation that persists into adulthood solely with psychopathology and understand it not as a product of the phylogenetic heritage of the species but rather as the result of pathological intrapsychic dissociation, which is a direct consequence of nonveridical intrapsychic caregiving. Pathological dissociation indicates a state of nature out of joint. Intrapsychic Treatment aims to produce a de novo intrapsychic agent-self, which has no need for a structural type of dissociation because the therapist's intrapsychic caregiving is veridical. In fact, structure building in treatment intrinsically entails mourning the loss represented by nonveridical well-being, which is protected by pathological dissociation. The patient mourns nonveridical well-being by becoming aware that it is inferior to the pleasure produced by the therapist's intrapsychic caregiving. In this process, the patient becomes uninterested in nonveridical well-being. When a patient loses interest in a nonveridical regulatory agency motive, the motive is destructuralized.

Intrapsychic Treatment does not focus on the *content* of the patient's pathological dissociation but instead aims to stabilize the functioning of the intrapsychic pleasure principle so that pathological dissociation becomes unappealing and acquires the meaning of loss. In contrast to psychoanalysis, Intrapsychic Treatment aims neither to make the unconscious conscious, nor to produce ego where id was, nor to provide a hermeneutic understanding of the patient's pathological dissociation. Since the content of pathological dissociation is fundamentally irrelevant to the process of the therapeutic action, its significance in treatment is limited to its role as a source of motives that interfere with the power of the therapeutic process to reawaken the veridical constitutive-intrapsychic motive, whose aim is the pleasure of intrapsychic caregiving intimacy.

From an intrapsychic caregiving perspective, invisible psychic pain originates in the pathological adaptation by which the child attaches the meaning of being the regulating agent-cause of veridical intrapsychic caregiving to the intrapsychic loss caused by nonveridical intrapsychic caregiving. Invisible psychic pain, therefore, is the process by which intrapsychic loss is misidentified as intrapsychic pleasure. The child's intrapsychic pain remains invisible to her/him, both because s/he has no idea that the well-being s/he feels is not ideal and also because s/he develops a motive for this nonveridical well-being. The reason that psychological treatment is such a long process, then, is that veridical care-getting pleasure must compete with an acquired motive for nonveridical care-getting pleasure.

Without exception, people come for treatment because they have an unreflective awareness that when they gratify pathological pleasurable self motives they feel more pleasure than when they gratify dysphoric self motives. Although a patient can have conscious psychic pain, s/he is unaware of the cause: no one comes to treatment with an awareness that the pain s/he feels is caused by the loss of veridical intrapsychic pleasure and by the delusional quality of her/his agent-self experience. Patients voluntarily come for psychological help because they experience more conscious psychic pain than feels reasonable, because they have significant difficulty in everyday functioning, or because of some combination of these factors. Each patient begins treatment with the primary aim of psychic pain relief. Her/his fundamental psychic pain is invisible because the patient's motive to pursue the delusional pleasure of the nonveridical caregiving s/he received from the original, psychopathogenic caregiver continuously undermines her/his ability to discern the relative differences between transference agent-self pleasure and veridical agent-self pleasure. In other words, initially the patient seeks delusional intrapsychic well-being more avidly than s/he seeks the pleasure of veridical intrapsychic mutuality generated by the intrapsychic caregiving intimacy of the treatment process.

The nonmediated masochist's acceptable psychic pain results from nonveridical *interpersonal* nurture, which strengthened her/his dysphoric self in relation to her/his pathological pleasurable self. Negative constitutive-interpersonal identifications are the most important proximal cause of nonmediated masochism and other clinical manifestations of constitutive-interpersonal self-rage. The underlying basis for constitutive-interpersonal manifestations of self-rage is regulatory-interpersonal self-rage and intrapsychic self-rage. We stress that intrapsychic self-rage and regulatory-interpersonal self-rage are not affects; they are personal meaning structures and, therefore, relationship structures. The irony in nonmediated masochism is that the individual introspectively associates the intense level of psychic pain s/he experiences with the drive to get relief, but, from an intrapsychic caregiving perspective, this conscious pain gratifies dysphoric self motives for unpleasure. In this syndrome, the patient uses her/his conscious suffering as a gratifying, pathological agent-self percept to confer the meaning of veridical agent-self, self-regulatory control.

The regulatory principles of therapeutic action are the same for all patients, including the nonmediated masochist. The therapist endeavors to enlist the nonfixated aspect of the patient's pathological positive transference in an effort to gratify and to cultivate the patient's newly formed motives for the pleasure of veridical intrapsychic caregiving mutuality. In this process, pathological positive transference motives become developmental transference motives, which gradually give way to non-transference motives for intrapsychic relationship pleasure. Essentially, treatment aims to help the patient to develop the reflective capacity to differentiate between veridical and delusional intrapsychic agency.[7] This ability results from exposure of the patient's nonfunctional veridical constitutive-intrapsychic motive to the unique care-getting pleasure produced by the therapist's veridical intrapsychic nurturing. The patient's capacity to choose the pleasure of veridical intrapsychic mutuality over the pleasure of delusional intrapsychic mutuality is the means by which the patient acquires the ability to mourn loss and to gratify her/his intrapsychic motive in a veridical manner.

AVERSIVE REACTIONS IN TREATMENT
Aversive Reactions to Care-getting Pleasure

The most important psychic conflict in Intrapsychic Treatment is a product of the treatment process itself. We term this conflict the ***aversive reaction to care-getting pleasure.*** It occurs neither in paradigmatic development nor in a person with psychopathology who is not in Intrapsychic Treatment. The aversive reaction to care-getting pleasure has its anlage in the aversive reaction to pleasure described in chapter 6. Unlike the aversive reaction to care-getting pleasure, the aversive reaction to pleasure characterizes all psychopathology. It results from the ongoing conflict between the two constitutive-interpersonal pathological centers of agency, the pathological pleasurable self and the dysphoric self. The aversive reaction to pleasure directly results from the temporary regulation of the motives of the pathological pleasurable self by the motives of the dysphoric self. Like the aversive reaction to pleasure, the aversive reaction to care-getting pleasure gratifies the dysphoric self's motive for psychic pain. The dysphoric self attaches the meaning of loss (pain) to each experience of intrapsychic care-getting pleasure because this pleasure interferes with the dysphoric self's use of relationship unpleasure as a gratifying, pathological agent-self percept. Constitutive-interpersonal self-rage is a major complication in treatment. For example, the mere fact of being in treatment, of making a commitment to care for oneself in a nondestructive (non-self-rageful) manner, represents ongoing loss to the dysphoric self. The dysphoric self restitutes this loss by an aversive reaction to care-getting pleasure.[8]

Aversive reactions to care-getting pleasure invariably cause the subject some form of constitutive-interpersonal pain, which s/he may or may not recognize as such. Such pain takes many possible forms, such as a psychogenic stomachache or being late for a therapy session. An aversive reaction to care-getting pleasure differs from an aversive reaction to pleasure in that it represents the dysphoric self's reaction to the pleasure of veridical intrapsychic care-getting. As the patient becomes able to appreciate the veridical pleasure of intrapsychic caregiving mutuality, s/he increasingly experiences the aversive reaction as a loss of veridical pleasure. After the patient develops a veridical, regulatory-intrapsychic agent-self and a veridical regulatory-interpersonal agent-self, aversive reactions to care-getting pleasure become aversive reactions to nontransference care-getting pleasure.

The aversive reaction to care-getting pleasure is characterized by a temporary regression in which the patient's dysphoric self dominates the patient's experience of the therapeutic relationship: the patient experiences the therapist as a source of pain and trouble rather than as a recognized and available ally. For example, a patient had the pleasurable thought of telling the therapist about something that went wrong at work and, thereby, of feeling better through the process of sharing the disappointment in the context of the caregiving relationship. In the actual session, however, the patient had an aversive reaction to anticipated care-getting pleasure and, instead of sharing the office problem with the therapist, said angrily, "Well, something went wrong today, but you would never be interested in hearing about it." This self-induced alienation from the therapeutic mutuality occurs in different forms. For example, in the early part of treatment, when the patient relates to the therapist only with pathological positive self motives and dysphoric self motives, regression caused by the aversive reaction to care-getting pleasure intensifies the patient's dysphoric self motives and weakens the patient's pathological positive self motives. Accordingly, early in treatment aversive reactions to care-getting pleasure threaten the therapeutic alliance, the survival of which depends on the resilience of the patient's motives for positive relationship experiences (the strength of which was an important part of the assessment of treatability). As treatment progresses, however, the patient's relationship with the therapist reflects the emergence of agent-self structures that evidence developmental transference and nontransference motives as well as psychopathological motives.

When the patient experiences an aversive reaction to care-getting pleasure, the therapist tries to help the patient to recover functional motives for positive intrapsychic relationship pleasure. Only after this occurs can the therapist help the patient embrace the exposed pain of the aversive reaction to care-getting pleasure. In an aversive reaction to care-getting pleasure, the rage directed at the self and at the therapist occurs within a functioning relationship of intrapsychic caregiving mutuality, the pleasure of which is superior to all others. Through aversive reactions to care-getting pleasure, therefore, the patient ultimately comes to know that gratifying her/his dysphoric self motives for relationship unpleasure is much less satisfying than gratifying her/his pathological pleasurable self motives for relationship pleasure. Subsequently, the patient realizes that gratifying her/his pathological pleasurable self motives for relationship pleasure is less satisfying than gratifying her/his nontransference motives for the pleasure of veridical intrapsychic mutuality.

Another example of an aversive reaction to care-getting pleasure is taken from the treatment of a five-year-old girl. This child had been referred to the therapist at the age of two by her pediatrician because, although she had no organic impairment, she did not speak a word. She was seen in Intrapsychic Treatment four times a week and after about six months, she had developed normal speech. By age five she was extremely articulate and above average for her age in both social and cognitive skills. In the session being discussed, the therapist had just returned from a two-week vacation. The child entered the session talking disgustedly about an "ugly" bug she had just seen in the waiting room. The child then announced that, "The two weeks seemed like forever. It's so good to see you!" Shortly after saying this, the child said that she hated bugs and was afraid one might have gotten on her. We would understand this statement as an aversive reaction to care-getting pleasure. In this example, the pleasure is both the child's pleasure at reentering the intrapsychic caregiving relationship and also the pleasure of the intimacy of a caregiving alliance in which the child could feel comfortable sharing both the loss she had felt at the missed sessions and the pleasure she was feeling at the reunion. The child associated to the unpleasure aroused by thoughts of bugs in order to gratify the motives of the dysphoric self for the pain of relationship unpleasure. The statement had the clear negative meaning, "You do not care about me enough to keep bugs out of the waiting room." The therapist correctly responded by pointing out the child's aversive reaction to care-getting pleasure. He said, "Maybe part of you was feeling a lot of pleasure at telling me how hard it felt to be apart and how good it feels to you to be back together, which made another part of you uncomfortable, so that part of you is thinking of something that feels bad." The child's association resulted from an active, though dissociated, dysphoric self motive for relationship unpleasure. In contrast, psychoanalysis and other psychodynamic treatment modalities would understand the child's hostility as a transference expression of preoedipal paranoid rage, oedipal rage, or narcissistic rage that is due to the reliving of archaic traumas (e.g., of separation).

Therapist-Present and Therapist-Absent Aversive Reactions

Some aversive reactions to care-getting pleasure occur in the physical presence of the therapist and others occur outside of the treatment session. The *therapist-present* form is a reaction to the intrapsychic pleasure caused by caregiver percepts that have their immediate source in the treatment session with the therapist. The *therapist-absent* form is a reaction to the intrapsychic pleasure produced by self-caretaking that occurs outside of the treatment session.

The following illustrates the therapist-absent form of aversive reaction to care-getting pleasure. A middle-aged man who had been in Intrapsychic Treatment for a year arrived for his session uncharacteristically late. He explained that because of a significant snowfall he had been concerned the night before that he would be late to his therapy session. He therefore had resolved to set his alarm one half hour earlier than usual the next morning in order to arrive on time. When he awoke in the morning, however, he discovered that he had mistakenly set his alarm later rather than earlier and that he was one half hour *behind* schedule. The self-caretaking pleasure that prompted the patient to have the conscious wish not to lose a moment of the intrapsychic caregiving mutuality of the treatment relationship had the meaning of loss to the patient's dysphoric self motives for isolation and relationship unpleasure. This loss was pathologically grieved when the dysphoric self gained control over the pathological pleasurable self's motives for self-caretaking pleasure.

From an intrapsychic caregiving perspective, the intrapsychic caregiving intimacy between therapist and patient signifies betrayal and danger to the patient's dysphoric self. Clinical examples of this process abound. For example, a patient who, after much struggle, unexpectedly shares with the therapist a positive feeling about the therapeutic process may react by saying that the therapist "forced" the positive statement from her/him and may miss the next appointment or assert that nothing ever changes as the result of therapy. When the patient mourns her/his paranoid reactions to the intrapsychic caregiving relationship and, thereby, becomes uninterested in them, s/he progressively develops the ability to make nontransference use of the therapeutic relationship. The therapist's veridical intrapsychic caregiving changes the meaning the patient attaches to the pain of her/his aversive reactions to care-getting pleasure from a gratifying, pathological agent-self percept (which, however, may have the conscious significance of pain or loss) to the loss of the superior pleasure represented by veridical intrapsychic mutuality. Psychic pain becomes less attractive to the patient, who is increasingly aware of the therapist's veridical intrapsychic caregiving availability and the superior pleasure this availability provides. The patient's demonstrated conflict-free ability to turn to the intrapsychic caregiving relationship in response to any loss, particularly the loss represented by paranoid reactions directed at the therapist, is a sign that the patient's involvement in the treatment process has become increasingly veridical.[9]

Aversive reactions to care-getting pleasure present the therapist with the challenge of determining whether the patient's aversive behavior is truly a transference manifestation of pain in response to care-getting pleasure or whether the patient is responding to pain with pain due to the therapist's nonveridical intrapsychic caregiving. In the latter case, the patient's negativity toward the therapist results when the patient accurately (even if nonreflectively) perceives the therapist's behavior as representing the same nonveridical caregiving as s/he received from the original caregivers.

THERAPEUTIC ACTION IN INTRAPSYCHIC TREATMENT

The term ***therapeutic action*** refers to the curative element in the treatment process, namely, intrapsychic structure building. In this section, we briefly review the most important components of the process of intrapsychic structure building.

Intrapsychic Treatment is analogous to development in childhood, but it differs from child development both in the maturational divergence between child and patient (if the patient is an adult) and also, and most importantly, in the fact that the motives regulated by the patient's psychic pain prevent the developmental process from unfolding straightforwardly. The therapist has the critical task of helping the patient acquire regulatory control over the set of motives opposing the course of paradigmatic development. In other words, the therapist helps the patient to realize that pathological gratification entails loss because it represents the use of the signified meaning of pain and rage to impart the illusion of effective agency. The therapist's veridical intrapsychic caregiving stimulates the patient to seek a pain-free inner well-being (to seek to actualize the ideals represented by the intrapsychic and the regulatory-interpersonal pleasure principles). This, in turn, stimulates the patient to mourn (to experience as a loss of veridical regulatory agency pleasure) well-being that rests upon both the dysphoric self's motive for constitutive-interpersonal unpleasure and also on the pathological positive transference self's motive for constitutive-interpersonal pleasure.

The patient reaches the therapeutic goal of developing a stable sense of inner well-being through an increasingly veridical involvement in the therapeutic relationship. Like the paradigmatic caregiver, the therapist has the regulatory intrapsychic capacity to choose intrapsychic caregiving pleasure over the pleasure of pursuing personal motives. Unlike the paradigmatic caregiver, however, the therapist must mourn the loss that (in contrast to paradigmatic development, in which the child always responds positively and with increased intimacy to veridical intrapsychic caregiving) the patient will react negatively to intrapsychic caregiving because of her/his aversive reactions to care-getting pleasure. Every patient has aversive reactions to care-getting pleasure, which may at times cause her/him to become withdrawn, depressed, angry, miserable, or scornful. Initially, the patient will respond to each moment of intrapsychic closeness with the therapist with an aversive reaction to care-getting pleasure. The therapist must have the self-regulatory agent-self capacity to react to the patient's negativity and lability with a functional commitment to intrapsychic caregiving ideals and motives rather than with personal motives, which can cause the therapist to experience unhappiness, distance, anger, placation, guilt, martyrdom, frustration, or hurt feelings. The therapist with functional intrapsychic caregiving ideals welcomes the patient's aversive reactions to care-getting pleasure as a means to help the patient realize that these reactions represent loss, namely, the loss of the superior pleasure provided by the patient's intrapsychic caregiving relationship with the therapist.

The patient's development of a veridical, regulatory-intrapsychic agent-self and a veridical regulatory-interpersonal agent-self is less a function of the patient's capacity to gratify any particular constitutive-interpersonal motive (including the motive for a cognitive understanding of her/his childhood or current behavior) than it is a function of the patient's dawning recognition of the superior pleasure provided by the therapist's active, veridical intrapsychic caregiving. A veridical therapeutic relationship is made possible by the therapist's capacity to have stable access to her/his intrapsychic caregiving motives in the context of having interpersonal personal motives. This capacity allows the therapist to mourn the relinquishing of her/his personal motives or needs (e.g., the motive to talk about the tennis tournament s/he had won the day before or the flat tire s/he got on the way to work) in the service of intrapsychic caregiving ideals. The therapist's veridical motive to respond to the patient with intrapsychic caregiving provides the patient with structuralizing caregiver percepts that convey a veridical reflection of effective agency and, therefore, stimulate the patient's intrapsychic pleasure principle.

Other psychological treatments (including psychodynamic, behavioral, and cognitive treatments) cannot help a patient develop the capacity veridically and stably to regulate her/his own motive experience because they provide the patient only with pain relief in the form of transference pleasure or transference pain. Psychodynamic therapists who rely on interpretation, for example, encourage the patient to grapple with her/his psychic pain on the level of cognitive reality, which is, by definition, nonempirical, solipsistic, and loss filled. Therapists who rely primarily on interpersonal empathy as the instrument of change (e.g., Rogers and, to a large extent, Kohut and A. Miller) achieve, at best, symptom alleviation through persuasion based on the patient's pathological positive transference motives.[10] In contrast, an intrapsychic therapist helps the patient to experience psychopathological psychic pain as the loss of veridical regulatory agency pleasure and to mourn this loss within the mutuality of the intrapsychic caregiving relationship. As a result, the patient's motive for psychic pain eventually loses all influence.

In untreated psychopathology, the individual has only a potential capacity for nontransference relating. Because the patient initially can have only a transference experience of the caregiving relationship, the therapist must both nurture the patient's *developmental* transference motives and also create an atmosphere in which all transference-based needs can be experienced by the patient as a loss. The patient's involvement in the therapeutic process occurs in the context of a nurtured intimacy, which results when the therapist either tacitly or expressly encourages the patient to become aware of and choose motives that represent to-be-actualized ideals of veridical intrapsychic caregiving intimacy.

Since the therapist realizes that during much of treatment the patient can only relate on a transference basis, the therapist does not accept at face value psychoanalytic notions such as the therapeutic alliance and working alliance (which are aspects of what psychoanalytic theory terms the real relationship). Because psychoanalytic clinical theory assumes that the patient enters the therapeutic relationship with the capacity for real (nontransference) relating, it asserts that the therapeutic and working alliances can and should commence early in the analytic relationship at a time when, from our perspective, the patient still lacks the capacity to experience a real (nontransference) relationship. In our view, the patient's capacity for veridical relationship experience occurs at a point well into the therapy and only by virtue of a hard-won developmental process.

In paradigmatic development and Intrapsychic Treatment, the patient's developmental transference precedes the patient's functional motive for reflective, nontransference, regulatory-intrapsychic agent-self meaning. When treatment commences, however, the patient's transference experience is exclusively pathological and only potentially developmental. The developmental transference only occurs in response to the therapist's veridical intrapsychic nurture. The pleasure produced by the therapist's veridical intrapsychic caregiving makes it possible for the patient to distinguish her/his transformable, potentially developmental transference motives from her/his obstructive, fixated pathological positive transference motives. In contrast to the pathological transference, the developmental transference is the basis for a relationship structure that, though transference in nature, is phase-appropriately free of conflict (i.e., nonparanoid, free of self-rage).

The therapist aims to stimulate selectively and to nourish that aspect of the patient's pathological positive transference that is not fixated so as to help this nonfixated pathological positive transference evolve into a developmental transference. In this process, the therapist needs to distinguish between: (1) the responsive part of the patient's pathological positive transference, which is regulated by the pursuit of the pleasure of intrapsychic caregiving ideals and (2) the motives of both the nonresponsive part of the pathological positive transference and the negative transference, which pursue the delusional pleasure that occurs in the context of isolation from the intrapsychic mutuality of the therapeutic relationship. The difference between the pathologically fixated part and the responsive part of the patient's pathological positive transference is illustrated by the first treatment sessions of a man who initially talked nonstop about his problems. He clearly felt a great deal of relief in unburdening himself, but the therapist realized that this rush of words primarily gratified the *fixated* part of his pathological positive transference, because it left the therapist no room to respond. The therapist listened carefully, but made no attempt to interfere with the man's need to talk uninterruptedly. After a few sessions had passed, the patient asked, "What do you think of what I've told you?" The therapist responded that she thought that the patient had both been trying to help her get to know him, and also that he had made clear his concern that the therapist would be intrusive. The man looked relieved and said that he hated being told what to do and was worried that the therapist would try to take over and make decisions for him. The fixated part of the patient's pathological positive transference was expressed as the motive to talk nonstop in the sessions, which was in the service of an isolated type of pleasure. The nonfixated part of the patient's pathological positive transference was expressed in the question the patient asked the therapist, which manifested a budding motive for caregiving mutuality.

When the therapist encourages the nonfixated part of the patient's pathological positive transference, s/he helps the patient acquire a developmental-transference-based agent-self, which can respond to the ideals of intrapsychic caregiving pleasure and begin to exert regulatory control over the patient's motives regarding the therapeutic relationship. The occurrence of the developmental transference marks the onset of the therapeutic developmental split.[11]

The patient takes an important step toward the stable pursuit of intrapsychic pleasure when s/he turns to the intrapsychic caregiving relationship with the therapist for help with the pain caused by aversive reactions to pleasure. An example is from the Intrapsychic Treatment of a 12-year-old girl who had been in therapy for two years. For the first time in her life, she was doing well in school and making friends. Two days after a short story she wrote appeared in the school newspaper, she showed the therapist that the jacket she was wearing was full of holes. She playfully said that her mother had tried to throw the jacket away but that the patient had "heard" the jacket in the garbage saying, "No, don't throw me away, I'll be lonely," and had "rescued" it. Because the patient had shared this experience, the therapist could help her with the pain generated by the dysphoric self, which was convincing her that she would feel lonely and miserable if she allowed herself the pleasure of succeeding.

A second example occurred in the treatment of a four-year-old boy whose inner life was characterized by constant and devastating aversive reactions to pleasure that left him unable to function adequately. He became increasingly able to share his conflict with the therapist. In one representative session, he asked the therapist, "Do you want me to tell you about all the parts of my mind?" When the therapist said, "Yes," the boy said, "I'll say them and you add them up. There are lots of vampire caves. They are gross and scary with twenty-five bats in there hanging upside down." The therapist said, "That sounds frightening, I'm glad you're telling us about it." The child went on, "Then there are sixty hundred meat-eating dinosaurs. How many is that?" The therapist responded, "Sixty hundred and twenty-five." The child continued, "Then there are a billion nice ones to go with the billion mean ones." The therapist said, "Sounds like a terrible tug of war," and the child looked relieved and said, "Yes!" The significance of this interaction is that the boy was increasingly turning to the therapeutic relationship to support his emerging motive for help with the pain generated by his dysphoric self.

As Intrapsychic Treatment continues, the therapist's encouragement of the responsive portion of the patient's pathological positive transference stimulates the reawakening of the developmental form of the patient's nonveridical constitutive-intrapsychic motive. This results in a nonfixated transference structure (the developmental transference), which marks the beginning of the therapeutic developmental split. Initially, the therapeutic developmental split is undifferentiated in that it includes only transference structures, one of which is developmental and one of which is pathological.

An illustration of a patient who had reached the developmental transference stage is an architect who, although highly skilled and professionally in demand, continued to work for a firm that treated him disrespectfully. He had been trying to leave the firm, but each time he began to look for another job, his employer would suddenly begin to treat him well and he would feel pleasure and decide to stay. Soon afterward, the abusiveness would recur. This cycle continued for nearly a year. One day the employer, perceiving that the patient was again becoming dissatisfied with the firm, offered the patient a large raise and a promotion. That night, the patient dreamed that he was trying to convince the therapist that the employer really liked and respected him, while, at the same time, another version of himself was standing to one side feeling happy in the knowledge that the therapist would never be convinced by his desire to stay with the firm. The employer's positive actions gratified the patient's pathological pleasurable agent-self motive, which caused a loss to the patient's developmental agent-self. Because at this point the patient's developmental agent-self lacked sufficient regulatory control to cause the patient to become disinterested in the pathological positive pleasure, the patient mourned the loss represented by the part of himself that was pursuing pathological positive pleasure by turning to the veridical caregiving relationship with the therapist.

Eventually, the rage-free pleasure of the developmental transference causes the reactivation of the patient's veridical intrapsychic precept. As a result, the therapeutic developmental split differentiates to include a nontransference component and a transference component. At this point, the patient's motives are increasingly regulated by the intrapsychic pleasure principle. Pathological transference motives remain functional only in the regressive process that causes aversive reactions to nontransference care-getting pleasure. The patient's newly developed, veridical, regulatory-intrapsychic agent-self and veridical regulatory-interpersonal agent-self give the patient the capacity for nontransference relationship experience.

If the therapist does not recognize the responsive part of the patient's pathological positive transference, the patient never acquires the potential for developmental transference experience. Until and unless a therapeutic developmental split occurs, the pathological intrapsychic transference prevents the patient from empirical contact with the therapist's intrapsychic motives. The patient's mind stays merged with the mind of the original nonveridical caregiver and all subjective personal meaning remains a function of delusional intrapsychic mutuality. The

patient, therefore, never develops the capacity for reality testing of veridical intrapsychic motive gratification.

From an intrapsychic caregiving perspective, each child knows of
her/his own agent-self capacity through her/his perceptions of the effects of the caregiver's caregiving. By virtue of the nature of consciousness, the child attributes to every effect the meaning of the caregiver's
intentional provision of veridical caregiving love which the child's agent-
self is causing. This teleological process explains a common aversive
reaction to care-getting pleasure in which the patient feels criticized by
the therapist. The feeling of being criticized represents the culmination of a transference loss experienced by the patient's dysphoric self,
which results when the patient experiences the pleasure of the veridical intrapsychic caregiving relationship with the therapist (experiences
her/himself as causing the therapist to make the positive choice of intrapsychic caregiving motives over personal motives). Like all pleasure,
the pleasure of veridical caregiving mutuality signifies loss to the dysphoric self, which responds to this pain with pathological grief work
(pain as pain relief). In keeping with the teleological principles that
govern developmental and psychopathological regulatory agency reality, this reactive psychic pain signifies the therapist's caregiving intentions to the patient. Thus, the patient experiences the *effect* of the
therapist's veridical intrapsychic caregiving (the pain generated by the
patient's dysphoric self) as intentionally caused by the therapist and
feels criticized.

Aversive reactions to care-getting pleasure complicate treatment in
that the patient's dysphoric self responds to veridical intrapsychic caregiving with reactive pain. The depth and frequency of the patient's
aversive reactions decrease as the developmental process proceeds and
the therapeutic developmental split comes to include nontransference
agent-self experience.

Like the goal of development, the goal of Intrapsychic Treatment
entails a developmental modification of the teleological organization of
the intrapsychic and regulatory-interpersonal agent-selves. Therapeutic action (psychic structure building) focuses on the conflict between
the motives for nonveridical intrapsychic pleasure and the motives for
veridical intrapsychic pleasure, that is, on the conflict between an inner
well-being rooted in the structure of delusional intrapsychic mutuality
and an inner well-being produced by an empirical, loss-free intrapsychic caregiving mutuality. The therapist's veridical intrapsychic caregiving enables the patient to know and to prefer her/his own motives for

veridical care-getting pleasure in a context in which the patient's inner well-being does not depend on the personal motives of another. This can only happen when the therapist has no motive for the nonveridical, delusional intimacy that had characterized the relationship between the patient and the patient's original, nonveridical caregivers.

The patient comes to treatment with motives to be helped. If these motives are sufficiently unencumbered by negative constitutive-interpersonal identifications in the form of structural, characterological paranoia, a therapeutic agreement can be made. From an intrapsychic caregiving perspective, the patient's most crucial strength in the beginning of the treatment lies in her/his pathological pleasurable self motives. Until the therapeutic developmental split occurs, the vicissitudes of treatment are explained by the dynamic conflict between: (1) the patient's nonfixated pathological positive transference motives and (2) the fixated pathological positive transference motives together with all of the negative transference motives.

The strengthening of the nonfixated part of the patient's pathological positive transference causes the onset of developmental transference motives in addition to pathological positive transference motives and negative transference motives. At this point, the patient has a therapeutic developmental split rather than a pathological split. The therapeutic developmental split includes a developmental (nonfixated) transference structure and a pathological (fixated) transference structure.

The therapeutic developmental split eventually differentiates to include both a pain-free, loss-free, veridical intrapsychic agent-self as well as a transference agent-self. The *differentiated therapeutic developmental split* is a structural separation between the patient's transference and nontransference centers of agency. As the patient's psychic structure progressively differentiates, the patient's capacity for self-awareness becomes increasingly veridical. From a structural viewpoint, the self-awareness associated with the differentiated therapeutic developmental split represents a new, pain-free, transference-free, mutualized mind experience per se (mutualized intrapsychic and regulatory-interpersonal consciousness). It does *not* result from solipsistic, nonempirical, constitutive-interpersonal introspection.

Once the therapeutic developmental split differentiates, the patient has the capacity for the veridical intrapsychic self-caretaking and regulatory-interpersonal self-caretaking described in chapters 3 and 4. The intrapsychic and regulatory-interpersonal pleasure principles now function to help the patient experience both her/his pathological transference center of agency and her/his developmental transference center of agency as the source of an inferior type of inner well-being. As a result, the patient begins to lose interest in these transference motives.

In summary, in the initial stages of Intrapsychic Treatment, the patient's relationship to the therapist is characterized by two forms of pathological transference, the *nonfixated* pathological positive transference and the *fixated* transference (which consists of the fixated part of the pathological positive transference and the negative transference). Subsequently, a therapeutic developmental transference emerges, which causes the therapeutic developmental split between developmental transference motives and pathological transference motives. Developmental transference motives resemble pathological positive transference motives in their pursuit of constitutive-interpersonal relationship pleasure to use for nonveridical agent-self percepts, but developmental transference motives are rage free. The therapeutic developmental split becomes differentiated when the patient develops the capacity for veridical agency. Finally, the increasing influence of the intrapsychic and regulatory-interpersonal pleasure principles facilitates the destructuralization of the pathological transference structure and, ultimately, of the developmental transference structure. As a result, the patient develops the capacity for a fully nontransference regulatory-intrapsychic and regulatory-interpersonal agent-self experience. The patient increasingly comes to experience and choose the pleasure of intrapsychic caregiving mutuality. This veridical pleasure differs from the pleasure of pain relief. That is, the stability of nontransference intrapsychic pleasure results from an emergent motive *not* to use transference pleasure or pain for pain relief, but, rather, to experience transference pleasure or pain as a loss that can be mourned by turning to the superior pleasure available within the intrapsychic caregiving relationship.

The patient can develop a veridical regulatory-intrapsychic agent-self through Intrapsychic Treatment because the intrapsychic pleasure principle performs the twofold function of inspiring the patient's intrapsychic agent-self to seek the intrapsychic pleasure provided by the therapist's intrapsychic caregiving and, simultaneously and synergistically, to pursue the goal of recognizing and mourning lifelong pain to which the patient has heretofore responded with a motive for escape. Because the patient develops a functional ability to recognize psychic pain in its different manifestations, especially those that had been invisible, s/he can recognize that psychic pain represents a delusional inner well-being that is inferior to the pleasure the patient experiences in the intrapsychic caregiving relationship with the therapist. Due to the fact that, from an intrapsychic caregiving perspective, the patient's core well-being prior to the treatment process has been the product of the patient's delusional use of the original caregiver's nonveridical intrapsychic caregiving for intrapsychic motive gratification, the patient's ability to experience the pleasure of delusional intrapsychic mutuality as a loss (as an inferior inner well-being) drives the therapeutic action of Intrapsychic Treatment.

The patient's capacity to mourn psychic pain in the mutual context of the intrapsychic caregiving relationship represents a monumental achievement.[12] This mourning process is a caregiving relationship experience rather than an interpretive experience of cognitive understanding. It only occurs when psychic pain acquires the meaning of loss in comparison with veridical intrapsychic care-getting pleasure. The patient's awareness that her/his lifelong agent-self experience has been delusional enables her/him to recognize that s/he has misconstrued the original caregiver's nonveridical intrapsychic caregiving as intentional, veridical caregiving love.

The phenomenon of bringing psychic pain to the therapeutic caregiving relationship occurs with increasing frequency as the regulatory-intrapsychic agent-self on the nontransference side of the differentiated therapeutic developmental split gradually acquires hegemony. The nontransference self-regulatory autonomy of this agent-self allows psychic pain (which heretofore had been excluded from awareness) to exist within reflective consciousness as an experience of loss, without engendering a motive for pain relief. In contrast to regression, decompensation, or fragmentation, the patient's ability to introduce into awareness previously invisible psychic pain in the form of observed aversive reactions to care-getting pleasure indicates the patient's availability to the mutuality of the therapeutic relationship. As a result, whereas the patient previously experienced psychic pain only within an intrapsychic reality characterized by isolation from the therapist's intrapsychic caregiving motives, the patient now experiences this psychic pain within the pleasure of the intrapsychic caregiving relationship. In this context, the patient can recognize that the psychic pain provides an inferior type of well-being and become uninterested in it. When the patient becomes uninterested in a given experience of pain, the pain acquires a permanent, structural alteration in meaning. It changes from a pathological agent-self percept that afforded unconscious intrapsychic and regulatory-interpersonal motive gratification to a representational event that has no significance whatsoever for inner well-being (for the meaning of effective agency). This mourning process can occur because the therapist's stable veridical intrapsychic caregiving helps the patient's nontransference agent-self both to maintain its consciously perceived, phase-appropriate sense of self-regulated, inner well-being and, simultaneously, to perceive the pain-dominated, pathological agent-self component of the therapeutic developmental split.

Although the intrapsychic differentiation that occurs in treatment is much more difficult to achieve than the intrapsychic differentiation that occurs during a paradigmatic childhood, the patient experiences a type of pleasure that does not occur during paradigmatic development. The patient experiences not only the pleasure that accrues from the veridical gratification of intrapsychic and regulatory-interpersonal motives but also the special pleasure that results from mourning pathological psychic pain. The latter pleasure occurs when the liberating effect of losing interest in psychic pain gives the patient the dual, reflectively experienced pleasure of the intimacy of the intrapsychic caregiving relationship and the sense of strength that ensues from the experience of not being enslaved by delusional pleasure.

As can be seen, the therapist facilitates the patient's capacity to recognize and prefer veridical therapeutic relationship pleasure neither by interpreting the patient's behavior as transference or nontransference, nor by emphasizing the patient's affect or emotional communication. The therapist's therapeutic power results from her/his stable capacity for veridical intrapsychic caregiving. Given the clear superiority of intrapsychic pleasure, it would seem that the treatment process would proceed in a straightforward manner. However, an intrinsic characteristic of the treatment process is that the patient experiences wide swings between dysphoric and positive emotions about her/himself, the therapist, and the treatment relationship. We are not referring to a treatment process episodically characterized by an occasional "good hour,"[13] but rather to a structural aspect of the treatment process that involves controlled, episodic, often prolonged, regressive processes. The sources of this structural regression are: (1) aversive reactions, at first to transference intrapsychic care-getting pleasure and, subsequently, to nontransference intrapsychic care-getting pleasure; (2) less importantly, transference reactions to intercurrent experiences within the patient's life; and (3) hopefully rare, the patient's reactions to the therapist's intrapsychic caregiving lapses. The therapist responds to the regressions caused by transference reactions to intercurrent events within the patient's life by using the same therapeutic approach that s/he uses to respond to aversive reactions to care-getting pleasure. The problem of caregiving lapses will be discussed shortly.

The patient cannot experience fully developed aversive reactions to nontransference caregiving pleasure until s/he has developed a non-transference regulatory-intrapsychic agent-self. The capacity for ve-ridical regulatory-intrapsychic agency occurs only if the therapist's in-trapsychic caregiving motives are sufficiently stable that the patient's regressive behavior does not become a source of transference loss for the therapist. The proper handling of the patient's aversive reactions to care-getting pleasure proves a constant challenge to the therapist who has any unregulated areas of therapeutic ambition.

Managing the Pathological Positive Transference

The patient's most easily recognized constitutive-interpersonal psy-chic pain is caused by the aversive reaction to care-getting pleasure, which occurs when the patient's dysphoric self is deprived of the agent-self reflections generated by constitutive-interpersonal percepts of pain and self-rage. The most therapeutically challenging psychic pain, how-ever, is the ongoing pain of delusional inner well-being caused when the patient misidentifies pathological pleasurable self pleasure as ve-ridical agent-self pleasure. Everyone with psychopathology has the fun-damental conviction that s/he received ideal caregiving. No one wants to know that s/he did not have the intrapsychic agent-self capacity stably to cause the caregiver to prefer intrapsychic caregiving pleasure to the pleasure of pursuing personal motives. This phenomenon is compatible with the fact that the patient may have strong motives to feel angry about memories of dreadful childhood experiences with the care-giver(s).[14] When the patient becomes able to recognize that pathological positive transference pleasure is the product of motives for a delusional type of inner well-being, that is, represents psychic pain, s/he becomes aware that the caregivers' caregiving was nonveridical (regulated by personal, noncaregiving motives) even during times that the patient either holds especially dear and keeps within an inner space of plea-surable, nostalgic fondness, or uses to create a protective disposition toward the caregivers. The patient's greatest challenge is to mourn her/his motive for pathological positive transference pleasure by recogniz-ing it as inferior well-being and losing interest in it.

An example of a patient's unreflective use of pathological positive transference pleasure with the original caregiver for delusional inner well-being is taken from the treatment of an eight-year-old girl. This child had great difficulty enjoying the therapeutic relationship and diluted it with compulsive drawing and reading. One day the child allowed herself to talk to the therapist for a relatively long time without distracting herself. Suddenly, the child began to sing a song about Mickey Mouse. She said that her mother had taught her this song over the weekend while showing home movies of the mother's childhood. The child continued to sing this song until the end of the session. She accompanied the song by drawing a picture of Mickey Mouse, which she asked to be allowed to take home to her mother. In this instance, the pleasure of the caregiving mutuality with the therapist caused the patient to react aversively and assert her motive for unpleasure by pursuing inferior, pathological care-getting pleasure. The motive for unpleasure was gratified by the child's memories of the pathological positive transference pleasure the child had had with her mother over the weekend. This caused the child to isolate and distance herself from the immediate, veridical pleasure with the therapist. As this example illustrates, once a patient has motives for developmental transference pleasure, aversive reactions to caregiving pleasure can represent the pursuit of pathological pleasurable self motives as well as dysphoric self motives.

A therapist faces a similar therapeutic challenge with the rare individual who is convinced that s/he has only feelings of dislike and disrespect for her/his parents. These negative feelings are a product of the patient's motive for pathological positive transference pleasure. They impart such a powerful sense of strength and independence that the patient has great difficulty in becoming uninterested in the nonveridical well-being they produce. This person experiences a severe loss when s/he perceives the hollowness of this oppositional strength (which actually represents an appetitive attitude toward the caregivers that is rooted in identifications with the caregivers' paranoia).

There are two types of transference pleasure within the therapeutic developmental split, each of which becomes destructuralized in an Intrapsychic Treatment process: pathological positive transference pleasure and developmental transference pleasure. These originate in two categorically different types of intrapsychic mutuality, delusional (psychopathological) and illusional (developmental). All pathological positive transference pleasure represents a motive to hold on to the meaning structure of pain and is the anchor of the patient's illness. The destructuralization of these two types of nonveridical pleasure occurs in part by mourning two types of aversive reaction to care-getting pleasure, namely the aversive reaction to care-getting pleasure and the aversive reaction to nontransference care-getting pleasure.

Since it enables the individual to survive defective nurture and also represents the fixation of mental illness, the pathological positive transference is at once the strength and the bane of the human species. From an intrapsychic caregiving viewpoint, the pathological positive transference embodies the individual's most tenacious motives to hold onto psychic pain. The need to hold on to pain does not refer to a need for interpersonal suffering, but rather refers to an innately driven, unconscious need to acquire inner well-being in a pathologically distorted way. The pathological positive transference is a structurally isolated and distorted version of the innately based, positive relationship motives represented by the smile response.

The therapist faces the subtle and challenging task of responding facilitatively to the patient's pathological positive transference. If the therapist unreflectively gratifies the fixated part of the patient's pathological positive transference, the patient will be encouraged to seek the delusional pleasure of pain relief rather than the veridical pleasure of mourning. This pain relief stimulates the dysphoric self to cause an aversive reaction to care-getting pleasure. The aversive reaction to pleasure may be subtle (e.g., a dissociated state, an unnoticed negative shift in the perceived meaning of a given experience) or patent (e.g., a resurgence of feelings of self-debasement). Thus, the immediate effect of the therapist's unreflective and nonveridical gratification of the patient's pathological positive transference is to alienate the patient from the intrapsychic caregiving relationship. Though the patient may seem to respond with a prodigious capacity for sensitive constitutive-interpersonal introspection, this introspection represents the defenses of intellectualization and compliance. Because every patient initially lacks a veridical capacity for intrapsychic and regulatory-interpersonal self-caretaking, the restimulation of the patient's self-rage by the therapist's unreflective gratification of the fixated part of the patient's pathological positive transference eventually instigates another cycle in which the patient seeks to gratify pathological positive transference motives. When the therapist gratifies the patient's fixated motive for pathological positive transference pleasure, the patient is sent into an ever-tightening spiral of self-rage (which can find conscious expression as paranoid rage and/ or self-rage), which deepens the patient's sense of inner isolation. By gratifying the fixated part of the patient's pathological positive transference, the therapist enhances the patient's delusional inner well-being, which is rooted in her/his denial of the painful reality that s/he never received veridical intrapsychic caregiving.

Our assertion that the therapist should not unreflectively provide the patient with pathological positive transference gratification does not imply that we endorse the psychoanalytic stance of extreme abstinence.[15] Classic psychoanalytic tenets of abstinence assume that an analyzable patient begins the treatment process with a functional capacity for a stable, real relationship and that the analyst needs to facilitate the patient's expression of transference (unreal) relationship behavior by relating to the patient with such neutrality that the patient will make the analyst the unprovoked object of the patient's instinctual drive derivatives. Psychoanalysis assumes that the analysand has a ready to use, relatively unrestricted, reflective capacity for introspection and, further, that the patient can simultaneously perceive the well-intentioned, real analyst and a transference-distorted analyst, who provides both negative (critical) and positive transference relationship experience.[16]

The therapeutic stance Freud describes as "a state of evenly suspended attention"[17] has the meaning to the patient of the therapist's preference for distance from the caregiving relationship. This meaning is reinforced by the analytic setting, in which the patient lies on the couch facing away from the analyst.[18] Because analytic deprivation overestimates the patient's inner stability, it causes the patient to regress. The patient with a pathological self-structure must not have her/his delusional intrapsychic well-being further stimulated and reinforced, either by inappropriate pathological positive transference gratification or by undue relationship deprivation. Undue deprivation is a gratifying percept for the motives of the dysphoric self; therefore, the most harmful aspect of harsh abstinence is that it unwittingly reinforces the dysphoric self's motives for pain as a gratifying, pathological agent-self percept.

Intrapsychic Treatment is a demanding form of intrapsychic caregiving because the therapist must be capable of identifying and facilitating the *nonfixated* part of the patient's pathological positive transference. In the initial stage of treatment, the therapist's selective gratification of the patient's nonfixated pathological positive transference enables the patient to become more veridically involved in the intrapsychic caregiving intimacy offered by the therapist. This veridical involvement corresponds to the activation of the patient's intrapsychic pleasure principle and the patient's growing capacity to discriminate between veridical and nonveridical forms of agency. Eventually this leads to the differentiation of the patient's regulatory-intrapsychic agent-self.

Role of Interpretation

If, as psychodynamic psychologies suggest, the etiology of psychopathology primarily concerns (constitutive-interpersonal) motives for conflict and self-rage, interpretation would be the primary or sufficient mode of therapeutic action (psychic structure building). However, since constitutive-interpersonal meaning structures of self-rage play a nonstructural role in psychopathology, the use of interpretation is a necessary but not sufficient cause of the therapeutic action. Since the cause of psychopathology, namely, nonveridical intrapsychic caregiving, is intrinsically metasemiotic, interpretation, which aims to correct semiotic confusions, cannot be the sufficient cause of intrapsychic therapeutic action.

Interpretations aim to make the patient aware of the significance of the pathological constitutive-interpersonal meaning structures that resulted from the original caregiver's psychopathological *interpersonal* caregiving. These pathological constitutive-interpersonal meaning structures can be unconscious or conscious. Treatment directed to constitutive-interpersonal meaning structures, however, can only decrease socially maladaptive interpersonal psychopathology (i.e., decrease the relative strength of the motives of the patient's dysphoric self structure vis à vis the motives of the patient's pathological pleasurable self structure). It cannot alter intrapsychic psychopathology. When the therapist relies solely on interpretations to effect structural change, any positive change in the patient's behavior represents patient compliance, which is a combination of positive identifications with the therapist and the pain relief afforded by the gratification of the patient's dysphoric self motives for self-rage.

The intrapsychic therapist uses interpretation judiciously to give the patient's innately determined ideal of veridical intrapsychic and veridical regulatory-interpersonal motive gratification leverage against invisible, distorted, agent-self meanings. A therapist will often interpret the patient's dysphoric self motives for isolation and discord. For example, one patient, who had great difficulty resisting her dysphoric self motives to cause herself unhappiness at work and in relationships, began to realize that she could in fact make self-caretaking choices. After a day when she had resisted the desire to do something she knew would irritate her boss, she dreamed that she had gone to a dress shop, where a salesperson had presented her with a choice of two dresses, each of which was equally ugly and certain to make her look unattractive. The therapist made the interpretation that the dream was an aversive reaction to pleasure in which the patient's dysphoric self was trying to convince her that making self-caretaking choices would be no better for her than making self-defeating choices. The therapist added that it was a positive sign that the patient's self-caretaking motives had regulated her *actions,* while the power of her self-defeating motives had been limited to regulating the content of the dream.

Although interpretations can provide the patient with an understanding of her/his conflict in response to her/his growing motives for veridical self-caretaking pleasure, all interpretation is a form of persuasion. The efficacy of interpretation lies not in corrected cognitive strategies or revisions in personal history, but rather in the deepening of the alliance between patient and therapist. Interpretation simply prepares for and fuels the sufficient cause of the therapeutic action, namely, the veridical intrapsychic caregiving relationship, which is the only therapeutic input that can allow the patient's fixated intrapsychic transference process to evolve into a developmental transference process. A structural alteration in psychopathological personal meaning structures occurs when the therapist's veridical intrapsychic caregiving stimulates and then makes functional that aspect of the patient's veridical intrapsychic motive that has remained both untouched by nonveridical nurture and sufficiently unregulated by the pathological transference to be potentially responsive to veridical intrapsychic caregiving.

The prime obstacle to a successful therapeutic process is the patient's aversive reactions to care-getting pleasure. The patient's dysphoric self experiences veridical intrapsychic care-getting pleasure as ungratifying, that is, as a loss of its sense of effective agency. The therapist's interpretations help the patient both to recognize her/his aversive reactions to care-getting pleasure, and, subsequently, to own and regulate her/his motive to be available to the therapist's veridical intrapsychic caregiving. It is, of course, vitally important that the therapist not make interpretations of the patient's unconscious motives in the service of gratifying the therapist's personal motives that the patient behave differently (e.g., be more positive toward the therapist or, even, more negative). As treatment progresses, the patient's commitment to veridical pleasure increases, and the allure of reactive pain decreases. This spiral of therapeutic process has three major phases. The initial phase contains a pathological split between the negative transference and the fixated pathological positive transference on the one side and the non-fixated pathological positive transference on the other side. The pathological split, in turn, changes to a therapeutic developmental split when it comes to include a functional, newly formed, developmental transference. Finally, there occurs a differentiated therapeutic developmental split, which now includes a transference-free self structure that evolves into a posttransference agent-self.[19]

Most psychodynamic and cognitive theories of psychopathology and treatment share the belief that the core of psychopathology exclusively consists of a set of meanings that are conflict ridden, irrational, and unreasonable and, therefore, are open to correction by a process of reality testing that the patient learns within the treatment process and combines with her/his motive to be helped. Whether the new edition of reality testing occurs by a reliving within the structure of the transference neurosis or by cognitive strategies, in both psychodynamic and cognitive psychotherapies the primary and sufficient therapeutic act is interpretation. The psychodynamic psychotherapist directs her/his interpretations to the patient's transference, and the cognitive therapist directs interpretations to illogical perceptions of reality. From our perspective, each type of therapy has the goal of enabling the patient to alter nonregulatory (solipsistic and nonempirical), constitutive-interpersonal meaning structures. The positive outcomes reported by other schools of psychotherapy represent a shift in the balance between competing constitutive-interpersonal motives, so that rational, adaptive cognitive meaning structures gain regulatory control over interpersonal reality testing. These changes, however, do not affect the intrapsychic or regulatory-interpersonal dimensions of psychopathology.

Process and Content Meanings in Intrapsychic Treatment

One of the most important and helpful distinctions a therapist can make is between the content and process meanings of a patient's associations during the therapy session. The distinction between content and process meanings does not reflect distinctions between manifest and latent, conscious and structurally unconscious, genetic and contemporary, or transference and nontransference meanings. Rather, the distinction between content and process meanings rests on the significance any association has in relation to the developmental goal that the patient acquire the capacity for stable involvement in the mutuality of the intrapsychic caregiving relationship. Consequently, this distinction is dynamic (person and situation dependent) rather than formal (static).

The *process* meaning of a patient's association is its meaning vis à vis the patient's conflicting motives for veridical intrapsychic intimacy with the therapist and for delusional intrapsychic mutuality. In other words, the process meaning of a communication is its significance in relation to the patient's movement toward or away from the pleasure of the intrapsychic caregiving relationship. Until the differentiated therapeutic developmental split, when the patient develops the capacity for veridical intrapsychic self-caretaking, the distinction between content and process meanings can be made only by the intrapsychic therapist. The content meaning of the patient's communication encompasses all other significance of that communication besides the process meaning.

One example of the distinction between process and content meanings is taken from the treatment of a patient who had serious conflicts about intimacy. This patient had planned a vacation, during which she would miss a therapy session. In the treatment sessions, the patient began to have many thoughts about separations (her boss leaving, a co-worker leaving). She also expressed many concerns about the upcoming vacation (she had never visited her destination and was afraid she would be unable to find her way around). The patient began to wonder about these thoughts and concluded that she was unconsciously conflicted about going on her vacation. The *content* meaning of these thoughts was an insightful understanding about her constitutive-interpersonal motives. While the therapist agreed with the patient's observations, it was also clear that the *process* meaning of the associations concerned the patient's unknowing use of the upcoming separation from the therapist to gratify dysphoric self motives for alienation from the intrapsychic caregiving relationship. The focus on the vacation caused the patient constantly to feel she had one foot already out the door.

In a second example, a lawyer in his fifties dejectedly reported that he had lost a case he had argued in court. He castigated himself severely, saying that the judge had asked him a question and he had not answered adequately. He had provided the judge with a number of good arguments, but felt that there was one argument he had left out. It seemed to the therapist that the judge simply did not favor the patient's position and that the omission of the one argument had not determined the decision. The therapist made the interpretation that the patient's self-castigation represented an attempt to maintain the esteem of the pathological all-powerful agent-self in the face of preconscious perceptions that the loss was a foregone conclusion regardless of any arguments the patient could have made. The patient immediately associated to a familiar and very painful childhood memory in which he had interviewed at the one college he really wanted to attend, assured by his college counselor that if the interview went well he would be accepted. The interview went badly, and the college rejected him. The patient's parents had responded to this loss by telling him that since he had done badly in the interview he was clearly destined to be unsuccessful, and they had used this rejection as the occasion to refuse to support his attempt to acquire a college education. The content meaning of the patient's association was his attempt to explain why the loss of the case was causing him so much misery. The process meaning, which the therapist interpreted, was that, by associating to a time when his actions had in fact caused a significant loss, the patient was unconsciously reacting to and rejecting the therapist's previous interpretation that the patient was having difficulty accepting the fact that the loss of the case had been inevitable.

In the following example, a young child's increasing capacity for veridical intrapsychic intimacy enabled her to distinguish between process and content meanings. The child had begun treatment at the age of 30 months, at which time she manifested a childhood psychosis that was characterized by an inability to separate from the mother even for short periods of time. At the age of five, she initiated a game with the therapist in which the therapist would say a word and the child would give a definition. When the therapist said, "Mother," the child said, "A mother is someone who takes care of you when you are sick." At this point, the child was beginning to recognize that the pleasure she felt with her mother depended on the ablation of her motives for veridical agency. A year later, during the last session before the weekend break in appointments, the child began playing with a doll. She had the doll throw a note to the parent dolls that said she was going away. Then the doll galloped off on her horse. Immediately, however, the patient had the doll come back and sleep near the mother doll. The mother doll said to the girl doll, "You are going to turn into a mummy and be dead." The patient told the therapist, "That's the mother's dream." There was a pause, and then the patient said, "Maybe I was thinking about dying because we don't have our appointment tomorrow." The child herself was able to recognize the process meaning of her association and to share this recognition with the therapist as a way of increasing her veridical self-caretaking pleasure.

One final example illustrates the contrast between Intrapsychic Treatment and psychoanalytic treatment in terms of the distinction between process and content meanings. A five-year-old boy who had been in Intrapsychic Treatment for about six months because of his unbridled aggression toward other children asked the therapist what kind of doctor he was. The therapist replied that he was the kind of doctor that "could help with feelings." The next day the boy came in with a ball in the shape of a monster's head that was cut open and had huge teeth and crooked eyes. The boy called it his "mad" ball. He said, "The mad ball kills everyone," and he had it "kill" all the dolls in sight except the baby doll. The boy had the baby doll start to cry and then had the mad ball comfort it. Then he made the baby doll curl up and go to sleep in the mad ball's mouth in order to be "safe." From the standpoint of classic psychoanalytic theory, this behavior would represent the fusion of libidinal and aggressive instinctual drives on the level of the oral psychosexual zone. In our opinion, this focus only addresses the content meaning of the child's behavior. The process meaning is that, in response to the pleasure of asking the therapist what the nature of their relationship was and being told it was to help the child feel better, the child had an aversive reaction to care-getting pleasure, which took the form of a manifest reliance on rage (pain) as a gratifying percept for the patient's dysphoric self motive.

There is no formula by which one can distinguish the process and content meanings of a patient's communication. The only sure way for a therapist to distinguish these levels is to possess a regulatory-intrapsychic agent-self. Because each patient is unique and, in addition, because each patient's ideals and motives change and evolve, a process meaning for one patient can be a content meaning for another, and what is a process meaning for one patient on a given day can be a content meaning for the same patient on a different day or even at a different point in the same session.

Nonveridical Treatment

Because the patient enters treatment with an intrapsychic agent-self and a regulatory-interpersonal agent-self that are pathologically fixated, if the therapist's caregiving is nonveridical, this nonveridical caregiving can only affect the balance of power between the patient's dysphoric self and the patient's pathological pleasurable self. In an obviously nonveridical treatment, the patient's dysphoric self is strengthened and her/his symptoms grow worse or new symptoms develop. The patient either becomes too psychologically regressed to continue the treatment or abruptly terminates the treatment. The more common nonveridical treatment process, however, is difficult to recognize as such, because the patient's pathological pleasurable self gains increasing control over the patient's interpersonal behavior. The patient's symptoms improve, s/he has positive feelings about the treatment, both patient and therapist ascribe lingering problems caused by the patient's pain to the patient's resistance to the therapeutic process or to an external cause, and the patient remains in treatment until the therapist feels the patient is ready to leave. But the underlying treatment process is the same in this example as in the more obviously nonveridical treatment process in that the therapist is using the patient as a gratifying percept for her/his pathological transference process. In other words, the therapist responds to the patient with personal needs rather than with intrapsychic caregiving motives.

Actually, the nonveridical treatment process we have labeled as obvious is also rarely recognized as such. For example, when a patient deteriorates to the point of psychosis as a result of nonveridical caregiving, the therapist usually concludes that the patient is either untreatable or is treatable only as an inpatient. The invisibility of psychic pain makes even the obvious category of nonveridical treatment difficult to recognize. Since the nonveridical therapist lacks the capacity for veridical intrapsychic self-caretaking, s/he has no functional motives to perceive the nonveridicality of her/his responses. The patient, of course, cannot her/himself recognize the nonveridical nature of the therapist's intrapsychic caregiving because s/he also lacks the capacity for intrapsychic reflectiveness.

Patients are a self-selected group in that they seek treatment because they possess functional motives for pathological positive transference gratification. These motives are usually coupled with unreflective ideals and longings to experience veridical intrapsychic caregiving. Given the existence of these positive ideals, the relative strength of the patient's pathological pleasurable self motives and dysphoric self motives will determine the patient's response when the therapist's caregiving is nonveridical. Usually the patient persists in finding some way to rationalize the therapist's behavior in order to maintain the needed representation of the therapist as a caring helper who is truly concerned about the patient. In other words, if the therapist uses the patient to gratify her/his own personal (noncaregiving) motives, the patient will often respond to this nonveridical caregiving as s/he responded to the original caregiver, namely by misidentifying it as needed, veridical caring. Just as the patient's most invisible and resistant motives are based on pathological positive identifications, in one sense the most damaging nonveridical therapist offers transference gratification in the form of stable, genuine interpersonal concern for the patient. From an intrapsychic caregiving perspective, the therapist's interpersonal kindness is actually in the service of gratifying the therapist's need for a pain-filled type of intimacy.

Patients, naturally, do not always comply with the therapist's nonveridical caregiving. The patient can usually recognize nonveridical *interpersonal* caregiving when the therapist has such extreme interpersonal psychopathology that even the patient's dysphoric self motive to use relationship-generated pain as a gratifying, pathological agent-self percept cannot cause the patient to confuse the therapist's behavior with acceptable caregiving. The patient fortunate enough to have had sufficiently benign interpersonal caregiving in childhood has a greater than usual ability to distinguish genuine from nonveridical *interpersonal* caregiving.

Nonveridical treatment is not defined by the occurrence of *caregiving lapses* per se, which occur in every treatment situation, but rather by the occurrence of caregiving lapses that the therapist cannot mourn. The nonveridical therapist cannot recognize and respond to the loss s/he has caused the patient without raging at the patient, at her/himself, or at both. When the therapist cannot mourn caregiving lapses, these lapses become *structural* caregiving lapses. Structural caregiving lapses are equivalent to ongoing nonveridical caregiving, because the ability to mourn constitutive-interpersonal loss is an all-or-nothing phenomenon. In other words, nonveridical treatment is nonveridical from its inception to its termination; it never follows or precedes a period of veridical treatment. While it is commonly held that a treatment process can go bad after a prior period of progress, this deterioration is a sign that the therapist's caregiving has been nonveridical. In a *veridical* therapeutic process, a patient may leave or deteriorate after some time has passed, but this interruption occurs in the course of an extended diagnostic phase and is not an unexpected decompensation in the treatment process per se. Accordingly, in veridical treatment, decompensation occurs before the establishment of the developmental transference and can be foreseen by the therapist.

A veridical therapeutic process depends on the therapist's ability to mourn two types of constitutive-interpersonal loss: the patient's aversive reactions to care-getting pleasure and the therapist's own caregiving lapses. When the therapist possesses a veridical, regulatory-intrapsychic agent-self, s/he has no need to use interpersonal experience for intra-psychic motive gratification. Therefore, the therapist will not use the patient as a source of nonveridical agent-self percepts. As a result, nei-ther the patient's aversive reactions to care-getting pleasure nor the therapist's caregiving lapses will cause the therapist to experience a loss of inner well-being. The following shows a therapist mourning a care-giving lapse and, in the process, giving the patient a veridical reflection of effective intrapsychic agency. In one treatment session with an eight-year-old boy, the therapist had a caregiving lapse, which he realized immediately after the end of the session. The next day, shortly after the boy came in, this interaction occurred:

> *Child:* You are not a regular doctor, you are a feelings doctor.
> When you need a feelings doctor, I know what you do.
> *Therapist:* What?
> *Child:* You go to yourself. (Pause) Actually, you can be my feelings doctor and I'll be your feelings doctor.
> *Therapist:* I think you are thinking I need a feelings doctor because yesterday I didn't stay with you (explains the process of his care-giving lapse).
> *Child:* Oh. I get it now. (Gave a big smile).
> *Therapist:* The really important thing is that you were able to come in and tell me that you didn't think I was taking care of you the way you deserve. That was terrific.

An indication that the child's expression of pleasure when the thera-pist shared his caregiving lapse did not represent compliance occurred when, in reaction to the therapist's responsiveness, the child proceeded to have an aversive reaction to care-getting pleasure in which he thought of a story about a teacher who was not doing a good job at teaching him basketball. The therapist interpreted the process meaning of this communication to the child by saying that the pleasure the child had when the therapist had shared his own caregiving lapse had been too much for a part of the child and that, therefore, the child had im-mediately tried to dilute or obliterate the pleasure by thinking of a pain-ful moment with someone else upon whom he relied for caregiving.

In most forms of psychological treatment, the most common type of nonveridical caregiving is probably the unreflective gratification of the patient's positive transference motives toward the therapist. However, nonveridical gratification of the patient's positive transference is not the predominant cause of the damage that occurs in psychoanalytic treatment. The most common unrecognized nonveridical caregiving in psychoanalysis probably consists of the analyst's interpersonal expressions of hostility toward the patient. These usually consist of interpretations accusing the patient of resistance. Such common analytic behaviors as giving the patient ultimatums (as Freud did with the Wolf Man), interpreting a patient's uncooperative behavior as resistance, telling the patient her/his needs are manipulative (e.g., complaining that the patient is treating the analyst as the patient's parents treated the patient), and deliberately stimulating the patient's negative transference reactions all express anger toward the patient. We believe that there is never any therapeutic justification for behaving in an angry or critical manner toward a patient and that all such behaviors constitute caregiving lapses. If the therapist cannot mourn these caregiving lapses and regain regulatory control over her/his personal motives, these caregiving lapses acquire the meaning of structural caregiving lapses (i.e., they signify a nonveridical treatment process).

The patient needs to experience the veridical, empirical mutuality that comes from being the agent cause of the therapist's intrapsychic caregiving. Consequently, the therapeutic relationship has an inherent tilt because, as in childhood, the relationship consists of one person having and giving what the other person needs and wants. The therapist's veridical, nurturing, intrapsychic responses facilitate the patient's progressively nontransference ability to recognize caregiving lapses. It is of paramount importance that the therapist have a functional motive to listen carefully to the patient's assertion that a given aspect of the therapist's interpersonal behavior is nonveridical. In other words, the therapist must be able to mourn—specifically, to experience deidealization by the patient without a loss of inner well-being. This portion of the therapeutic process is analogous to the caregiver's capacity to respond with pleasure to the child's desire that the caregiver put aside personal motives and choose intrapsychic caregiving motives. As a part of veridical intrapsychic caregiving, the therapist reinforces the patient's ideal of rejecting nonveridical caregiving.

Therapists who are incapable of veridical intrapsychic caregiving commonly fall into one of three categories of nonveridical interpersonal caregiving: (1) the therapist who has difficulty tolerating the intrapsychic caregiving intimacy pursued by the patient and avoids this intimacy by unconsciously stimulating the motives of the patient's dysphoric self for distance and isolation; (2) the therapist who needs the patient's pathological positive transference as a gratifying percept for her/his pathological pleasurable self motive and, hence, both stimulates the patient's positive transference and does not help the patient experience her/his reliance on pathological positive transference gratification as a loss to be mourned; and (3) the therapist who cannot tolerate the inevitable moments of being deidealized by the patient or of being the object of the patient's anger, which occur when the therapist has a caregiving lapse or the patient has an aversive reaction to care-getting pleasure.

One of the therapist's most difficult tasks is to ascertain whether the patient's negative behavior toward her/him is the result of the patient's aversive reaction to care-getting pleasure or is a reaction to a caregiving lapse. There are certain guidelines that indicate the treatment process is on the right track, such as the therapeutic use made of aversive reactions to care-getting pleasure and the therapist's ability to mourn being deidealized by the patient. Because of the invisibility of psychic pain, however, a therapist without the capacity for veridical intrapsychic self-caretaking might have the illusion that these criteria are being met when they are not. In contrast, the therapist with the capacity for veridical self-caretaking will recognize her/his caregiving lapses in a context devoid of self-rage. The caregiving lapse acquires the meaning of a loss to be mourned, that is, the caregiving lapse represents the loss of the pleasure the therapist experiences when s/he provides the patient with veridical intrapsychic caregiving.

We have described the process by which Intrapsychic Treatment provides the patient with an opportunity to develop a loss-free inner well-being. In addition, the intrapsychic therapist can experience the pleasure of intrapsychic caregiving mutuality in a context in which the patient's negative responses can be fully understood and do not cause the therapist to experience a loss of inner esteem.

In summary, Intrapsychic Treatment can be conceptualized as an attempt to compensate for the generally deleterious effects that the evolution and specialization of the human capacity for symbolic representational thought has had on human caregiving. In psychopathology, the human capacity to create and pursue myriad forms of vocational and recreational pleasure interferes with intrapsychic caregiving motives. At the same time, however, in the context of an intrapsychic therapeutic relationship, the human capacity for self-reflectiveness facilitates the patient's ability to come to know that the pleasure of veridical intrapsychic mutuality is superior to the pleasure of nonveridical intrapsychic mutuality.

Identification[1]

The construct of identity, or identification, is important to our exposition of Intrapsychic Humanism.[2] On the most abstract level, we posit an
identity between (1) our construct of a paradigmatic subjective experience of psychic reality and (2) the ontological, phenomenological real
of paradigmatic psychic reality. This equivalence underlies our assertion that Intrapsychic Humanism represents both a philosophy of mind
and also a general psychology. A second way in which the construct of
identification is important to Intrapsychic Humanism is that identification (as we define it) shares an intimate relationship with psychological
meaning, specifically, causal-ontological, personal meaning structures.
For example, we identify a new category of identification that is a determinant of the subjective experience of personal existence. This appendix will address the following subjects: (1) the nature and forms of identifications; (2) the distinction between identifications and associated
motives for relationship pleasure and other phenomena, especially imitation and affect; (3) constitutive-interpersonal (nonregulatory) identifications; and (4) nonveridical identifications.[3]

The Nature and Types of Identification in Intrapsychic Humanism

The many meanings of identification can generally be divided into
two categories: meanings common to the term identification and meanings that are unique to Intrapsychic Humanism. We will refer primarily
to our unique definition of identification; however, when we intend the
usual meanings of identification, the context should make this transi-
tion clear. The type of identification that is unique to Intrapsychic Humanism occurs solely within regulatory agency reality. It is an act of
self-recognition produced by the veridical, empirical recognition of the
self-reflection discovered within the caregiver's caregiving ideals.[4]

Certain ontologically distinct types of identification need to be distinguished. Identifications can be classified according to whether the motive for relationship pleasure that stimulates the identification originates in nonagency or agency reality. If this motive originates in agency reality, the identification can be further classified according to whether the motive (and, hence, the identification) stems from intrapsychic, regulatory-interpersonal, or social-interpersonal consciousness. If an identification stems from either intrapsychic or regulatory interpersonal consciousness, it has *regulatory agency reality*, that is, causal-ontological status with regard to the regulatory control of psychic reality. Social-interpersonal identifications, on the other hand, partake of *nonregulatory agency reality*. The distinction between regulatory and nonregulatory agency identifications can also be made in terms of the type of regulatory ideal (pleasure principle) that informs the identification. Regulatory agency identifications are guided by the intrapsychic and regulatory-interpersonal pleasure principles. Nonregulatory agency identifications are guided by the constitutive-interpersonal pleasure principle. Alternatively, psychological identifications of any type can be classified according to whether the sense of agency they signify occurs within a paradigmatic or psychopathological self system.

An act of identification involves both a process of reality testing and also the experience of an idealized meaning of self. Positive relationship experience, by definition, is based upon the conviction that one will find, to some degree, a desired sense of oneself within the experience of relating to the other, that is, that relationship experience will provide an experiential identity between oneself and a sought-after ideal. This phenomenon is important for the determination of the veridicality of a regulatory identification. A veridical regulatory identification can only be recognized through determining whether or not the object of identification is "truly real,"[5] that is, identical to the veridical precept. Nonveridical identifications occur only in development and psychopathology. In psychopathology, the nonveridicality can result from either a flaw in the validity of the judgment regarding the presence of identity or from a mistaken judgment about the nature of the object of identification. In other words, a regulatory identification is veridical if and only if: (1) the sought-after ideal represents genuine self-caretaking, and (2) the to-be-identified-with caregiver represents a veridical, actual form of the ideal. Except for a brief section at the end of this appendix, here we will discuss only paradigmatic types of identifications. We discussed psychopathological identifications in chapter 6.

Viewed as a product of motive, identifications originate in the reflective nature of consciousness. The reflective act associated with regulatory agency reality concerns the capacity to "see" oneself from a perspective outside of oneself, which is equivalent to the reflection of agent-self as agent-self.[6] As we described in chapters 2 and 3, this reflective act occurs when the child can recognize the identity of her/his own regulatory intrapsychic agent-self motive and the extracranial intrapsychic caregiving motive of the caregiver.

Intrapsychic identification is the process by which innately determined, dissociated personal meaning structures become conscious, empirical, mutual, and self-regulatory. In paradigmatic development, this capacity for self-regulatory stability occurs as the result of the child's mutual, empirical recognition of and identification with the caregiver's veridical intrapsychic caregiving ideals and motives. In psychopathology, delusional intrapsychic mutuality is the regulating cause of subjective personal existence. It results from the child's innately determined motive to accept and emulate even nonveridical intrapsychic caregiving. Delusional intrapsychic mutuality occurs because the child's sought-after ideal—to be the agent-cause of the caregiver's intrapsychic caregiving—is not matched by the caregiver's functional intrapsychic motives. Due to the caregiver's intrapsychic psychopathology, her/his pathologically distorted regulating intrapsychic motives prevent her/him from stably pursuing the pleasure of intrapsychic caregiving mutuality, that is, these motives prevent the caregiver from making the child's intrapsychic agent-self the regulating cause of her/his intrapsychic caregiving behavior.

Nonregulatory, constitutive-interpersonal identifications, such as identifications with the caregiver's identity as a farmer, express the social-interpersonal form of the motive for relationship pleasure. While they are not structuralizations and do not in themselves represent structures of regulatory agency, constitutive-interpersonal identifications do have the ability to guide behavior because they are ideals that specify motives (e.g., the motive to harvest at the right time so as to get in a good crop). Further, constitutive-interpersonal identifications serve the critical unifying function of integrating diverse experiences so that these experiences make sense to the agent-self.

The psychoanalytic literature generally discusses identification in terms of emotion, affect, instinctual drives, and cognitive schemata. The identifications described in psychoanalytic theory occur on what we term the constitutive-interpersonal level of consciousness; however, they differ from our construct of constitutive-interpersonal identifications. Neither Freud nor his followers could ever consistently relate affects and instinctual drives. In keeping with this, most contemporary psychodynamic authors who have tried to integrate the notions of ego and self blur the distinction between the notions of innate instinctual drives, affect, and affect as an innate motivational system.[7]

Freud postulated that identifications arise in two primary ways: (1) a Lamarckian type of acquired inheritance,[8] and (2) as an innately based response to loss, in which the lost object is restituted by means of an ego identification.[9] In our view, Freud based the latter explanation on the faulty premises that the instinctual drives are the causal-ontological basis of psychic reality and that identification with the lost object represents the normative response to loss. We agree that the motive for identification is an inherent component of human nature, but argue that identifications represent the process of gratifying the consciousness-generated motive for relationship pleasure. Further, the act of identification is neither exclusively nor primarily a form of imitation or assimilation.

We have not presented an encompassing review of the psychoanalytic constructs concerned with identification (e.g., incorporation, introjection, and internalization) because these constructs are not relevant to the paradigmatic development of the capacity for veridical agent-self, self-regulatory control of psychic reality. In our view, the phenomena referred to by the psychoanalytic notions of introjection, incorporation, and internalization are aberrant forms of constitutive-interpersonal identifications, and their occurrence indicates the presence of psychopathology.

Identifications Distinguished from Imitation and Affect

We believe that the relationship between identification and imitation is more apparent than real. That is, in our view identifications and imitations represent distinctly different motives and acts. Only an identification can produce a lasting change in ideals. Second, unlike identification, meaningful involvement with the objects to be copied is not a prerequisite for imitation. Imitation has no fixed relationship to the act of identification; although at times it may represent a preliminary stage in an act of identification, it is not a prerequisite to the process of identification. In development, the most important function of imitation is as a facilitator of the learning process (e.g., motor mimicry, echolalia). In psychopathology, however, time-limited imitations may have the significance of as-if identifications.

Identification hitherto has been conflated with affect as well as with imitation. The conflation of identification and affect is one cause of the psychological and philosophical misunderstanding of the nature and sources of personal identity. Discussions of personal identity usually distinguish two types of personal identity: a subjective experience of agency reality which is a function of memory (the sense of sameness of the I in the present, the I in the past, and the I imagined in the future), and an objective view of nonagency reality in which personal identity is equated with material, nonagency reality (e.g., fingerprints and photographs).

Intrapsychic Humanism recognizes four types of personal identity:

1. the subjective experience of regulatory agency reality based on the unifying meaning of intrapsychic and regulatory-interpersonal agent-self, which is generated by the capacity for the reflective experience of agent-self as agent-self;

2. the subjective experience of personal identity based on nonregulatory agency reality (this is identical to that traditional form of personal identity which is a function of memory);

3. the objective category of personal identity based on nonagency reality; and

4. the social category of personal identity that refers to the consistency or lack of consistency in an individual's behavior. The referent for this identity is the nature of the ideals regulating the individual's manifest behavior. This is the category of identity referred to in statements such as, "She is a changed person."

Affect refers to a category of sensations that are "neurally generated and introspectively perceived signals that generally do—but may not—physiologically induce action."[10] Affects are innately based, universal patterns of sensation. Tomkins has distinguished nine innate affects.[11] Darwin posited that there is a basic set of emotional expressions common to man and animals.[12] The various affective responses of the autonomic nervous system can have adaptive significance for both the individual and also for other members of the species who are attuned to the individual experiencing the affect.

Nonagency-based meaning structures that signify affect can have the felt impact of arising simultaneously within the body yet external to the agent-self. Though not an innate meaning structure, affect stimulates the generation of paralinguistic meaning structures which, from the viewpoint of the agent-self, have the paradoxical quality of being simultaneously both labile and nonvolitional and also motivating.

The terms "affect," "feelings," "emotion," and "mood" all refer to the basic phenomenological experience of personal existence—the spectrum of pleasure-unpleasure which plays a crucial role in the teleological experience that characterizes sentient, purposive life forms. We use *affect* as the central term denoting experiences of pleasure or unpleasure that arise in physiological nonagency reality. *Emotion* refers to the subjective experience of an affect and, therefore, to its meaning for the agent-self. *Mood* refers to an emotion of prolonged duration. *Feeling* is used as a general term that includes affect, mood, and emotions.

The relationship of affect to identification is highly complex. On the level of regulatory agency reality, affect is only a signifier of an identification; the affect (sensible pleasure or unpleasure) merely signifies that an identification is occurring. The signifying affect has no causal ontology; however, the identification it signifies does have structure-building, causal-ontological significance. In other words, although affect accompanies the motives for relationship pleasure (and, therefore, the identifications) that occur on the level of regulatory agency reality, the affect itself has no causal-ontological significance. On the level of nonregulatory agency reality, affect not only signifies a nonregulatory identification, but also affect itself may stimulate a (social-interpersonal) motive for identification. In the latter case, the affect both stimulates and signifies the (nonregulatory) identification. To summarize, affect is an innately determined system of pleasure and unpleasure, which, in and of itself, has no intrinsic regulatory significance for psychic reality, but which is intimately related to (i.e., accompanies) identifications, some of which have regulatory (causal ontological) significance for psychic reality.

Motives for relationship pleasure are the primary cause of identifications (and, hence, are fundamental to the notion of personal identity). Like affect, these motives can be described as "prewired" structures; however, motives for relationship pleasure are generated by consciousness (which is contingent on the central nervous system) rather than by the autonomic nervous system (which generates affect). The experiential pleasure produced by meaning structures of relationship pleasure is sentient experience that represents a type of sensibility which is not a type of affect. Although they are not intrinsically related, the system of motives for relationship pleasure and the system of affect have not previously been distinguished.

The primary origin of the motive for relationship pleasure can be either regulatory agency reality or nonregulatory agency reality. With regard to regulatory agency reality, the origin can be intrapsychic or regulatory-interpersonal, and the motive can be either primarily innately based or primarily nurture based. Regulatory agency motives for relationship pleasure occur in the form of a purposive, appetitive need for recognition by the other, as manifested by the intrapsychic motive. Innately based motives for relationship pleasure are an important source of emotional contagion. In our view, emotional contagion is one cause of group psychology, that is, the dynamics of the relationship between the leader and the led. In contrast to this are causes of emotional contagion that are primarily functions of stimuli belonging to non-agency reality (e.g., anxiety caused by someone else's realistic fear of an external danger, or a sense of patriotism stimulated by martial music).[13]

Affect has occupied a unique and problematic position in philosophical and psychological discussions both because the experience of affect may have agent-self significance and also because, in psychopathology and development, affect's capacity to have hegemony over agency has been recognized from the earliest times (e.g., the stories of Abel and Cain, Helen of Troy, Samson and Delilah). The relationship between cognition and the emotions has resisted elucidation, especially because, despite the attempts of Hegelian mentalism, it was hard to imagine that any form of reason could conclusively regulate affective experience.[14]

Some philosophical and psychological theories presuppose that pleasure and/or unpleasure have a regulatory influence over an individual's experience of identity. However, this leads to a view of humankind as hedonistic and impulse-ridden. This view fails to recognize the fundamental distinction between motives for pleasure that arise in the innately determined system of motives for relationship pleasure and motives for pleasure or unpleasure that are induced by the prewired system of affect. In the affective system of communication generated by the autonomic nervous system, pleasure and unpleasure refer only to biological, physical nonagency reality in the form of sensations. In contrast, when the referent is the system of motives for relationship pleasure, pleasure and unpleasure refer only to biological, physical agency reality in the form of meaning structures endogenous to consciousness, which is contingent on the central nervous system. This system of motives for relationship pleasure is composed of two types of meaning structures: regulatory agency reality (personal meaning structures) and nonregulatory agency reality (self meaning structures). Personal meaning structures have causal-ontological status. They are generated solely by intrapsychic consciousness or by the regulatory level of interpersonal consciousness. The nonpersonal category of self meaning structures are generated by constitutive-interpersonal consciousness.[15]

In relation to personal meaning structures, the primary referent for pleasure and unpleasure is the veridical or nonveridical nature of the subjective experience of personal existence rather than affect. The intrapsychic well-being of paradigmatic, conflict-free psychic reality is an apperception of an existential meaning, not an affect; regulatory agency experience has no intrinsic relationship to the autonomic nervous system. Since the affect of pleasure can be used to signify this type of existential meaning, the two systems of meaning are vulnerable to conflation.

In paradigmatic development, the function of the meaning structure of unpleasure in the system of motives for relationship pleasure categorically differs from the function of the affect of unpleasure. With the time-limited exception of the occurrence of intrapsychic and regulatory-interpersonal developmental loss, the meaning structure of unpleasure serves no regulatory function in paradigmatic regulatory agency reality. That is, an individual who has completed a paradigmatic development will experience only pleasure on the level of regulatory agency reality. Even when an individual has psychopathology, that is, psychic pain caused by nonveridical caregiving, this pain cannot be known on the regulatory agency level except from an intrapsychic caregiving perspective. In addition, all unpleasure that an individual with a psychopathological self system experiences on the nonregulatory agency level is under the hegemony of regulatory agency motives for delusional intrapsychic and regulatory-interpersonal relationship pleasure.

In the system of affect, the pleasure-pain continuum of induced meaning structures occurs only on the level of constitutive-interpersonal consciousness and, therefore, does not have causal-ontological status with regard to subjective personal existence. However, both affective pain and affective pleasure exert non-causal-ontological influence with respect to the individual's capacity for self-caretaking. Unpleasurable affect can either signify nonregulatory agency meaning structures of unpleasure (e.g., the experience of hurt feelings) or it can both act as the signifier and also represent the signified (as in the case of a stomachache). Innate patterns of negative affect are also a phylogenetic form of adaptive behavior in the service of fight-or-flight response patterns. Further, the sole interface between unpleasurable affect and regulatory agency reality occurs when the affect signifies the temporary appearance of the regulatory agency meaning structure of unpleasure at the time either of the intrapsychic developmental losses (expressed as stranger anxiety, separation anxiety, and care-getting anxiety), which occur during the pre-eidetic stage and the regulatory-intrapsychic self stage, or of the regulatory-interpersonal developmental losses, which occur during the regulatory-interpersonal self stage.

Many authors believe that innately determined patterns of negative affect signify the meaning of human nature. In our view, however, in paradigmatic development negative affect represents adaptive fight-or-flight behavior on the level of constitutive-interpersonal consciousness. As discussed in the text of this volume, the survival capacity conferred by the child's ability to use nonveridical percepts for intrapsychic motive gratification has the paradoxical effect of making humans vulnerable to mental illness while ensuring physical survival. In psychopathology, negative affects can serve as pathological agent-self percepts for the nonveridical perceptual identity process that misidentifies psychic pain as signifying intrapsychic pleasure. In paradigmatic development, patterns of negative affect do not acquire this function.[16]

The power of affective (nonagency-based) expression to induce identification has given considerable support to the materialistic, reductionistic, psychoanalytic view of the developmental basis of psychic reality.[17] Psychoanalytic theory does not give consciousness per se a causal role in the individual's development of a regulatory agency capacity. Instead, psychoanalytic theory posits that the capacity for agency arises from two distinct sources: the developmental vicissitudes of innate patterns of affect and the developmental vicissitudes of cognitive development.[18] That is, psychoanalytic theory postulates that psychological agency results from a process whereby the occurrence of biological states of pain and pleasure are associated with symbolic meanings both of self and also of self in relation to other. For this reason, psychoanalytic theory asserts that the development of regulatory agency (as usually defined) corresponds to the onset (at roughly 18 months) of the capacity for speech, symbolic thinking, and cognitive awareness of the inanimate world.[19] Because psychoanalytic theory incorrectly ascribes the essence of psychic reality to nonagency reality and to nonregulatory agency reality, psychoanalytic theory does not distinguish between the following distinctly different components of the smile response: the facial expression of pleasure, the affect of pleasure, and the regulatory agency meaning structure of pleasure.[20]

The issue of how affect, which arises in nonagency reality, influences the regulatory control of psychic reality is part of the broader issue of the interrelationship of pleasure, truth, and goodness. The way in which this issue is viewed, in turn, influences one's understanding of the way in which the meaning of pain relates to the problem of evil. In contrast to the notion of truth based on nonagency reality (e.g., the natural sciences), in which truth is usually defined in terms of consistency and correspondence, the referent of the truth being discussed here is causal-ontological meaning structures, specifically, the conflict-free, autonomous regulatory agency capacity for self-regulatory stability. Pleasure may or may not have causal-ontological status with reference to the regulation of subjective personal existence. Unpleasure never has veridical causal-ontological status. Causal-ontological pleasure has the significance of causal-ontological psychic truth; it is the basis for action and agency, and is incompatible with delusional convictions regarding the nature of an individual's own psychic reality.

Types of pleasure and unpleasure that lack causal-ontological status with reference to regulating subjective personal existence occur on the constitutive-interpersonal level of consciousness. This type of pleasure-unpleasure can arise within agency reality or nonagency reality. In posttransference existence, unpleasure that arises within nonagency reality (e.g., a sore throat) will not cause unpleasure on the level of agency reality because the individual will not respond to loss with self-rage. Further, unpleasure that arises in nonagency reality will never have the meaning of pleasure, as often is the case in psychopathology. The posttransference individual's constitutive-interpersonal introspection about the pleasure or unpleasure which arises in nonagency reality will be regulated by the same precepts of constitutive-interpersonal introspection that regulate the constitutive-interpersonal introspection of other posttransference individuals.[21] In contrast, in the presence of the motives for psychic pain that occur in psychopathology, consensual validation of introspection about nonagency-based pleasure or unpleasure is highly problematic because the signifying process is regulated by self-rage. Consequently, psychoanalytic theory has had difficulty in creating a coherent theory of affect. The significance that an individual with psychic pain attaches to a given affect will be the idiosyncratic outcome of her/his character structure (see chap. 6). For example, an infusion of adrenalin will normally stimulate unpleasure, but an individual with psychopathology could report this unpleasure as an experience of pleasure.

Causal-ontological pleasure is a product of the perceptual identity process of intrapsychic and regulatory-interpersonal consciousness. It has no primary association with nonagency reality, which plays a secondary role as signifier. For example, in infancy, the perceptual identity process that produces the smile response creates causal-ontological pleasure (which builds psychic structure) and is signified by the sensation of pleasurable affect. Primary types of nonagency-based pleasure or unpleasure (e.g., sexual pleasure or a toothache) are not predicated on motive experience but, instead, stimulate a secondary type of meaning structure. The nonagency experience of pleasure or unpleasure functions as sign and signifier and is the referent for that which is signified. An example is the introspective experience stimulated by an infusion of pentobarbital. This barbiturate induces sleepiness (signifier), which initiates a motive to sleep (signified), which has as its referent the infusion of the barbiturate.

Constitutive-Interpersonal Identifications

The social-interpersonal agent-self and its associated motive for relationship pleasure emerge in the regulatory-interpersonal self stage. From that point on, the social-interpersonal agent-self is the sole form of agency by which any of the categories (i.e., regulatory agency or nonregulatory agency, innate or nurture based) of the motive for relationship pleasure can be expressed. In paradigmatic development, the nontransference form of the social-interpersonal motive for relationship pleasure is under the hegemony of the regulatory-interpersonal agent-self and has hegemony over all other constitutive-interpersonal motives, including the motives for relationship pleasure that originate in nonagency reality (e.g., the motive for genital gratification). Conversely, in its developmental transference form, where, by definition, the sense of agency is illusional, the social-interpersonal motive for relationship pleasure is vulnerable to regulation by nonagency, constitutive-interpersonal motives. For example, in the conjugally competitive agent-self phase of the regulatory-interpersonal self stage, the child's motive for conjugal gratification by the heterosexual caregiver acquires temporary hegemony over the child's motive for social-interpersonal pleasure with the caregivers. When the child mourns triadic conjugally competitive loss, her/his social-interpersonal motive again gains hegemony over all other constitutive-interpersonal motives and over nonagency motives.

Because of its hegemonic position in relation to the other constitutive-interpersonal motives, the social-interpersonal agent-self motive is the nexus of constitutive-interpersonal psychic structure and, accordingly, goes through a unique identification process. Because they arise within constitutive-interpersonal consciousness, social-interpersonal identifications are based on a nonempirical experience of the other's motives and ideals. By their nature, social-interpersonal identifications are easily stimulated by the nonagency type of signifier, which, by definition, is vulnerable to losses caused by positive entropy and chance. Social-interpersonal identification always entails the hierarchy and interrelationship of more than one form of influence. This phenomenon is exemplified by human sexuality, which is a biological activity sustained by a cultural process. It involves an array of self meaning structures, which are, in part, organized by and, in part, are responses to conjugal motives, which, in turn, have been stimulated by gonadal metabolism.

The essence of the relationship between the social-interpersonal agent-self and nonagency-based agent-self meanings (e.g., sexual impulse) is that the physiologically induced motive leads to an activity sustained by a meaning experience that originates in agency reality. Put differently, the social-interpersonal agent-self neither acts as a vehicle for nor mediates physiologically induced motives, but rather governs a specific meaning experience that consists of pursuing simultaneous gratification of two distinct to-be-actualized ideals: (1) an aim determined by a physiological stimulus and (2) the purposive meaning to the self signified by successful gratification of the physiological aim.

The phenomenological experience of the social-interpersonal agent-self differs from the phenomenological experience of the regulatory-intrapsychic agent-self and the regulatory-interpersonal agent-self in that: (1) the social-interpersonal agent-self is under the hegemony of the regulatory-intrapsychic agent-self and the regulatory-interpersonal agent-self and (2) introspectively, social-interpersonal self-experience seems to be regulated by the capacity for effective agency that originates in agency reality, but, from an intrapsychic caregiving perspective, it is proximally regulated by the positive entropy of nonagency reality.

Identifications related to gender occur on the constitutive-interpersonal level of consciousness (i.e., accord with the commonly used definitions of identification). On the level of nonregulatory agency reality (constitutive-interpersonal consciousness), gender is the most important identification-based organizational structure in human sexuality. Paradigmatically, that aspect of personal identity related to gender develops through an identification process that entails: a male or female sexual organ, the social-interpersonal agent-self's relationship to the sexual anatomy and the sexual motives engendered by gonadal metabolism, and the reflections for sexual identity given the child by family and culture. These reflections include the caregivers' valuation of the child's gender and the caregivers' outlook on how the child should relate to her/his own conjugal motives (which involves the comfort with which the caregivers respond to the child's experience of her/his own genital motives).

Motives for relationship pleasure that are stimulated by nonagency reality (e.g., the sexual drive) are, by definition, secondary to and facilitative of the needs of nonagency reality (e.g. homeostatic vegetative motives, such as to eat and to be warm). The extent to which one has regulatory control of these motives is a function of the degree of differentiation of the intrapsychic self.

Nonveridical Identifications

Because the developmental transference and pathological transference forms of social-interpersonal identifications entail the illusion of self-regulatory control over psychic reality, the pleasure and pain generated within nonagency reality (e.g., the pleasure of eating, the pain of a cut finger) can acquire the meaning of the presence or absence of (nonveridical) agent-self percepts. Accordingly, transference identifications have such power that, in effect, constitutive-interpersonal meaning structures can have the (illusional) personal meaning significance of mutualized, nontransference intrapsychic meaning structures. Even though transference constitutive-interpersonal identifications with the caregivers' motives are nonempirical, the effect of these identifications is similar to that caused by the child's awareness of the caregiver's intrapsychic caregiving motives that occurs in the undifferentiated phase of the regulatory-intrapsychic self stage. It can be speculated that the power of transference forms of constitutive-interpersonal identifications to convey the illusion of causal-ontological power (effective agency) is one reason for the fact that intrapsychic consciousness has never previously been recognized.

From the viewpoint of the subjective experience of personal existence, structures of regulatory control are products of an individual's identifications. Therefore, the identification process is the fulcrum for the pleasure and pain subjectively experienced by an individual. Pathological development distorts the innately based motive for relationship pleasure, that is, distorts the child's need to feel intrapsychically loved. In the presence of nonveridical caregiving, the child is driven to take what, from an intrapsychic caregiving viewpoint, is the experience of not being loved (in the sense of not being given the gift of the stable, veridical power to regulate the caregiver's caregiving) and to attach to this experience the meaning of being loved (of having the veridical capacity for effective agency in relation to the caregiver's intrapsychic caregiving motives). This occurs through the dynamic that "to be like is to be liked," which leaves the child vulnerable to misidentify defective caregiving as veridical caregiving. Psychopathology originates in the caregiver's nonveridical caregiving, which unintentionally alters the child's needed experience of being loved by the caregiver to the opposite, in which the child loves to be like the caregiver.

The possibility of the regulatory control of desire has remained problematic in philosophy and psychology primarily because interpersonal and/or intrapsychic psychopathology has been mistaken for paradigmatic psychic reality. In psychopathology there are two competing structures of regulatory control produced by two categorically different types of identification: (1) identifications responsible for the sense of personal identity (which is generated by motives stemming from consciousness per se) and (2) identifications proximally caused by nonagency motives. Conflicts and difficulties that center around the regulatory control of desire are caused by nonveridical intrapsychic nurture, which can cause nonagency-based identifications to be used as gratifying agent-self percepts for the psychopathological transference and thus cause nonagency-based identifications to gain hegemony over agent-self based identifications. An example is the person whose conscious source of identity arises from being a successful lover and who constantly moves on to new conquests.

NOTES

1 We have been practicing and teaching Intrapsychic Humanism for over fifteen years.

2 Detailed applications of Intrapsychic Humanism to parenting and psychological treatment will be presented in subsequent publications.

3 Freud, *Three Essays on the Theory of Sexuality, Standard Edition* (hereafter abbreviated as *S.E.*), vol. 7, p. 158, n. 2.

4 **Ontology** is defined as, "a particular theory about the nature of being or the kinds of existents" (*Webster's Ninth New Collegiate Dictionary*, p. 825) and **epistemology** is defined as, "the study or a theory of the nature and grounds of knowledge esp. with reference to its limits and validity" (p. 419).

5 Freud, "The Psychotherapy of Hysteria," *S.E.*, vol. 2, p. 305.

6 While we present here a nonderivative psychology and philosophy of the human condition that is based on a specific understanding of human consciousness, we write in a historical context in which the past is prologue. This work would not have been possible without Freud and his predecessors. The history of ideas can be organized according to relationships of coincidence, affinity, influence and derivation. Overall, what we present is sui generis; however, certain components of our work do have relationships either of influence or affinity to previous theorists. Most obviously, Intrapsychic Humanism has been influenced by certain clinical observations and theoretical constructs in the psychoanalytic literature, of which the most central psychoanalytic influence has been the work of René Spitz. The influence of certain of Freud's contributions is manifest in some of the terms we use, such as transference and identification. The meanings we ascribe to these observations, constructs, and terms, however, are categorically different from the significance given them by psychoanalytic theory. For example, in our work psychic determinism is not a principle of regulatory control, but has a time-limited appearance in conflict-free form in paradigmatic development. Only in psychopathology is psychic determinism a permanent and conflicted feature of psychic reality.

Freud's influence can also be seen in what we term the conjugally competitive self phase. However, while we posit that a generic form of genitally organized behavior, aspects of which Freud termed the oedipal stage, is important as a developmental milestone in paradigmatic development, we believe that the infantile neurosis described by Freud has only epiphenomenal etiological significance in psychopathology and does not occur in paradigmatic development.

One central influence on our work has been Spitz's delineation of the discrete infant behaviors he termed the smiling response, eight-month anxiety, and the semantic "no" gesture. However, the meaning that we attach to these discrete developmental phenomena is categorically different from the meaning that Spitz attaches to them, as he places his discoveries within the context of the instinctual drive model of mind.

With regard to general relations of affinity and influence, we position ourselves within a well-established tradition of Western thought: our positive, humanistic, nontranscendental viewpoint with regard to the nature of human nature stands within the tradition of such thinkers as Aristotle, Shaftesbury, Rousseau, Feuerbach, Marx, and Macmurray. Although Intrapsychic Humanism differs from the work of these philosophers, it shares certain assumptions: that humans are intrinsically social, that human satisfaction and goals are realizable only within a community, that human nature includes feelings of natural affiliation and concern, and that relationship experience can open up a new and higher form of existence which, to paraphrase Rousseau, allows individuals to perfect and enlighten one another (*The Social Contract*). As will be seen, while we present a psychology of autonomy and responsibility, we have neither a reformist nor a utopian orientation.

Intrapsychic Humanism should not be confused with the humanistic psychology that has evolved in American academia. Traditionally, *humanism* refers both to a perspective about the human condition and also to a specific school of thought within American psychology (see, generally, the *Encyclopedia of Psychology*, pp. 155–161). As a perspective, humanism traditionally embraces two distinct, contrasting views of human nature: (1) the existential, tragic viewpoint, exemplified in the work of Rollo May and Victor Frankl and (2) an extremely sanguine view of human nature, exemplified by the writings of Norman Vincent Peale and Mary Baker Eddy. Between these extreme viewpoints lies the work of such psychologists as Allport, Murray, Murphy, Kelly, Rogers, and Maslow. Intrapsychic Humanism has no relation to the tradition of humanistic psychology primarily because we do not posit an exclusively semiotic basis for the phenomenon of agent-self experience. Further, we do not render human nature in terms of an assumed tendency toward self-actualization, as do authors such as Rogers and Maslow. Also, though the view we offer is identitarian and transformationalist, it is not a type of essentialism (Mayr, *The Growth of Biological Thought*, pp. 45–47); it does not posit separate ontological bases for continuity and sameness in structure and for changes in structure.

Our work has a strong affinity with one particular tradition in Western thought, the school of moral philosophy developed during the eighteenth-century Scottish Enlightenment, especially by Hutcheson. Hutcheson conceived of an innate moral sense, which he distinguished from the notion of innate ideas. In this usage, moral does not have a prescriptive meaning, but rather refers to a sense of the good in human relationship experience. In answering the epistemic question of how one may know the moral experience, Hutcheson disallowed reason, which seemed to him too weak to undergird moral judgments. Hutcheson addressed the question of how regulatory moral ideas are acquired by positing that the moral sense resides in human nature and responds to human relationships with an act of moral knowing that motivates actions (regulates acts of decision). In other words, Hutcheson posited that moral knowledge was intelligible by virtue of its intrinsic connection with the experience of everyday life (*Illustrations upon the Moral Sense*, p. 194). Hutcheson's notion of a moral sense adumbrated Spitz's discovery of the smile response by two centuries. Hutcheson located this innate trait in unconflicted human nature, whereas Spitz's discoveries are consonant with Freud's postulation of a pain-ridden human nature.

Our discussions of ontology, causality, and the nature of scientific theories have been informed by contemporary philosophers of science, esp. Roy Bhaskar, Herbert Simon, and William Wimsatt. Finally, we wish to comment in advance on what are likely to be, from the perspective of the analytic tradition in philosophy, the two most frequent misunderstandings of Intrapsychic Humanism. The first is the application to it of the charge Ryle made against the Cartesian "I." Ryle claimed that the Cartesian "I" was an arbitrary, unfounded explanation for human behavior, that is, a "ghost in the machine" (*The Concept of Mind*, p. 15). In contrast to the dualistic context of the Cartesian "I," Intrapsychic Humanism posits an "I" of "We"ness in a monistic context of intrapsychic mutuality.

The second potential misunderstanding is that Intrapsychic Humanism is inherently mentalistic and, therefore, logically incoherent because it relies on what analytic philosophy calls intentional idioms, that is, it is based on an appeal to meaning. However, such a criticism would reflect the fundamental bias of analytic philosophy that the problem of truth can be addressed solely through linguistic analysis, which denies validity to epistemological and ontological concerns. We argue that the ontology of analytic philosophy is reductionistically materialistic and is, therefore, incompatible with our ontology of regulatory agency reality.

While we believe that our constructs reflect the true ontology of psychic reality, we recognize that, like all ontological presuppositions, this view cannot be proved. We do assert, however, that Intrapsychic Humanism has more manifestly robust, heuristic, explanatory power than other psychologies or philosophies of mind. Intrapsychic Humanism offers experience-near, heuristic explanations of important human problems such as suicide, mental illness, unprovoked aggression, and other forms of self-defeating behavior. With respect to understanding the human condition, Intrapsychic Humanism offers a rational, metacognitive, experience-near explanation for the age-old issues relating to the presence of evil and the question of free will.

7 The *subjective experience of personal existence* refers to one's experience of the nature and quality of being alive.

8 While there may be an unintentional implication that Intrapsychic Humanism is a mixture of philosophy and psychology and, therefore, is essentially

speculative and nonclinical, this is not the case. Our sole focus is the experience of personal meaning, which we investigate by means of an epistemology made possible by a developmental, caregiving, structure-building context. Philosophy inquires into the meaning of meaning. We describe an epistemic act that is tailored to knowing the subjective experience of personal existence and enables the investigation of the meaning of meaning to occur at the locus of psychobiological unity, where the concerns and approach of both clinical psychological theory and metaphysics become one and the same. Accordingly, the differences between the disciplines of moral philosophy, metaphysics, and metapsychology disappear, and the distinction between metapsychology and clinical psychology collapses. Allowing for the imprecision of any label, our system can be termed ***metapsychics,*** or philosophy in practice.

9 *Reality* here refers to *physical reality*, that is, to all forms of nontranscendental existence. The epistemology specific to Intrapsychic Humanism apprehends a new ontology of human consciousness. In order to find an ontology and epistemology appropriate to knowing the subjective experience of personal existence, it is heuristic to posit two major categories of physical reality: biological and nonbiological. This work focuses on the biological category of physical reality. Although the revolutionary expansion of knowledge of molecular biology has blurred the distinction between biological and nonbiological categories of physical reality, in general, biological reality refers to any manifestation of a life process, which is understood as a generic category of physical functioning and not as an epiphenomenal residue of such functioning or as a type of transcendental vitalism. Sentient biological reality entails some form of purposiveness. For an excellent discussion of the explanatory value of teleology in biological systems, see Wimsatt, "Teleology and the Logical Structure of Function Statement."

10 In its common usage, the teleological viewpoint characterizes organized beings in terms of the kind of adaptation that conforms to Aristotle's concept of final causality. The focus on the end to which a given behavior appears to be directed easily lends itself to an anthropomorphism that conflates goals and purpose. As a result, the teleological viewpoint has often been misused to attribute an unwarranted kind of purpose to nature (Mayr, *The Growth of Biological Thought,* pp. 47–53).

11 Overall, we take a constructivist approach to the relation of mind to the external, sensible world. With regard to knowing another's regulatory agency reality, however, paradigmatic development will make it possible for an individual to make veridical (in the sense of correspondence to essential reality) perceptions about another's regulatory-intrapsychic agent-self in the context of an intrapsychic caregiving relationship. The truth on which we focus is the causal-ontological reality of the regulatory agency that controls psychic reality. This veridical regulatory agency capacity is created within the intrapsychic caregiving relationship.

Intrapsychic veridicality refers to whether subjective judgments of intrapsychic agency capacity objectively correspond to the external reality of the caregiver's intrapsychic caregiving motives. This capacity for veridical assessment of the quality of intrapsychic agency is the result of a transformation of intrapsychic meaning structures as a consequence of empirical, mutual contact with the caregiver's veridical caregiving motives (the specifics of which constitute the majority of this book). This transformation is different from the innate linguistic structures of transformational grammar proposed by Chomsky in that our referent for *transformational* is an intrinsic change in nonlinguistic structures from dissociated and nonempirical to reflective and empirically based (mutual). (See, e.g., Wimsatt, "Developmental Constraints, Generative Entrenchment and the Innate-Acquired Distinction.") Further, innate interpersonal linguistic structures and innate intrapsychic personal meaning structures refer to innate structures of meaning that occur on distinctly different levels of consciousness. Innate interpersonal linguistic structures are one of the inherent components of the agency reality associated with the constitutive-interpersonal "I." In contrast, innate intrapsychic personal meaning structures represent the fabric of intrapsychic agency reality, which has one referent: the psychic reality of the self-regulation of inner well-being. Language has a *facilitative* function in relation to the "I" of intrapsychic regulatory agency reality, whereas it has a *mediative* function in relation to the constitutive-interpersonal "I." Misapplication of the mediative function of language in constitutive-interpersonal reality to all psychic reality has contributed to the pessimistic view that humans are incapable of direct perceptual contact with either their own agent-self experience or another's agent-self experience.

As we discuss in detail in chaps. 2 and 3, we posit a bifurcated model of innate intrapsychic meaning structures. The undifferentiated form has the characteristic of an innateness that is contingent on, but is not derived from, experience. In contrast, the differentiated form significantly derives from experience. With regard to the capacity of the intrapsychic agent-self to exert autonomous regulatory control, our model of innateness includes two categorically different forms of nonveridicality, developmental and psychopathological. The developmental form, which occurs only in paradigmatic development, can evolve, whereas the pathological form becomes fixated. In other words, meaning structures are both innate and also open to modification.

12 As we use the term, the referent for paradigmatic development is empirical intrapsychic mutuality (see chap. 3) not interpersonal behavior. Therefore, we emphasize that paradigmatic development is not meant to imply that any cultural style of caregiving, childhood, or adulthood is inherently superior.

13 While the history of the idea of consciousness since Parmenides is vast, the critical watershed in terms of whether consciousness per se can be a source of knowable, valid reality was Descartes's conviction that the introspective reasoning of the privileged first-person case could represent a certain basis for the fact of one's personal existence as a thinking being. The history of the idea of consciousness since Descartes can be organized in many ways. Still controversial is the question of the validity of the subjective experience of mind. This issue is often formulated as the question of whether introspection constitutes a valid epistemic act. In one sense, this controversy revolves around the solipsism of the Cartesian knower and the question of how, if at

all, the privileged first-person—case accessibility of introspection can demonstrate the physical existence of the introspector. Descartes's inability to use the experience of physical pain to prove his own physical existence reflects the problem of whether introspection can be a reliable source of knowledge of one's own mind, much less of another's mind. Leibniz remarked that, "At that point, M. Descartes withdrew from the game" (quoted in Gilson, *The Unity of Philosophical Experience,* p. 185). In psychological terms, this is the problem of ascertaining a mode of knowing consciousness that will afford the self-regulatory control of subjective personal existence.

In the context of historical consciousness, each age frames the enduring problems of human nature in terms unique to itself. For Kant, the focus of Intrapsychic Humanism, namely the possibility of a self-knowledge that can afford the self-regulatory control of psychic reality, would have been a contradiction in terms. His paradigm assumed the mutual exclusivity between knowledge and the freedom of moral agency. He accepted the premise that the world that can be known represents a deterministic reality, which precludes an agency of moral freedom based on self-knowledge. In pursuit of his aim of establishing the possibility of both an objectively valid cognitive judgment and an objectively valid moral judgment, Kant proposed a dualistic regulatory reality. Overall, this reality allowed for a subjective personal existence in which the exclusive substrate to-be-known, which consists of a limited category of sensible reality (the appearance of things, not things in themselves), precludes a regulatory reality of personal existence grounded in self-knowledge. Kant's view of self-as-known followed from his doctrine of the unknowable reality of things-in-themselves. Unlike Descartes's experiential self-as-knower, Kant's agency of knowing, the transcendental unity of apperception, is not subject to introspection. Kant said, "There can be in us no modes of knowledge, no connection or unity of one mode of knowledge with another, without that unity of consciousness which precedes all data of intuitions, and by relation to which representation of objects is alone possible. This pure, original, unchangeable consciousness, I shall name *transcendental apperception*" (italic in original; Kant, *Critique of Pure Reason,* p. 136). The knowable Kantian self, the empirical self, can be known only as an object. Knowledge of it is limited, as is that of any sensible object, to appearance not substance. For Kant, personal existence is experienced not by the knowing self of speculative reason but rather by the acting self of practical reason, a self that has introspective freedom of moral choice but no capacity for veridical moral knowledge. Kant concluded that introspective self-knowledge, much less knowledge of others' minds, is a transcendental illusion. Kant's humanism was expressed in his postulation that humans have an innate autonomous moral agency founded on respect for others.

It is not surprising that Kant's work contributed to the occurrence of the extreme subjectivism of nineteenth-century idealism. Many of those who followed Kant found the prospect of an inborn incapacity for self-knowledge abhorrent and wished to ground introspective knowledge of the regulatory reality of personal existence in the knowable experience of consciousness per se rather than in an unknowable categorical moral imperative. For example, nineteenth-century idealism aimed to reinstate the privileged state of the first-person case. Kant's assertion that valid, objective scientific knowledge ensues

from a reason-regulated activity of the productive imagination encouraged
the idealist view that knowledge of both suprasensible and sensible reality
could be had by means of introspective self-knowledge. The resultant metaphysical excesses, especially those of Hegelian idealism, were succeeded by a
renewed commitment to the Kantian goal of establishing a valid form of empirical knowledge as an answer to skepticism. This renewed quest, however,
did not use strictly Kantian means. Rather the quest split ultimately into two
epistemic paths: phenomenology and logical positivism (which turned away
from introspection altogether). Positivism represented the attempt to purge
science of metaphysical concerns by concentrating on "hard" data, which
could be apprehended by the five senses, as the criteria for meaningfulness.

In contrast, Husserl followed Brentano in attempting to establish the validity of the first-person case by analyzing the phenomenological basis of the
introspective act. Husserl attempted to demonstrate the existence of a category of introspection that is distinct from but has the same validity as the
epistemic act of the natural sciences. In actuality, however, because Husserl's
act of phenomenological reduction is, in essence, merely a type of Cartesian
res cogitans, it does not provide a workable basis for a privileged first-person
case. Wittgenstein asserted the accessibility of the conscious experience of self
and other, but, in the process, denied legitimacy to the first-person case altogether and gave priority only to the third-person case.

When one accords a highly qualified legitimacy to the direct or indirect
apprehension of self-experience in a context in which the introspected agent-
self has no reflection of itself as itself (no reflection of agent-self as agent-
self), one has no way to be certain that one's experience of regulatory agency
is veridical. If introspection remains the sole method of self-knowledge
(which is not the case in paradigmatic development), it leads to an inescapable sense of inner alienation. This missing reflection of agent-self as agent-
self causes the existential despair so tellingly described by Kierkegaard, Dostoevsky, Sartre, et al.

Current continental philosophers of mind have continued to uphold the
validity of the first-person case. Some of these philosophers, such as Merleau-
Ponty and Marcel, rely on principles of phenomenology. A second group,
whose thinking is exemplified by the ontological hermeneutics of Heidegger
and Gadamer, supports the validity of the first-person case on the basis of
semiotics (which asserts the identity of being and semiosis). In contrast to this
viewpoint stands the theory of deconstructionist dialectics, as elaborated in
the writings of Derrida, which critiques the premise of Heideggerian Being.

On the basis of history alone, it would seem reasonable to conclude that
despair is indigenous to human nature. From our perspective, however, existential despair is the incapacity to have certain knowledge of one's own mind
(the incapacity for the control of subjective personal existence). The pain of
despair follows from the belief that one can never acquire the capacity for
effective regulatory agency or have even a potential capacity to maintain a
sense of inner well-being. Despair represents a pathological, interpersonalized meaning of permanent incompleteness, which occurs because the center
of intrapsychic agent purpose remains external to the agent-self.

14 It does not denote a *property* of mental states.

15 Nietzsche, *Ecce Homo,* p. 84.

16 Freud thought introspection posed vastly more problems than exteroception. In a letter to Fluss, he said introspection "is unfortunately not a firm basis for self-knowledge" (quoted in Trosman, "The Cryptomnesic Fragment in the Discovery of Free Association," p. 245).

17 See Bhaskar, *The Possibility of Naturalism.*

18 While we believe that intrapsychic and interpersonal consciousness are ontologically distinct, we insist only on the weaker claim that distinguishing these two types of consciousness is heuristic and conforms to introspective experience.

19 This is in keeping with the construct of negative entropy. It is heuristic to view positive and negative entropy as forming one continuum. While *positive entropy* is the thermodynamic notion of invariant change in the direction of disorder, *negative entropy* is the invariant change in the direction of order or increasing structure that is a property of all life forms. The notion of negative entropy is illustrated by Wendell Stanley's description of the two ontologically distinct forms of the tobacco mosaic virus: molecules organized as inert crystals and molecules organized as an infectious agent of the tobacco plant (Stanley, "Isolation of a Crystalline Protein Possessing the Properties of Tobacco-Mosaic Virus," pp. 644–645). In this instance, a physical reality is in two forms, nonbiological and biological, each of which demonstrates mutually exclusive forms of regulatory behavior. This illustrates that a force for disorder (positive entropy) can be reversible to a force for structure building (negative entropy) in an open system. In the context of understanding the subjective experience of personal existence, living matter displays an organization of molecules that exhibits negative entropy, or the inherent regulatory capacity to utilize energy for structure building (for change in the direction of order). This energy is the consequence of the hegemonic, inherent property of matter to change in the direction of disorder. The inherent capacity of living matter for stable growth even in the face of a universal positive entropic force is equivalent to a conditional ability to utilize free energy to provide a constant infusion of new units of structure.

This process makes possible the adaptive equilibrium between ordered and disordered states of energy that is necessary to support life. Negative entropy plays as important a role in agency physical reality as it does in the rest of biological physical reality; it provides the most heuristic explanation for the ceaseless quest for meaning (structure) exhibited by sentient beings. It explains the phenomenon that noncorporeal biological physical reality in the form of regulatory agency reality is as fundamental as corporeal biological physical reality (e.g., one's hand) in counteracting stasis (which is incompatible with an organism's integrity). One can reasonably postulate that sentient life forms have an ongoing purposiveness and, therefore, some form of perceptual identity process. This process becomes most evident when it goes awry. An illustration, taken from nonvertebrate behavior, of the hierarchical, regulatory nature of innate ideals (precepts) and to-be-actualized ideals (motives) is that the precept regarding light is sufficiently hegemonic in the caterpillar that this creature will remain at the light end of a jar and starve to

death even though there is accessible food at the dark end and the tempera-
ture there will support caterpillar life (Wimsatt, "Purposiveness and Intentionality in Nature," pp. 2–3). The analogy with the human syndromes of
marasmus and anorexia nervosa is striking.

20 D'Arcy, *The Mind and Heart of Love*, pp. 276–304.

21 Intrapsychic subjectivity is made possible only by a veridical intrapsychic caregiving relationship, that is, only in a paradigmatic childhood or in Intrapsychic Treatment. One can only know (in the sense of own and regulate in a
loss-free manner) one's own consciousness by a process of mutualizing that
consciousness. The relationship construct we term the mutualizing of consciousness is not a mediation process and bears no similarity to Schleiermacher's projective imagination (*Schleiermacher's Soliloquies*, pp. 33, 82), the
Hegelian master-slave dialectic, Nietzsche's perspectivism, Dilthey's intersubjective I and Thou (Brown, *Structure, Consciousness and History*, p. 43),
Mead's social behaviorist view of self as a "generalized other" (*Mind, Self, and
Society*, p. 154), Buber's I and Thou, Macmurray's relationship-based agent-
self, Gadamer's hermeneutical I and Thou (Gadamer, *Truth and Method*,
pp. 321–325), or Vygotsky's notion of the transformation of an interpersonal
process into an intrapersonal process (*Mind in Society*, p. 57).

22 Used in this generic sense, the notions of meaning and purposiveness do not
necessarily connote a consciously intentional form of agency.

23 Psychoanalytic theory makes very different use of the concept of perceptual
identity. Freud's explanation of the process by which the individual evaluates
the fit between idea and percept reflects his materialistic ontology of the instinctual drives. In consequence, Freud's act of perception is an act of "re-
finding" ("Negation," *S.E.*, vol. 19, p. 237).

24 In other words, it has causal-ontological status in relation to the subjective
experience of personal existence.

25 Our constructs of the "we"ness of the "I" and the "I" of "we"ness are only
superficially akin to similarly named constructs in the tradition of dialectical
agency. For example, Hegel's teleological dialectic of desire is expressed
in terms of an "'I' that is 'we' and 'we' that is 'I'" (*Phenomenology of Spirit*,
p. 110). However, Hegel's mutuality represents an intersubjective relationship that is regulated by the need to destroy the otherness discovered within
the consciousness of the developing self (see Ver Eecke, "Hegel as Lacan's
Source for Necessity in Psychoanalytic Theory," in Smith and Kerrigan, eds.,
Interpreting Lacan, p. 123). In contrast, we represent a pleasurable relationship of intrapsychic mutuality which is the product of the empirical experience of extracranial motives (see chap. 3).

The psychoanalytic authors Erikson, Lacan, and G. Klein have constructs
of mutuality that have an apparent but not substantive similarity to our construct of intrapsychic mutuality. In general, Lacan's referent for the otherness of the I is the unconscious subject disguised in the individual's conscious
thoughts. This conclusion is in keeping with Lacan's view that language accounts for the uniqueness of humans (Lacan, *Ecrits*, pp. 146–178, and *The
Language of the Self*, pp. 263–270).

Erikson posits an innately determined responsive mutuality between infant and caregiver that regulates the infant-caregiver relationship: "Babies control and bring up their families as much as they are controlled by them; in fact, we may say that the family brings up a baby by being brought up by him" (*Childhood and Society*, p. 65). Erikson's notion of mutuality represents an intersubjective type of relationship experience. Further, Erikson's view of the infant-caregiver relationship differs from ours in that he believes every infant experiences an unavoidable "residue of a primary sense of evil and doom and of a universal nostalgia for a lost paradise" (p. 75). In our view, in paradigmatic development true inner paradise is the pleasure of veridical intrapsychic mutuality which the child experiences with the caregiver (see chap. 3) and which forms the fabric of the individual's subjective experience of personal existence.

More recently, G. Klein has asserted that there is a gap in the psychoanalytic constructs of the ego because these constructs refer only to separateness from others and ignore the universal, appetitive, noninstinctual human needs for relationship. He posits that "we" identities are intrinsic components of self. He also argues that psychoanalytic theory lacks a focus on "we-go" to complement its focus on the ego and that the "we" is as important as the "I" in demarcating self and other. His constructs refer to meaning structures that occur only on the level of solipsistic, constitutive-interpersonal consciousness and are grounded in the deterministic materialism that characterizes psychoanalytic theory (*Psychoanalytic Theory*, pp. 174–181).

26 Intrapsychic meaning structures are accessible to and can be transformed by public experience with the caregiver. While the innate intrapsychic meaning structure needs a minimal level of public experience (caregiving) in order to function, this functioning does not depend on its structural transformation. Whether or not innate intrapsychic meaning structures evolve into nurture-based, self-regulatory meaning structures depends on the functional integrity of the caregiver's intrapsychic caregiving ideals and motives.

As will be seen, we offer a constructivist approach to the ontological basis of subjective personal existence that entails both *preexperiential* meaning structures of regulatory control and *nurture-based* meaning structures of regulatory control that have the same causal-ontological power as the preexperiential meaning structures. Veridical knowledge of our own minds presupposes knowledge of, in the sense of empirical contact with, the caregiving ideals and motives of the significant other(s).

27 The most important referent for the term *caregiver* is intrapsychic caregiving (which will be discussed subsequently); therefore, caregiver refers only to the person or persons with sustained intrapsychic significance for the child.

28 The issue of innateness involves the age-old question, Does phenomenological experience determine the significance of a meaning structure, or does a preexperiential type of meaning structure determine the significance of phenomenological experience? Since Kant it has been possible to cast this issue in other than stark, either/or terms.

The construct of innate intrapsychic meaning structures is one of our primary notions. The notion of innateness has most often been used to refer to cognitive reality, moral reality, or the nonintrapsychic type of psychological reality (e.g., Jungian archetypes) rather than to intrapsychic reality. If we exclude preternatural and supernatural viewpoints, in Western thought until this century the notion of innate ideas has been predominantly discussed in philosophy. In the latter half of the twentieth century, however, the issue of innateness has been predominantly discussed from the standpoint of developmental psychology (see, e.g., Trevarthen, "The Foundations of Intersubjectivity" and "Neurological Development and the Growth of Psychological Functions").

The notion of a knowledge that comes from within (innate ideas) has persisted in Western thought from the pre-Socratic age and entails three general problems: (1) mysticism, which pertains to the problem of the origination of ideas; (2) prejudice, which occurs when the notion of innateness is applied as a doctrine; and (3) solipsism, which is the problem of reconciling the apparent contradiction that a truth can be at once logical, necessary, universal, and independent of empirical refutation.

The theory of innate ideas refers to knowledge that is both prior to and also independent of sense experience. Western philosophers have generally postulated two fundamental types of innate ideas: actual and virtual (for this discussion, see generally *Encyclopedia of Philosophy*, vol. 4, pp. 196–198). *Actual* innate ideas are explicitly present in the mind before it has begun to experience anything at all. An example is Plato's ideal form, which is known by the epistemic act of recollection. *Virtual* innate ideas are a priori forms of thought that are neither derived from sense experience nor distinct from the capacity to reason. They are not inborn, fully formal objects of thought that are temporally antecedent to sense experience; rather, they are the products of the mind's innate structure and are known by the act of reasoning. Examples include Descartes's clear and distinct ideas, Leibniz's truths of reason, and Chomsky's notion of an innate universal grammar. Both actual and virtual types of innate ideas refer to the knowledge content of ideas, have logical and epistemological a priori status, and do not derive from sensory experience (the actual type is temporally antecedent to sensory experience).

The opposing assessment of the problem of innateness is exemplified by Locke's view that nothing in the mind was not first in the senses; the mind begins as a blank slate. Locke argued that the theory of virtual innate ideas is a superfluous hypothesis (Coppleston, *A History of Philosophy*, vol. 5, p. 76). Calling ideas innate explains nothing and adds nothing. When Locke asserted that all knowledge is derived from experience, however, he used experience to mean the information produced by two types of perception: sensation (exteroception) and reflection (introspection). Unfortunately, Locke could not demonstrate how the reality perceived by introspection could be the same as the reality perceived by exteroception. This failure renders meaningless the view that all knowledge arises from sense experience. In stark contrast is Leibniz's balanced view of virtual innateness, in which reason does not copy the world but actually interprets and expresses it.

The need for certainty drove the controversy between the empiricists and rationalists during the Age of Reason. The prevailing paradigm of knowledge, which reflected Cartesian dualism, supported conflicting views of two distinct ontological substances (mind and matter) and, accordingly, two distinct approaches to certainty. In both views, certainty referred to a nondelusional, fundamental form of the real. The empiricists opted for the felt security of a publicly knowable, sensible experience, whereas the rationalists were concerned with certainty in terms of self-evident demonstrability, logical necessity, and universality. The empiricist approach led to Hume's skeptical use of reason to denigrate reason, and the rationalist approach led to the scholasticism of Wolff's metaphysics.

Kant responded to the challenge of Hume's empiricism, Wolff's rationalism (Gilson, *Being and Some Philosophers*, pp. 113–131), and Hamann's spiritualism (see Beiser, *The Fate of Reason*, pp. 16–43) by examining the conditions that makes knowing possible rather than by examining the notion of knowledge per se. Consequently, he denied the possibility of innate ideas and transformed the issue into the problem of a priori judgments. He replaced the problem of innateness with what he termed the problem of pure reason. This was the problem of demonstrating that there could be judgments (termed synthetic a priori) that were valid generalizations about experience, even though their universality could not be derived from experience. His core assertion was that sense impressions are perceiver dependent; the objects of knowledge conform to the mind; the mind cannot conform to objects of knowledge.

Kant's revolution in epistemology was elaborated in terms of his system of transcendental pure a priori concepts. The notion of a priori judgments emphasizes the importance of distinguishing between the notions of innate ideas, a priori ideas, and apriorism. The notion of a priori ideas, which is often conflated with the notion of innate ideas, is a distinction based on the organization of a specific type of knowledge. An a priori proposition can be known to be true or false without reference to experience except in so far as experience is necessary for understanding its terms (Flew, *A Dictionary of Philosophy*, p. 16). In contrast, apriorism is a philosophical position opposed to empiricism that asserts both the possibility of knowledge that is independent of experience and also that the mind contains innate ideas.

Kant distinguished two types of a priori knowing: relative and pure. Relative a priori knowledge refers to that which is implicit in the meanings of ideas already accepted; by definition, it has no intrinsic reference to the state of being preexperiential. Kant's construct of pure a priori concepts refers to structures that are not derived from experience and that make their appearance as knowledge only on the occasion of experience. For Kant, the act of knowing is an activity of constructing knowledge. Kant's pure a priori concepts represent transcendental structures which, under the regulation of pure reason (reason uninfluenced by experience), actively synthesize knowledge only on the occasion of experience. These transcendental structures are neither concepts nor possible objects of experience, but are inherent mental structures that transcendentally synthesize knowledge (see generally, Jones, *A History of Western Philosophy*, vol. 4, pp. 34–42).

Before Kant, the notion of innate ideas generally focused on the content of preexperiential ideas in a passively unfolding mind (Coppleston, *A History of Philosophy*, vol. 6, p. 397). In contrast, Kant's construct of pure a priori concepts presents a model of mind in which a constructive imagination functions by means of transcendental forms of synthetic activity, which makes external, sensible experience both possible and organized. As is well known, Kant's transcendental idealism, which presents a model in which the synthetic function of the imagination is under the hegemony of reason, ironically became an important stimulus to the development of the radical idealism of the Romantic period, which Kant had intended his view of transcendental idealism to refute.

In this century, there has been an explosion of experimental studies that, in one way or another, have taken a positive position on the notion of innateness. This literature has predominantly occurred in the fields of developmental psychology and linguistics; the work at Harvard's Center for Cognitive Studies is an example of the former, and the work of Chomsky is an example of the latter. Two important contemporary sources for the construct of innate structures of relationship experience are the disciplines of evolutionary biology and developmental psychology. In evolutionary biology, Wimsatt's concept of "generative entrenchment" seems to have robust explanatory power with reference to innateness (Wimsatt, "Developmental Constraints, Generative Entrenchment and the Innate-Acquired Distinction"). In developmental psychology, there is increasing evidence to support the notion of innate meaning structures of relationship experience (e.g., Bowlby, "Developmental Psychiatry Comes of Age;" Kaye, *The Mental and Social Life of Babies;* Meltzoff, "Imitation, Intermodal Co-ordination and Representation in Early Infancy;" Stern, *The Interpersonal World of the Infant;* and Trevarthen, "Instincts for Human Understanding and for Cultural Cooperation"). One viewpoint in developmental psychology is that innateness is ethological (e.g., Bowlby); another view is that the neonate's capacity for relationship experience cannot fully be explained by ethological theory. Trevarthen, e.g., argues that: "the phenomenon of mother-infant communication cannot be reduced to any nonhuman description such as [a] physical or physiological one. Nor, it would appear, is animal behavior as described by ethologists, with Fixed Action Patterns and Innate Release Mechanisms, an adequate model. The way is open to conclude that the endowment that makes possible learning how to behave from how others behave must include being to some degree human or personal to start with" ("The Foundations of Intersubjectivity," p. 318).

The behavior associated with our construct of innate meaning structures differs from that referred to by the ethological constructs of innate release mechanisms and fixed action patterns, because the intrapsychic meaning structures we posit are accessible to, and can be transformed by, public experience with the caregiver.

29 An innate intrapsychic meaning structure is a self-regulatory identity, which, though not derived from experience, makes its appearance as a functioning structure only on the occasion of experience. This structure of regulatory agency is not transcendental in the Kantian sense of that which cannot be an aspect of perceived experience and its presence is a prerequisite for the individual's continued biological existence.

30 Which can *potentially* be attained by anyone with normal brain functioning.

31 That is to say, interpersonal consciousness generates motives (to-be-actualized ideals) which are gratified by percepts that are signified through a perceptual identity process as matching consciousness-generated precepts (ideals of actualized ideals).

32 On the *constitutive* level of interpersonal consciousness, it makes sense to posit two types of meaning structures: innate (e.g., generative structures of language) and acquired (e.g., language itself). Chomsky's structuralism is congruent with our assertion that constitutive-interpersonal consciousness contains innate meaning structures.

One hallmark of the meaning structures of constitutive-interpersonal consciousness is that when they are exposed to the minimal amount of nurture sufficient to actualize them, they function autonomously. An example is language. Constitutive-interpersonal motive choice and gratification have causal-ontological status only in regard to nonagency reality and do not have causal-ontological status with regard to the subjective experience of personal existence. Causal-ontological status with regard to nonagency reality operates under the hegemony of positive entropy and is not generative. Examples of the causal-ontological status of constitutive-interpersonal consciousness with regard to nonagency reality are painting a picture or cooking a meal. The picture and meal are the proximate result of the creator's motives rather than the result simply of the ingredients of the picture or the ingredients of the meal.

The *regulatory* level of *interpersonal* consciousness generates motives for regulatory-interpersonal agency. Regulatory-interpersonal motives are motives for the reflection of agent-self as agent-self that arise from the (illusional or veridical) capacity for regulatory control over the choice and pursuit of constitutive-interpersonal motives. In paradigmatic development, the gratification of the motive for an effective regulatory-interpersonal agent-self ultimately becomes uncoupled from the gratification of specific constitutive-interpersonal motives. For example, the experience of effective regulatory-interpersonal agency will neither depend on winning a game nor be affected by losing a game.

33 Current thinking is that the number of sequentially regressive reflective steps that can be managed in short term memory is limited to four to seven (G. Miller, "The Magical Number Seven, Plus or Minus Two," p. 92).

34 Interpersonal introspection is, as Ryle pointed out, retrospection because introspection about introspection produces an infinitely regressive series of reflections about reflections, in which each observational pair consists of a relationship between an object to be perceived and the agent doing the perceiving (See Flew, *A Dictionary of Philosophy*, p. 177).

35 Sartre terms this phenomenon prereflective consciousness. The loss per se is the referent for Sartre's term nothingness, which forms the basis of the type of agency he terms absolute freedom (*Being and Nothingness*, p. 742).

As will be described in chaps. 4 and 5, to remedy the missing reflection of agent-self as agent-self of interpersonal consciousness the individual must acquire a stable, autonomous capacity for a veridical, effective, *regulatory-interpersonal* agent-self that receives gratifying reflections for its regulatory agency capacity from a source that was originally extracranial (the caregiver's intrapsychic caregiving) but that is now structuralized within the individual's *intrapsychic* center of agency. When this occurs, the regulatory-interpersonal agent-self is not experienced as an object self as is the case in sequentially regressive, constitutive-interpersonal introspection (which is limited by the constraints of short-term memory). Therefore, in the paradigmatic form of subjective experience we are describing, the capacity for interpersonal agency is not self-enclosed. In paradigmatic development, this freeing up of the regulatory and constitutive-interpersonal agent-selves from illusional experience occurs comprehensively in the posttransference stage of development.

36 Marasmus is a syndrome of progressive emaciation. Here, marasmus always refers to the psychologically caused form of the syndrome.

37 While genic inheritance can affect constitutive-interpersonal capacities and predilections, as a general rule it does not cause either mental health or psychopathology. Studies (e.g., of identical twins who have been separated at birth) that indicate that genic inheritance is a proximal cause of behavior focus on what we term constitutive-interpersonal behavior rather than on the veridical or nonveridical nature of an individual's intrapsychic agent-self experience.

38 In early childhood, every effect has the significance of being intentionally caused. Thus, regardless of the caregiver's purpose, when the caregiver's intrapsychic caregiving is nonveridical and, as a result, causes the child a loss, from an intrapsychic caregiving viewpoint, this loss acquires the unconscious meaning that the caregiver is intentionally causing the child pain. Concurrently, however, because the nature of intrapsychic experience is that, by definition, every caregiving act (veridical or nonveridical) signifies to the child an intentional act of love (not loss) the child unconsciously interprets psychic pain as agent-self-caused caregiver love. It can be seen, therefore, that psychopathology in actuality emerges from a life instinct rather than a death instinct—it is the coopting of the child's intrapsychic motive for mutualized pleasure by the effects of the nonveridical caregiver's need for relief from intrapsychic psychic pain.

39 The classification of behavior as interpersonally psychopathological, that is, as abnormal, is to a large extent culture dependent. While our examples of interpersonal psychopathology are usually drawn from American culture in the 1980s, we do not mean to imply that the behaviors we describe necessarily would be psychopathological in all other cultures or eras.·

40 Interpersonal psychopathology is the referent for other psychologies' categories of abnormal behavior and has multiple causes, although the underlying cause is always intrapsychic psychopathology. We, therefore, agree with critiques of reductionistic accounts of interpersonal psychopathogenesis. For example, we would essentially agree with Rubovits-Seitz's criticism of Kohut's theory of unitary psychopathogenesis and interpretation ("Kohut's Method of Interpretation"), although we disagree with the epistemic and ontologic basis of his argument.

41 The terms *experience near* and *experience distant* refer both to the degree of abstraction from the immediacy of lived experience conveyed by a given concept and also to the nature of the consciousness involved in the act of knowing. With reference to the degree of immediacy and abstraction involved in knowing, the natural sciences generally presuppose that experience-distant constructs produce the most valuable knowledge. When the social sciences try

to achieve scientific acceptability by emulating the ontology and epistemology of the natural sciences, they, too, make experience-distant concepts privileged. For example, in psychoanalysis the regulatory control of psychic reality resides in the experience-distant construct of the instinctual drives.

With reference to the type of consciousness involved in knowing, the attribute of experience-far refers to mediated knowledge, which is the product of interpersonal consciousness, and the attribute of experience-near refers to nonmediated knowledge, which is the product of intrapsychic consciousness. The constructs of Intrapsychic Humanism are particularly appropriate to the ontology being studied (regulatory agency reality) because they are experience near in that they focus on the veridical nonmediated knowing of the immediacy of the subject's regulatory agency reality.

Empathy and introspection have been criticized (e.g., by Hartmann, *Essays on Ego Psychology*, pp. 390–396) as experience near and, therefore, unreliable for producing truth. We consider that their unreliability is due to the fact that they are experience distant when contrasted to the experience nearness of intrapsychic caregiving.

42 When empathy and introspection are applied to the subjective experience of personal existence, they are inaccurate because, by definition, the knower makes indirect perceptions through the lens of her/his solipsistic, constitutive-interpersonal motives.

43 Skeptics have traditionally used epistemological solipsism as the justification for metaphysical skepticism.

44 Examples of this confusion are Descartes's discussion of the cogito and Kant's transcendental unity of apperception.

45 Constitutive-interpersonal meaning structures that do not entail the subjective experience of personal agency (are nonintrospective) are generally considered to be accessible with regard to the determination of validity in terms of consistency and completeness (i.e., in terms of the various linguistic and mathematical modes of logic).

46 Common usage excludes the viewpoint of absolute idealism exemplified by the dyadic solipsism of Hegel's master-slave dialectic.

47 Historically, those (such as Heidegger) who define the human being as "the entity which talks" (Heidegger, *Being and Time*, p. 208) and who seek to remedy the state of inner alienation attributed to the inherent solipsism of introspective experience have tried to solve the problem of alienation by a reliance on linguistic phenomena. However, because thoughts cannot be communicated directly and even speech, which makes thought as available as possible, still remains an indirect expression, language produces a problematic type of meaning. It is in this context that the school of deconstructionism reacted against the demonstrated failure of the various schools of hermeneutics, such as those proposed by Dilthey, Heidegger, Gadamer, and Habermas.

48 Initially, this mutuality is empirical because it is the experience of intrapsychic caregiving and care-getting. Subsequently, when this mutuality is structuralized within the child's regulatory-intrapsychic agent-self, this mutuality is still empirically based (see the differentiated phase of the regulatory-intrapsychic self stage).

314

49 As will be explained in chap. 4, although regulatory-interpersonal agency experience is solipsistic with regard to extracranial agent-selves, in paradigmatic development it becomes mutualized in the intracranial context of its relationship with intrapsychic consciousness.

50 The intrapsychic type of empirical, mutual knowledge is further distinguished by the characteristic that veridical knowledge of the child's or patient's intrapsychic agent-self requires that the caregiver or therapist possess a veridical intrapsychic agent-self.

51 This was a stimulus for the contemporary deconstructionist movement.

52 In contrast to interpersonal consciousness, intrapsychic consciousness is potentially both empirically accessible and mutualized. While *interpersonal* consciousness is never empirically accessible, it is mutualized in paradigmatic development because of the presence of the empirically based well-being of the maturated intrapsychic agent-self (see chap. 4). In contrast, the knowing of internal bodily sensations is both nonempirical and solipsistic. Parenthetically, this caused Descartes to fail in his attempt to assert that the experience of pain was a clear and distinct idea that could be used to demonstrate the existence of the external world (see Gilson, *The Unity of Philosophical Experience*, pp. 182–183).

As will be shown, our ontology does not unidirectionally dictate our epistemology. In this volume, the terms *epistemology* and *ontology* refer to the unified intrapsychic agent-self experience of what we have termed **metapsychics** rather than the distinct regulatory and constitutive meaning categories of metaphysics. In other words, epistemology and ontology refer to a level of existence (regulatory agency reality) that is not transcendental (is not beyond the phenomenological) but rather is a part of the commonly understood meaning of physicality that comprises human nature.

The epistemology associated with the ontology we propose can be described as **knowing as being.** There are two categorically different modes of knowing subjective experience. One is the inherently solipsistic and nonempirical knowledge of constitutive-interpersonal motives. In paradigmatic development, the agent-self associated with constitutive-interpersonal motives comes under the hegemony of the mutualized, veridical, regulatory form of agency that we term the regulatory-intrapsychic agent-self. The second type of epistemology for knowing subjective experience focuses on knowing intrapsychic regulatory agency reality. Because this epistemology is empirical and mutual, it deals with substance rather than with appearance and avoids the isolation and distance that results from an exclusive reliance on cognition. In this epistemology, the organ of knowing is mutualized consciousness rather than cognition.

Our ontology of regulatory agency reality rests on the assumption that in the appropriate context meaning can have the significance of efficient cause. Accordingly, the causal-ontological real of regulatory agency reality lies in intrapsychic and regulatory-interpersonal personal meaning, which is a manifestation of gratified motive experience. The most important motive being gratified is the motive for the reflection of effective agency. The individual acquires this reflection of effective agency via a specific relationship experience, the intrapsychic caregiving relationship. This relationship is equivalent to intrapsychic motive gratification (to intrapsychic perceptual identity). The *meaning* structure of veridical regulatory-intrapsychic agency is the veridical regulatory *cause* of the stable inner well-being that characterizes a paradigmatic subjective experience of personal existence. As will be discussed in chap. 3, the superior pleasure represented by the meaning of veridical intrapsychic agency causes the individual to have an ongoing, stable motive to experience nothing but veridical agent-self meaning and, conversely, to have a stable motive to avoid illusional agent-self meaning.

53 Referents of empathy date back at least to Herder in the eighteenth century (Berlin, *Vico and Herder,* pp. 154–155).

54 Kohut, "Introspection, Empathy and Psychoanalysis," in *The Search for the Self,* vol. 1, p. 206. Consistent with his view of empathy as vicarious introspection, Kohut asserts that empathy originates from the vicissitudes of narcissism ("Forms and Transformations of Narcissism," ibid., p. 450).

55 Kohut, *The Restoration of the Self.*

56 Because empathy stems from the observer's constitutive-interpersonal motives and focuses on the constitutive-interpersonal motives of the observed, it is, by definition, solipsistic and nonempirical and, therefore, unreliable for knowing with certainty the motives of the person being observed. The use of empathy can never result in a mutualized consciousness, i.e., in empirical contact between the agent-self of the observed and the agent-self of the observer. Thus, empathy is a form of hermeneutic activity.

   Our epistemic basis for perceiving the regulatory intrapsychic motives of the child or patient is quite different. First, our epistemology is the product of a mutual involvement in an intrapsychic caregiving relationship and cannot occur unilaterally. Second, it can only occur when the caregiver or intrapsychic therapist has a veridical regulatory-intrapsychic agent-self and a veridical regulatory-interpersonal agent-self, the possession of which enables her/him to distinguish between veridical and nonveridical forms of intrapsychic and regulatory-interpersonal agent-self experience in her/himself and in the other. In development, these two capacities make it possible for the caregiver to respond to the child with stable, veridical intrapsychic caregiving. The caregiver can veridically recognize intrapsychic and (after the child completes the regulatory-intrapsychic self stage) regulatory-interpersonal agent-self purpose in the child's behavior. In Intrapsychic Treatment, the therapist can stably and veridically respond to the veridical intrapsychic and regulatory-interpersonal motives that underlie the patient's pathological, distorted, learned, pain-ridden forms of intrapsychic and regulatory-interpersonal motive gratification.

57 While the construct of empathy remains perplexing, there is general agreement that empathy can represent both a type of affective communication, the aim of which is to know what another mind is experiencing, and also an act of caregiving. In its common usage, empathy represents a conflation of the experience of affective communication and the ideal both to know and to be known by the mind of another. Affective communication is based upon the capacity to imitate states of autonomic nervous system excitement that occurs in another. This capacity arises from the basic emotional expressions common to humans and other animals (Darwin, *The Expression of the Emotions*

in Man and Animals, pp. 120, 347, 366). The ideal both to know and to be known by the constitutive-interpersonal mind of another represents the influence of the intrapsychic form of the motive for relationship pleasure experienced within the psychopathological context of intrapsychic isolation. Interestingly, Hartmann, himself, had strong reservations about the veridicality of empathic knowledge. He said that "the nature of empathetic experience is still poorly understood, and its value in knowing other minds is still quite uncertain" ("Understanding and Explanation" in *Essays on Ego Psychology,* p. 379).

58 Used in this sense, *knowing* has no intrinsic relation to language.

59 McKenna, "Primate Infant Caregiving Behavior," p. 409.

60 Neither the drive model nor the object relations model advanced by psychoanalysis afford an ontological basis for understanding the crucial personal meaning arising from the relationship between personal agency and intended motive. Therefore, to the degree that either model focuses on personal meaning (in contrast to instinctual drive meaning), this meaning is restricted to the semiosis of constitutive-interpersonal consciousness.

Semiosis cannot serve as the basis of a regulatory agency reality that regulates the subjective experience of personal existence. Accordingly, prevailing psychological theories, such as those of Kohut, A. Miller, Lacan, Klein, Schafer, Habermas, and Gill, which rely for their validity and regulatory power on semiosis, are nonveridical and are psychotoxic when applied to psychological treatment or childrearing.

Mahler's perspective on human nature is that of Freud's. The fundamentals of her separation-individuation paradigm of development, such as hatching, simply elaborate Freud's notions of the primary autoerotic stage, pure pleasure ego stage, primary narcissism, and secondary narcissism in the context of an emphasis on object relations. Mahler approaches the child's self experience from the same external vantage point from which Freud approaches introspection. Thus, despite an intended emphasis on object relationship experience, Mahler's theory displays the instinctual reductionism of Freud.

Kohut tries to remedy the limitations imposed by the instinctual reductionism of psychoanalysis. He differs from Kernberg in that he does not treat object relations primarily as a mechanism for expressing the vicissitudes of instinctual drive derivatives. Kohut emphasizes the child's subjective experience of the parent and, analogously, the patient's introspective experience of the therapist. Ultimately, however, Kohut's outlook on introspection operates from the same experience-distant vantage point as do the views of Freud and Mahler. For example, Kohut advances the construct of the grandiose self as a normative structure and also as the centerpiece of his theory of narcissistic psychopathology. While Kohut asserts that his perspective gives priority to an experience-near perspective, grandiosity is clearly an experience-distant noun that does not reflect the child's or patient's inner experience. Like Freud and Mahler, Kohut mistakes psychopathology for normality. He cannot conceive of subjective personal experience which does not entail psychic conflict. Kohut's theory of parenting, e.g., offers no way to distinguish between a truly nurturing parental smile and an as-if smile that is a cover for the parent's nonveridical caregiving. Consequently, he provides no way to distinguish a well-functioning adult with an illusional (psychopathological) inner well-being from a well-functioning adult with a veridical (paradigmatic) type of self-experience.

61 See chap. 6.

62 See Bhaskar, *The Possibility of Naturalism.*

63 All intrapsychic meaning structures are *personal meaning structures.* Paradigmatically, intrapsychic meaning structures are veridical and can be effortlessly and reflectively recognized by the veridical intrapsychic caregiver or therapist or by the person who has completed a paradigmatic development. Thus, intrapsychic personal meaning structures are categorically different from meaning structures produced by thinking about consciousness by means of empathy or introspection.

   In contrast to intrapsychic knowing, constitutive-interpersonal knowing results from the perceptual identity process specific to constitutive-interpersonal consciousness. Depending on the nature of the object-to-be-known, constitutive-interpersonal knowing can be separated into the two Lockean categories of reflection (introspection) and exteroception. Intrapsychic and regulatory-interpersonal types of knowing, however, do not generate information about nonagency reality. Unlike those meaning structures that are products of the cognitive motives of constitutive-interpersonal consciousness, matured intrapsychic meaning structures are not inherently solipsistic, or nonempirical, or derivative, or descriptive, or associated with language. They originate extracranially in the caregiver's veridical intrapsychic caregiving. Mutualized intrapsychic consciousness is identical neither to what has been termed the collective unconscious (Jung, *The Collected Works of Carl Jung*) nor to the Hegelian teleological dialectic of master-slave (both of which in our view represent interpersonalized residues of intrapsychic pain).

64 Nonpersonal meaning structures occur on the level of constitutive-interpersonal consciousness and, therefore, fall under the hegemony of the regulatory-interpersonal type of personal meaning structure, which is, in turn, under the hegemony of intrapsychic personal meaning structures.

65 Piaget's constructivist epistemology, however, categorically differs from Freud's (Gruber and Vonèche, eds., *The Essential Piaget.* pp. 832–842).

66 Freud and Piaget also concurred in the premise that growth occurs as a response to loss. See Piaget's notion of disequilibrium (Wolff, *The Developmental Psychologies of Jean Piaget and Psychoanalysis,* p. 25).

67 In arguing for mind as an emergent quality of brain, Sperry concludes, "the conscious properties of cerebral activity are conceived to have analogous causal effects in brain function that control subset events in the flow pattern of neural excitation. In this holistic sense the present proposal may be said to place mind over matter, but not as any disembodied or supernatural agent" ("A Modified Concept of Consciousness," p. 533). Wimsatt strengthens Sperry's assertions by interpreting them in the context of Wimsatt's framework of multi-level reductionism ("Reductionism, Levels of Organization, and the Mind-Body Problem").

68 In contrast, we adopt a monistic paradigm of biology that avoids ontological reductionism without resorting to panpsychism, transcendentalism, or vitalism. See Wimsatt's construct of an alternate levels account of reductionism ("Reductionism, Levels of Organization, and the Mind-Body Problem," pp. 200, 219–224). Our version of monism bears no relation to the monistic viewpoints of: Spinoza, who asserted that body and mind are two modes of the same substance; Hegel, who asserted a monistic radical idealism in which all existence ultimately consists of one substrate, which is a thinking agent; or Schopenhauer, who asserted that through introspection one can discover that one's will has primacy over one's reason and sensation and, therefore, that all else, including one's body, is an expression of, or objectification of, Will. Other constructs of monism that can be distinguished from our version of monism include Davidson's recently proposed "anomalous monism" ("Mental Events" in *Essays on Actions and Events,* p. 214) and the monism proposed by Merleau-Ponty, which is associated with the belief that the condition of intentionality is associated with an irreducible solipsism. The monism we propose is superficially similar to the monism of William James, which Russell later elaborated in his *Analysis of Mind.* The ontology posited by William James partakes of the Cartesian view of substance in that the ontological real is defined as a type of primary stuff that represents the basic units of reality. In other words, James's ontological real is not characterized by a Hegelian dialectic or by efficient causality. James's ontology is neither dualistic nor materialistic, nor, by his account, is it mentalistic. Rather, James asserts a peculiar type of monism. His radical empiricism states that mind and body are separate but reconcilable in that they represent different arrangements of one kind of stuff—pure experience, which is neither mental nor physical. James defines pure experience as the immediate present, which has not evolved into theory, thought, subject, or object. Russell misinterpreted James's viewpoint as a form of what Russell called neutral monism. But James explicitly stated that his pure experience (the basic unit of reality) consists of the vast variety of sensations composing neutral reality that can be considered neither mental nor physical, but encompasses both mind and matter. Myers concluded that James's type of monism is most accurately depicted by the term neutral pluralism (Myers, *William James: His Life and Thought,* p. 566, n. 1. Also see William James, *The Writings of William James,* p. 170, and Bertrand Russell, *The Analysis of Mind,* pp. 24–25).

69 *Intrapsychic* agency reality refers exclusively to a biological physical reality with the power to be a regulating cause of subjective personal existence. *Interpersonal* agency reality includes: (1) a type of regulatory agency reality with causal-ontological status with regard to the regulation of subjective personal existence and (2) a type of nonregulatory agency reality with causal-ontological status with regard to the conditional regulation of nonagency reality (via the regulation of constitutive-interpersonal motives). An example of the latter is the manipulation of material resources to produce a desired product.

70 Our principle of intrapsychic reality testing is grounded in an empirical rationalism and a nontranscendental reflective idealism: we construct the criteria for intrapsychic reality testing from an empirical and mutualized context, and we use as our reference point timeless forms of relationship experience.

71 As we asserted in n. 69, this point of view is not anthropocentric, pantheistic, panpsychic, transcendental, or a disguised form of vitalism. The truly knowable is a veridical regulatory-intrapsychic agent-self and a veridical regulatory-interpersonal agent-self, both of which are grounded in the caregiving mutuality of a paradigmatic developmental process. As the source of regulatory control over all types of knowing, intrapsychic and regulatory-interpersonal forms of knowing represent the limiting boundary of all reality experience (of reality per se and of experience per se). Because we posit an ontologically distinct, empirical, mutual, regulatory agency reality that coexists with nonregulatory forms of agency reality, we avoid the pitfalls inherent in the four ontologies that could most easily be confused with ours. These are: (1) the reductionistic, teleological dialectic that generates the Hegelian model; (2) Husserl's transcendental phenomenological essence that is apprehended by the epistemic act of eidetic reduction (Jones, *A History of Western Philosophy*, vol. 5, pp. 269–279); (3) Heidegger's notion of modes of being that acquire ontological status to the degree that an individual nonsolipsistically regulates his personal existence; and (4) Mead's psychosocial model of mind, which asserts that mind arises out of or comes into being from, "the matrix of social relations and interactions among individuals which is supposed by it" (*Mind, Self and Society*, p. 223, n. 25).

72 In scientific circles, teleology normally conjures up visions of a naive application of the notion of Aristotelian teleological causality, in which the goal of an act (telos) is the regulating cause of the act (in conjunction with the efficient, material, and formal causes). When applied to the natural sciences, this type of teleological explanation is a form of panpsychism, in which purposiveness is attributed to nonbiological or nonsentient biological phenomena.

73 The intrapsychic motive entails causality, not just meaning or significance. This is in spite of the fact that, since Kant separated the notions of reason and causality, Western thought has unsuccessfully tried to explain the undeniable experience of intentionality associated with personal agency without positing the operation of subjective causality.

74 Thus, an intrapsychic teleological process forms the basis of a causal-ontological type of personal meaning structure that, contrary to hermeneutic theory, is a species of reason that also functions as a cause. Intrapsychic motive gratification has causal-ontological status in and of itself, but it does not have the same logic of explanation as the efficient causality used by the natural sciences. It is not an example of Grunbaum's causal relevance (*The Foundations of Psychoanalysis*, pp. 69–73) and does not conform to Davidson's proposed notion of a causal type of reason based on linguistic, analytical logic, which gives privileged priority only to the third-person case and uses an impersonal, experience-distant method to distinguish between events and actions (Davidson, *Essays on Actions and Events*, pp. 149–162).

Because, in relation to the regulation of subjective personal existence, cause is the product of the motives and ideals generated by intrapsychic consciousness and is not intrinsically the product of the semiosis of interpersonal consciousness, it is not regulated by the logic of explanatory reasons, by the hermeneutic principles of *verstehen* (understanding) philosophy, or by the principles of the ontological hermeneutic proposed by Heidegger and Gadamer. Further, the intrapsychic perceptual identity process conforms neither to Hegel's distinction between the causality of nature and the causality of fate nor to Kant's distinction between the laws of nature and the laws of freedom. Intrapsychic causality is concerned with the agent-self regulation of ends and intentionality.

In the second half of the nineteenth century, the philosopher Franz Brentano reacted to the excesses of idealism and positivism by attempting to establish an authentic type of privileged first-person basis for a nonsolipsistic experience of mind that was not a type of physical phenomenon. This model of mind was based on a specific introspective experience he termed *intentionality* (see Gregory, *The Oxford Companion to the Mind,* pp. 383–386). Brentano used intentionality in the sense given to it by medieval scholastic philosophy (to aim at, or point at) and argued that intentionality only applies to mental states and can be used to distinguish the mental and the physical. Brentano thought intentional meaning structures (beliefs, desires, etc.) proved the non-solipsistic nature of mind, because intentional states aimed or pointed at something other than themselves. Brentano used the fact that only mental phenomena possess this attribute to demonstrate the categorical difference between mind and matter. The school of phenomenology carried on Brentano's pursuit of a nonreductionistic bridge over both the Cartesian gap between mind and matter and also the Kantian gap between speculative reason and practical reason.

Freud and Husserl were students of Brentano, whose influence can be seen in both psychoanalysis and phenomenology. Brentano's influence on Husserl is more evident in that phenomenology was founded on Brentano's construct of intentionality. Freud seems to have had extensive personal contact with Brentano (Gedo and Pollock, *Freud: The Fusion of Science and Humanism,* p. 13). A number of Freud's notions, such as cathexis, psychic energy, and the evolution of primary-process to secondary-process meanings, can be traced to Brentano's thought, especially his concept of intentional existence (Ellenberger, *The Discovery of the Unconscious,* pp. 541–542).

Brentano's influence on Freud is most obvious in Freud's pre-1895 model of mind, which he based on the premise that meaning structures can be both nonsolipsistic and also regulating causes of psychic reality. This model of mind was based on *verstehen* psychology rather than on an explanation based on physical causality.

Freud employed the construct of intentionality in two categorically distinct ways. In his pre-1895 phase of theory construction, he postulated that psychopathology is caused by a conscious act of intentionality motivated by a "dominant mass of ideas constituting the ego" (Breuer and Freud, "Case Histories: 3, Miss Lucy R," *Studies on Hysteria, S.E.,* vol. 2, p. 16). However, following his introduction of a psychosexual genetic theory of personality development grounded in his instinctually based theory of human nature (*Three Essays on the Theory of Sexuality, S.E.,* vol. 7, pp. 1–122), Freud restricted the construct of intentionality to the observable aims of the instinctual forces that drive consciousness. In this later use, Freud employs intentionality in the technical sense of a linguistic representation of a somatically generated intentional state. Accordingly, it has no primary reference to a purposive act.

75 A differentiated (regulatory) intrapsychic agent-self has the following characteristics: (1) it is empirical and mutual, (2) it is the basis of the capacity for
veridical caregiving and self-caretaking, (3) the immediacy of self-awareness
of the first-person case is characterized by a subjective experience that has an
incontrovertible veridicality, and (4) efficient causality is associated with intention (agent cause) and is not inferred from the nature of the completed
act. We agree with Hume that desire can be regulated effectively only by desire and not by reason, but we do not think it is appropriate to apply Hume's
critique of causality to regulatory agency reality.

Further, the loss-free, causal capacity of differentiated regulatory agency
reality is one solution to the riddle of free will versus determinism. Free will
and determinism refer to the locus of the regulation of desire. True free will
(which we define as the power to regulate veridically one's inner well-being)
occurs only as a result of a paradigmatic developmental process, whereas determinism ultimately refers to the hegemony of the to-be-gratified ideal over
the agent-self. Determinism operates when the regulating cause is external to
the agent-self and is the result either of immaturity or of psychopathology.

76 Teleology embraces the dimension of the purposive in human behavior. The
construct of causality has been controversial in Western thought since Hume.
Our view of causality is consonant with Kant's bifurcation of the notions of
meaning and causality to the extent that this bifurcation is applied to nonregulatory agency meaning structures. However, because the mutualized
intrapsychic personal meaning structure (regulatory-intrapsychic agency) is
both empirical and mutual, it has a causal ontology that is equivalent to the
natural sciences' notion of an ontological form of efficient causality.

There are two ways in which teleological causality applies to the regulation
of subjective personal existence. First, the nature of consciousness is such
that all purpose and intentionality ultimately derive from consciousness-
generated, to-be-actualized ideals, which function as teleological causes in relation to subjective personal existence. Second, as will be explained in later
chapters, in early development and permanently in untreated psychopathology, the locus of the to-be-actualized ideal and the locus of the means
(perceptual input) necessary to gratify it are, from an intrapsychic caregiving
perspective, outside of the veridical regulatory control of the individual's intrapsychic agent-self and regulatory-interpersonal agent-self. Consequently,
in early development (and permanently in untreated psychopathology) the
individual can only have an illusional experience of agency with regard to the
regulation of her/his inner well-being. Introspectively, however, the individual always believes that her/his intrapsychic and regulatory-interpersonal
agent-selves have hegemonic agent cause capacity.

At the completion of a paradigmatic development, because the child has
had the veridical, reflective experience of being the agent cause of the caregiver's intrapsychic caregiving, the child's to-be-actualized ideals (motives) for
hegemonic agent-cause capacity and the percepts necessary to gratify these
motives become structuralized within the child's intrapsychic agent-self.

When applied to the teleological process of intrapsychic and regulatory-
interpersonal motive gratification, the specifics of causality (the veridical locus both of the regulatory control over motives and of the gratification of

those motives) determine an individual's capacity for conscious, intentional, self-regulatory control of her/his subjective personal existence. In a psychological context, teleology is a specific approach to meaning, that is, to the subjective dimension of the gratification of consciousness-generated motives. In contrast, one of the few universally accepted tenets of psychoanalytic theory is that psychoanalytic explanations only narrowly focus on causal factors; they include the *how* and the *what* but never the *why*. Because it does not encompass intrapsychic and regulatory-interpersonal consciousness, psychoanalysis does not formally recognize the crucial role of intrapsychic teleological cause in human development.

Hume's perceptive remarks on associational psychology notwithstanding, Aristotle is one of the most penetrating observers of causal processes. Aristotle discussed human behavior from the subjective viewpoint of psychological causality. In chaps. 6 and 7 of *De Motu Animalium*, Aristotle presents the thesis that the phenomena of desire and cognition are efficient causes of intentional behavior. Further, as Nussbaum points out *(The Fragility of Goodness,* p. 286), Aristotle posits two types of reason, or consciousness: a category of reason associated with cognition and a category of reason that is the basis for an agency which is "like that which listens to a parent" (ibid.). Aristotle's construct of practical reason (which includes the notion of efficient causal agency) has a marked affinity to our view of a type of consciousness with causal ontological status. However, unlike Aristotle's practical reason, which represents a solipsistic, constitutive-interpersonal type of self-regulatory capacity that remains vulnerable to the loss of self-regulatory stability, our self-sufficient agency rests on an empirical intrapsychic mutuality, which provides a loss-free self-regulatory stability.

77 This capacity for a false hermeneutic process illustrates Hume's dictum that an *ought* cannot be derived from an *is* (*A Treatise of Human Nature,* p. 469).

78 Because human consciousness generates ideals (precepts) and to-be-actualized ideals (motives) that must be gratified by perceptual experiences (percepts) that (illusionally or veridically) are accepted as matching the precepts, the application of a teleological viewpoint that is unique to intrapsychic consciousness generates the most heuristic explanation for human behavior and experience. In contrast to interpersonal consciousness, one aspect of the nature of intrapsychic consciousness is that the regulative and constitutive are combined within the one ideal of self-regulatory autonomy with regard to intrapsychic motive gratification. Once paradigmatic development is complete, the gratified intrapsychic motive is both the act of knowing (veridical intrapsychic self-caretaking or intrapsychic caregiving) and also the essence of the known (the regulatory-intrapsychic agent-self). The veridical intrapsychic reflection of agent-self as agent-self that results from being the agent cause of the caregiver's intrapsychic caregiving is both the essence of the content of intrapsychic motive gratification and also the motivating ideal. This ideal combines the regulatory (being the agent cause of the caregiver's intrapsychic caregiving) and constitutive (the agent-self that has causal hegemony over the teleological cause, which is the ideal to-be-actualized) aspects of intrapsy-

chic consciousness. The content of the gratified intrapsychic motive is an agent-self-caused extracranial reflection of agent-self as agent-self that is the meaning conveyed by being the agent cause of the caregiver's intrapsychic caregiving.

79 Paradigmatic development releases the intrapsychic agent-self from the influence of an external regulating cause because the to-be-actualized ideal (intrapsychic motive) and the percepts gratifying that motive become structuralized within the intrapsychic agent-self (see chap. 3). After the completion of a paradigmatic developmental process, intrapsychic consciousness includes an element of teleological (external to the agent-self) causality in that consciousness continues to generate to-be-actualized ideals (motives) that must be gratified for consciousness to function and life to be maintained. Within this context, however, the intrapsychic agent-self has loss-free, regulatory control over the gratification of these intrapsychic motives, regardless of the vicissitudes of others' motives or of the workings of positive entropy and chance.

80 See chap. 3.

81 In a young child or in an individual with intrapsychic psychopathology, the primary causal center of purpose is *external* to the experienced sense of agent-self. This externality can be either extracranial or intracranial. It is *extracranial* in the sense that in early development intrapsychic motive gratification depends on the caregiver's intrapsychic caregiving. The externality of the center of purpose is *intracranial* in that, from an intrapsychic caregiving viewpoint, the to-be-actualized ideal, which has agent-cause significance, is intracranial but external to the agent-self. The resultant lack of veridical regulatory control due to this externality is the source of an ongoing loss for the intrapsychic agent-self. The goal of psychological development is to bridge the gaps: (1) between the intrapsychic agent-self and the source of the percepts (the caregiver) necessary to gratify the intrapsychic motive and (2) between the intrapsychic agent-self and the center of purposive causality that is intracranial but external to the agent-self within the to-be-actualized ideal.

82 Psychodynamic theories characterize the nature of the neonate's psychological state as universally paranoid or as-if. These opposite perspectives can be illustrated by the Kleinian premise that the infant takes a primary paranoid position (M. Klein, *The Psychoanalysis of Children*) and by the notions of primary narcissism (Freud, *The Ego and the Id, S.E.,* vol. 19, pp. 64–66) and the grandiose-self (Kohut, *The Analysis of the Self*). Other psychoanalytic misperceptions of the neonate derive from the presupposition that human nature is inherently conflicted and that the cause of psychic pain is instinctual and results either from object conflict or narcissistic conflict. In contrast, we posit that, except in psychopathology, the most important motive, the intrapsychic motive, is conflict free. In paradigmatic development, the regulatory center of causal agency becomes veridically internalized within the intrapsychic agent-self only by means of genuine intrapsychic intimacy, and not through loss and conflict. This is in stark contrast to the paranoid position, in which the child is thought to relate to the other in a conflicted manner that precludes the experience of true intimacy.

324

83 In this usage, psychoanalytic theory encompasses all psychodynamic psychologies, which ultimately derive from Freud's work. Heinz Hartmann, who devoted himself to developing psychoanalytic theory, concluded that psychoanalysis is: "an inductive science of the connections between complex mental structures. Its propositions are obtained empirically and have to be verified empirically" (*Essays on Ego Psychology*, p. 401). He went on to describe psychoanalysis as an explanatory rather than an understanding psychology. Hartmann argued that the object of psychoanalysis is to form theories, "regardless of whether the inductively established connections are also understandable" (ibid., p. 401). In other words, in asserting that psychoanalysis is scientific, Hartmann further concluded that it is not "capable of preserving in its concepts the lived immediacy of its primary material and that any psychology has to sacrifice to its scientific goal the illusion of that 'deeper penetration' into its subject which belongs to immediate experience" (ibid., p. 402). Accordingly, psychoanalysis views any psychology that defines psychic reality in terms of meanings derived from the lived immediacy of experience as a psychology of descriptive understanding rather than as a psychology of genuine causal explanation. As Hartmann says, "But what can this lived experience tell us about *actual* mental connections? What knowledge can it give us? How can experiencing itself contain within it the criterion for the real givenness of mental connections" (italic in original; ibid., p. 379). Ironically, for reasons quite different from Hartmann's we are in qualified agreement with Hartmann's critique of *verstehen*, or knowledge based on an immediacy of understanding, in so far as the referent for this type of understanding has been solipsistic constitutive-interpersonal introspection.

  Freud concluded that thinking and knowing do not exhibit the established characteristics of the biological and, therefore, when they are used to explain the experience of mind, thinking and knowing are symptoms of intellectualization. He posited that instinctual drive derivatives, or mental experiences that he thought directly represent nonmental biological processes, are the empirical reality basis for a self-consciously conscious, veridical mind experience with the reliability Freud thought belonged solely to the natural sciences.

84 In psychoanalytic theory, mind represents an epiphenomenal manifestation of biological, materialistic physical reality. The choice of this ontology made it inevitable that psychoanalytic authors would conclude that ontological and epistemological discussions of psychoanalytic issues that are not guided by positivist assumptions are symptoms of intellectualization. It is true that epistemological and ontological issues do not help in understanding the subjective experience of personal existence if these terms are used to refer to purely cognitive processes. Also, when consciousness is used to refer solely to what Freud termed an organ of perception, a definition which Hartmann further elaborated into the categories of primary autonomous apparatus and secondary autonomous apparatus (Hartmann, *Ego-Psychology and the Problem of Adaptation*, pp. 100–108), the constructs of epistemology and ontology indeed have no contribution to make to psychological discourse.

  Given the historical context in which Freud wrote (a world defined by, among others, Descartes, Newton, Hume, Kant, Comte, Helmholtz, and Nietzsche), it is understandable that he never conceived of the possibility of a direct apprehension of psychic reality. Accordingly, Freud adopted what he construed as the most foolproof way to know psychic reality, namely, a form of introspection based on the positivist paradigm of the physical sciences. Given this paradigm and the fact that his sole focus was the personal experience of mind per se, Freud was most concerned with avoiding the charge of solipsism (in the sense of the impossibility of consensual validation). Subsequently, the combined influence of the positivist value system of the Helmholtz school (transmitted to Freud through his mentor Brucke) and Freud's own research on hypnosis (hypnosis being the most dramatic form of persuasion) led Freud to conclude that consciousness, in the form of motive and intentionality, could not be trusted with regard to the need for objectivity (the need to avoid solipsism).

85 Freud did not believe that consciousness could be the basis for a self-reflection that could regulate an ontological category of psychic reality. He only recognized that type of consciousness that is an organ of perception or is characterized by the solipsism of the Cartesian subjective certainty.

86 See Freud, "Project for a Scientific Psychology," *S.E.*, vol. 1, pp. 281–387.

87 Therefore, in psychoanalytic treatment, explanation is the outcome of an experience-distant process, the transference neurosis, which provides the solipsistic data that are to be "objectively" observed and interpreted within the intersubjective field of patient and analyst.

88 Freud, *Totem and Taboo, S.E.*, vol. 13, pp. 148–150.

89 Freud, "Instincts and Their Vicissitudes," *S.E.*, vol. 14, p. 115; *Beyond the Pleasure Principle, S.E.*, vol. 18, p. 50.

90 Freud, *Beyond the Pleasure Principle, S.E.*, vol. 18, pp. 51–54.

91 Freud, *The Ego and the Id, S.E.*, vol. 19, pp. 54–58.

92 Unlike Schopenhauer, Freud does not assert that death is the only aim of life. Freud remarked, "We are not overlooking the fact that there is life as well as death" (*New Introductory Lectures on Psycho-Analysis, S.E.*, vol. 22, p. 107). However, in the context of his premise that the life and death instincts were fused, Freud ultimately concluded that the death instinct has hegemony over the life instincts and their vicissitudes. In "Analysis Terminable and Interminable," he wrote, "For the moment we must bow to the superiority of the forces against which we see our efforts come to nothing" (*S.E.*, vol. 23, p. 243). He based the hegemony of the death instinct on the needs of the life instinct as well as on the strength of the death instinct in that the death instinct became destructive to others in the interest of self-preservation: "The organism preserves its own life, so to say, by destroying an extraneous one" ("Why War," *S.E.*, vol. 22, p. 211).

93 Freud, "The Psychotherapy of Hysteria," *S.E.*, vol. 2, p. 305.

94 Sulloway, *Freud: Biologist of the Mind*, pp. 390–391.

95 Though Freud admittedly had to use a teleological viewpoint for many purposes, in keeping with Kant's *Critique of Pure Reason* he never ascribed an equivalent of the efficient causality of the natural sciences to his teleological

explanation of mental processes. For example, he asserted that psychoanalysis never ascribed efficient causality solely to psychological phenomena per se. According to Hartmann, this view was not contradicted by the fact that Freud's case histories are organized by the principle of teleological causality because these behavioral explanations refer to the vicissitudes of innately determined physical events, e.g., instinctual wishes (Hartmann, *Essays on Ego Psychology*, pp. 402–403).

96 Freud, *The Ego and the Id, S.E.*, vol. 19, p. 15.

97 Freud, "The Psychotherapy of Hysteria," *S.E.*, vol. 2, p. 305.

98 Ibid.

99 The experience-distant quality of psychoanalytic theory was inevitable, given that the experience-distant experience of the waking mind recalling the solipsistic dreaming mind was considered the closest approximation of a causal-ontological category of pure consciousness.

100 Freud's *Interpretation of Dreams* is based on two mutually exclusive *reals* of psychic reality: (1) meanings subsumed under the primary process (dreams and irrational thinking) and (2) a psychic apparatus in which instinctual drives are regulated by the pleasure principle within a context in which the aim and object of the drives are determined by experience. Freud never completely explained how the instinctual drives (nonpsychic reality) could be mediated by meaning structures (psychic reality) in the form of the instinctual drive derivatives of the primary process. He posited that primary-process meaning structures (unconscious irrational thoughts termed *thing-presentations*) became expressed in waking, conscious, rational thoughts (the *word-presentations* of the secondary-process meaning structures) when the thing presentations become hypercathected by association with the corresponding word presentations. He supposed that these hypercathexes "make it possible for the primary process to be succeeded by the secondary process which is dominant in the Preconscious" ("The Unconscious," *S.E.*, vol. 14, p. 202). Freud's assertion that the primary process is succeeded by the secondary process when the *thing* cathexis is transferred onto a *word* cathexis underscores his conviction that the only apprehendable form of the real of psychic reality is that which can be captured within what we would term constitutive-interpersonal consciousness.

101 Freud, *The Ego and the Id, S.E.*, vol. 19, pp. 1–59.

102 Freud, "On Narcissism," *S.E.*, vol. 14, pp. 75–76.

103 Freud, "Formulations on the Two Principles of Mental Functioning," *S.E.*, vol. 12, p. 219.

104 Even then, Spitz made the smile response a function of the instinctual drives.

105 For example, Sartre's will to act, which signifies radical freedom (Sartre, *Being and Nothingness*), Heidegger's pursuit of Dasein, Maslow, etc.

106 For example, in hunting societies the category of the real that can (illusionally) signify the capacity for veridical, regulatory control over one's subjective personal existence may be represented in terms of a successful hunt blessed

by a symbolic experience based on some form of animism, such as the rendering of the animal's image on the wall of a cave.

107 Intrapsychic Humanism is a new approach to the conflict between reason and historical contingency. A given culture's view of human nature has often been understood as the regulatory effect of historical contingency on reason. In our view, however, this conclusion describes psychopathological human nature.

　　We suggest that paradigmatic personal existence is solely contingent on the history of the intrapsychic caregiving relationship with the caregivers. Correspondingly, the impact on subjective experience ascribed to historical contingency and historical consciousness actually depicts the corrosive effects of the pain-filled need to use every day interpersonal experience for illusional intrapsychic motive gratification on the individual's capacity for self-regulatory stability.

　　We argue that, in reference to subjective experience, historical contingency and historical consciousness apply solely to biological, not cultural evolution. Specifically, psychopathological subjective experience refers to the infant's developmental capacity mistakenly to attach the significance of caregiving love to a caregiving act that has the objective meaning of loss (see chap. 6).

108 Aristotle, *Nicomachean Ethics*, bk. I, chap. 7, 1097.9, p. 317.

109 Gellner, *Plough, Sword and Book*, p. 105.

110 Freud's view can be characterized as an inverted Platonism in that he posits an extramental reality (the instinctual drives) as the ontological basis of the experience of mind. Paradoxically, psychoanalytic thinkers are skeptics who mistrust mind experience and cannot separate mind from references to psychic pain, which they see as the common ground of psychic reality. Freud focused cultural consciousness on the experience of mind, which he reified in order to attain the reductionistic goal of explaining mind in terms of nonmind. We reexamine the question of what is mind and, more specifically, of how the experience of mind can best be understood. We adopt a holistic, non-Manichean approach to mind without equating mind with language.

111 Those who thought it valuable to be introspective but also recognized that cognition could not exert veridical regulatory control over the subjective experience of the human condition were forced to adopt some type of Manichean resolution. Conversely, those who were convinced that the need for certainty could best be satisfied by a radical skepticism of the experience of mind were only too happy to equate mind with cognition. This allowed them to construct a straw person whose demolition readily facilitated the promulgation of one of two possible alternative views: radical skepticism or radical empiricism. We fundamentally agree with the outlook promulgated by, among others, the British Jesuit Martin D'Arcy, which states that, since mind as knower is also the only possible type of subjective known, it is fruitless to mistrust mind or to attempt to get outside of mind in order to understand the subjective experience of it. To the question What is the subjective experience of mind? we reply that there are two minds and, therefore, two types of

knowing and two types of ontological known and, consequently, two categorically distinct types of meaning: *intrapsychic* and *interpersonal*.

112 One of the best known examples is the tradition of French thinking that began with Descartes's skepticism and ended with Comte's positivism. For a good discussion, see Gilson, *The Unity of Philosophical Experience*, pp. 248–270.

NOTES TO CHAPTER TWO

1 "At birth" does not imply that in the last trimester of pregnancy the fetus lacks a richly sentient existence that contributes to postnatal self-regulatory stability.

2 These first two behaviors were first identified by Spitz. He termed them the "smiling response" and "eight-month anxiety" *(The First Year of Life)*.

3 The smile response refers to the infant's smile of pleasure in response to relationship experience. At times we also use the smile response to refer to the infant's entire spectrum of attachment behaviors.

4 Spitz, *Dialogues from Infancy*, p. 298. Because children's developmental time tables are so varied, we always give the dates of onset of specific developmental capacities in the form of a range of time. This range does not imply a rigid time-frame, but only indicates the general period that corresponds to the onset of the specific developmental capacity.

5 As we described in chap. 1, the term caregiver: (1) refers only to intrapsychic, not interpersonal, caregiving, although it includes the intrapsychic significance of interpersonal caregiving and, therefore, (2) refers only to the person or persons with intrapsychic significance for the child (with the capacity to serve as a stable source of caregiver percepts that gratify the child's intrapsychic motive). We use caregiver in the singular until the third stage of development, the regulatory-interpersonal self stage, because until then, from the standpoint of intrapsychic development, the child experiences each caregiver primarily as a source of gratifying intrapsychic percepts.

6 Spitz, *Dialogues from Infancy*, pp. 114–119.

7 It is reasonable to suppose that in early infancy visual experience is most important in terms of the motive for social relationship experience (see, e.g., Brothers, "A Biological Perspective on Empathy," pp. 13–14).

8 While the infant has functional constitutive-interpersonal motives (e.g., to eat, to play) and, therefore, purposive agency, constitutive-interpersonal motive gratification has only the intrapsychic meaning of regulating the caregiver's intrapsychic caregiving.

9 The construct of innate meaning structures is associated with the question of the different ways in which caregiving affects development, especially with regard to the distinctly different situations entailed by innate and noninnate developmental capacities. Gottleib and Aslin, e.g., have developed a model that depicts five different ways in which caregiving can affect the emergence of innate and noninnate meaning structures. These are maturation, mainte-

nance, facilitation, attunement, and induction. Beginning with maintenance and ending with induction, caregiving experience plays an increasingly influential role in the development of the phenotypes. Maintenance occurs when a specific capacity is fully developed prior to the onset of the caregiving behavior that must occur in order for the developmental capacity to remain functional.

Werker has applied the model of maintenance to the development of (constitutive-interpersonal) linguistic capacities. She says that, given that infants "are able to discriminate nearly every phonetic contrast on which they have been tested, including those they have never before heard . . . the ability to discriminate phones from the universal phonetic inventory may be present at birth" (Werker, "Becoming a Native Listener," p. 54). In accordance with Gottlieb's model of maintenance, Werker found that "young infants can discriminate phonetic contrasts before they have gained experience listening but that experience hearing the phones used in their own language is necessary to maintain the ability to discriminate at least some pairs of phones" (ibid., p. 57). While this structural transformation pertains to a reorganization of innate meaning structures within constitutive-interpersonal consciousness, the parallels between the effects of interpersonal caregiving on innate meaning structures and the structural transformation in intrapsychic meaning structures on which we focus are quite striking.

10 In early infancy, the criterion that determines whether the intrapsychic caregiving mutuality is veridical or illusional is whether or not the caregiver's behavior matches the veridical ideal (precept) generated by the child's intrapsychic consciousness.

11 Psychoanalysts (e.g., Lacan and Kohut) have spoken of the infant discovering her/his face and, thereby, a form of her/his self, in some form of mirroring experience. In the *Phaedrus*, Socrates says that in a love relationship each lover's experience of the other is that "the lover is his mirror in whom he is beholding himself, but he is not aware of this" (*The Dialogues of Plato*, p. 259).

12 Stern, *The First Relationship*, pp. 34–37.

13 For example, see Spitz, "Hospitalism," pp. 53–74, and Freedman, "Maturational and Developmental Issues in the First Year," pp. 135–139.

14 Spitz, *The First Year of Life*, pp. 86–107.

15 While there is a broad spectrum of interpersonal caregiving behaviors that are consonant with a paradigmatic intrapsychic developmental process, in general, interpersonal caregiving that causes the infant to feel significant amounts of conscious unhappiness is likely to cause her/him to develop intrapsychic psychopathology. The presence of intrapsychic psychopathology, of course, does not prevent an individual's interpersonal actions and self-experience from falling within average social norms.

16 Lorenz, "Companionship in Bird Life," in *Instinctive Behavior*.

17 Unless, of course, the interpersonal caregiving is so psychotoxic that the child dies of marasmus or develops a manifest or somaticized infantile psychosis.

18 See chap. 4 for a more extensive discussion.

19 Unlike the intrapsychic motive, which is the basis for a nurture-based, mutualized autonomy of regulatory intrapsychic agency only when the caregiver's
intrapsychic caregiving is veridical, the acquired autonomy of innately based,
constitutive-interpersonal, cognitive motives requires only minimally sufficient
interpersonal caregiving. Because of the solipsistic and nonempirical nature
of constitutive-interpersonal introspection, the relative autonomy of constitutive-interpersonal, cognitive motives is never based on an empirical mutuality.

20 See chap. 4 for more about the regulatory-interpersonal self stage.

21 When we suggest that certain interpersonal caregiving behaviors can cause
intrapsychic psychopathology, we limit the applicability of these examples to
our own time and culture and eschew the ethnocentric conclusion that only
one set of interpersonal caregiving behaviors can produce an individual with
a paradigmatic regulatory-intrapsychic agent-self. Obviously, culturally diverse styles of interpersonal caregiving can produce children with veridical,
empirically based, inner well-being. On the other hand, we believe that cultures that prescribe styles of interpersonal caregiving that cause children to
experience significant periods of conscious unhappiness will produce fewer
children whose intrapsychic meaning structures are veridical. This does not
mean, however, that these cultures will have fewer adults who are interpersonally successful, consciously happy, and accepted by the culture as normal.

22 Accessibility of constitutive-interpersonal knowledge is limited to the first-
person case and reporting is the sole means of public accessibility.

23 This does not imply that constitutive-interpersonal introspection can develop
outside of interpersonal relationships, which are, in fact, a necessary and po-
tentiating force in the development of language and other cognitive functions. The terms *intersubjectivity, intersubjective relationship,* and *intersubjective
field,* which refer to the notion of interpersonal relationship experience, reflect the indirect, mediated quality of the sense of experiential contact with
another's subjective experience that characterizes the interpersonal form of
relationship experience. For good discussions of intersubjectivity, see Wertsch,
Vygotsky and the Social Formation of Mind, pp. 158–183; Owens, *Phenomenology
and Intersubjectivity,* pp. 1–13; Schutz, *The Phenomenology of the Social World,*
pp. 97–138; and Kaye, *The Mental and Social Life of Babies,* pp. 117–154.

24 Even in the first year of life the infant's self-experience does not conform to
the egg-hatching metaphor of the monadic model of primary narcissism, to
Bruner's cognitive model, or to Stern's model of interpersonal agency.

25 Mahler and McDevitt, "Separation-Individuation and Identity," pp. 399–400.

26 For example, Spitz interprets the smile response by means of explanatory
constructs that are compatible with notions of autoeroticism, primary narcissism, the pure pleasure ego, and the process of hatching.

27 The reality testing implied by Freud's hypothesis of the infant hallucinating
the breast is merely a contingent event of the infant's instinctually driven need
for oral pleasure. See "Formulations on the Two Principles of Mental Functioning," *S.E.,* vol. 12, pp. 219–222.

28 Freud's drive-structural model (*The Ego and the Id, S.E.*, vol. 19, pp. 1–66), which occurred many years after his hallucinated breast model, does not offer a more satisfactory explanation of how an autoerotic psychic reality based on the instinctual drives can become structurally transformed to a psychic reality that is contingent on external reality. The drive-structural model fails because it begs the question. As early as 1914, Freud posited the unexamined premise that "we are bound to suppose that a unity comparable to the ego cannot exist in the individual from the start; the ego has to be developed" ("On Narcissism," *S.E.*, vol. 14, p. 77). In 1917, Freud asserted that this unity comes about by identification, i.e., by means of a process that reinstates the lost object within the ego ("Mourning and Melancholia," *S.E.*, vol. 14, pp. 237–258). This undemonstrated assertion was elaborated in *The Ego and the Id* (pp. 29, 63–66).

29 In "Formulations on the Two Principles of Mental Functioning," Freud asserted: "Actually the substitution of the reality principle for the pleasure principle implies no deposing of the pleasure principle, but only a safeguarding of it" (*S.E.*, vol. 12, p. 223). For a good discussion of Freud's contradictory statements about the pleasure principle and the reality principle, see Yankelovich and Barrett, *Ego and Instinct*, pp. 73–87.

30 By definition, the Freudian breast model excludes the paradigmatic developmental phenomenon of an illusional, in contrast to a hallucinatory, level of reflective agent-self experience. The restrictive reality of transference experience in psychoanalytic theory reflects the defect in the hallucinated breast model. Freud believed transference phenomena were the inevitable result of an instinctually based, structurally unconscious id. Freud saw transference as obstructing the individual's capacity for veridical regulatory control of her/his subjective experience of personal existence. Freud's metaphor for normal psychic functioning, namely, the rider astride, but incompletely in control of a horse (*The Ego and the Id, S.E.*, vol. 19, p. 25), illustrates the fact that the Freudian model does not posit any stable regulatory agency form of psychic reality.

31 Examples of investigators with this viewpoint whose work has had a widespread influence are Bowlby, Brazelton, Bruner, Kagan, Kaye, Meltzoff, Stern, Trevarthen, and White. In addition, M. Klein posited that the neonate begins life actively engaged in a paranoid transference relationship with the caregiver. In contrast to Intrapsychic Humanism, Klein addressed a reality that represents epiphenomena of constitutive-interpersonal consciousness and she posited that the infant-caregiver relationship is overwhelmingly determined by innate forces that nurture may influence but not structurally change. For Klein, actual caregiver behaviors represent little more than a lattice or framework within which the child's innately preformed relationship meaning structures unfold.

32 Stern's writings exemplify this emphasis on early relationship experience. Stern postulates that the neonate actively engages in the caregiving relationship and that s/he first finds her/himself in the significant other. In contrast to our view, Stern locates the mother-child relationship exclusively on the level of motive experience we term constitutive-interpersonal motive experience.

Accordingly, Stern's theory contains the same anthropomorphic fallacies as does mainstream psychoanalytic theory. Given the inherent solipsism of constitutive-interpersonal consciousness, Stern has to conclude that the infant's subjective experience is inaccessible. As a result, he describes the infant's experience of agency almost exclusively in terms of the experience-distant construct of "motor plans" and focuses on "affect attunement" between mother and child (Stern, *The Interpersonal World of the Infant*, pp. 77, 140). While Stern acknowledges that there are certain epigenetic moments in development, such as the no response, in contrast to our view, he sees these as neurological responses rather than motivational signs and accords them no ontological significance with regard to psychic reality. He attributes psychopathology to an accretion of small incidents and assumes psychic imbalances (which we would classify as psychopathology) are normal.

33 See Mahler et al., *The Psychological Birth of the Human Infant*, and Kohut, *The Analysis of the Self*, for examples of viewing child development from the perspective of cognition, language, and interpersonal social relationships.

34 *Webster's Ninth New Collegiate Dictionary*, p. 618.

35 Bettleheim, *The Empty Fortress*, exemplifies the view of autism as a retreat to internal emptiness.

36 Psychodynamic treatment of these malignant syndromes aims to modify the internalized psychotic caregiving relationship based on interpretations of the child's linguistic and motor behavior. In contrast, Intrapsychic Treatment offers the afflicted child a de novo veridical intrapsychic caregiving relationship as a radical alternative to the internalized, malignant relationship in which s/he finds her/his continuous source of nourishment (see chap. 7).

37 Anxiety is used generically to refer to an expression of distress.

38 Though to our knowledge Spitz's data relating to the phenomenon he termed eight-month anxiety has never been discredited, stranger anxiety is not usually viewed as a universal milestone in infancy. Greenspan, e.g., asserted in an interview that "many infants who are quite healthy emotionally don't have stranger anxiety at all" (Daniel Goleman, "New Research Overturns a Milestone of Infancy," *New York Times*, June 6, 1989, p. C1). In contrast, psychoanalytic theory endorses Spitz's emphasis on the importance of eight-month anxiety.

While we agree that eight-month anxiety universally occurs in paradigmatic development, our explanation for this phenomenon differs from Spitz's. Spitz concluded that eight-month anxiety is a response to the child's "perception that the stranger's face is not identical with the memory traces of the mother's face" (*First Year of Life*, p. 155), which causes the child to experience the "fear of having lost his mother (the libidinal object)" (p. 160). We argue that the loss expressed as stranger anxiety is the loss of intrapsychic motive gratification which results from the effects of the intrusion of the child's constitutive-interpersonal motives into the intrapsychic motive gratification process. It is not due to a process of object conservation and object permanence which depends on evocative memory.

One reason that stranger anxiety is not recognized more frequently as a

333

universal developmental milestone is that it is often confused with separation anxiety. Katan has pointed out that "In the literature, as well as in psychoanalytic discussions, this phenomenon of distress at the sight of a stranger's face is often referred to as 'separation anxiety'" ("The Infant's First Reaction to Strangers," p. 502). Another problem with discussions of stranger anxiety by clinicians and developmental psychologists is that the child's fear of strangers has been used as a test of whether the child can be consoled—which then becomes a test of the child's mental health. Ainsworth, e.g., has developed a test termed "The Strange Situation," which exposes the baby to experiences that test the "use of mother as a secure base for exploration, response to separation, and response to a stranger—all in an unfamiliar environment" (Ainsworth, et al., *Patterns of Attachment,* p. 321).

We distinguish stranger anxiety from separation anxiety and also postulate that stranger anxiety is a milestone that occurs in both paradigmatic development and in all but the most severe forms of psychopathological development. Therefore, the occurrence of stranger anxiety is not a sign of mental health.

Another reason for the problematic status of stranger anxiety in the child development literature is that the infant's aversive behavior to strangers may be very transient and, therefore, can be overlooked easily. While the intruding percept, the strange face, remains a constant in stranger anxiety, the ease and rapidity with which the infant can be soothed is contingent on numerous factors, including the context in which the stranger's face appears. For example, the child may respond very differently at home or in a crowded airport.

Interestingly, many nonhuman animals exhibit behaviors similar to human stranger anxiety. For example, soon after certain species of nestlings open their eyes they "learn to distinguish their parents from contrasting forms, gaping toward the former but crouching down into the nest if a strange object approaches" (Skutch, *Parent Birds and Their Young,* p. 317).

39 Therefore, our construct of intrapsychic loss differs from the loss of instinctual drive gratification that psychoanalytic theory posits as the sine qua non of all forms of individual development.

40 While primary intrapsychic loss is complete, it is not absolute. While the loss of the intrapsychic motive gratification caused by the phase-specific caregiver percept is inclusive, the initial registration of this loss immediately precipitates an alternate, regressed form of gratification. In this way, the infant's experience of intrapsychic motive gratification is unbroken.

41 See chap. 3.

42 In psychopathology the most important external complexity is the caregiver's intrapsychic psychopathology and, frequently, manifest interpersonal psychopathology.

43 *Perception,* of course, refers to a constructivist activity that is regulated by constitutive-interpersonal agent-self motives. We do not intend to imply the possibility of the unalloyed registration of empirical constitutive-interpersonal experience.

44 While there is general agreement that separation anxiety occurs in infancy, it has not been conceptualized as a developmental milestone. Freud discussed the loss the infant experiences during separation from the mother as a danger situation that stimulates a "signal of anxiety" (*Inhibitions, Symptoms and Anxiety*, p. 138). Freud, accordingly, emphasized that it is crucial for the infant to develop the ability to defend against the mother's absence, which is made possible when the ego acquires the capacity for instinctual renunciation (*Beyond the Pleasure Principle*, p. 15). Spitz does not include separation anxiety in his organizers of psychic development. Further, prominent developmental psychologists, e.g., Stern and Kaye, do not discuss separation anxiety as a developmental milestone. Bowlby is one author who emphasizes the developmental significance of separation and loss. He posits that there is an innately determined infant-caregiver bonding process and asserts both that the quality of this attachment is an important determinant of an individual's mental health and also that the quality of attachment is most importantly determined by the caregiver's responsiveness to the infant's distress at separation. Though Bowlby characterizes the infant's distress when the caregiver becomes inaccessible as anxious, he does not assert that separation anxiety is a phase-specific developmental milestone ("Developmental Psychiatry Comes of Age," pp. 1–5).

   Discussions of separation anxiety in the first year of life generally question whether separation anxiety can be explained solely on the basis of recall memory or whether separation anxiety necessarily entails the infant's capacity to predict future events and devise responses to these predictions (for a good summary of this literature, see Stern, *The Interpersonal World of the Infant*, p. 117). In our view, separation anxiety is not memory dependent in the usual sense. Separation anxiety is due to the loss of intrapsychic motive gratification that results from the failure of the current percepts to satisfy the meaning attachment criteria of the nonveridical intrapsychic precept.

45 Bruner, et al., *Studies in Cognitive Growth*, p. 1.

46 Eidetic memory does not refer to eidetic imagery, which is the capacity "to hold in short-term memory visual images that are almost photographic in clarity" (Hilgard, Atkinson, and Atkinson, *Introduction to Psychology*, p. 224).

47 In contrast, the term structuralization denotes the process that produces veridical, nurture-based psychic structure. It occurs only in paradigmatic development and will be discussed in chaps. 3 and 4.

48 Authors on child development disagree about the onset of evocative memory, which is a crucial component of the process we term eidetic internalization. We place the onset of eidetic internalization between 12 and 14 months. Many authors who focus on the evocative memory of inanimate objects place the onset of this capacity later than 14 months. However, the caregiver, who provides the child with her/his deepest and most important type of gratification, will be the very first percept to be eidetically internalized. Further, since the child at this stage has little or no language, the experience-distant method of investigation used in observing children is ill suited to produce information about the child's subjective ability to evoke memories stored in long-term memory in

order to provide her/himself with soothing. Therefore, the methodology of child development investigators actually prevents them from assessing the onset of evocative memory.

When the method of knowing is intrapsychic caregiving, it appears that eidetic internalization is the consequence of and solution to separation anxiety. The child does become relatively impervious to separation anxiety at about 12 to 14 months. This change could occur either by regression or by the onset of an endogenous capacity to generate (nonveridical) caregiver percepts. Since the child at this age is becoming less dissociated, not more dissociated (is not regressing), eidetic internalization is the most reasonable explanation for the child's new-found ability to experience relatively short separations from the caregiver without a loss of inner well-being. We should also add that like the onset of all capacities, eidetic internalization becomes fully functional only gradually.

49 We wish to emphasize that the construct of the transitional intrapsychic caregiver only superficially resembles the psychoanalytic constructs of "internalized libidinal object" (Mahler, The Psychological Birth of the Human Infant, p. 112); "good introject" (Schafer, *Aspects of Internalization*, p. 116; or "self-object" (Kohut, *The Analysis of the Self*, p. 3). The transitional intrapsychic caregiver is dissimilar because: (1) although it is part of paradigmatic development, it is time-limited; (2) it is the basis of the intrapsychic transference, which is an agent-self experience that is not recognized by other psychologies; and (3) the transitional intrapsychic caregiver is not generated by instinctual drive derivatives but by ideals and motives generated within consciousness per se.

The psychoanalytic notion of the internalization of the libidinal internal object refers to a static structure of a memory of the caregiver per se. Because the libidinal object is, by definition, need gratifying (is created by the needs and aims of the instinctual drives), the object's meaning inheres in its image. There is no referent to the caregiver's motives, because the psychoanalytic object is contingent not necessary. Similarly, psychoanalytic theory distinguishes between symbolic thoughts of the caregiver as object and the image of the caregiver that is experienced as need gratifying. The latter does not refer to the regulation of the caregiver's motives by the child's care-getting motives. In other words, the psychoanalytic libidinal object is signified by the attribute of physical presence rather than by the attribute of being a representation of intrapsychic caregiving intentionality.

NOTES TO CHAPTER THREE

1 Freud used the term transference on two levels: metapsychological theory and clinical theory. In metapsychological theory, transference refers to the unconscious transfer of repressed instinctual content across the repression barrier. In clinical theory, transference refers to the phenomenon of an unconscious, compulsive repetition of a conflicted experience of infantile sexuality.

2 Mahler and McDevitt, "The Separation-Individuation Process and Identity Formation," in *The Course of Life*, pp. 403–404, and Parens, "Psychic Development during the Second and Third Years of Life," in *The Course of Life*, pp. 467–72.

3 The nonveridical, caregiving caregiver percept becomes functional at a time when the infant-caregiver relationship is increasingly founded on verbal communication. Accordingly, in addition to the visual signifiers of the caregiver's caregiving (e.g., the caregiver's smile), which characterized the caregiver percept in the veridical gratification phase of the pre-eidetic stage, the caregiving caregiver percept in the undifferentiated regulatory-intrapsychic self stage uses linguistic signifiers to convey information about the caregiver's intrapsychic caregiving motives.

4 Freud, *Inhibitions, Symptoms and Anxiety*, S. E., vol. 20, p. 170.

5 The intrapsychic no is dissimilar from and occurs prior to what Spitz has termed the "semantic 'No' gesture" (*No and Yes*, p. 144). The intrapsychic no is the child's insistence on veridical intrapsychic caregiving, whereas, in our terms, the referent for Spitz's no response is the child's negation of the caregiver's attempt to interfere with a *constitutive-interpersonal* motive being pursued by the child. We understand Spitz's no response as a transference constitutive-interpersonal response, which is an innately determined, maturational event that marks the onset of the capacity for the introspective recognition of interpersonal motives (interpersonal agency). This process is discussed in chap. 4.

6 Writers, such as Ricoeur and Lacan, who view the ontological basis of psychic reality from the viewpoint that Hegel described as a "dialectic of desire" (*Phenomenology of Spirit*, pp. 109–110) assert that human nature is such that this dialectic of desire can never produce stable gratification, and they accept the conclusion that loss is an intrinsic component of psychic reality. In other words, the dialectic of desire these authors formulate excludes the capacity for pain-free, rage-free, and, therefore, loss-free agent-self experience (excludes the capacity for an intrapsychic mourning process). Because the referent for the dialectic of desire these authors posit is constitutive-interpersonal motives, all ontological categories of desire (e.g., oedipal desire as posited by Ricoeur and desire for the other as posited by Lacan) are necessarily associated with loss (as discussed in Richardson, "Psychoanalysis and the Being-Question," p. 154).

7 For example, three of the most gifted introspectors in the history of Western civilization—Saint Augustine, Descartes, and Nietzsche—clearly did not have the good fortune to receive paradigmatic caregiving.

8 As will be explained in chap. 6, in the context of the missing reflection of agent-self as agent-self that occurs in psychopathology, introspection invariantly has the meaning of loss, which goes unrecognized because the nature of language is to signify a listener (see Bakhtin, *The Dialogical Imagination;* also Vygotsky, *Thought and Language*, and Wittgenstein, *Philosophical Investigations*). This experience of a listener hearing one's introspection acquires the illu-

sional significance of the reflection of intrapsychic agent-self as agent-self. The gratification implicit in interpersonally shared introspection is not an exception to this assertion, but can be understood as the subject unconsciously creating the illusion of an intrapsychic caregiver in the external world (e.g., the intended listener). The social context acquires the illusional meaning of an intrapsychic context. This form of introspection is actually an externalized form of an imagined dialogue.

9 There are several categorical differences between (1) our constructs of the intrapsychic caregiver, eidetic internalization, and autonomous, self-regulatory stability and (2) the psychoanalytic constructs of libidinal object and object constancy. Some of these differences pertain to the definition of object, the nature of the caregiving relationship, the developmental period in which internalization occurs, the function and functional duration of the internalized object, and, finally, the basis of the child's capacity for self-regulatory stability.

The libidinal object posited by psychoanalytic theory is a need-gratifying experience for the instinctual drives. The object being internalized changes from inanimate to animate and becomes a source of "sustenance, comfort and love" (Mahler and Furer, *On Human Symbiosis and the Vicissitudes of Individuation*, p. 222). As described in psychoanalytic theory, in time the internalized libidinal object becomes a stable, life-long source of reassuring love and acquires the attribute of object constancy. Mahler says object constancy has occurred when "the maternal image has become intrapsychically available to the child in the same way as the actual mother had been libidinally available for sustenance, comfort and love" (ibid., p. 3. See also, Joffe and Sandler, "Notes on Pain, Depression, and Individuation," pp. 394–424).

However, psychoanalytic theory has never provided a robust theory to explain the transformation of the original need-gratifying object to an internalized object with the characteristic of object constancy. As Hartmann, who introduced the notion of object constancy, said: "there is a long way from the object that exists only as long as it is need satisfying to that form of satisfactory object relations that includes object constancy" (Hartmann, *Essays on Ego Psychology*, p. 163). Part of the difficulty with the psychoanalytic theory of object constancy is the ambivalence of psychoanalysis about the importance of the caregiver in child development. Hartmann spoke of the "danger of overemphasizing and oversimplifying" the importance of "satisfactory object relations." He argued that maternal rejection should not be made "responsible for nearly all varieties of later pathological developments and particularly of ego disturbances" and concluded that "poor" early object relations may be compensated for by later ego development and "so-called 'good' object relations may become a developmental handicap" (ibid., p. 163). For a more recent example of minimizing the harmful effects of caregiver rejection on psychological development, see Anthony and Cohler, *The Invulnerable Child.*

Psychoanalytic theory views the internalization process as occurring through cognitive maturation of the capacity for symbolic thought. The meaning of internalized libidinal object occurs when the child ascribes to the cognitive memory of the caregiver the personal meaning that the caregiver's representation signifies the child's self-regulatory stability. In this way, the notion of object constancy attributes the source of inner well-being to a causal agency (object representation) that is external to the individual's constitutive-interpersonal agent-self. In other words, psychoanalytic theory posits that the human capacity for (intrinsically conflicted) inner well-being resides in the cognitive memory of the caregiver to which the meaning of inner well-being has been assigned.

In contrast, our understanding of the capacity for autonomous, loss-free self-regulatory stability is that it derives from the stable, empirical reflection of agent-self as agent-self with regard to being the regulating cause of the caregiver's intrapsychic caregiving.

10 See, e.g., Bowlby, *Attachment and Loss,* vol. 1; Erikson, *Childhood and Society;* Ainsworth, "Infant-Mother Attachment;" and Provence, *Infants in Institutions.*

NOTES TO CHAPTER FOUR

1 Once the intrapsychic motive is differentiated as a result of the intrapsychic no, the regulatory-intrapsychic agent-self motive can be gratified only by empirical, mutual percepts of the caregiver's intrapsychic caregiving and it no longer can be gratified by gratified constitutive-interpersonal motives.

2 In nonhuman species, there seems to be a permanently undifferentiated (merged) relationship between intrapsychic and interpersonal agent-self meaning. Intrapsychic agent-self needs also have ultimate regulatory control, as can be illustrated by animals who experience an important loss, become "depressed," and starve to death in the presence of abundant nourishment. As with humans, the intrapsychic motives that keep the animal organized and functional (the need for intrapsychic perceptual identity, for the reflection of effective intrapsychic agency) have regulatory supremacy and, in psychopathological form, can result in the animal's death.

3 Stern cites a wealth of experimental data to support this contention (see *The Interpersonal World of the Infant,* esp. pp. 37–68). Because in his view the neonatal forms of motive and intentionality are not invariantly associated, Stern sees the first two months of life as a period of "emergent relatedness" (p. 67) of self and other. He does not assign an agency capacity to the infant until eight weeks of age, and this agency is interpersonal in nature. Also, he bases his notion of agency on a viewpoint designed to apprehend external, nonagency reality and, therefore, concludes that the infant's relationship motives are not directly knowable. While he calls his model of development subjective, the referent for this subjectivity is the experience-distant, solipsistic relatedness characteristic of the intersubjective field of interpersonal meaning.

4 Winnicott's notion of agency is suggested by his view that the transitional object represented the initial stage in the developmental line of self-object differentiation. He said that the child creatively fashions this object, which represents an intermediate structure of self and other (Winnicott, "Transitional Objects and Transitional Phenomena," in *Collected Papers,* pp. 229–247). In contrast, we assert that the favorite blanket or teddy bear does not have the undifferentiated meaning of infant-caregiver, but rather has the illusional significance of the child's capacity to be the regulating cause of the caregiver's intrapsychic caregiving.

5 As we will describe, on the nontransference side of the developmental split, regulatory-interpersonal motive gratification is produced by the stable, empirically based well-being of the regulatory-intrapsychic agent-self and, on the transference side of the developmental split, either by gratified constitutive-interpersonal motives or by gratified nonveridical intrapsychic motives.

6 Paradigmatically, the caregiver's frustration of the child's constitutive-interpersonal motives will not entail the expression of disapproval toward the child. In contrast, in keeping with his postulation of the acquired nature of the no behavior, Spitz sees the phenomenon he terms the child's semantic "no" gesture as an identification with the parents' negative gestures, such as head shaking and finger wagging (*No and Yes*, p. 43). He says the no is an example of identification with the aggressor (ibid., p. 46).

7 The capacity for veridical intrapsychic personal meaning first appears briefly and unreflectively in the veridical gratification phase of the pre-eidetic stage, becomes nonfunctional in the illusional gratification phase of the pre-eidetic stage, and is subsequently reactivated and then structuralized (made reflective) in the differentiated phase of the regulatory-intrapsychic self stage. The veridical, regulatory-intrapsychic agent-self coexists with a nonveridical intrapsychic agent-self until the end of the regulatory-interpersonal self stage. The capacity for *veridical regulatory-interpersonal personal meaning* first appears with the onset of the veridical regulatory-interpersonal agent-self in the interpersonal no phase of the regulatory-interpersonal self stage. Veridical regulatory-interpersonal meaning coexists with transference regulatory-interpersonal personal meaning until the posttransference stage of development.

Constitutive-interpersonal meaning structures can have only illusional personal meaning because, by their nature, they have no capacity to be regulating causes of a loss-free psychic reality. Thus, while a given constitutive-interpersonal meaning structure may have the interpersonal meaning of self (in contrast to the category of nonself), it will not have veridical personal meaning. An example is the introspection, "My thought about this toy is that it looks cute there." Here, "thought" signifies a self meaning structure and "toy" signifies a nonself meaning structure. However, neither "thought" nor "toy" signifies veridical regulatory-intrapsychic agency or regulatory-interpersonal agency with regard to the subjective experience of personal existence. While nonself and self meaning structures acquire indirect personal meaning only through a *transference* process, this process is not a function of the content of the gratifying percept, but rather of the relationship between the constitutive-interpersonal meaning per se and the transference form of the intrapsychic or regulatory-interpersonal perceptual identity process, which attaches personal meaning significance to constitutive-interpersonal meaning. In other words, whether or not a constitutive-interpersonal meaning of self or nonself has the added, illusional significance of personal meaning depends upon whether or not the significance of regulatory agency reality becomes attached to the constitutive-interpersonal gratification (meaning), which is, thereby, used for illusional intrapsychic or regulatory-interpersonal motive gratification. For example, in a developmental transference process, the pleasure of the thought, "This is my strong right arm," signifies self meaning and also may have the (illusional) personal meaning significance of the inner well-being associated with the reflection of effective agent-self, self-regulatory control over subjective personal existence. In contrast, in *posttransference* existence whether or not interpersonal self meaning is also personal meaning depends upon whether or not it matches the veridical precept (ideal) of regulatory-interpersonal agency. In posttransference existence, constitutive-interpersonal meaning (e.g., the thought, "I am happy because this job was well done") would never have personal meaning significance (e.g., the meaning, "I am a good person"). At this point, constitutive-interpersonal motive gratification will signify only self or nonself meanings and will never be used to provide the meaning of regulatory-intrapsychic or regulatory-interpersonal agency. In other words, the meaning of regulatory agency becomes uncoupled from the gratification of specific constitutive-interpersonal aims.

8   As will be explained in chap. 6, the regulatory hegemony exerted by pathological transference motives stimulates a pain-induced motivation for identifications that function as self meaning structures which can regulate central personal values. An example is when the child who has a racially prejudiced nonveridical caregiver identifies with this prejudice as a way of life that has meaning for the child's own self.

9   The problem of personal identity has been insoluble because it has only focused on constitutive-interpersonal introspection. With regard to the agency reality involved in the problem of personal identity, we define two categories of personal identity: intrapsychic and interpersonal. Paradigmatically, an individual's awareness of intrapsychic personal identity is a function of the presence or absence of the capacity for veridical, regulatory-intrapsychic agency, and an individual's awareness of interpersonal personal identity is a function of the presence or absence of the individual's capacity for veridical regulatory-interpersonal agency. Regulatory-interpersonal personal identity is under the hegemony of intrapsychic personal identity.

10 Most authors who have addressed the problem of how the child acquires the capacity to discriminate self from nonself have concluded that this occurs on the basis of loss (pain). Piaget, e.g., posits that states of disequilibrium (loss) are necessary for cognitive development (Wolff, *The Developmental Psychologies of Jean Piaget and Psychoanalysis*, p. 25). Other examples are Winnicott's "gradual failing of adaptation" (*The Maturational Processes and the Facilitating Environment*, pp. 87–89), Aboulafia's "no" (*The Mediating Self*, p. 74), and Macmurray's "negative phase" (Macmurray, *Persons in Relation*, p. 94).

Piaget posited that the child's capacity to distinguish between self and nonself occurs strictly as a function of cognitive development (Gruber and Vonèche, eds., *The Essential Piaget*, pp. 272–277). Also, though Freud's notions of the nature and development of the capacity to discriminate self from nonself changed over time, he consistently grounded the evolution of the capacity to discriminate self and nonself in the individual's reaction to the loss of instinctual gratification. This reaction entailed behavior we would term self-rage (see, e.g., Freud, *The Ego and the Id, S. E.*, vol. 19, pp. 25–26). Within the explicit context of the psychoanalytic instinctual drive model, Mahler posits a pleasure-pain equation based upon a trial and error separation-individuation process, and Kohut talks about the impact of unavoidable shortfalls of care-giving, which disturb the state of narcissistic equilibrium between grandiose and exhibitionistic selves.

11 That is, have causal-ontological status.

12 The "I"ness of constitutive-interpersonal introspection is the "I" of Descartes's cogito, Kant's empirical self, Nietzsche's will to power, the ego in Freud's earliest model of mind, the self subjected to Heidegger's thrownness, Sartre's radical freedom, the propositional self of linguistic analysis, Meissner's construct of self-representation, and Schafer's notion of the self-as-agent that can know its self only as self-as-object. (Our term regulatory-interpersonal agent-self does not correspond to Schafer's construct of self-as-agent.) Constitutive-interpersonal introspection is also the "I" component of what has been termed intersubjective space, in which Dilthey's empathic reliving, Buber's I and Thou, and Kohut's empathic perception function.

13 In contrast to the two commonly understood forms of personal identity, physical continuity (e.g., fingerprints) and a subjectively experienced "I"ness, we posit a third, ontological identity of psychic reality. This is stable and, though memory has a facilitating role in this identity, it is founded on an inner sense of effective agency. This ontological type of personal identity only occurs in paradigmatic development. It is a function of that agent intentionality that is empirically created by the pleasure of veridical intrapsychic mutuality.

14 Innately based cognitive, perceptual, and motor capacities roughly correspond to what Hartmann defined as the primary autonomous apparatus of the ego (*Ego Psychology and the Problem of Adaptation*, pp. 100–108). Psychoanalytic theory places these functions under the potential hegemony of the instinctual drives. In contrast, we view these capacities as representing inherent strengths, which, in paradigmatic development, are regulated by the regulatory-interpersonal agent-self.

15 For current thinking on the capacity of short-term memory to store sequential operations, see G. Miller, "The Magical Number Seven, Plus or Minus Two: Some Limits on Our Capacity for Processing Information," p. 92.

16 Though the notion denoted by intersubjectivity has been taken for granted in most societies, there has never been agreement about how or whether intersubjectivity is possible. Intersubjectivity refers to the sharing of subjective states of meaning that originate in cranially distinct centers of solipsistic consciousness. The notion ultimately refers to the problem of other minds, that is, to the question of how one can know of the existence and contents of minds other than one's own. Following the excesses of nineteenth century romantic idealism and positivism, the notion of intersubjectivity was advanced as one possible answer to the problem of other minds. The term intersubjective is associated with Husserl and phenomenology, but the notion (not the term) was also suggested by Dilthey and, in the twentieth century, by Mead, Schutz, and other social scientists, by Wittgenstein and other contemporary analytic philosophers, and by Bakhtin and other linguists.

In psychiatry, approaches consonant with the notion of intersubjectivity were espoused by Sullivan and by the continental school of phenomenological psychiatry most prominently associated with Jaspers. While the premises that underlie psychoanalytic theory prevent it from seriously entertaining the notion of intersubjectivity, some authors, including Kohut, Stolorow, Atwood, and Basch, have tried to assert the possibility of intersubjective relatedness.

The issue of intersubjectivity has been imported to developmental psychology by authors such as Trevarthen, Kaye, Stern, and Fogel. There has been no general agreement about when and in what manner intersubjectivity occurs (i.e., whether it is fundamentally innate, constructed, or learned). Trevarthen argues for an innate basis for intersubjectivity and for its occurrence in primary form early in the first year of life.

In our view, because intersubjective relatedness occurs in the context of the incorrigible solipsism of constitutive-interpersonal consciousness, it is necessarily a mediated process and, therefore, inherently indirect and only approximately veridical. Empirical, nonmediated relatedness occurs only in paradigmatic development and intrapsychic treatment as a consequence of intrapsychic mutuality. In paradigmatic development and intrapsychic treatment, interpersonal intimacy remains mediated, proximate, and indirect, but it is veridical in the sense that motives regarding the subject are free of rage.

17 See Appendix.

18 On the constitutive-interpersonal level of consciousness, the "I" of language is both signifier and signified. On the level of regulatory agency, however, the "I" of language is a signifier but is not part of that which is signified.

19 Ultimately, of course, all motive experience is regulated by positive entropy. However, on the level of current, proximal experience, only the physiological category of motives is regulated by positive entropy.

20 See Gruber and Vonèche, *The Essential Piaget*, pp. 353–358.

21 For example, Freud said, "The ego is first and foremost a bodily ego" (*The Ego and the Id, S.E.*, vol. 19, p. 27).

22 Cognition is broadly defined here to include motives for understanding, mastering, and exploring the environment, and also for understanding and creatively employing one's own constitutive-interpersonal thought processes.

23 Hegel's *Phenomenology of Spirit* provides an example of this use of negation.

24 Freud, "Negation," *S.E.*, vol. 19, pp. 235–239.

25 Other authors have advanced forms of negation as *ontological* that are actually pathological examples of the logical or psychological categories of negation. An example is Parmenides (*Fragments, a Text and Translation*, p. 67), who was one of the earliest Western authors to assign to logical negation the significance of ontological negation. This conflation was in keeping with his monistic view of the unified oneness of all being. A prominent and influential example of assigning ontological status to psychological negation is the Hegelian dialectic of master and slave. Sartre's attribution of a fundamental, existential significance to negation is exemplified by his definition of the ontological form

343

of consciousness as a spontaneous nothing. In our judgment, this spontaneous nothing ultimately refers to an act of self-rage that occurs in response to the lack of the veridical reflection of agent-self as agent-self. Recently, Ricoeur and Aboulafia have built on Hegel's dialectic of desire in ascribing a prominent role to negation in their theories. Also, Lamiell has advanced the notion of dialectical negation (*The Psychology of Personality*, pp. 183–184).

26 This was discussed in chap. 3.

27 All psychodynamic explanatory systems can be categorized according to their view of the significance of acquired experience, especially the nurturing relationships of early childhood, for personality development. The spectrum of theories is defined on one end by Freud's drive–structure model, in which the drives are intrinsically objectless and objects become recognized only by virtue of their use for drive gratification. On the other end of the spectrum, the Sullivanian school of interpersonal psychiatry, the British school of object relations (e.g., Klein, Balint, Winnicott, Fairbairn, Guntrip, and Bion), the attachment school of object relations (e.g., Bowlby, and Ainsworth), and developmental psychologists (e.g., Trevarthen and Stern) all posit that caregiving relationships have intrinsic importance. However, none of these authors advance an ontological basis for the regulatory agency reality they ascribe to the caregiving relationship. Fairbairn, e.g., asserted that libido is object seeking, not pleasure seeking (Fairbairn, *An Object Relations Theory of the Personality*, pp. 127,137). Stern and other psychodynamic authors who emphasize object relations assign some degree of importance to an innate capacity for intentional agency organized and regulated with reference to relationship experience with the primary object. Further, much of the childrearing literature tends to impute what we would term interpersonal agent-self intentionality to the infant from birth on, or at least from the early part of the first year of life.

Two different origins are most frequently postulated to explain the emergence of the infant's capacity for personal agency: (1) innate species-specific sets of invariant relationship experiences or (2) an emergent process of a phase-appropriate capacity for (interpersonal) introspection, or self-awareness. The innate explanation is represented by Melanie Klein, who posits an innate universe of preoedipal and oedipal relationship structures organized within a context of epigenetic paranoid and depressive positions. Klein sees the child's self and object experiences as solipsistic; in the Kleinian model, important others serve as a basic lattice around which innate experiences of personal meaning become organized.

Sullivan and Stern are representative of authors who believe in the existence of an emergent capacity for self-awareness. Sullivan's outlook is regulated by a positivist ontology based on Bridgman's operationalism. His notion of a field of interpersonal relations (*The Fusion of Psychiatry and Social Science*, pp. 70–73) represents self-consciousness as initiated by the infant's capacity to distinguish between the two alternating, global states of euphoria (the good mother) and tension (the bad mother).

Recently, Stern has posited that the infant has a very early capacity for interpersonal relationship intentionality associated with a phase-appropriate capacity for (interpersonal) introspection. Although Stern emphasizes the importance of the child's agency and of the caregiving relationship in promoting the child's psychic growth, like the other authors just mentioned, he does not explain how caregiving relationships promote the growth of self-regulatory control of psychic reality given the solipsism of interpersonal introspection. Stern characterizes his model of development as prospective and normative (rather than retrospective and pathomorphic). However, because he does not recognize the possibility of a rage-free mourning process, his paradigm of normality in reality represents intrapsychic and, usually, interpersonal psychopathology (*The Interpersonal World of the Infant*, p. 20). Like Freud, Stern mistakenly assumes that he can use his patients' verbal and other behaviors (psychopathological agent-self experience) to make inferences about paradigmatic development.

28 Tausk offered an early discussion of the significance of the child's discovery that the parent cannot read her/his mind to the development of psychopathology ("On the Origin of the 'Influencing Machine' in Schizophrenia," pp. 535–536).

29 The transference well-being associated with the all-powerful agent-self is phenomenologically akin to the notion of overweening pride that historically has been referred to as hubris, delusions of grandeur, and, more recently, the grandiose self. Our construct of all-powerful agent-self differs from Kohut's construct of grandiose self in several respects. Kohut never explains the origin of his construct except by an allusion to innateness (Kohut, *The Analysis of the Self*, pp. 27–32). He does not envision a nontransference form of self structure as paradigmatically superseding the grandiose self. He attributes regulatory functions to his grandiose self, which we believe are inherently contradictory due to the grandiose self's illusional nature. Further, the adjective "grandiose" is distant from the child's experience of her/himself in that grandiose has pejorative connotations that arise from the caregiver's noncaregiving motives (e.g., irritation).

30 In the West, an early contribution to the tradition of nonreligious morality (in the form of obeying one's own conscience) was Socrates's well-known assertion of the sufficiency of knowledge for virtue. Socrates claimed that one who acts wrongly acts from ignorance. Plato postulated that self-regulation is possible by means of reason alone if and only if reason operates in the context of an existence based on an ethical ideal of extreme self-abnegation. In contrast, Aristotle grounded ethics in human nature rather than in reasoned argument. He thought that loss due to unregulated desire could be reduced to a reasonable degree if an individual based her/his life on ethical ideals. In contrast, the stoics thought that reason could control desire through the practice of self-abnegation. This ideal of self-abnegation did not mandate abstinence from the gratification of desire, but did require self-restraint based on the acceptance of loss as an essential component of the meaning of life. This outlook was subordinated to the notion that the potential for suicide provides each person with the capability to attain an absolute form of self-regulatory stability.

   Hume and Freud exemplify those who assert that the ideal of a nonillusional form of regulatory control of desire is an impossibility. They both believed that desire has hegemony over reason. Hume thought "reason is and ought to be the only slave of the passions" (*A Treatise of Human Nature*,

p. 415), that desire could only be regulated by desire and not by reason, and, further, that the relationship between reason and desire is such that the sole function of reason is to provide the means to satisfy desire. Hume expressed his ethical skepticism in the view that one cannot get an ought from an is (p. 469). In contrast to Hume, who did posit an innate moral sense, Freud proposed a reductionistic model of the psychic apparatus that, because of its somatic origin, denied that any mind experience per se could exert hegemony over desire.

Kant tacitly dealt with this problem by postulating that free will could exclude the possibility of loss caused by committing an immoral act. Kant's assumption that a specific type of reason, practical reason, could regulate desire is based on the premise of the existence of an innate moral sense in the form of a categorical imperative with a priori validity. Kant's free will is based on a regulatory relationship between the categorical imperative and the capacity for rational, autonomous agency. In postulating a capacity for a loss-free type of free will, Kant separated truth and goodness, which he said were known differently: truth is known by the understanding and the good is chosen by practical reason. Accordingly, Kant asserted that, while an individual can decide what s/he ought to do, s/he cannot veridically assess the truthfulness of her/his moral choice.

Hegel and Nietzsche both suggested that desire could be regulated by idiosyncratic forms of desire. Hegel's regulatory control of desire is based on a dialectical teleology of radical idealism organized by conflict. Since Hegel advances no notion of mourning, loss must be grieved by a process based on conflicted competition within the master-slave dialectic. Nietzsche, via his notion of a will to power possessed only by the *ubermensch,* in effect asserted that desire could be regulated by desire. He based the capacity for the regulatory control of desire on the successful desire to dominate.

Marxism best exemplifies the systems that propose a model of regulatory control of desire by means of a social movement. Marxist utopianism rests on the radical restructuring of society by means of a dialectical materialism. The behaviorist model for the regulatory control of desire, as elaborated in Skinner's *Walden Two,* is based on a social movement.

During the Scottish Enlightenment, Hutcheson, writing from the viewpoint of ethical naturalism, proposed an innate moral sense as the basis of the regulatory control of desire. Though he did not posit the possibility of a loss-free regulatory control of desire, his viewpoint has affinity with ours.

31 McDevitt and Mahler, "Object Constancy, Individuality, and Internalization," p. 412.

32 One reader pointed out that a fitting illustration of this denial is the title of Vinette Carroll's play "Your Arm's Too Short to Box with God" (Fay Sawyier, personal communication, November 1986).

33 Lovejoy argues forcefully that the success of early hominids is due more to the nuclear family than to the development of sophisticated cognitive capacities ("The Origin of Man," p. 348).

34 Ibid., p. 343. See also, Gubernick and Klopfer, eds., *Parental Care in Mammals.*

35 Another effect of the human's evolved cognitive capacities on the caregiving relationship is that interpersonal caregiving behaviors have become especially vulnerable to cultural and other social-interpersonal extrafamilial influences (e.g., Kagan, Kearsley and Zelazo, *Infancy*, pp. 1–51). While social-interpersonal extrafamilial influences on caregiving may produce individuals with diverse configurations of interpersonal characteristics, they need not affect a caregiver's ability to give intrapsychic care. There may be instances, however, in which a society's need for a specific type of adult may entail styles of interpersonal caregiving that, if adhered to, would make veridical intrapsychic caregiving especially difficult.

36 This is the etiology of many of the behaviors that are included in the syndrome labeled attention deficit disorder.

37 Of course, we recognize that many children are growing up in families that are headed by one caregiver or are characterized by unstable relationships. If a second caregiver participates in the child's life, the conjugally competitive agent-self phase will occur in actual but somewhat distorted form. If no second caregiver is present, then the child's conjugally competitive agent-self experience will occur only on a fantasy level. In living arrangements such as these, it is important that the caregiver(s) remain simultaneously aware of the child's actual responses to her/his own phase-specific, conjugally competitive agent-self motives and of the loss the child undergoes due to the fact that s/he is not living with caregivers who are involved in a loving conjugal relationship.

38 See, for example, Freud, "From the History of an Infantile Neurosis," *S.E.*, vol. 17, p. 99.

39 The psychoanalytic tenet that women are unavoidably burdened by the sense of inferiority that results from experiencing their vulva as an open wound caused by castration is a pathological, projective identification of male anxiety that may be reinforced by the fact that men acquire their primal identifications early in life through experiences with a caregiver with a profoundly different anatomy.

40 See Appendix for a discussion of the identification process in general and see chap. 6 for a discussion of pathological identifications.

41 The constitutive types of reflections offered by the relationship ideal are relevant to an issue that has sparked much discussion but little agreement in psychology, psychoanalysis, and philosophy—the perennial issue of personal identity. Modern Continental philosophers, such as Heidegger and Sartre, treat the problem of personal identity by asserting that being and semiosis are one and the same (Heidegger) or by asserting that personal existence precedes essence (Sartre). Psychoanalysis, on the other hand, is permanently saddled with the incompatible constructs of ego and self, which occur on two different levels of abstraction.

42 Examples are Socrates and the Plato of the *Phaedo, Symposium,* and *Republic.*

43 For example, the Sybarites exemplify self-indulgence. Between these extremes of denial and indulgence lie the practical reason of Aristotle, Thomis-

tic free will, the naturalistic moral sense of Hutcheson, the categorical imperative of the practical reason of Kant, and the will to power of Nietzsche.

44 This is in contrast to Heidegger's assertion that the most meaningful form of personal existence is gained through a motive for the active acceptance of the moment of death.

45 Gruber and Vonèche, eds., *The Essential Piaget*, pp. 456–463.

NOTES TO CHAPTER FIVE

1 When the child has just begun to acquire the cognitive capacity Piaget termed "concrete operational thinking" (Piaget, *The Psychology of Intelligence*, p. 123).

2 See *The Psychology of Intelligence*, p. 65, for a discussion of decentering.

3 The death of a parent before the posttransference stage always means that the child will need psychological help in order to avoid handling this loss in psychopathological ways.

NOTES TO CHAPTER SIX

1 This chap. presents an overview of Intrapsychic Humanism's theory of psychopathology. A more detailed consideration of psychopathology will be included in subsequent publications. In this volume we discuss only psychopathology that does not have a physiological basis (i.e., we exclude mental retardation). Future publications will deal with the treatment of organically based mental disorders.

2 We do not mean to suggest that the evolution of culture could only have occurred by transference-based motive experience; we are only commenting on the process of evolution as we believe it actually occurred.

3 The distinction between intrapsychic and interpersonal psychopathology also elucidates a phenomenon that has long been observed, namely that when one psychological symptom improves the patient commonly discovers that a new symptom has emerged.

4 In the terminology of the psychoanalytic structural model, we understand all psychopathology as a structural, intrasystemic conflict caused by developmental defects.

5 It is interesting that Freud's second model of psychological conflict, which succeeded the early defense model used in the Miss Lucy case (*Studies on Hysteria, S.E.*, vol. 2, pp. 106–124), postulated that the "neuro-psychoses of defense" (symptoms of hysteria) were intrinsically related to the trauma of childhood sexual seduction by an adult or by older children ("Further Remarks on the Neuro-Psychoses of Defence," *S.E.*, vol. 3, p. 163). Freud quickly renounced his childhood sexual trauma model (*Three Essays on the Theory of Sexuality, S.E.*, vol. 7, p. 190 , and "My Views on the Part Played by Sexuality in the Aetiology of the Neuroses," *S.E.*, vol. 7, pp. 274–279). Freud came to the oedipus complex (*The Interpretation of Dreams, S.E.*, vol. 4, pp. 261–263) through his self-

analysis (*Three Essays on the Theory of Sexuality*, S.E., vol. 7, p. 128, n. 1). This discovery convinced Freud that infantile sexuality is universal and that the childhood sexual traumas reported by his patients were fantasies, not memories. From that time on, Freud viewed psychopathogenesis as the consequence of innate, biologically based conflicts that he conceptualized in terms of intrapsychic conflict between opposing instinctual drives (*Three Essays on the Theory of Sexuality*, S.E., vol. 7, pp. 130–243, and "Instincts and Their Vicissitudes," S.E., vol. 14, pp. 117–140). In Freudian terms, then, intrapsychic conflicts are ahistorical; the intrinsic cause of psychic pain is biological. By 1905, Freud had evolved the genetic (etiological) view of psychosexual development (*Three Essays on the Theory of Sexuality*, S. E., vol. 7, pp. 130–243). Rappaport among others has described the evolution of Freud's views from a nurture-based to a nature-based etiology of mental illness (Rappaport, "A Historical Survey of Psychoanalytic Ego Psychology," pp. 5–17). The radical changes in Freud's understanding of the etiology of psychopathology have been sensationally reported by Masson in *The Assault on Truth: Freud's Suppression of the Seduction Theory*.

Given the constraints of his nineteenth-century ontology and the fact that he was searching for a source of reliable knowledge about psychic reality, Freud's shift away from an etiology based on meaning structures was unavoidable, even though it did not prove to be heuristic. Freud had created a theory of meaning in his constructs of primary process and secondary process, but he felt the need to anchor this theory in nonagency reality (in the instinctual drives). This change was probably inevitable, since the meaning structures with which Freud dealt belong to nonempirical, interpersonal consciousness and, therefore, cannot provide the foundation for a sound ontology of psychic reality. The evolution of the psychoanalytic theory of ego psychology illustrates the problem with founding an ontology of psychic reality on an epistemic method that reductionistically assumes that the primary fabric of personal existence consists of nonagency reality. When Hartmann, whose ideas Freud explicitly endorsed, posited that the ego has innate adaptive cognitive capacities, Freud's notion of a personal existence based on a purely nonagency type of physical reality was expanded to include meaning structures of nonregulatory, constitutive-interpersonal agency reality.

Some psychodynamically oriented writers outside of mainstream psychoanalysis (e.g., Balint, Winnicott, Fairbairn, Guntrip, Kohut, and A. Miller) have postulated that psychopathology is caused by traumatic early relationship experiences, although they also conclude that psychic pain is inevitable. Like theorists of ego psychology, however, these authors have no reliable epistemology for apprehending regulatory agency reality because they posit as ontological personal meaning structures a type of experience that really represents the subject's solipsistic, nonempirical, constitutive-interpersonal motive experience. Of these authors, only Fairbairn and Guntrip assert that psychopathology is *exclusively* caused by traumatic early relationship experience. Further, with the exception of Fairbairn and Guntrip, these authors all base the ontological validity of their respective concepts of self on Freud's reductionistic model of mind. Fairbairn and, following him, Guntrip, explicitly disavow Freud's instinctual drive model. They believe that psychic structure arises from experience generated by a primary need for object relationships (i.e., by the vicissitudes of relationship pleasure) rather than as a consequence of the needs of the unstructured drive energies of Freud's libido theory (the need for pleasure per se). For Fairbairn and Guntrip, psychopathology results from psychotoxic caregiving, but neither author provides a coherent theory of development and both base their model of normal psychic development on the psychopathological behavior of their patients.

6 When we refer to an intrapsychic caregiving perspective in the context of nonveridical caregiving, we mean to indicate the understanding of the nonveridical caregiver's regulatory agent-self that would result from an intrapsychic therapist's therapeutic relationship with the nonveridical caregiver. Similarly, when a child has psychopathology, her/his regulatory agency reality can only be known by her/his intrapsychic therapist. We do not mean to imply that the nonveridical caregiver can have a veridical understanding of the child's regulatory agency, as that knowledge can only occur by means of veridical intrapsychic caregiving.

7 Freud disavowed the notion that there was a unitary cause of psychopathology: "A single pathogenic influence is scarcely ever sufficient . . . a *number* of aetiological factors are required" (italic in original) ("My Views on the Part Played by Sexuality in the Aetiology of the Neuroses," *S.E.*, vol. 7, p. 279). His notion of a multifactorial basis of psychopathogenesis was grounded in the importance he accorded sexuality in the etiology of psychopathology. However, Freud reached these conclusions because he mistook constitutive-interpersonal meaning structures for the ontological basis of psychic reality.

8 Freud, "From the History of an Infantile Neurosis," *S.E.*, vol. 17, pp. 97–103.

9 In contrast, psychoanalytic theory postulates that the oedipal conflict universally resolves into an infantile neurosis, which is understood as an ineluctable part of normal development.

10 See Hess, *Imprinting*, pp. 70–81.

11 Freud, "The Psychotherapy of Hysteria" (*S.E.*, vol. 2, p. 305). Freud also said, "Every normal person, in fact, is only normal on the average. His ego approximates to that of the psychotic in some part or other and to a greater or lesser extent" ("Analysis Terminable and Interminable," *S.E.*, vol. 23, p. 235). See also Kohut's assumption that a grandiose self occurs in all development, and Winnicott's premise that the normative true self is unalterably "incommunicado" (*The Maturational Process and the Facilitating Environment*, p. 187).

12 Nontransference intrapsychic pleasure has no relation to loss or pain because it results from a loss-free intrapsychic mutuality. Intrapsychic mutuality is pain free rather than painless because it is not part of an antipodal system of interpersonal pleasure and interpersonal pain.

13 Freud grappled inconclusively with the problem of negative identifications in a number of papers (two of the more notable are *Beyond the Pleasure Principle*, *S.E.*, vol. 18, pp. 1–64, and "The Economic Problem of Masochism," *S.E.*, vol. 19, pp. 155–172). Anna Freud built on her father's work with the construct she termed identification with the aggressor (*The Ego and the Mechanisms of Defense*, pp. 117–131).

14 See Green, Campbell, and Raphael, "Psychosocial Dwarfism."

15 A word should be said about the infant's intrapsychic vulnerability to the effects of serious physical illness in the pre-eidetic stage. The infant's marked physiological immaturity grounds her/his functional psychic adaptability (the capacity for mental illness in response to psychotoxic nurture). However, physical immaturity also makes the infant more vulnerable now than at any other time to psychopathology caused by the subjective effects of physiological malfunctioning that results from significant physical illness. This syndrome of severe regression that is easily fixated most commonly appears with abnormally high fevers, with or without manifest convulsions, in infants under a year of age.

   Because of the immaturity of the pre-eidetic infant, dynamic and structural regressions are synonymous. Therefore, acute, intense physical illness, especially that characterized by high fevers, represents a psychological emergency. We will present a full discussion of this syndrome in a forthcoming volume on the psychopathology and treatment of childhood disorders. For now, we wish only to emphasize that, in addition to the obvious need for crisis management to control the fever and prevent or control convulsions, there needs to be an immediate psychological intervention, which consists of the urgent, persistent penetration of the infant's potentially malignant, regressed, dissociated state by active, stimulating caregiving ministrations aimed primarily at preserving the infant's capacity for the smile response.

16 Developmental intrapsychic pain categorically differs from pathological intrapsychic pain. Each type of intrapsychic psychic pain is a meaning structure that can neither be associated with affect nor perceived directly. Unlike developmental intrapsychic pain, however, psychopathological intrapsychic pain includes meanings of delusional intrapsychic mutuality and isolation.

17 For the view that "generative entrenchment" is a constraint in biology, see Wimsatt, "Developmental Constraints, Generative Entrenchment and the Innate-Acquired Distinction," pp. 185–208.

18 In contrast, psychoanalytic theory explains interpersonal symptoms from the genetic viewpoint, which suggests that the diverse universe of the possible aims and objects of the instinctual drives should be given nosological prominence.

19 Because of space constraints, we do not always specify the characteristics that frame a specific use of the term rage, for example, whether the rage is conscious or unconscious, or what the observing vantage point is. Accordingly, we rely on the general context to supply the meaning.

20 The construct of rage as a personal meaning structure bears no resemblance to narcissistic rage as defined in the psychoanalytic literature. The lack of universal agreement on a psychoanalytic definition of narcissistic rage is partly a product of the confusion in the psychoanalytic theory of affect. The problematic state of the psychoanalytic theory of affect (and, accordingly, of the construct of rage) is evidenced by the proliferation in the psychoanalytic literature of divergent, competing theories of affect.

21 Freud, "The Economic Problem of Masochism," *S.E.*, vol. 19, p. 166, n. 1.

22 See Freud's *The Psychopathology of Everyday Life, S.E.,* vol. 6.

23 This construct bears only a superficial similarity to Freud's construct of negative therapeutic reaction. A more comprehensive comparison of these two
constructs will be made in chap. 7. At this point, we wish to emphasize only
that the notion of negative therapeutic reaction was conceived by Freud to
depict his patients' paradoxical reactions to what he saw as therapeutic success
and to explain these by positing the existence of an unconscious guilt primarily derived from instinctually based rage. In contrast, Intrapsychic Humanism's construct of aversive reaction to pleasure mainly refers to the trauma
caused by nonveridical intrapsychic nurture.

24 Stevenson, *The Strange Case of Dr. Jekyll and Mr. Hyde,* pp. 44–45.

25 When the caregiver does not offer the child this alliance and, in fact, relates to
the child with nearly constant constitutive-interpersonal rage, the child will be
driven to gratify her/his need for care-getting pleasure by identifying with the
caregiver's paranoid orientation. This phenomenon illustrates the subjective
experience that to be like is to be liked.

26 Freud came to recognize the following clinical manifestations of what we term
constitutive-interpersonal self-rage as the patient behaviors that are most resistant to therapeutic modification: the ego's fear of being overwhelmed
(Freud, "The Neuro-Psychoses of Defence," *S.E.,* vol. 3, p. 55, and *The Ego
and the Id, S.E.,* vol. 19, p. 57); negative therapeutic reactions (*The Ego and the
Id,* pp. 49–50); the compulsion to repeat (*Beyond the Pleasure Principle, S.E.,*
vol. 18, pp. 35–36); and masochism (*Three Essays on the Theory of Sexuality,
S.E.,* vol. 7, pp. 157–160). In fact, one of the reasons that Freud introduced
his structural model of the psyche was his need to explain his patients' driven,
self-destructive behavior. The structural model made it possible to ground the
ego and superego within a structurally unconscious ego (*The Ego and the Id,
S.E.,* vol. 19, pp. 3–66) and, thereby, to explain internally directed instinctual
rage that had no obvious origin in the libidinal instinctual drives of the id
(which constitutes the unconscious segment of the topographic model). As a
result, Freud was able to make some sense of his growing awareness of the
ineffectiveness of psychoanalysis as a treatment for mental illness ("Analysis
Terminable and Interminable," *S.E,* vol. 23, p. 241).

27 Unlike Schopenhauer, Freud did not say that death is the only aim of life. He
cautioned, "We are not overlooking the fact that there is life as well as death"
(*New Introductory Lectures on Psycho-Analysis, S.E.,* vol. 22, p. 107). However,
Freud's many statements about the death instinct amply support the conclusion that, given that Freud posited that the life and death instincts are fused,
he accorded the death instinct hegemony in terms of the regulatory control
of the instincts and their vicissitudes (e.g., *Beyond the Pleasure Principle, S.E.,*
vol. 18, pp. 3–64, and *An Outline of Psycho-Analysis, S.E.,* vol. 23, pp. 141–207).

28 Freud, "The Economic Problem of Masochism," *S.E.,* vol. 19, pp. 161–164.

29 Although Freud saw an intrinsic erotic component in all masochism other
than the type of masochism he termed moral masochism, in our opinion, a
character structure composed largely of manifest constitutive-interpersonal
motives for self-rage does not intrinsically include an erotic component. We

include Freud's category of moral masochism in our category of nonmediated masochism. Freud characterized moral masochism as "chiefly remarkable for having loosened its connection with what we recognize as sexuality. . . . The suffering itself is what matters" ("The Economic Problem of Masochism," *S.E.*, vol. 19, p. 165).

30   Although Freud's constructs of primary-process thinking and secondary-process thinking were rooted in the thought of his time (including both theories of associational thinking and also of hypnoid states and other types of dissociated thought stimulated by a widespread scholarly and popular interest in hypnosis), taken together, they represented an original theory of meaning structures. In our terms, *The Psychopathology of Everyday Life* (*S.E.*, vol. 6) describes the regulatory control possessed by nonveridical, psychopathological, constitutive-interpersonal meaning structures. On an unconscious basis, these constitutive-interpersonal meaning structures can exert continuous regulatory control over conscious decisions. In Freud's terms, the primary process can exert hegemony over the secondary process. The same motives that have regulatory control over the constitutive-interpersonal irrational thought processes of the dream work can exert continuous control over constitutive-interpersonal irrational thought during everyday waking life. A slip of the tongue dramatically illustrates the hegemony of this type of irrational thought process over the rational type of thought process. Slips of the tongue can also elucidate the forces at work in constitutive-interpersonal psychopathology. Two of the most important characteristics of slips of the tongue are: (1) the motives with regulatory control function unconsciously on the constitutive-interpersonal level of consciousness and aim to make the speaker deaf to the irrational or forbidden thought *after* as well as before it is actualized and (2) the statement in question is often identified as a slip only by means of a hermeneutic process on the part of another.

   Slips of the tongue are powerful examples of Freud's view that, given the inevitability of psychic pain, the irrational (primary process) has ultimate hegemony over the rational (secondary process). Freud implemented this view in the psychoanalytic analysis of free associational trains of thought. In Freud's theory of meaning, cognition is the basis for reality testing (the criterion of veridicality and security), and reality testing is, at bottom, a hermeneutic process, that is, an interpretation ("The Unconscious," *S.E.*, vol. 14, pp. 201–204; "A Metapsychological Supplement to the Theory of Dreams," *S.E.*, vol. 14, pp. 228–229; "Mourning and Melancholia," *S.E.*, vol. 14, pp. 256–258). By definition, then, Freud's constructs of rationality and irrationality (his theories of primary and secondary thought processes) exclusively concern constitutive-interpersonal meaning structures. In this usage, *rational* refers to the appropriate use of cognitive meaning structures. *Irrationality* is a rationally defective act that can only be identified by an individual with a sufficiently conflict-free set of cognitive motives. In our terms, the type of irrationality defined by Freud results from the hegemony of psychic pain over the agent-self that has regulatory control over cognitive motives.

31   Freud also discussed irrationality in terms of a defective reality testing of relationship experience on the level of the oedipal transference relationship. However, because oedipal relating is a product of constitutive-interpersonal

motives, it does not directly pertain to the intrapsychic motive for relationship pleasure. The same is true of Fairbairn's notion of endopsychic structures, Kohut's notions of the primal idealizing transference, A. Miller's notion of self, and Winnicott's true self.

32 Freud, *Leonardo da Vinci and a Memory of his Childhood*, S.E., vol. 11, pp. 63–137.

33 For example, the *Diagnostic and Statistical Manual III-R*.

34 Freud, "The Psychotherapy of Hysteria," *S.E.*, vol. 2, p. 305.

35 Intrapsychic Humanism has been successfully used with violent institutionalized adolescents (demonstration project with the State of Illinois, Department of Child and Family Services, 1974–1978).

36 Freud, *Civilization and Its Discontents*, S.E., vol. 21, p. 86.

37 The diagnostic process entailed by psychoanalytic nosology synthesizes five viewpoints: genetic, dynamic, structural, topographic, and adaptive (Rappaport and Gill, "The Points of View and Assumptions of Metapsychology," pp. 153–162). The psychoanalytic explanatory system, however, is regulated by the ontology implicit in the psychosexual theory of development.

38 Freud, "The Disposition to Obsessional Neurosis," *S.E.*, vol. 12, pp. 313–326.

39 The reason is that, outside of Intrapsychic Treatment, the hegemonic motive to subordinate personal motives to caregiving motives without any kind of reciprocity would represent self-rage. The child's caregiver cannot her/himself provide the child with veridical intrapsychic caregiving because of the nonveridical nature of this caregiver's regulatory-intrapsychic agent-self.

NOTES TO CHAPTER SEVEN

1 At this time we will present only an overview of the new form of treatment that is based on the principles of Intrapsychic Humanism.

2 While Freud and Hartmann claim that psychoanalysis is a scientific psychology because it uses the ontology and epistemology of the natural sciences, the *method* of psychoanalysis is hermeneutic. The method of psychoanalytic theory is embodied in the transference neurosis and its interpretation, which represent both the psychic reality postulated by psychoanalysis and the epistemic mode of knowing this psychic reality. In psychoanalytic theory, the psychic reality apprehended in the transference neurosis is a form of materialistic, nonagency reality and the interpretation of the transference neurosis is claimed to be an act of direct observation of the nonagency reality of psychic reality. According to psychoanalytic theory, interpretation is not a hermeneutic act, and psychoanalysis is a scientific psychology, or natural science, which acquires knowledge through induction (Hartmann, *Essays on Ego Psychology*, pp. 400–403).

In our view, the constructs of transference neurosis and interpretation refer to the two conflicting ontologies entailed by Freud's model of the psychic apparatus: a theory of ontological meaning that is a teleological explanation of psychic reality (primary and secondary process), and a nonteleological ontology of a psychic reality composed of physical forces (the construct of the instinctual drives). Freud conflated these two models of psychic reality when he asserted that the secondary-process system of meaning, within which primary-process meanings are manifested, is not ontological because it represents only the conscious signification of the intrapsychic real with true ontologic status—the instinctual drives. Freud tried to synthesize these two systems in statements such as, "Thinking was endowed with characteristics which made it possible for the mental apparatus to tolerate an increased tension of stimulus while the process of discharge was postponed" ("Formulations on the Two Principles of Mental Functioning," *S.E.*, vol. 12, p. 221). He asserted that the individual interacts with the external world only for purposes of energy discharge (the satisfaction of instinctual aims). Accordingly, Freud thought that both psychic structure and object relations represent responses to the organism's needs to regulate the level of excitation in the mental apparatus. In this way, the psychoanalytic view of human nature entails an impoverished view of the subjective experience of personal existence; it essentially excludes any motive the infant has other than the motive for instinctual-drive-gratifying relationship experience.

Since the 1920s, psychoanalytic theory has increasingly concerned itself with redressing Freud's impoverished vision of human nature. Psychoanalytic theory has tried to establish an ontological basis for the teleological nature of thought and for primary relationship experience. Taken as a whole, the movement in psychoanalytic theory to establish a satisfactory way to know the teleological category of psychic reality began with a shift from an instinctual drive model of the psychic apparatus to an object relations model. This change was initiated by Freud's introduction of the structural model (*The Ego and the Id*) as a replacement for the topographic model. Freud's structural model was modified by the work done in the area of ego psychology that sprang from the work of, among others, A. Freud (*The Ego and the Mechanisms of Defense*), Reich (*Character Analysis*), and Hartmann (*The Ego and the Problem of Adaptation*). In addition to ego psychology, attempts to redress the defects in psychoanalytic theory include the efforts of the British school of object relations theory (Balint, Fairbairn, Guntrip, Klein, and Winnicott) and the work of Lacan. One of the most important departures from the object relations/ structural model was the Self Psychology pioneered by Kohut. Despite the affiliation with psychoanalysis expressed in his final book, Kohut denigrated the psychosexual model by assigning a subsidiary role to Freud's primary construct—the oedipal conflict. He did not consider the vicissitudes of oedipal desire to play a critical role in either psychopathology or paradigmatic development. However, attempts by psychoanalytic theorists such as Kohut to construe a reliable (nonsolipsistic, empirical) way of knowing a psychic reality that is in essence teleological are destined to fail. Every psychodynamic author who has struggled with the problem has been forced to wrestle with two types of compromise: (1) a need to reconcile the Freudian drive model with the object relations model of ego psychology and (2) the need for a theory that will provide a structural basis for the relationship between the constructs of ego and self that preserves them as categorically distinct, yet compatible and empirical, and also ensures their accessibility to reflective first-person experience.

The attempt to integrate the notions of self and ego is analogous to trying to mix oil and water because the construct of ego was conceived from a nonteleological viewpoint and the construct of self is a statement in and of itself of teleological experience. This impasse is reflected in Meissner's article, "Can Psychoanalysis Find Its Self," in which Meissner asserts that the fundamental existential characteristic of self is its "heterogeneity" (p. 391). This heterogeneity is based on the phenomenon that the introspecting subject is neither representable nor introspectable. In our terms, this assertion accurately depicts the phenomenology of mind that characterizes pathological agency reality, namely, that there is no mutualized intrapsychic pleasure to counteract the limitation of the introspection of the constitutive-interpersonal "I" to the constraints of short-term memory. It reflects the limits of an introspection that manifests the primary structural defect of intrapsychic and regulatory-interpersonal psychopathology, namely, the lack of the veridical reflection of agent-self as agent-self. Meissner's assertion, therefore, illustrates the common fallacy of positing as normative that which is actually psychopathological.

Authors who are committed to preserving the psychoanalytic focus on nonagency reality have been unable to resolve the problem of relating an instinctual drive model to an explanatory system in which the goal is to understand the ontological basis of the subjective experience of personal existence. Accordingly, no school of psychology that employs the notion of self has been able to demonstrate that the form of self-knowledge it posits derives from a reliable epistemology. Like other psychologies, Self Psychology is a form of persuasion: at best it produces modifications in pathological interpersonal transference structures.

Another, competing, psychoanalytic viewpoint is based on hermeneutics. This approach has gained increasing acceptance in America in the 1980s. Like psychologies that emphasize the self, the hermeneutic approach emerged from dissatisfaction with the reductionism that characterizes both the drive-structural model and the object-structural model of mind. A number of analysts and social scientists (e.g., Gill, Habermas, G. Klein, Lacan, and Schafer) propose that psychoanalysis is not a biological science but rather should be seen as a hermeneutic enterprise in which intersubjective communication and the act of interpretation are the primary instruments of the psychoanalytic process. This view holds that psychopathogenesis results from faulty developmental affective experiences in the intersubjective field of child-caregiver relationships. Accordingly, this theory emphasizes the significance of systematically unempathic parenting in the etiology of psychopathology (see e.g., Stolorow and Branschaft, "Developmental Failure and Psychic Conflict," pp. 241–253). The essence of the psychoanalytic process, the means of knowing the subjective experience of personal existence, is presented in terms of understanding and reinterpreting signs and meanings of autobiographical (historical) experience. However, no creditable epistemic basis for a hermeneutics of privileged first–person knowledge has ever been established. Lacan's assertion that "the unconscious is structured like a language" (Smith and Kerrigan, *Interpreting Lacan,* vol. 6, p. 35) and Heidegger's assertion that "man shows himself as the entity which talks" (Heidegger, *Being and Time,* p. 208) are attempts to base the epistemic validity of a hermeneutic approach to agency reality on the phenomenon of the innate, biological basis of the primary structures of language (that is, on the assertion that semiosis is the onto-logical basis of personal existence). This equation, however, is not veridical because meaning structures of language are solipsistic and nonempirical and, therefore, invalid as the basis of a reliable form of knowing the self or another.

A psychoanalytic offshoot of the hermeneutic approach employs the prin-ciples of narrative prose structure (Sass and Woofolk, "Psychoanalysis and the Hermeneutic Turn"). It is based on the premise that there is a valid, cate-gorical distinction between narrative and historical knowledge. This view em-phasizes narrative structure in contrast to historical knowledge of genetic re-constructions. The therapeutic act consists of changes and reorganizations of self-narrations. The reality of the newly created autobiography is not only id-iosyncratic and solipsistic, but also, and more important, its primary criterion is not truth but rather the patient's judgment about the coherence and useful-ness of the autobiographical revisions. The regulating principles of the con-struction of the autobiography have as their referent narrative prose struc-ture rather than historical veridicality.

Clearly, no viewpoint could be more contrary to the principles underlying Freud's instinctual drive model than the narrative model. In fact, Freud aban-doned his first two models because of his need to establish a model that, in his judgment, avoided the idiosyncrasy of narrative structure.

In psychoanalysis, the patient's neurosis is treated by interpretation within a developed transference neurosis. The patient works through neurotic con-flict by replacing an unconscious repetition compulsion (repeated attempts to gratify a repressed forbidden instinctual wish of infantile sexuality) with a re-living of the original conflicted instinctual wishes of early childhood within the context of the therapeutic transference relationship in order to replace unconsciously motivated reexperiencing with conscious remembering. Freud asserted that this process fulfills his dictum, "where id was, there ego shall be" (*New Introductory Lectures on Psycho-Analysis, S.E.,* vol. 22, p. 80).

3 As will be clear, this is entirely different than theories of psychoanalytic treat-ment which prescribe interpretations of the transference in the "here and now" (Gill, "The Analysis of Transference," p. 265).

4 Hugo, *Les Miserables,* p. 111.

5 See chap. 6.

6 Freud, *The Ego and the Id,* vol. 19, p. 15.

7 Delusional intrapsychic mutuality, of course, always has the subjective mean-ing of veridical caregiving mutuality. The determination of veridicality is only made from an intrapsychic caregiving perspective, not from the introspective experience of the subject.

8 The most critical distinction between the psychoanalytic construct of negative therapeutic reaction and Intrapsychic Humanism's construct of aversive reac-tions to care-getting pleasure is the cause attributed to each. Though most fully developed in *The Ego and the Id* (*S.E.,* vol. 19, pp. 49–50), the psycho-analytic construct of negative therapeutic reaction was initially discussed by Freud in "From the History of an Infantile Neurosis" (*S.E.,* vol. 17, p. 69), where it was termed a "negative reaction." Freud defined the negative reac-

tion as the phenomenon in which the patient never "gave way to fresh ideas without making one last attempt at clinging to what had lost its values for him" (p. 68). In *The Ego and the Id*, the definition of negative therapeutic reaction expanded to include the phenomenon that such people "cannot endure any praise or appreciation, but that they react inversely to the progress of treatment" (*The Ego and the Id*, S.E., vol. 19, p. 49). Freud distinguished between the negative therapeutic reaction and three other clinical conditions associated with the patient's resistance to improvement: (1) narcissistic inaccessibility, (2) a negative attitude toward the therapist, and (3) the clinging to gain from illness (p. 49). In the same discussion, Freud characterized the negative therapeutic reaction as temporary and did not believe it affected all patients, whereas we assert that aversive reactions to pleasure characterize all psychopathology.

Freud defined negative therapeutic reactions as regressive behaviors that occur in reaction to pleasurable therapeutic experience. In our terms, the negative therapeutic reactions Freud described were either reactions to nonveridical caregiving or aversive reactions to pleasure. Freud thought negative therapeutic reactions resulted from unconscious guilt and were unpredictable. Kris's notion of the "good analytic hour" ("On Some Vicissitudes of Insight in Psychoanalysis," p. 266) is an example of the fact that negative therapeutic reactions as found in psychoanalytic treatment are characterized by wide, uncontrollable, regressive swings. Freud ascribed the source of the negative therapeutic reaction to the patient's need for punishment, which he made synonymous with an unconscious sense of guilt. He saw this guilt as the ego's reaction to the superego's criticism. Superego aggression was attributed to the death instinct, which Freud thought had ultimate power over the life instinct. (See discussion in chap. 1, Freud, *An Outline of Psycho-Analysis*, S.E., vol. 23, pp. 141–207, and *Beyond the Pleasure Principle*, S.E., vol. 18, pp. 3–64.)

In contrast to Freud's instinctual drive explanation for negative therapeutic reactions, two psychoanalysts who propose that psychoanalysis is essentially a hermeneutic enterprise assert that "'negative therapeutic reactions' are most often produced by prolonged unrecognized intersubjective disjunctions wherein the patient's selfobject transference needs are consistently misunderstood and thereby relentlessly rejected by the analyst" (Atwood and Stolorow, *Structures of Subjectivity*, p. 53). In our view, however, aversive reactions to care-getting pleasure are the consequence of the distorting effects of nonveridical nurture on an innately based motive for veridical intrapsychic relationship pleasure. Care-getting pleasure signifies a loss to the dysphoric self, which relies on meanings of psychic pain to gratify its motive for effective agency meaning. Thus, whereas Freud thought negative reactions are the result of nature, we believe aversive reactions reflect the effects of nonveridical nurture on innately determined ideals.

9 A related issue is the problem of patient compliance, which is pathological pleasurable self behavior that is under the hegemony of motives for pain and isolation, which stem from the structure of delusional intrapsychic mutuality. Freud thought patient compliance does not pose a serious problem because the patient's "conflicts will only be successfully solved and his resistances overcome if the anticipatory ideas he is given tally with what is real in him. Whatever in the doctor's conjecture is inaccurate drops out in the course of

the analysis . . . . it has to be withdrawn and replaced by something more correct" (*Introductory Lectures on Psycho-Analysis, S.E.,* vol. 16, p. 452). Others have pointed out that Freud's tally is not viable. Grunbaum termed Freud's assertion the "tally argument" and proceeded to negate it (*The Foundations of Psychoanalysis,* p. 166).

10 That is, they rely on empathy as a therapeutic act in addition to empathy as an act of perception.

11 We equate the therapeutic split described in psychoanalytic theory to our construct of the pathological split between the dysphoric self and the pathological pleasurable self in untreated psychopathology. We believe the psychoanalytic construct of the therapeutic split between the patient's observing and experiencing ego rests solely on transference experience and (solipsistic and nonempirical) constitutive-interpersonal introspection. From our perspective, psychoanalysis misunderstands shifts in the dynamic balance between the two sides of the pathological split (between the pathological pleasurable self structure and the dysphoric self structure) as the patient's development of the capacity for nontransference self-experience.

12 The pleasure-stimulated motive to mourn pain by bringing it into the therapeutic relationship differs entirely from the psychoanalytic principles of abreaction, reliving within the transference, genetic understanding, or the restoration of some functional, transference sector of the patient's personality. To mourn psychic pain within the therapeutic relationship is to lose interest in it because it has come to signify an inferior type of inner well-being.

13 Kris, *Selected Papers of Ernst Kris,* p. 266.

14 An example of mistaking rage at the original caregivers as representing an achieved inner freedom from the pain caused by them is A. Miller's use of Igor Stravinsky's bitter recollection of his childhood, "as an example of successful mourning" (*Prisoners of Childhood,* p. 43, n. 1).

15 As exemplified in the writings of Brenner.

16 Those authors, such as Balint, Bowlby, Fairbairn, Guntrip, Spitz, and Winnicott, who emphasize early object relations tacitly or overtly recognize that each child comes endowed with a species inheritance of a biological, innately determined set of drives or motives that, in effect, program the child to participate actively in an emerging relationship with the caregiver. The structure of innate relationships differs significantly from innate language structures, in that it is not intrinsically tied to cognition, even though it obviously has a synergistic relationship with grammar structures. The authors just mentioned do not distinguish the innate capacity for relationship experience that they posit from what Chomsky has called the deep structures of grammar. In an attempt to legitimize the notion of an incipient adult capacity for a real relationship experience that is present at the inception of therapy and on which a therapeutic alliance can be built, these authors mistakenly assume that their notion of an innate childhood capacity for a healthy relationship experience applies to the therapeutic relationship. They overestimate the patient's capacity to respond in a genuinely growth-promoting manner to relationship deprivation caused by therapeutic abstinence. These authors either mistake dynamic shifts

359

in character defenses (i.e., the strengthening of the motives of the pathological pleasurable self in relation to the motives of the dysphoric self) for a structure-building process, or, like Brenner, assert that analysis should not be concerned with structure building (Brenner, *Psychoanalytic Technique and Psychic Conflict,* p. 109).

17 Freud, "Two Encyclopaedia Articles," *S.E.,* vol. 18, p. 239.

18 The requirement that the patient lie on the analytic couch facing away from the analyst was introduced by Freud in an attempt both to establish distance from his patients ("I cannot put up with being stared at by other people for eight hours a day"), and also in order to give himself over to his unconscious thoughts without influencing the patient by virtue of his own facial expressions ("On Beginning the Treatment," *S.E.,* vol. 12, p. 134). In our view, this requirement represents the hegemony of the therapist's personal motives (e.g., not to be stared at, not to have to control her/his facial expressions) over her/his intrapsychic caregiving motives (represents nonveridical intrapsychic caregiving). This nonveridical intrapsychic caregiving is compounded when the analyst understands the patient's regressive responses to the analytic couch as caused by traumatic early experience or instinctual drive derivatives rather than by the therapist's nonveridical caregiving. For example, one analyst saw his patient's regressive associations to the couch as an indication of the presence of a deepening but mistrustful transference, which was based on earlier disappointments with the patient's primary objects (Waugaman, "Falling Off the Couch"). Another analyst understood his patient's tendency to fall asleep on the couch as the result of preoedipal and oedipal conflicts that were being expressed in the transference neurosis (Inderbitzin, "Patients' Sleep on the Analytic Couch").

19 In contrast, the classic psychoanalytic understanding of the therapeutic action consists of helping the patient reexperience (the neurotic symptoms that represent repetitive attempts to gratify repressed, conflicted instinctual drive derivatives), relive (by means of the transference neurosis interpretation), reconstruct (by means of genetic interpretation), and remember and work through (establish a self-analytic function that allows for remembering instead of the neurotic action of repetition). Freud wrote:

> It has been the physician's endeavor to keep this transference neurosis within the narrowest limits: to force as much as possible into the channel of memory and to allow as little as possible to emerge as repetition . . . . [the physician] must get him to re-experience some portion of his forgotten life, but must see to it, on the other hand, that the patient retains some degree of aloofness, which will enable him, in spite of everything, to recognize that what appears to be reality is in fact only a reflection of a forgotten past. If this can be successfully achieved, the patient's sense of conviction is won, together with the therapeutic success that is dependent on it (*Beyond the Pleasure Principle, S.E.,* vol. 18, p. 19).

This schema shows the logical outcome of the psychoanalytic view of psychopathology as primarily a biologically based conflict (universal infantile neurosis) overlaid by acquired conflict and internalized rage. Psychoanalytic treatment aims to bring the patient's repressed, conflicted instinctual drive derivatives under the hegemony of rational motives and, thereby, to enable the patient to live on a level of reality testing. In contrast, Kohut focused on a different set of psychic conflicts, and, thus, saw the aim of treatment as the "restoration of the self," that is, as the rehabilitation of what he termed the compensatory sectors of a patient's self structure (Kohut, *The Restoration of the Self*).

NOTES TO APPENDIX

1 We wish to acknowledge Jessica Heineman-Pieper's help with this Appendix.

2 Unless otherwise specified, we will use identity and identification interchangeably, since the construct of identification refers to an act or process that generates an identity.

3 In the body of this volume we discussed identification as a process of perceptual identity. Here our focus is on identification as a product of motive. The traditional construct of intentional meaning may appear to correspond to our application of motive to identity. However, with the exception of phenomenology (whose approach is unlike ours in being interpersonal and solipsistic), the traditional construct of intentional meaning is nearly always approached from a non-agency, third-person perspective.

4 Our construct of a form of identification defined by self-recognition is not an instance of the "mirror transference" posited by Kohut (*The Analysis of the Self*, pp. 123–124). "Caregiver" in our usage does not represent the self-object Kohut depicts (ibid., p. 3). The identity of self-recognition we describe intrinsically includes the caregiver's purposive motive to have her/his intrapsychic caregiving regulated by the child's intrapsychic agent-self. As a result, the child's sense of agency acquires the empirical meaning of self-regulatory causality.

5 This distinction must be qualified both with regard to the type of real that is in focus (e.g., the psychic reality of personal existence or the nonagency reality that is the object of the natural sciences and experimental psychology) and also with regard to the epistemic act per se, which differs according to the type of reality that is to be known.

6 In psychopathology, this experience of seeing oneself from a viewpoint outside of oneself can occur only solipsistically by means of the cognitive process Piaget termed "decentering" (*The Essential Piaget*, pp. 439–441).

7 For a recent example, see Robert N. Emde, "Development Terminable and Interminable," pp. 23–42.

8 Freud, *The Ego and the Id*, S.E., vol. 19, pp. 29–33, 37–39.

9 See Freud, "Mourning and Melancholia," *S.E.*, vol. 14, p. 249; *The Ego and the Id*, S.E., vol. 19, p. 48; and *New Introductory Lectures on Psycho-Analysis*, S.E., vol. 22, pp. 63–68.
   In addition to these two main types of identification, Freud had an abiding interest in identifications that occurred in the syndrome of hysteria and in

group psychology. He sometimes discussed these types of identifications in terms of imitation. To be consistent with his instinctual drive theory, it was especially important to Freud that he disprove the notion of an identification caused by herd behavior. Freud stated, "There is no doubt that something exists in us which, when we become aware of signs of an emotion in someone else, tends to make us fall into the same emotion . . . . we should have to say that what compels us to obey this tendency is imitation" (*Beyond the Pleasure Principle, S.E.*, vol. 18, p. 89). In response to his question of what induces imitation, Freud concludes that the proximal cause is the influence of suggestion, which, in turn, occurs on the basis of transference relationships that are determined by the instinctual drives. Instinctually derived identifications are intrinsic to Freud's reductionistic view of human nature.

10 Schwartz, "Drives, Affects, Behavior—and Learning," p. 475.

11 The positive affects he lists are: interest or excitement, enjoyment or joy, and surprise or startle. The negative affects are distress or anguish, fear or terror, shame or humiliation, contempt, disgust, and anger or rage (Tomkins, *Affect as Amplification*, pp. 142–143).

12 See Darwin, *The Expression of the Emotions in Man and Animals*, pp. 120, 347, 366.

13 During the classical age in Athens, the concern that identifications could lead to intense, unregulated, potentially harmful emotions is illustrated by the anecdote told about a performance of Aeschylus's "Eumenides," where several women spontaneously aborted after they were swept up by emotions stimulated by the tragic action (David Grene, public lecture, University of Chicago, February 22, 1987). This phenomenon of "emotional contagion" manifests the intrinsic relationship between identifications and affect. The question of the social significance of identifications that can be induced by emotional reactions stimulated by involvement with a work of art remains important.

14 The Western viewpoint that agency reality cannot maintain autonomous regulatory control over affect (nonagency reality) is exemplified by Plato's thoughts about the ethical significance of poetry and by Augustine's writings about carnal desire. As we discussed in the text, two important exceptions are Aristotle's notion of practical reason and Hutcheson's moral sense. However, neither Aristotle nor Hutcheson thought the potential exists for a conflict-free and pain-free type of self-regulatory stability.

15 From the viewpoint of evolutionary biology, Brooks and Wiley make an analogous assertion in their claim that in an organism instructional information (in a psychological context, this corresponds to our term agency reality) both has physical reality and also takes precedence over energy (in a psychological context, this corresponds to our term nonagency reality). That is, within the obvious limits of the effects of positive entropy, instructional information (agency reality) determines how energy (nonagency reality) will flow, that is, will be regulated (Brooks and Wiley, *Evolution as Entropy*, pp. 34–35).

16 It is interesting to note that ethological studies of imprinting suggest that nonveridical imprinting (appetitive nonveridical relationship behavior) will occur more strongly in animals in response to pain. See A. J. Riopelle, "Imprinting," *Encyclopedia of Psychology*, vol. 2, pp. 190–191.

17 Many Western thinkers have noted the indispensable role identification plays in the development and management of a stable society. Its role in maintaining the social order is the basis for the difference of opinion between Aristotle and Plato about the value of tragedy. Plato asserts in *The Republic* that moral virtue and happiness are inseparable. He argues that tragedy should be banned because it depends on a disparity between moral virtue and happiness. Though he agreed that the ethical ideal of happiness is a measure of moral virtue, Aristotle disagreed with Plato's view that tragedy should be banned.

18 See, e.g., Emde, "Development Terminable and Interminable," p. 32.

19 See, e.g. Basch, "The Concept of Affect," pp. 766–771 and "Empathic Understanding," pp. 101–128, and Lane and Schwartz, "Levels of Emotional Awareness," pp. 135–139.

20 After Freud, those psychoanalysts who conclude that prior to 18 months-of-age the infant has only a biological, in contrast to a reflective, psychological experience base this conclusion on studies (e.g., the work of Piaget) that focus on the infant's knowledge of the inanimate world. However, studies in the field of developmental psychology have begun to question the practice of using experimental findings from studies concerning the infant's knowledge of the inanimate world as a basis from which to speculate about the infant's capacity to have conscious, reflective thoughts about relationship experience with the animate world of caregiving relationships. Meltzoff, e.g., has reported studies that support the view that infants are capable of both representational thoughts and intermodal coordination at birth (Meltzoff, "Imitation, Intermodal Co-ordination and Representation in Early Infancy," pp. 108–109).

21 Subject, of course, to cultural, linguistic, and other environmental influences.

BIBLIOGRAPHY

Aboulafia, Mitchell. *The Mediating Self: Mead, Sartre, and Self-Determination.* New Haven, Conn.: Yale University Press, 1986.

Achinstein, Peter, and Barker, Stephen. *The Legacy of Logical Positivism.* Baltimore: Johns Hopkins University Press, 1969.

Adorno, Theodor W. *Against Epistemology.* Cambridge, Mass: MIT Press, 1985.

Adorno, Theodor. *Authoritarian Personality.* New York: Harper, 1950.

Adorno, Theodor. *Negative Dialects.* Translated by E. B. Ashton. New York: Seabury Press, 1973.

Ainsworth, Mary. "Infant-Mother Attachment." *American Psychologist* 34 (1979): 932−937.

Ainsworth, Mary. "Patterns of Infant-Mother Attachments: Antecedents and Effects on Development." *Bulletin of the New York Academy of Medicine* 61 (1985): 771−791.

Ainsworth, Mary, et al. *Patterns of Attachment: A Psychological Study of the Strange Situation.* Hillsdale, N.J.: Lawrence Erlbaum Associates, 1978.

Alexander, Franz. *Fundamentals of Psychoanalysis.* New York: W. W. Norton, 1948.

Alexander, Franz. *Psychoanalysis and Psychotherapy: Developments in Theory, Technique and Training.* London: Allen & Unwin, 1957.

Alexander, F.; French, T. M.; with Bacon, C. L., et al. *Psychoanalytic Therapy: Principles and Application.* New York: Ronald Press, 1946.

Alexander, Franz, and Ross, Helen. *Dynamic Psychiatry.* Chicago: University of Chicago Press, 1952.

Alexander, Franz, and Ross, Helen, eds. *The Impact of Freudian Psychiatry.* Chicago: University of Chicago Press, 1961.

Allport, Gordon W. *The Person in Psychology: Selected Essays.* Boston: Beacon Press, 1968.

Altmann, Jeanne. *Baboon Mothers and Infants.* Cambridge, Mass.: Harvard University Press, 1980.

Anthony, E. James, and Cohler, Bertram, eds. *The Invulnerable Child*. New York: Guilford Press, 1987.

Aristotle. *Aristotle's De Motu Animalium*. Translated by Martha Craven Nussbaum. Princeton, N.J.: Princeton University Press, 1985.

Aristotle. *Metaphysics*. Translated by W. D. Ross. In *The Complete Works of Aristotle*. Edited by Jonathan Barnes, pp. 1552–1728. Princeton, N.J.: Princeton University Press, 1984.

Aristotle. *Nicomachean Ethics*. Translated by W. D. Ross. In *Introduction to Aristotle*. Edited by Richard McKeon, pp. 1337–1581. New York: Random House, 1947.

Aristotle. *On the Soul*. Translated by J. A. Smith. In *The Complete Works of Aristotle*. Edited by Jonathan Barnes, pp. 641–692. Princeton, N.J.: Princeton University Press, 1984.

Aslin, R. N. "Experiential Influences and Sensitive Periods in Perceptual Development: A Unified Model." In *Development of Perception*. Vol. 2. Edited by R. N. Aslin, pp. 45–49. Hillsdale, N.J.: Academic Press, 1981.

Asquith, Peter, and Kyberg, Henry, eds. *Current Research in the Philosophy of Science*. East Lansing, Mich.: Philosophy of Science Association, 1979.

Atkinson, R. F. *Knowledge and Explanation in History: An Introduction to the Philosophy of History*. Ithaca, N.Y.: Cornell University Press, 1978.

Atwood, George, and Stolorow, R. D. *Structures of Subjectivity: Explorations in Psychoanalytic Phenomenology*. Hillsdale, N.J.: Analytic Press, 1984.

Ayer, A. J., ed. *Logical Positivism*. New York: Free Press, 1959.

Bakhtin, M. M. *The Dialogical Imagination: Four Essays*. Austin: University of Texas Press, 1981.

Balint, Michael. *The Basic Fault*. London: Tavistock, 1968.

Barratt, Barnaby B. *Psychic Reality and Psychoanalytic Knowing*. New York: Analytic Press, 1984.

Basch, Michael. "The Concept of Affect: A Re-examination." *Journal of the American Psychoanalytic Society* 24 (1976): 759–777.

Basch, Michael. *Doing Psychotherapy*. New York: Basic Books, 1980.

Basch, Michael F. "Empathic Understanding: A Review of the Concept and Some Theoretical Considerations." *Journal of the American Psychoanalytic Association* 31 (1983): 101–126.

Basch, Michael. *Understanding Psychotherapy: The Science Behind the Art*. New York: Basic Books, 1988.

Beck, Lewis W. "What Have We Learned from Kant?" In *Self and Nature in Kant's Philosophy*. Edited by A. W. Wood, pp. 17–30. Ithaca, N.Y.: Cornell University Press, 1984.

Beiser, Frederick C. *The Fate of Reason: German Philosophy from Kant to Fichte*. Cambridge, Mass.: Harvard University Press, 1987.

Bellak, Leopold. "Free Association: Conceptual and Clinical Aspects." *International Journal of Psychoanalysis* 42 (1961): 9–20.

Bellak, Leopold, and Small, S. *Emergency Psychotherapy and Brief Psychotherapy.* New York: Grune & Stratton, 1965.

Bergson, Henri. *Creative Evolution.* Translated by Arthur Mitchel. New York: H. Holt, 1911.

Berlin, Isaiah. *Vico and Herder: Two Studies in the History of Ideas.* London: Chatto & Windus, 1980.

Bernard, Claude. *An Introduction to the Study of Experimental Medicine.* Translated by Henry C. Green. New York: Dover Publications, 1957.

Berneld, S. "Freud's Earliest Theories and the School of Helmholtz." *Psychoanalytic Quarterly* 13 (1944): 341–362.

Bernstein, Mary, ed. *Maternal Responsiveness: Characteristics and Consequences.* San Francisco: Jossey-Bass, 1989.

Bettelheim, Bruno. *The Empty Fortress.* New York: The Free Press, 1967.

Bettelheim, Bruno. *Love Is Not Enough: The Treatment of Emotionally Disturbed Children.* Glencoe, Ill.: The Free Press, 1950.

Bhaskar, Roy. *The Possibility of Naturalism: A Philosophical Critique of the Contemporary Human Sciences.* Atlantic Highlands, N.J.: Humanities Press, 1979.

Bhaskar, Roy. *A Realist Theory of Science.* Atlantic Highlands, N.J.: Humanities Press, 1978.

Bion, W. R. *Attention and Interpretation.* London: Tavistock, 1970.

Bion, W. R. *Elements of Psycho-Analysis.* London: Heinemann, 1963.

Bion, W. R. *Experiences in Groups.* New York: Basic Books, 1959.

Bion, W. R. "Group Dynamics: A Re-View." *International Journal of Psychoanalysis* 33 (1952): 235–247.

Blatt, Sidney. "Levels of Object Representation in Anaclitic and Introjective Depression." *Psychoanalytic Study of the Child* 29 (1974): 107–157.

Blum, Harold. *Time's Arrow and Evolution.* 2d ed. Princeton, N.J.: Princeton University Press, 1955.

Boring, Edwin. *A History of Experimental Psychology.* New York: Century, 1929.

Bowlby, John. *Attachment and Loss.* 2d ed. 2 vols. New York: Basic Books, 1982.

Bowlby, John. "Developmental Psychiatry Comes of Age." *American Journal of Psychiatry* 145 (1988): 1–10.

Bowlby, John. "Psychoanalysis and Child Care." In *Psychoanalysis and Contemporary Theory.* Edited by J. D. Sutherland. London: Hogarth Press, 1958.

Brazelton, T. Berry. *Infants and Mothers: Differences and Development.* New York: Delta, 1969.

Brazelton, T. Berry, and Yogman, Michael, eds. *Affective Development in Infancy.* Norwood, N.J.: Ablex, 1986.

Breier, Alan; Kelsoe, John; Kirwin, Paul; et al. "Early Parental Loss and Development of Adult Psychopathology." *Archives of General Psychiatry* 45 (1988): 987–993.

Brenner, Charles. *Psychoanalytic Technique and Psychic Conflict.* New York: International Universities Press, 1970.

Brenner, Charles, and Arlow, Jacob. *Psychoanalytic Concepts and the Structural Theory.* New York: International Universities Press, 1964.

Brentano, Franz. *Psychology from an Empirical Standpoint.* Translated by A. C. Rancurello, D. B. Terrel, and L. L. McAllister. English edition edited by L. L. McAllister. New York: Humanities Press, 1973.

Bridgman, Percy Williams. *The Logic of Modern Physics.* New York: Macmillan, 1927.

Brooks, Daniel R., and Wiley, E. O. *Evolution as Entropy: Toward a Unified Theory of Biology.* Chicago: University of Chicago Press, 1988.

Brothers, Leslie. "A Biological Perspective on Empathy." *American Journal of Psychiatry* 146 (1989): 10–19.

Brown, Harold. *Perception, Theory and Commitment: The New Philosophy of Science.* Chicago: University of Chicago Press, 1977.

Brown, Richard; Harvey, Lyman; and Stanford, M. *Structure, Consciousness and History.* Cambridge: Cambridge University Press, 1978.

Bruner, Jerome. *Actual Minds, Possible Worlds.* Cambridge, Mass.: Harvard University Press, 1986.

Bruner, Jerome. *In Search of Mind.* New York: Harper & Row, 1983.

Bruner, Jerome. *On Knowing: Essays for the Left Hand.* Cambridge, Mass.: Belknap Press of Harvard University Press, 1979.

Bruner, Jerome, et al. *Studies in Cognitive Growth.* New York: John Wiley & Sons, 1966.

Bruner, Jerome. *Under Five in Britain.* London: Grant McIntyre, 1980.

Bruner, Jerome, and Garton, Alison, eds. *Human Growth and Development.* Oxford: Clarendon Press, 1978.

Bruner, Jerome, and Haste, Helen, eds. *Making Sense: The Child's Construction of the World.* London: Metheun, 1987.

Bruner, Jerome, with Watson, Anita. *Child's Talk.* New York: W. W. Norton, 1983.

Buber, Martin. *I and Thou.* Translated by Walter Kaufmann. New York: Scribner, 1970.

Buck-Morss, Susan. *The Origin of Negative Dialectics: Theodor W. Adorno, Walter Benjamin, and the Frankfurt Institute.* New York: Free Press, 1977.

Carnap, Rudolf. *The Logical Structure of the World and Pseudoproblems in Philosophy.* Translated by Rolf E. George. Berkeley: University of California Press, 1967.

Carnap, Rudolf. *Philosophy and Logical Syntax.* London: Kegan Paul, Trench, Trubner & Co., 1935.

Carroll, Lewis. *Alice's Adventures in Wonderland.* New York: New American Library, 1960.

Cassirer, Ernst. *The Problem of Knowledge: Philosophy, Science, and History Since Hegel.* Translated by William H. Woglom, M.D., and Charles W. Hendel. New Haven, Conn.: Yale University Press, 1978.

Chambers, Winifred. "Clinical Interpretations and the Debate over the Scientific Acceptability of Psychoanalysis." Ph.D. Dissertation, University of Chicago, 1975.

Charcot, Jean Martin. *Lectures on the Disease of the Nervous System.* Translated and edited by George Sigerson. New York: Hafner, 1962

Chomsky, Noam. *Aspects of the Theory of Syntax.* Cambridge, Mass.: MIT Press, 1965.

Clarke-Stewart, Alison. "And Daddy Makes Three: The Father's Impact on Mother and Young Child." *Child Development* 49 (1978): 466–478.

Clarke-Stewart, Alison. "Dealing with the Complexity of Mother-Child Interaction." Paper presented at the Society for Research in Child Development, Denver, April 1975.

Coles, Gerald. *The Learning Mystique: A Critical Look at "Learning Disabilities."* New York: Pantheon Books, 1987.

Coles, Robert. *Children of Crisis: A Study of Courage and Fear.* Boston: Little Brown, 1964.

Colodny, Robert, ed. *Mind and Cosmos: Essays in Contemporary Science and Philosophy.* Pittsburgh: University of Pittsburgh Press, 1966.

Comte, Auguste. *Auguste Comte and Positivism: The Essential Writings.* Translated and edited by Gertrud Lenzer. New York: Harper & Row, 1975.

Coppleston, Frederick. *A History of Philosophy.* 9 vols. New York: Doubleday, 1960.

Cronbach, Lee. "Beyond the Two Disciplines of Scientific Psychology." *American Psychologist* 30 (1975): 116–127.

D'Arcy, Martin. *The Mind and Heart of Love: Lion and Unicorn, a Study in Eros and Agape.* New York: Henry Holt, 1947.

Darwin, Charles. *The Expression of the Emotions in Man and Animals.* Chicago: University of Chicago Press, 1965.

Darwin, Charles. *On the Origin of the Species: A Facsimile of the First Edition.* Cambridge, Mass.: Harvard University Press, 1966.

Davidson, Donald. *Essays on Actions and Events.* Oxford: Clarendon Press, 1980.

Derrida, Jacques. *Of Grammatology*. Translated by Gayatri Chakravorty Spivak. Baltimore: Johns Hopkins University Press, 1976.

Descartes, René. *Discourse on Method and Meditations*. Translated by Lawrence J. Lafleur. New York: Liberal Arts Press, 1980.

Diagnostic and Statistical Manual of Mental Disorders: DSM-III. 3d ed., rev. Prepared by the Task Force on Nomenclature and Statistics of the American Psychiatric Association. Washington, D.C.: American Psychiatric Association, 1987.

Dilthey, Wilhelm. *Descriptive Psychology and Human Understanding*. Translated by Richard M. Zaner and Kenneth L. Heiges. The Hague: Martinus Nijhoff, 1977.

Dilthey, Wilhelm. *Meaning in History: W. Dilthey's Thoughts on History and Society*. Translated and edited by H. P. Rickman. London: Allen & Unwin, 1981.

Dostoevsky, Fyodor. *Crime and Punishment*. Translated by David Magarshak. Harmondsworth: Penguin Books, 1952.

Dostoevsky, Fyodor. *Notes from the Underground*. Translated by Jesse Coulson. Harmondsworth: Penguin Books, 1972.

Dreyfus, Hubert L., and Rabinow, Paul. *Michel Foucault: Beyond Structuralism and Hermeneutics*. Chicago: University of Chicago Press, 1983.

Eagle, Morris. *Recent Developments in Psychoanalysis: A Critical Evaluation*. Cambridge, Mass.: Harvard University Press, 1987.

Eissler, Kurt R. *Leonardo da Vinci: Psychoanalytic Notes on the Enigma*. New York: International Universities Press, 1961.

Ellenberger, Henri F. *The Discovery of the Unconscious: The History and Evolution of Dynamic Psychiatry*. New York: Basic Books, 1970.

Elsa, Irene. *The Female Animal*. New York: H. Holt, 1988.

Emde, Robert N. "Development Terminable and Interminable." *International Journal of Psychoanalysis* 69 (1988): 23–42.

Encyclopedia of Psychology. Edited by Raymond Corsini. 4 vols. New York: John Wiley & Sons, 1984.

Erikson, Eric. *Childhood and Society*. New York: W. W. Norton, 1950.

Fairbairn, W. R. D. *An Object-Relations Theory of Personality*. New York: Basic Books, 1952.

Fairbairn, W. R. D. *Psychoanalytic Studies of the Personality*. London: Tavistock, 1952.

Feuerbach, Ludwig Andreas. *Principles of the Philosophy of the Future*. Translated by Manfred Vogel. Indianapolis, Ind.: Hackett, 1986.

Feuerbach, Ludwig Andreas. *Thoughts on Death and Immortality*. Translated by James Massey. Berkeley: University of California Press, 1980.

Feyerabend, Paul. "Problems of Empiricism." In *Beyond the Edge of Certainty: Essays in Contemporary Science and Philosophy*. Edited by Robert Colodny, pp. 145–260. Englewood Cliffs, N.J.: Prentice Hall, 1965.

Field, Tiffany, and Fogel, Alan. *Emotion and Early Interaction.* Hillsdale, N.J.: Lawrence Erlbaum Associates, 1982.

Flew, Anthony, ed. *A Dictionary of Philosophy.* 2d ed., rev. New York: St. Martin's Press, 1984.

Flew, Antony, and Vesey, Godfrey. *Agency and Necessity.* New York: Basil Blackwell, 1987.

Fodor, Jerry. *Psychosemantics: The Problem of Meaning in the Philosophy of Mind.* Cambridge, Mass.: MIT Press, 1987.

Fogel, Alan. *Infancy: Infant, Family and Society.* St. Paul, Minn.: West, 1984.

Fogel, Alan, and Melson, Gail, eds. *Origins of Nurturance: Developmental, Biological, and Cultural Perspective on Caregiving.* Hillsdale, N.J.: Lawrence Erlbaum Associates, 1986.

Frankl, Victor E. *The Will to Meaning: Foundations and Applications of Logotherapy.* New York: New American Library, 1981.

Freedman, David A. "Maturational and Developmental Issues in the First Year." In *The Course of Life: Psychoanalytic Contributions toward Understanding Personality Development.* Vol. 1, *Infancy and Early Childhood.* Edited by Stanley Greenspan and George Pollock, pp. 129–145. East Adelphi, Md.: U.S. Department of Health and Human Services, Public Health Service, 1980.

French, Thomas M. "Brief Psychotherapy in Bronchial Asthma." In *Psychoanalytic Interpretations: The Selected Papers of Thomas M. French.* Chicago: Quadrangle Books, 1970.

Freud, Anna. *The Ego and the Mechanisms of Defense.* New York: International Universities Press, 1936.

Freud, Sigmund. *The Standard Edition of the Complete Psychological Works of Sigmund Freud.* 24 vols. Edited by James Strachey in collaboration with Anna Freud. London: Hogarth Press, 1953–1974.

Gadamer, Hans-Georg. *Truth and Method.* Translated by Sheed and Ward. Edited by Garrett Barden and John Cumming. New York: Crossroads, 1986.

Gadlin, Howard, and Ingle, Grant. "Through the One-Way Mirror: The Limits of Experimental Self-Reflection." *American Psychologist* 30 (1975): 1003–1009.

Gay, Peter. *Freud: A Life for Our Time.* New York: W. W. Norton, 1988.

Gedo, John E., and Goldberg, Arnold. *Models of the Mind: A Psychoanalytic Theory.* Chicago: University of Chicago Press, 1973.

Gedo, John, and Pollock, George, eds. *Freud: The Fusion of Science and Humanism; the Intellectual History of Psychoanalysis.* New York: International Universities Press, 1976.

Geertz, Clifford. "The Impact of the Concept of Culture on the Concept of Man." *Bulletin of the Atomic Scientists* 12 (1966): 1–8.

Gellner, Ernest. *Plough, Sword, and Book: The Structure of Human History.* Chicago: University of Chicago Press, 1989.

Gill, Merton. "The Analysis of Transference." *Journal of the American Psychoanalytic Association Supplement* 27 (1979): 263–288.

Gill, Merton, and Holzman, Philip. *Psychology versus Metapsychology.* Psychological Issues Monographs, no. 36. New York: International Universities Press, 1976.

Gilson, Etienne. *Linguistics and Philosophy: An Essay on the Philosophical Constants of Language.* Translated by John Lyon. Notre Dame, Ind.: University of Notre Dame Press, 1988.

Gilson, Etienne. *The Unity of Philosophical Experience.* New York: Scribner's Sons, 1937.

Gleick, James. *Chaos: Making a New Science.* New York: Penguin Books, 1987.

Glover, Jonathan. *The Philosophy of Mind.* New York: Oxford University Press, 1976.

Gottlieb, Gilbert. "Roles of Early Experience in Species-Specific Perceptual Development." In *Development of Perception.* Edited by R. N. Aslin, J. R. Alberts, and M. R. Petersen. Vol. 1, pp. 5–44. New York: Academic Press, 1981.

Gottlieb, Gilbert, ed. *Studies on the Development of Behavior and the Nervous System.* 3 Vols. New York: Academic Press, 1976.

Green, Wayne H.; Campbell, Magda; and David, Raphael. "Psychosocial Dwarfism: A Critical Review of the Evidence." *Journal of the American Academy of Child Psychiatry* 23 (1984): 39–48.

Greenberg, Jay R., and Mitchell, Stephen A. *Object Relations and Psychoanalytic Theory.* Cambridge, Mass.: Harvard University Press, 1983.

Greenson, Ralph. *Technique and Practice of Psychoanalysis.* New York: International Universities Press, 1967.

Greenspan, Stanley. "The Development of the Ego: Insights from Clinical Work with Infants and Young Children." *Journal of the American Psychoanalytic Association* 36 (1988): 3–56.

Greenspan, Stanley, and Pollock, George, eds. *The Course of Life: Psychoanalytic Contributions toward Understanding Personality Development.* Vol. 1, *Infancy and Early Childhood.* East Adelphi, Md.: U.S. Department of Health and Human Services, Public Health Service, 1980.

Gregory, Richard L., ed. *The Oxford Companion of the Mind.* New York: Oxford University Press, 1987.

Grice, H. Paul. "Logic and Conversation." In *Syntax and Semantics 3: Speech Acts.* Edited by Peter Cole and Jerry Morgan, pp. 41–58. New York: Academic Press, 1975.

Grice, H. Paul. "Meaning." *Philosophical Review* 66 (1957): 377–388.

Griffin, Donald. "Animal Thinking." *American Scientist* 72 (1984): 456–464.

Grunbaum, Adolf. *The Foundations of Psychoanalysis: A Philosophical Critique.* Berkeley: University of California Press, 1984.

Gubernick, David, and Klopfer, Peter. *Parental Care in Mammals.* New York: Plenum, 1981.

Guntrip, Harry. *Personality Structure and Human Interaction.* New York: International Universities Press, 1961.

Habermas, Jurgen. *Knowledge and Human Interests.* Translated by J. Shapiro. Boston: Beacon Press, 1971.

Haeckel, Ernst H. *The History of Creation, or The Development of the Earth and its Inhabitants by the Action of Natural Causes.* New York: D. Appleton, 1876.

Haeckel, Ernst H. *The Riddle of the Universe.* New York: Harper & Bros., 1902.

Hampshire, Stuart. *Spinoza.* London: Faber & Faber, 1956.

Hanson, Norwood. *Patterns of Discovery.* Cambridge: Cambridge University Press, 1958.

Harré, R. *The Philosophies of Science: An Introductory Survey.* Oxford: Oxford University Press, 1972.

Hartmann, Heinz. *Ego Psychology and the Problem of Adaptation.* Translated by David Rappaport. New York: International Universities Press, 1958.

Hartmann, Heinz. *Essays on Ego Psychology: Selected Problems in Psychoanalytic Theory.* New York: International Universities Press, 1964.

Hegel, Georg W. F. *The Phenomenology of Mind.* Translated by J. B. Baillie. London: Allen & Unwin, 1949.

Hegel, Georg W. F. *Phenomenology of Spirit.* Translated by A. V. Miller. Edited by J. N. Findlay. Oxford: Oxford University Press, 1977.

Heidegger, Martin. *Being and Time.* Translated by J. Macquarrie. New York: Harper, 1962.

Heidegger, Martin. *An Introduction to Metaphysics.* Translated by Ralph Manheim. New Haven, Conn.: Yale University Press, 1959.

Heidegger, Martin. *What Is Called Thinking?* Translated by J. Glenn Gray. New York: Harper & Row, 1968.

Heineman (Pieper), Martha. "The Obsolete Scientific Imperative in Social Work Research." *Social Service Review* 55 (1981): 371–397.

Helmholtz, Hermann von. *Physiological Optics.* Leipzig: Vosos, 1856–1866.

Hempel, Carl. *Aspects of Scientific Explanation and Other Essays in the Philosophy of Science.* New York: Free Press, 1965.

Hempel, Carl. "Recent Problems of Induction." In *Mind and Cosmos: Essays in Contemporary Science and Philosophy.* Edited by Robert Colodny, pp. 112–134. Pittsburgh: University of Pittsburgh Press, 1966.

Heraclitus of Ephesis. *Fragments.* Translated by T. M. Robinson. Toronto and Buffalo: University of Toronto Press, 1987.

Herder, Johann Gottfried. *Reflections on the Philosophy of the History of Mankind.* Translated by T. O. Churchill. Chicago: University of Chicago Press, 1968.

Hess, Eckhard H. *Imprinting: Early Experience and the Developmental Psychobiology of Attachment.* New York: Nostrand Reinhold, 1973.

Hilgard, Ernest; Atkinson, Rita; and Atkinson, Richard. *Introduction to Psychology.* 7th ed. New York: Harcourt Brace Jovanovich, 1953.

Hollis, Martin. *Models of Man: Philosophical Thoughts on Social Action.* Cambridge: Cambridge University Press, 1977.

Holt, Robert. "A Review of Some of Freud's Biological Assumptions and Their Influence on His Theories." In *Psychoanalysis and Current Biological Thought.* Edited by Norman Greenfield and William Lewis, pp. 93–124. Madison: University of Wisconsin Press, 1963.

Holt, Robert. "Drive or Wish? A Reconsideration of the Psychoanalytic Theory of Motivation." *Psychological Issues* 9 (1976): 158–197.

Hook, Sidney. "Science and Mythology in Psychoanalysis." In *Psychoanalysis, Scientific Method and Philosophy.* Edited by Sidney Hook, pp. 212–224. New York: New York University Press, 1969.

Horan, Patrick. "Is Status Attainment Research Atheoretical?" *American Sociological Review* 43 (1978): 534–541.

Hugo, Victor. *Les Miserables.* Translated by Norman Denny. Harmondsworth: Penguin Books, 1982.

Hull, David. "The Operational Imperative: Sense and Nonsense in Operationalism." *Systematic Zoology* 17 (1968): 438–457.

Hume, David. *A Treatise of Human Nature.* Edited by L. A. Selby-Bigge and P. H. Nidditch. Oxford: Oxford University Press, 1978.

Hume, David. *Enquiries Concerning Human Understanding and Concerning the Principles of Morals.* 3d ed. Edited by P. H. Nidditch. Oxford: Clarendon Press, 1975.

Husserl, Edmund. *Cartesian Meditations: An Introduction to Phenomenology.* Translated by Dorian Cairns. The Hague: Martinus Nijhoff, 1960.

Hutcheson, Francis. *Illustrations on the Moral Sense.* Edited by Bernard Peach. Cambridge, Mass.: Belknap Press, 1971.

Inderbitzin, L. B. "Patient's Sleep on the Analytic Couch." *Journal of the American Psychoanalytic Association* (1988): 673–695.

Jakacki, Regina. "Pulsatile Secretion of Luteinizing Hormone in Children." *Journal of Clinical Endocrinology and Metabolism* 55 (1982): 453–458.

Jakobson, Roman, and Halle, Morris. *Fundamentals of Language.* The Hague: Mouton, 1971.

James, William. "Does Consciousness Exist?" In *Essays in Radical Empiricism,* pp. 3–20. Cambridge, Mass.: Harvard University Press, 1976.

James, William. *Varieties of Religious Experience.* New York: Random House, 1929.

374

Bibliography

James, William. "The Will to Believe." In *Essays in Pragmatism*. Edited by Alburey Castell, pp. 88–109. New York: Hafner, 1948.

James, William. *The Writings of William James*. Edited by John McDermott. Chicago: University of Chicago Press, 1977.

Jaspers, Karl. *General Psychopathology*. Chicago: University of Chicago Press, 1963.

Jaspers, Karl. *Philosophy*. 3 vols. Chicago: University of Chicago Press, 1960.

Jay, Martin. *Adorno*. Cambridge, Mass.: Harvard University Press, 1984.

Joffe, W. J., and Sandler, J. "Notes on Pain, Depression, and Individuation." *The Psychoanalytic Study of the Child* 20 (1965): 394–424.

Jones, Ernest. *The Life and Work of Sigmund Freud*. 3 vols. New York: Basic Books, 1953–1957.

Jones, W. T. *A History of Western Philosophy*. 4 vols. New York: Harcourt Brace Jovanovich, 1975.

Jung, Carl G. *Analytical Psychology: Its Theory and Practice*. New York: Random House, 1970.

Jung, Carl. *The Collected Works of Carl Jung*. Edited by Sir Herbert Read, et al. Translated by R. F. C. Hull. Princeton, N.J.: Princeton University Press, 1969.

Kagan, Jerome. *Change and Continuity in Infancy*. New York: John Wiley, 1971.

Kagan, Jerome. *The Growth of the Child*. New York: W. W. Norton, 1978.

Kagan, Jerome. *The Second Year*. Cambridge, Mass.: Harvard University Press, 1981.

Kagan, Jerome; Kearsley, Richard; and Zelazo, Philip. *Infancy: Its Place in Human Development*. Cambridge, Mass.: Harvard University Press, 1980.

Kahneman, Daniel; Slovic, Paul; and Tversky, Amos, eds. *Judgment under Uncertainty: Heuristics and Biases*. New York: Cambridge University Press, 1987.

Kant, Immanuel. *Critique of Judgment*. Translated by J. H. Bernard. New York: Hafner, 1951.

Kant, Immanuel. *Critique of Practical Reason*. Translated by Lewis Beck. Indianapolis, Ind.: Bobbs-Merrill, 1956.

Kant, Immanuel. *Critique of Pure Reason*. Translated by Norman Kemp Smith. London: Macmillan, 1933.

Katan, Anny. "The Infant's First Reaction to Strangers: Distress or Anxiety." *International Journal of Psychoanalysis* 53 (1972): 501–503.

Kaye, Kenneth. *The Mental and Social Life of Babies: How Parents Create Persons*. Chicago: University of Chicago Press, 1982.

Keat, Russell. "Positivism, Naturalism, and Anti-Naturalism in the Social Sciences." *Journal for the Theory of Social Behaviour* 1 (1971): 3–17.

Keats, John. "Letter to George and Thomas Keats, Sunday, Dec. 22, 1817." In *The Poetical Works and Other Writings of John Keats*. Edited by H. Buxton Forman. Vol. 6, pp. 101–104. New York: Charles Scribner, 1939.

Kegan, Robert. *The Evolving Self: Problem and Process in Human Development.* Cambridge, Mass.: Harvard University Press, 1982.

Kelley, Harold H. "The Process of Causal Attribution." *American Psychologist* 28 (1973): 107–128.

Kelly, George. "A Psychology of the Optimal Man." In *Personal Construct Psychology: Psychotherapy and Personality.* Edited by A. W. Landfield and L. M. Leitner. New York: John Wiley, 1980.

Kernberg, Otto. *Borderline Conditions and Pathological Narcissism.* New York: J. Aronson, 1975.

Kierkegaard, Soren. *Concluding Unscientific Postscript.* Translated by David Swanson. Edited by Walter Lowrie. Princeton, N.J.: Princeton University Press, 1946.

Kierkegaard, Soren. *Fear and Trembling.* Translated by Walter Lowrie. Princeton, N.J.: Princeton University Press, 1941.

Kierkegaard, Soren, *The Sickness Unto Death.* Translated by Walter Lowrie. Princeton, N.J.: Princeton University Press, 1968.

Klein, George. *Perception, Motive and Personality.* New York: Knopf, 1970.

Klein, George. "Peremptory Ideation: Structure and Force in Motivated Ideas." *Psychological Issues.* Vol. 5, pp. 80–128. New York: International Universities Press, 1967.

Klein, George. *Psychoanalytic Theory: An Exploration of Essentials.* New York: International Universities Press, 1976.

Klein, Melanie. *Contributions to Psychoanalysis, 1921–1945.* London: Hogarth Press, 1948.

Klein, Melanie. *Envy and Gratitude and Other Works, 1946–1963.* London: Hogarth Press, 1975.

Klein, Melanie. *Narrative of a Child Analysis: The Conduct of the Psycho-analysis of Children as Seen in the Treatment of a Ten-Year-Old Boy.* New York: Delacorte Press, 1975.

Klein, Melanie. *Our Adult World and Other Essays.* New York: Basic Books, 1963.

Klein, Melanie. *The Psychoanalysis of Children.* Rev. ed. Translated by Alix Strachey. Edited by H. A. Thorner with the collaboration of Alix Strachey. New York: Delacorte Press, 1975.

Kline, Morris. *Mathematics: The Loss of Certainty.* New York: Oxford University Press, 1980.

Kohut, Heinz. *The Analysis of the Self: A Systematic Approach to the Psychoanalytic Treatment of Narcissistic Personality Disorders.* New York: International Universities Press, 1971.

Kohut, Heinz. *How Does Analysis Cure?* Edited by Arnold Goldberg with the collaboration of Paul Stepansky. Chicago: University of Chicago Press, 1984.

Kohut, Heinz. *The Search for the Self: Selected Writings of Heinz Kohut, 1950–1978.* 2 vols. Edited by Paul H. Ornstein. New York: International Universities Press, 1978.

Kohut, Heinz. *The Restoration of the Self*. New York: International Universities Press, 1977.

Kohut, Heinz. *Self-psychology and the Humanities: Reflections on a New Psychoanalytic Approach*. Edited by Charles B. Strozier. New York: W. W. Norton, 1985.

Kris, Ernst. *Psychoanalytic Explorations in Art*. New York: International Universities Press, 1952.

Kris, Ernst. *Selected Papers of Ernst Kris*. New Haven, Conn.: Yale University Press, 1975.

Kuhn, Thomas. *The Structure of Scientific Revolutions*. 2d ed. Chicago: University of Chicago Press, 1977.

Kulin, Howard; Moore, Robert; and Santner, Steven. "Circadian Rhythms in Gonadotropin Excretion in Prepubertal and Pubertal Children." *Journal of Clinical Endocrinology and Metabolism* 46 (1976): 770–773.

Kulin, Howard, and Reiter, Edward. "Gonadotropins During Childhood and Adolescence: A Review." *Pediatrics* 51 (1973): 260–171.

Lacan, Jacques. *Ecrits: A Selection*. Translated and edited by Alan Sheridan. New York: W. W. Norton, 1977.

Lacan, Jacques. *The Four Fundamental Concepts of Psychoanalysis*. Translated by Alan Sheridan. Edited by Jacques-Alain Miller. London: Hogarth Press, 1977.

Lacan, Jacques. *The Language of the Self: The Function of Language in Psychoanalysis*. Translated by Anthony Wilden. Baltimore: Johns Hopkins University Press, 1968.

Lamarck, Jean Baptiste. *Zoological Philosophy: An Exposition with Regard to the Natural History of Animals*. Translated by Hugh Elliot. Chicago: University of Chicago Press, 1984.

Lamiell, James T. *The Psychology of Personality: An Epistemological Inquiry*. New York: Columbia University Press, 1987.

Lane, Richard D., and Schwartz, Gary. "Levels of Emotional Awareness: A Cognitive-Developmental Theory and Its Application to Psychopathology." *American Journal of Psychiatry* 144 (1987): 133–143.

Lange, Carl Georg, and James, William. *The Emotions*. Baltimore: Williams & Wilkins, 1922.

Langer, Susanne. *Mind: An Essay on Human Feeling*. 2 vols. Baltimore, Md.: Johns Hopkins University Press, 1967.

Langer, Susanne. *Philosophy in a New Key: A Study in the Symbolism of Reason, Rite, and Art*. 3d ed. Cambridge, Mass.: Harvard University Press, 1980.

Laudan, Larry. "Historical Methodologies: An Overview and Manifesto." In *Current Research in the Philosophy of Science*. Edited by Peter Asquith and Henry Kyberg, pp. 40–54. East Lansing, Mich.: Philosophy of Science Association, 1979.

Lehrer, Keith. *Knowledge*. Oxford: Clarendon Press, 1974.

Leibniz, Gotthold. *New Essays on Human Understanding*. Translated and edited by P. Remnant and J. Bennett. Cambridge: Cambridge University Press, 1951.

LeVine, Robert A. *Culture, Behavior, and Personality: An Introduction to the Comparative Study of Psychosocial Adaptation*. New York: Aldine, 1982.

LeVine, Robert A. "Knowledge and Fallibility in Anthropological Field Research." In *Scientific Inquiry and the Social Sciences*. Edited by Marilyn Brewer and Barry Collins. San Francisco: Jossey-Bass, 1981.

LeVine, Robert; Miller, Patrice; and West, Mary, eds. *Parental Behavior in Diverse Societies*. San Francisco: Jossey-Bass, 1988.

Levins, Richard, and Lewontin, Richard. *The Dialectical Biologist*. Cambridge, Mass.: Harvard University Press, 1985.

Lewin, Karl K. *Brief Psychotherapy, Brief Encounters*. New York: Bruner/Mazel, 1971.

Lewontin, Richard. "Adaptation." *Scientific American* 239 (1978): 213–229.

Lichtenberg, Joseph. "A Theory of Motivational-functional Systems as Psychic Structures." *Journal of the American Psychoanalytic Association* 36 (1988): 57–73.

Locke, John. *An Essay Concerning Human Understanding*. Edited by P. H. Nidditch. Oxford: Clarendon Press, 1975.

Lorenz, Konrad. *On Aggression*. Translated by Marjorie Kerr Wilson. New York: Harcourt, Brace and World, 1966.

Lorenz, Konrad. "Companionship in Bird Life" In *Instinctive Behavior*. Translated and edited by Claire Schiller, pp. 83–128. New York: International Universities Press, 1957.

Lorenz, Konrad. *Evolution and Modification of Behavior*. Chicago: University of Chicago Press, 1986.

Lorenz, Konrad. *The Foundations of Ethology*. Translated by K. Lorenz and R. W. Kickert. New York: Springer-Verlag, 1981.

Lovejoy, Arthur O. *Reflections on Human Nature*. Baltimore: Johns Hopkins University Press, 1961.

Lovejoy, C. Owen. "The Origin of Man." *Science* 23 (1981): 341–350.

McKenna, James J. "Primate Infant Caregiving Behavior: Origins, Consequences and Variability with Emphasis on the Common Indian Langur Monkey." In *Parental Care in Mammals*. Edited by David J. Gubernik and Peter H. Klopfer. New York: Plenum, 1981.

Mackenzie, Brian. "Darwinism and Positivism as Methodological Influences on the Development of Psychology." *Journal of the History of the Behavioral Sciences* 12 (1976): 330–337.

Macmurray, John. *The Self As Agent*. London: Faber & Faber, 1952.

Macmurray, John. *Persons in Relation*. London: Faber & Faber, 1961.

Mahler, Margaret. *The Selected Papers of Margaret Mahler*. New York: J. Aronson, 1979.

Mahler, Margaret, with Furer, Manuel. *On Human Symbiosis and the Vicissitudes of Individuation*. New York: International Universities Press, 1968.

Mahler, Margaret, and Gosliner, B. J. "On Symbiotic Child Psychosis: Genetic, Dynamic and Restitutive Aspects." In *The Psychoanalytic Study of the Child.* Vol. 10, pp. 195–212. New York: International Universities Press, 1955.

Mahler, Margaret, and McDevitt, John. "The Separation-Individuation Process and Identity Formation." In *The Course of Life: Psychoanalytic Contributions toward Understanding Personality Development.* Edited by Stanley Greenspan and George Pollock, pp. 395–406. East Adelphi, Md.: U.S. Department of Health and Human Services, Public Health Service, 1980.

Mahler, Margaret, with Pine, Fred, and Bergman, Anni. *The Psychological Birth of the Human Infant: Symbiosis and Individuation.* New York: Basic Books, 1975.

Malan, D. *A Study of Brief Psychotherapy.* London: Tavistock, 1963.

Malcolm, Janet. *In the Freud Archives.* New York: Knopf, 1984.

Malcolm, Janet. *Psychoanalysis, the Impossible Profession.* New York: Knopf, 1981.

Marcel, Gabriel. *Being and Having: An Existentialist Diary.* Translated by Katherine Farrer. Westminster: Dacre Press, 1949.

Marcel, Gabriel. *The Philosophy of Existentialism.* Translated by Marya Harari. New York: Citadel Press, 1961.

Margulies, Alfred. *The Empathic Imagination.* New York: W. W. Norton, 1989.

Marshall, John C., and Kelch, Robert. "Gonadotropin-Releasing Hormone: Role of Pulsatile Secretion in the Regulation of Reproduction." *New England Journal of Medicine* 23 (1986): 1459–1468.

Marx, Karl. *A Contribution to the Critique of Political Economy.* Translated by S. W. Ryazanskaya. New York: International Publishers, 1981.

Marx, Karl, and Engels, Friedrich. *The Communist Manifesto.* Translated by Samuel Moore. Harmondsworth: Penguin Books, 1967.

Marcus Aurelius. *The Meditations.* Translated by G. M. A. Grube. Indianapolis, Ind.: Hackett, 1983.

Maslow, Abraham H. *Dominance, Self-esteem, Self-actualization: Germinal Papers of A. H. Maslow.* Edited by Richard J. Lowry. Monterey, Calif.: Brooks-Cole, 1973.

Maslow, Abraham, H. *Motivation and Personality.* 2d ed. New York: Harper & Row, 1970.

Maslow, Abraham H. *Toward a Psychology of Being.* Princeton, N.J.: Van Nostrand, 1952.

Masson, J. Moussaieff. *The Assault on Truth: Freud's Suppression of the Seduction Theory.* New York: Farrar, Straus, & Giroux, 1984.

Matas, Leah; Arend, Richard; and Stroufe, Alan. "Continuity of Adaptation in the Second Year: The Relationship between Quality of Attachment and Later Competence." *Child Development* 49 (1978): 547–556.

Maurer, Daphne, and Maurer, Charles. *The World of the Newborn.* New York: Basic Books, 1988.

May, Rollo. *Psychology and the Human Dilemma.* New York: W. W. Norton, 1980.

Mayr, Ernst. *The Growth of Biological Thought: Diversity, Evolution, and Inheritance.* Cambridge, Mass.: The Belknap Press, 1982.

Mead, George H. *Mind, Self, and Society: From the Standpoint of a Social Behaviorist.* Edited by Charles W. Morris. Chicago: University of Chicago Press, 1934.

Mead, Margaret. *Continuities in Cultural Evolution.* New Haven, Conn.: Yale University Press, 1964.

Meissner, W. W. "Can Psychoanalysis Find Its Self?" *Journal of the American Psychoanalytic Association* 34 (1986): 379–400.

Meltzoff, Andrew. "Imitation, Intermodal Co-ordination and Representation in Early Infancy." In *Infancy and Epistemology.* Edited by George Butterworth, pp. 85–114. New York: St. Martins, 1982.

Meltzoff, Andrew. "Infant Imitation After a 1-Week Delay: Long-Term Memory for Novel Acts and Multiple Stimuli." *Developmental Psychology* 24 (1988): 470–476.

Meltzoff, A. N., and Moore, M. K. "Imitation of Facial and Manual Gestures by Human Neonates." *Science* 198 (1977): 75–78.

Merleau-Ponty, Maurice. *Adventures of the Dialectic.* Translated by Joseph J. Bien. Evanston, Ill.: Northwestern University Press, 1973.

Merleau-Ponty, Maurice. *Consciousness and the Acquisition of Language.* Translated by Hugh J. Silverman. Evanston, Ill.: Northwestern University Press, 1973.

Merleau-Ponty, Maurice. *Phenomenology of Perception.* Edited by James M. Edie. Translated by William Cobb et al. Evanston, Ill.: Northwestern University Press, 1964.

Mesmer, Franz Antoine. *Mesmerism, A Translation of the Original Medical and Scientific Writings of F. A. Mesmer.* Translated by George Bloch. Los Altos, California: W. Kaufmann, 1980.

Miller, Alice. *For Your Own Good: Hidden Cruelty in Child-rearing and the Roots of Violence.* Translated by Hildegarde Hanmen and Hunter Hanmen. New York: Farrar, Straus, & Giroux, 1983.

Miller, Alice. *Prisoners of Childhood: The Drama of the Gifted Child and the Search for the Self.* Translated by Ruth Ward. New York: Basic Books, 1981.

Miller, George. "The Magical Number Seven, Plus or Minus Two: Some Limits on Our Capacity for Processing Information." *Psychological Review* 63 (1956): 81–97.

Mishler, Eliot. "Meaning in Context: Is There Any Other Kind?" *Harvard Educational Review* 49 (1979): 1–19

Mitroff, Ian. "Systems, Inquiry, and the Meanings of Falsification." *Philosophy of Science* 40 (1973): 255–276.

Mitroff, Ian, and Bonoma, Thomas. "Psychological Assumptions, Experimentation, and Real World Problems." *Evaluation Quarterly* 2 (1978): 235–259.

Mitroff, Ian, and Featheringham, Tom. "On Systemic Problem Solving and the Error of the Third Kind." *Behavioral Science* 19 (1974): 383–393.

Moran, John H., trans. and ed. *On the Origin of Language: Jean-Jacques Rousseau, Essay on the Origin of Language; Johann Gottfried Herder, Essay on the Origin of Language.* New York: F. Ungar, 1967.

Moser, Paul K., ed. *A Priori Knowledge.* New York: Oxford University Press, 1987.

Murphy, Gardner. *Personality: A Biosocial Approach to Origins and Structure.* New York: Harper, 1947.

Murphy, J. M., et al. *The Widening World of Childhood.* New York: Basic Books, 1962.

Murphy, L., and Moriarty, A. *Development, Vulnerability, Growth, and Resilience.* New Haven, Conn.: Yale University Press, 1975.

Murray, Henry A. "This I Believe." In *Endeavors in Psychology: Selections from the Personology of Henry A. Murray.* Edited by E. S. Shneidman. New York: Harper & Row, 1981.

Murray, H. S. *Explorations in Personality.* New York: Oxford University Press, 1938.

Myers, Gerald E. *William James: His Life and Thought.* New Haven, Conn.: Yale University Press, 1986.

Newton, Isaac. *Principia.* Translated by Andrew Motte. New York: D. Adee, 1848.

Nichols, Christopher. "Science or Reflection: Habermas on Freud." *Philosophy of Social Science* 2 (1972): 261–270.

Nietzsche, Friedrich. *Beyond Good and Evil.* Translated by Walter Kaufmann. New York: Vintage Books, 1966.

Nietzsche, Friedrich. *Ecce Homo.* Translated by Walter Kaufmann. New York: Random House, 1968.

Nietzsche, Friedrich. *On the Genealogy of Morals.* Translated by Walter Kaufmann. New York, Vintage Books, 1969.

Nietzsche, Friedrich. *Thus Spoke Zarathustra.* Translated by Walter Kaufmann. Harmondsworth: Penguin Books, 1978.

Nietzsche, Friedrich. *The Will to Power.* Translated and edited by Walter Kaufmann. New York: Random House, 1967.

Nussbaum, Martha. *The Fragility of Goodness: Luck and Ethics in Greek Tragedy and Philosophy.* Cambridge: Cambridge University Press, 1986.

Ockham, William. *Ockham's Theory of Terms.* Translated by Michael J. Loux. Notre Dame, Ind.: University of Notre Dame Press, 1974.

Orne, Martin. "Demand Characteristics and the Concept of Quasi-Controls." In *Artifact in Behavioral Research.* Edited by Robert Rosenthal and Ralph Rosnow, pp. 143–179. New York: Academic Press, 1969.

Ovid. *The Metamorphoses.* Translated and edited by Horace Gregory. New York: Viking Press, 1958.

Owens, Thomas J. *Phenomenology and Intersubjectivity: Contemporary Interpretations of the Interpersonal Situation.* The Hague: Martinus Nijhoff, 1970.

Palmer, Richard E. *Hermeneutics: Interpretation Theory in Schleiermacher, Dilthey, Heidegger, and Gadamer.* Evanston, Ill.: Northwestern University Press, 1969.

Parens, Henri. "Psychological Development during the Second and Third Years of Life." In *The Course of Life: Psychoanalytic Contributions toward Understanding Personality Development.* Edited by Stanley Greenspan and George Pollock. East Adelphi, Md.: U. S. Department of Health and Human Services, Public Health Service, 1980.

Parmenides. *Fragments, a Text and Translation.* Translated by David Gallop. Toronto: University of Toronto Press, 1984.

Penny, Robert; Olambiwonnu, N. Olatunji; and Frasier, Douglas. "Episodic Fluctuations of Serum Gonadotropins in Pre- and Post-Pubertal Girls and Boys." *Journal of Clinical Endocrinology and Metabolism* 45 (1977): 307–311.

Piaget, Jean. *Adaptation and Intelligence: Organic Selection and Phenocopy.* Translated by Stewart Eames. Chicago: University of Chicago Press, 1980.

Piaget, Jean. *The Construction of Reality in the Child.* Translated by Margaret Cook. New York: Basic Books, 1954.

Piaget, Jean. *The Essential Piaget.* Edited by Howard E. Gruber and Jacques Vonèche. New York: Basic Books, 1977.

Piaget, Jean. *The Origins of Intelligence in Children.* New York: W. W. Norton, 1963.

Piaget, Jean. *The Principles of Genetic Epistemology.* Translated by W. Mays. New York: Basic Books, 1972.

Piaget, Jean. *The Psychology of Intelligence.* Translated by Malcolm Piercy and D. E. Berlyne. New York: Harcourt, Brace, 1950.

Pieper, Martha Heineman. "The Future of Social Work Research." *Social Work Research and Abstracts* 21 (1985): 3–11.

Pieper, Martha Heineman. "The Heuristic Paradigm: A Unifying and Comprehensive Approach to Social Work Research." Brown Foundation Lecture, Smith College School for Social Work, July 10, 1989. *Smith College Studies in Social Work,* in press.

Plato. *The Dialogues of Plato.* Translated by B. Jowett. New York: Random House, 1937.

Plato. *The Phaedo.* Translated by David Gallop. Oxford: Clarendon Press, 1975.

Plato. *Phaedrus.* In *The Dialogues of Plato.* Vol. 1. Translated by B. Jowett. New York: Random House, 1937.

Plato. *The Republic.* Translated by B. Jowett. New York: Prometheus Books, 1986.

Plato. *The Symposium.* Translated and edited by K. Dover. Cambridge: Cambridge University Press, 1980.

Pribriam, Karl, and Gill, Merton. *Freud's "Project" Reassessed.* New York: Basic Books, 1976.

Provence, S., and Lipton, R. C. *Infants in Institutions.* New York: International Universities Press, 1963.

Pumpian-Mindlin, E. *Psychoanalysis as Science*. Stanford, Calif.: Stanford University Press, 1952.

Quine, Willard V. O. *From a Logical Point of View*. Cambridge, Mass.: Harvard University Press, 1953.

Quine, Willard V. O. *Word and Object*. Cambridge, Mass.: MIT Press, 1960.

Randall, John. *The Career of Philosophy*. New York: Columbia University Press, 1965.

Rappaport, David. "A Historical Survey of Psychoanalytic Ego Psychology." *Psychological Issues*. Vol. 1, pp. 5–17. New York: International Universities Press, 1959.

Rappaport, David. *The History of the Concept of the Association of Ideas*. New York: International Universities Press, 1974.

Rappaport, David. *Organization and Pathology of Thought*. New York: Columbia University Press, 1965.

Rappaport, David, and Gill, Merton. "The Points of View and Assumptions of Metapsychology." *The International Journal of Psychoanalysis* 40 (1959): 153–162.

Reese, William L. *Dictionary of Philosophy and Religion: Eastern and Western Thought*. Atlantic Highlands, N.J.: Humanities Press, 1980.

Regier, Darrel; Boyd, Jeffrey; Burke, Jack; et al. "One-Month Prevalence of Mental Disorders in the United States." *Archives of General Psychiatry* 45 (1988): 977–986.

Reich, Wilhelm. *Character Analysis*. Translated by Theodore P. Wolfe. New York: Orgone Institute Press, 1949.

Richardson, William J. "Psychoanalysis and the Being-Question." In *Interpreting Lacan: Psychiatry and the Humanities*. Edited by J. H. Smith and W. Kerrigan. Vol. 6, pp. 139–159. New Haven, Conn.: Yale University Press, 1983.

Ricoeur, Paul. *Freud and Philosophy: An Essay on Interpretation*. Translated by Denis Savage. New Haven, Conn.: Yale University Press, 1970.

Ricoeur, Paul. "The Question of Proof in Freud's Psychoanalytic Writings." *Journal of the American Psychoanalytic Association* 25 (1977): 835–872.

Rifkin, Jeremy. *Entropy: A New World View*. Toronto: Bantam Books, 1980.

Rifkind, Arleen; Kulin, Howard; and Ross, Griff. "Follicle-Stimulating Hormone (FSH) and Luteinizing Hormone (LH) in the Urine of Prepubertal Children." *Journal of Clinical Investigation* 46 (1967): 1925–1931.

Rogers, Carl R. *Carl Rogers on Personal Power*. New York: Delacorte, 1977.

Rogers, Carl. *The Clinical Treatment of the Problem Child*. Boston: Houghton-Mifflin, 1939.

Rogers, Carl. *Counseling and Psychotherapy: Newer Concepts in Practice*. Boston: Houghton-Mifflin, 1942.

Rogers, Carl, and Dymond, R., eds. *Psychotherapy and Personality Change*. Chicago: University of Chicago Press, 1954.

Rosenthal, David. *Materialism and the Mind-Body Problem.* Englewood Cliffs, N.J.: Prentice Hall, 1971.

Rosenthal, Robert. *Experimenter Effects in Behavioral Research.* New York: Appleton-Century-Crofts, 1966.

Rosenthal, Robert, and Rosnow, Ralph, eds. *Artifact in Behavioral Research.* New York: Academic Press, 1969.

Ross, Judith; Loriaux, D. Lynn; and Cutler, Gordon, Jr. "Developmental Changes in Neuroendocrine Regulation of Gonadotropin Secretion in Gonadal Dysgenesis." *Journal of Clinical Endocrinology and Metabolism* 57 (1982): 288–293.

Rousseau, Jean-Jacques. "A Discourse on the Origin of Inequality of Mankind." In *The Social Contract and Discourses.* Translated by G. D. H. Cole, pp. 199–234. New York: E. P. Dutton, 1950.

Rousseau, Jean-Jacques. *The Social Contract.* Translated by M. Cranston. Harmondsworth: Penguin Books, 1968.

Rubovits-Seitz, Philip. "Kohut's Method of Interpretation: A Critique." *American Journal of Psychoanalysis* 36 (1988): 933–959.

Russell, Bertrand. *The Analysis of Mind.* London: Allen & Unwin, 1921.

Ryle, Gilbert. *The Concept of Mind.* London: Hutchinson's University Library, 1949.

Salmon, Wesley. *Statistical Explanation and Statistical Relevance.* Pittsburgh: University of Pittsburgh Press, 1971.

Sartre, Jean-Paul. *Being and Nothingness: An Essay on Phenomenological Ontology.* Translated by H. E. Barnes. New York: Philosophical Library, 1956.

Sartre, Jean-Paul. *Existentialism and Humanism.* Translated by Philip Mairet. Brooklyn: Haskell House, 1977.

Sartre, Jean-Paul. *Nausea.* Translated by Lloyd Alexander. New York: New Directions, 1949.

Sartre, Jean-Paul. *No Exit and The Flies.* Translated by Stuart Gilbert. New York: A. A. Knopf, 1947.

Sartre, Jean-Paul. *The Wall and Other Stories.* Translated by Lloyd Alexander. New York: New Directions, 1948.

Sass, Louisa, and Woofolk, Robert. "Psychoanalysis and the Hermeneutic Turn: A Critique of Narrative Truth and Historical Truth." *Journal of the American Psychoanalytic Association* 36 (1988): 429–454.

Saussure, Ferdinand de. *Course in General Linguistics.* Translated by Wade Baskin. Edited by C. S. Bally and A. Sechehaye. New York: McGraw-Hill, 1966.

Schafer, Roy. *The Analytic Attitude.* New York: Basic Books, 1983.

Schafer, Roy. *Aspects of Internalization.* New York: International Universities Press, 1968.

Schafer, Roy. *Language and Insight.* New Haven, Conn.: Yale University Press, 1978.

Schafer, Roy. *Narrative Actions in Psychoanalysis*. Worcester, Mass.: Clark University Press, 1981.

Schafer, Roy. *A New Language for Psychoanalysis*. New Haven, Conn.: Yale University Press, 1976.

Schleiermacher, Friedrich. *The Christian Faith*. Translated and edited by H. R. Mackintosh and J. S. Stewart. Philadelphia: Fortress Press, 1976.

Schleiermacher, Friedrich. *Schleiermacher's Soliloquies: An English Translation of the Monologen*. Translated by Horace L. Friess. Chicago: Open Court, 1926.

Schlick, M. *General Theory of Knowledge*. Translated by A. E. Blumberg. New York: Springer-Verlag, 1974.

Schlick, M. *Problems of Ethics*. Translated by David Rynn. Englewood Cliffs, N.J.: Prentice Hall, 1939.

Schopenhauer, Arthur. *Essay on the Freedom of the Will*. Translated by Konstantin Kolenda. New York: Liberal Arts Press, 1960.

Schopenhauer, Arthur. *The World as Will and Idea*. 3 vols. Translated by R. B. Haldane and J. Kemp. London: Kegan Paul, 1883.

Schultz, Duane. "Psychology: A World with Man Left Out." *Journal of Theory in Social Behaviour* 1 (1971): 99–107.

Schutz, Alfred. *The Phenomenology of the Social World*. Translated by George Walsh and Frederick Lehnert. Evanston, Ill.: Northwestern University Press, 1967.

Schwartz, Andrew. "Drives, Affects, Behavior—and Learning: Approaches to a Psychobiology of Emotion and to an Integration of Psychoanalytic and Neurobiologic Thought." *Journal of the American Psychoanalytic Association* 35 (1987): 467–506.

Segall, Marshall; Campbell, Donald; and Herskovits, Melville. *The Influence of Culture on Visual Perception*. New York: Bobbs-Merrill, 1966.

Shaftesbury, Anthony Ashley Cooper. *Characteristics of Men, Manners, Opinions, Times*. London, 1727.

Sheldrake, Rupert. *A New Science of Life: The Hypothesis of Formative Causation*. Los Angeles: J. P. Tarcher, 1981.

Shweder, Richard and LeVine Robert, eds. *Culture Theory: Essays on Mind, Self, and Emotion*. Cambridge: Cambridge University Press, 1984.

Simon, Herbert. *Models of Discovery: and Other Topics in the Methods of Science*. Dordrecht: D. Reidel, 1977.

Simon, Herbert. *Models of Man: Social and Rational*. New York: John Wiley, 1957.

Simon, Herbert. *Models of Thought*. New Haven, Conn.: Yale University Press, 1979.

Simon, Herbert. *The Sciences of the Artificial*. Cambridge, Mass.: MIT Press, 1981.

Simon, Herbert. "The Structure of Ill-Structured Problems." *American International Journal* 3 (1972): 181–201.

Skinner, B. F. *Beyond Freedom and Dignity*. New York: Bantam Books, 1972.

Skinner, B. F. "The Phylogeny and Ontogeny of Behavior." *Science* 153 (1966): 1205–1213.

Skinner, B. F. *Walden Two*. New York: Macmillan, 1976.

Skutch, Alexander. *Parent Birds and Their Young*. Austin: University of Texas Press, 1976.

Small, Leonard. *The Briefer Psychotherapies*. New York: Brunner/Mazel, 1971.

Smith, J. H., and Kerrigan, W., eds. *Interpreting Lacan: Psychiatry and the Humanities*. Vol. 6. New Haven, Conn.: Yale University Press, 1983.

Solomon, Robert. "Freud's Neurological Theory of Mind." In *Freud: A Collection of Critical Essays*. Edited by Richard Wollheim, pp. 25–52. New York: Anchor, 1974.

Sperry, Roger W. "A Modified Concept of Consciousness." *Psychological Review* 76 (1969): 532–536.

Sperry, Roger. *Science and Moral Priority: Merging Mind, Brain and Human Values*. New York: Columbia University Press, 1983.

Sperry, Roger W. "Structure and Significance of the Consciousness Revolution," *Journal of Mind and Behavior* 8 (1987): 37–66.

Spinoza, Baruch. *The Ethics and Selected Letters*. Translated by S. Shirley. Edited by S. Feldman. Indianapolis, Ind.: Hackett, 1982.

Spitz, René. *Dialogues from Infancy: Selected Papers*. Edited by Robert E. Emde. New York: International Universities Press, 1983.

Spitz, René. *A Genetic Field Theory of Ego Formation*. New York: International Universities Press, 1962.

Spitz, René. "Hospitalism." In *The Psychoanalytic Study of the Child*. Vol. 1, pp. 53–74. New York: International Universities Press, 1945.

Spitz, René. "A Note on the Extrapolation of Ethological Findings." *International Journal of Psychoanalysis* 36 (1955): 162–165.

Spitz, René. *No and Yes: On the Genesis of Human Communication*. New York: International Universities Press, 1957.

Spitz, René, with Cobliner, W. G. *The First Year of Life: A Psychoanalytic Study of Normal and Deviant Development of Object Relations*. New York: International Universities Press, 1965.

Spock, Benjamin. *Baby and Child Care*. Rev. ed. New York: Pocket Books, 1968.

Stanley, Wendell M. "Isolation of a Crystalline Protein Possessing the Properties of Tobacco-Mosaic Virus." *Science* 81 (1935): 644–645.

Steiner, George. *Martin Heidegger*. New York: Viking Press, 1978.

Stent, Gunther. "Limits to the Scientific Understanding of Man." *Science* 187 (1975): 1052–1057.

Sterba, R. "The Fate of the Ego in Analytic Therapy." *International Journal of Psychoanalysis* 15 (1934): 117–126.

Stern, Daniel H. *The First Relationship: Infant and Mother.* Cambridge, Mass.: Harvard University Press, 1977.

Stern, Daniel H. *The Interpersonal World of the Infant: A View from Psychoanalysis and Developmental Psychology.* New York: Basic Books, 1985.

Stevenson, C. L. *Ethics and Language.* New Haven, Conn.: Yale University Press, 1944.

Stevenson, Robert Louis. *The Strange Case of Dr. Jekyll and Mr. Hyde.* Philadelphia: Running Press, 1987.

Stolorow, R., and Branschaft, B. "Developmental Failure and Psychic Conflict." *Psychoanalytic Psychology* 4 (1987): 241–253.

Stone, Leo. "Psychoanalysis and Brief Psychotherapy." *Psychoanalytic Quarterly* 20 (1951): 215–236.

Stone, Leo. *Transference and Its Context: Selected Papers on Psychoanalysis.* New York: J. Aronson, 1984.

Stone, W.; Smith, H. T.; and Murphy, B. B., eds. *The Competent Infant.* New York: Basic Books, 1973.

Sturrock, John. *Structuralism and Since: From Lévi-Strauss to Derrida.* New York: Oxford University Press, 1979.

Sullivan, Harry Stack. *Clinical Studies in Psychiatry.* New York: W. W. Norton, 1956.

Sullivan, Harry Stack. *The Fusion of Psychiatry and Social Science.* New York: W. W. Norton, 1964.

Sullivan, Harry Stack. *The Interpersonal Theory of Psychiatry.* New York: W. W. Norton, 1953.

Sullivan, Harry Stack. *The Psychiatric Interview.* New York: W. W. Norton, 1954.

Sullivan, Harry Stack. *Schizophrenia as a Human Process.* New York: W. W. Norton, 1962.

Sulloway, Frank J. *Freud: Biologist of the Mind—Beyond the Psychoanalytic Legend.* New York: Basic Books, 1979.

Taub, David M., ed. *Primate Paternalism.* New York: Von Nostrand Reinhold, 1984.

Tausk, Victor. "On the Origin of the 'Influencing Machine' in Schizophrenia." *Psychoanalytic Quarterly* 2 (1933): 519–556

Tennant, Christopher. "Parental Loss in Childhood." *Archives of General Psychiatry* 45 (1988): 1045–1055.

Theunissen, Michael. *The Other: Studies in the Social Ontology of Husserl, Heidegger, Sartre, and Buber.* Translated by Christopher Macann. Cambridge, Mass.: MIT Press, 1986.

Thomas Aquinas. *Summa Theologica.* Translated by the Fathers of the English Dominican Province. Westminster, Md.: Christian Classics, 1981.

Bibliography

Titchner, Edward. *Lectures on the Elementary Psychology of Feeling and Attention*. New York: Macmillan, 1908.

Tomkins, Silvan S. "Affect as Amplification: Some Modifications in Theory. In *Emotion: Theory, Research, and Experience*. Vol. 1. Edited by Robert Plutchik and Henry Kellerman, pp. 141–164. New York: Academic Press, 1980.

Toulmin, Stephen. *Foresight and Understanding: An Enquiry into the Aims of Science*. New York: Harper Torchbooks, 1961.

Toulmin, Stephen, with discussion by Ricoeur, Paul, and Swanson, D. R. "Psycho-analysis, Physics, and the Mind-Body Problem." In *The Annual of Psychoanalysis*. Vol. 6, pp. 315–352. New York: International Universities Press, 1978.

Tracy, David. *Plurality and Ambiguity: Hermeneutics, Religion, Hope*. San Francisco: Harper & Row, 1987.

Trevarthen, Colwyn. "Communication and Cooperation in Early Infancy: A Description of Primary Intersubjectivity." In *Before Speech: The Beginning of Interpersonal Communication*. Edited by M. M. Bullowa. New York: Cambridge University Press, 1979.

Trevarthen, Colwyn. "Descriptive Analyses of Infant Communicative Behavior. In *Studies in Mother-Infant Interaction*. Edited by H. R. Schaffer. New York: Academic Press, 1977.

Trevarthen, Colwyn. "The Foundations of Intersubjectivity: Development of Interpersonal and Cooperative Understanding in Infants." In *Essays in Honor of Jerome Bruner*. Edited by David R. Olson. New York: W. W. Norton, 1980.

Trevarthen, Colwyn. "Instincts for Human Understanding and for Cultural Cooperation: Their Development in Infancy." In *Human Ethology: Claims and Limits of a New Discipline*. Edited by Mario von Cranach; K. Foppa; W. Lepenies; and G. Ploog, pp. 530–571. Cambridge: Cambridge University Press, 1979.

Trevarthen, Colwyn. "Neurological Development and the Growth of Psychological Function." In *Developmental Psychology and Society*. Edited by J. Sants, pp. 46–95. London: Macmillan, 1979.

Trevarthen, Colwyn. "Psychobiology of Speech Development." In *Language and Brain: Developmental Aspects*. Neurobiology Science Research Program Bulletin no. 12, 1974.

Tversky, Amos, and Kahneman, Daniel. "The Framing of Decisions and the Psychology of Choice." *Science* 211 (1981): 453–458.

Tyson, Phyllis. "Psychic Structure Formation: The Complementary Roles of Affects, Drives, Object Relations, and Conflict." *Journal of the American Psychoanalytic Association* 36 (1988): 73–101.

Vygotsky, Lev S. *Mind in Society*. Edited by Michael Cole, Vera John-Steiner, Sylvia Scrigner, and Ellen Sauberman. Cambridge, Mass.: Harvard University Press, 1978.

Vygotsky, Lev. S. *Thought and Language*. Translated by Eugenia Hanfmann and Gertrude Vakar. Cambridge, Mass.: MIT Press, 1962.

Wachtel, Paul. "Psychodynamics, Behavior Therapy, and the Implacable Experimenter." *Journal of Abnormal Psychology* 82 (1973): 324–334.

Waelder, Robert. "Psychoanalysis, Scientific Method and Philosophy." In *Psychoanalysis: Observation, Theory and Application*. Edited by Samuel A. Guttman, pp. 248–274. New York: International Universities Press, 1976.

Wallace, Edwin R. *Historiography and Causation in Psychoanalysis*. Hillsdale, N.J.: Analytic Press, 1985.

Waugaman, R. M. "Falling Off the Couch." *Journal of the American Psychoanalytic Association* 35 (1987): 861–876.

Webster, Murray. "Psychological Reductionism, Methodological Individualism, and Large-Scale Problems." *American Sociological Review* 38 (1973): 258–273.

Werker, Janet F. "Becoming a Native Listener." *American Scientist* 77 (1989): 54–59.

Wertsch, James V. *Vygotsky and the Social Formation of Mind*. Cambridge, Mass.: Harvard University Press, 1985.

Whorf, Benjamin. "Science and Linguistics." In *Psycholinguistics: A Book of Readings*. Edited by Sol Saporta, pp. 460–467. New York: Holt, Rhinehart, & Winston, 1961.

Whyte, Lancelot L. *The Unconscious Before Freud*. London: Julian Friedmann, 1978.

Wilson, Peter J. *Man, The Promising Primate: The Conditions of Human Evolution*. New Haven, Conn.: Yale University Press, 1980.

Wimsatt, William C. "Complexity and Organization." In *Boston Studies in the Philosophy of Science*. Vol. 20. Edited by K. F. Schaffner and R. S. Cohen, pp. 67–86. Dordrecht: Reidel, 1974.

Wimsatt, William C. "Developmental Constraints, Generative Entrenchment and the Innate-Acquired Distinction." In *Integrating Scientific Disciplines*. Edited by P. W. Bechtell, pp. 185–208. Dordrecht: Martinus-Nijhoff, 1986.

Wimsatt, William C. "Forms of Aggregativity." In *Human Nature and Natural Knowledge*. Edited by A. Donegan, S. N. Perovich, and N. V. Wettin, pp. 259–298. Dordrecht: Reidel, 1986.

Wimsatt, William C. "Heuristics and the Study of Human Behavior." In *Metatheory in the Social Sciences*. Edited by D. Fiske and R. Schweder, pp. 293–314. Chicago: University of Chicago Press, 1986.

Wimsatt, William C. "Purposiveness and Intentionality in Nature." Unpublished manuscript, University of Chicago, 1968.

Wimsatt, William C. "Reduction and Reductionism." In *Current Problems in the Philosophy of Science*. Edited by H. Kyburg and P. Q. Asquith, pp. 353–377. East Lansing, Mich.: Philosophy of Science Association, 1979.

Wimsatt, William C. "Reductionism, Levels of Organization, and the Mind-Body Problem." In *Consciousness and the Brain*. Edited by G. G. Globus, G. Maxwell, and I. Savodnik, pp. 199–267. New York: Plenum, 1976.

389

Wimsatt, William C. "Reductionist Research Strategies and Their Biases in the Units of Selection Controversy." In *Scientific Discovery*. Edited by T. Nickles, pp. 213–259. Dordrecht: Reidel, 1980.

Wimsatt, William C. "Reductive Explanation: A Functional Account." In *Boston Studies in the Philosophy of Science*, vol. 32. Edited by R. S. Cohen, C. A. C. Michalos, and J. Van Evra, pp. 671–710. Dordrecht: Reidel, 1976.

Wimsatt, William C. "Robustness and Functional Localization: Heuristics for Determining the Boundaries of Systems and Their Biases." In *Scientific Inquiry and Knowing and Validating in the Social Sciences: A Tribute to Donald T. Campbell*. Edited by M. Brewer and B. Collins, pp. 124–163. San Francisco: Jossey-Bass, 1980.

Wimsatt, William. "Teleology and the Logical Structure of Function Statements." *Studies in the History of the Philosophy of Science* 3 (1972): 1–79.

Winnicott, Donald. *Collected Papers: Through Paediatrics to Psychoanalysis*. London: Tavistock, 1958.

Winnicott, Donald. *The Maturational Processes and the Facilitating Environment: Studies in the Theory of Emotional Development*. New York: International Universities Press, 1965.

Winnicott, Donald. *Playing and Reality*. New York: Basic Books, 1971.

Wittgenstein, Ludwig. *Philosophical Investigations*. Translated by G. E. M. Anscombe. New York: Macmillan, 1953.

Wolff, Christian. *Preliminary Discourse on Philosophy in General*. Translated by Richard J. Blackwell. Indianapolis, Ind.: Bobbs-Merrill, 1963.

Wolff, Peter. "The Developmental Psychologies of Jean Piaget and Psychoanalysis." *Psychological Issues*. Vol. 2. New York: International Universities Press, 1960.

Worringer, Wilhelm. *Abstraction and Empathy: A Contribution to the Psychology of Style*. New York: International Universities Press, 1967.

Yankelovich, Daniel, and Barrett, William. *Ego and Instinct: The Psychoanalytic View of Human Nature—Revised*. New York: Random House, 1970.

Zetzel, E. R. *The Capacity for Emotional Growth*. New York: International Universities Press, 1970.

Zilboorg, G. "Some Sidelights on Free Association." *International Journal of Psychoanalysis* 33 (1952): 489–495.

INDEX